Nature's Ambassador:
THE LEGACY OF THORNTON W. BURGESS

CHRISTIE PALMER LOWRANCE

4880 Lower Valley Road • Atglen, PA 19310

Published by Schiffer Publishing, Ltd.
4880 Lower Valley Road
Atglen, PA 19310
Phone: (610) 593-1777; Fax: (610) 593-2002
E-mail: Info@schifferbooks.com

For our complete selection of fine books on this and related subjects, please visit our website at **www.schifferbooks.com**. You may also write for a free catalog.

This book may be purchased from the publisher. Please try your bookstore first.

We are always looking for people to write books on new and related subjects. If you have an idea for a book, please contact us at **proposals@schifferbooks.com**.

Schiffer Publishing's titles are available at special discounts for bulk purchases for sales promotions or premiums. Special editions, including personalized covers, corporate imprints, and excerpts can be created in large quantities for special needs. For more information, contact the publisher.

In Europe, Schiffer books are distributed by:
Bushwood Books
6 Marksbury Ave.
Kew Gardens
Surrey TW9 4JF England
Phone: 44 (0) 20 8392 8585; Fax: 44 (0) 20 8392 9876
E-mail: info@bushwoodbooks.co.uk
Website: www.bushwoodbooks.co.uk

Unless otherwise specified, the Thornton W. Burgess Society in Sandwich, Massachusetts has provided the photographs and artwork used throughout this book.

COPYRIGHT © 2013 by Christie Palmer Lowrance

LIBRARY OF CONGRESS CONTROL NUMBER: 2013936749

All rights reserved. No part of this work may be reproduced or used in any form or by any means—graphic, electronic, or mechanical, including photocopying or information storage and retrieval systems—without written permission from the publisher.

The scanning, uploading, and distribution of this book or any part thereof via the Internet or via any other means without the permission of the publisher is illegal and punishable by law. Please purchase only authorized editions and do not participate in or encourage the electronic piracy of copyrighted materials.
"Schiffer," "Schiffer Publishing, Ltd. & Design," and the "Design of pen and inkwell" are registered trademarks of Schiffer Publishing, Ltd.

DESIGNED BY RoS
TYPE SET IN CloisterOpenFace BT/Garamond

ISBN: 978-0-7643-4445-9
Printed in China

Dedicated to Kai, Robby, Gwendolyn, and Jorin,
the ones Thornton Burgess wrote for

EPIGRAPH

"I would rather write for, and talk to, children than to be a bestselling novelist. For the child mind is open and it receives truth without question. And I would rather be Mother Nature's Ambassador to the Kingdom of Childhood wherein the passing of years means nothing than to be President."

THORNTON W. BURGESS
"WRITING SEVEN THOUSAND ARTICLES"
PICTORIAL REVIEW (1935)

"No kind of writing lodges itself so deeply into our memory, echoing there for the rest of our lives, as the books that we met in our childhood…To enter and hold the mind of a child or young person is one of the hardest of all a writer's tasks."

WILLIAM ZINSSER
THE ART AND CRAFT OF WRITING FOR CHILDREN (1990)

CONTENTS

FOREWORD

My favorite Thornton Burgess story is one you have never read: "The Naturalist and the Heath Hen." It is one of many tales artfully told in this wonderful new biography. Although best known for the fictitious Peter Rabbit, Burgess was just as familiar with the real wildlife of his native Massachusetts landscape. Born into the agrarian conservation of John Burroughs, Burgess died a year after Rachel Carson and the advent of the modern environmental movement. His life encompassed dramatic changes in both the environmental movement and his New England landscape, but his work remained rooted in his outlook as both a naturalist and a translator of nature for the public.

I first came to know Burgess as a conservationist through some breathtaking film footage he shot of the last heath hens on Martha's Vineyard, shortly before their extinction. For a conservation historian, this was a revelation. Imagine if we had film footage of the last dodos or passenger pigeons? It was with that level of excitement that I saw this grainy 1931 footage of the famous children's author capturing for posterity this bird's last few years on the planet. It was both homage to the bird and a rebuke to Americans who had so carelessly let it go extinct. After this epiphany, I wanted to learn more about Burgess as both an author and citizen conservationist. Luckily, now I have this book to fill that gap.

Christie Lowrance's new biography raises the critical question about our ongoing debt to Burgess. Obviously he has provided many hours of enjoyment for children and their parents who delighted in his anthropomorphic animals, but Lowrance has recovered a whole community of conservationists who worked closely with Burgess or were inspired by him. A close collaborator with many of the conservation luminaries of his day, Burgess used his children's stories to educate readers about the need to protect and support native and migratory birds and other wildlife.

Burgess was a pioneer in helping protect migratory birds. He created the first bird refuges and educated the public about vanishing species. He used radio, the newest technology of his day, to introduce adults and a generation of youths to the wonders of nature through his popular Radio Nature League program. Burgess was both a key actor in the early American Conservation Movement and an inspiration for many of the leaders of the modern environmental movement. By appealing to both children and their parents, by publishing both children's stories and rigorous natural history, Burgess transcended narrow niches with interests as broad and diverse as the landscapes he chronicled. In many ways, his naturalist work may be his more enduring legacy on the literal (vs. literary) landscape.

What a charmingly apt title Lowrance chose: "Nature's Ambassador." If the past is indeed a foreign country, then Christie Lowrance is the perfect tour guide: knowledgeable about her subject, fluent in the discourse of literature and science, and passionate about her work. Burgess was indeed the true ambassador for all wild things. He had studied wildlife all his life and dedicated himself to translating their mores and modes of existence for young readers. Today our children live in a world disconnected from nature, a world never far from the nearest electrical outlet. Burgess harkened back to a world more intimately connected to the natural environment. As Lowrance chronicles, Burgess used the newest technologies of the day to try to keep America's youth in relationship with nature via books, newspapers, and radios. She reminds us we need a new Burgess for the twenty-first century to combine an intimate knowledge of nature with the most effective new technologies. Burgess's most enduring legacy would be a world where we never again need to film a vanishing species, but instead finally achieve his dream of humans and wildlife coexisting in harmony.

Mark Madison, Historian
U.S. Fish and Wildlife Service

INTRODUCTION

One of the most prolific and beloved twentieth-century children's writers, Thornton Waldo Burgess created a pathway to books and nature with one enticing package: a storyteller's animal tale. After his first children's book *Old Mother West Wind* was published in 1910, scores followed, all filled with such wildlife characters as Jimmy Skunk, Reddy Fox, and Bob White who ate beetles, berries, and mice, built dens and nests, raised families, and eluded hunger and danger every day. As a literary naturalist, Burgess' work earned the gratitude of environmental conservationists, the respect and friendship of prestigious scientists and artists, the appreciation of teachers and parents, and the affection of an international fan base that has endured for a century. Early twentieth century conservationist Dr. William T. Hornaday wrote a warm, personal note in Burgess' copy of his book *The Minds and Manners of Wild Animals*: "To my distinguished colleague and Gold Medal worker in the field of Wild Life Protection, Thornton W. Burgess. With the imperishable regard of the Author, May 9, 1922. W.T. Hornaday."[1]

A tireless writer, Burgess produced seventy full-scale children's books, scores of minor publications, poems, songs, and more than 15,000 syndicated newspaper articles during his lengthy, productive career. The 1987 corporate history of his longtime publisher Little, Brown and Company noted that Thornton Burgess was "by far" its most prolific author.[2] He was as popular in Canada as he was in the United States. Forty-five of his books were published in England and twenty of his titles were translated into Japanese. Some titles appeared in French, Swedish, Norwegian, Chinese, and Braille.

Burgess' official mid-century sales of seven and a half million books represented totals from only two of his numerous publishers and a Book-of-the-Month Club edition[3]; fifteen books were later released. Sixty-four of Burgess' seventy books were still in print when he died in 1965, and more than half are currently available through standard publishing, print-on-demand, or Kindle. "A child's book today goes out of print in an average of three years," notes Carol Chittenden, a veteran bookseller in Falmouth, Massachusetts. "Not many writers' work survives one hundred years."

Millions of readers were touched by Burgess' animal stories. Among them was H. Bradford Washburn, mountain climber, explorer, and revered director of the Boston Museum of Science. When Washburn asked that his institution honor the three men who most influenced his life's path, he named Kirtley Mather, Harvard University geology professor; Gilbert Grosvenor, first editor of *National Geographic*; and Thornton Burgess, children's author.

Sierra Club president and Nobel Peace Prize nominee David Brower also credits Burgess with giving him a foundation from which to examine the relationship between wildlife and humanity: "How do you cross the species barrier? Talk to creatures who have no way of understanding your words? ... What took the wholeness we were part of and separated us out? ... It is very helpful to have a parent or grandparent... invite you to think about these things. And it was certainly helpful to me to have my mother read bedtime stories to me from Thornton W. Burgess and suggest that I read more of them myself."[4]

Drive, discipline, a rich imagination, as well as an acute sense of audience and a hunger for natural science, account for Burgess' effectiveness as a writer. As a young journalist/editor for newspapers and magazines, his assignments covered such diverse topics as fertilizers, bicycle racing, catamaran construction, wild flowers, child-rearing, bird migration, and commercial fishing. The chance invitation to submit a children's book to Little, Brown and Company transformed Burgess' career. Eventual fame as a children's author and a naturalist led to speaking invitations at the Boston Public Library, the Smithsonian Institution, National Museum of Natural History, and the Boston Museum of Science.

Charles "Chuck" Roth, former Massachusetts Audubon Society interpretive director, knew Burgess personally and lauds his contributions to the early conservation movement as well as to children's literature. "John Muir was one voice, John Burroughs was another, and Thornton Burgess was another," says Roth. "I think they were all bringing the same message through different routes to the public at large, but Burgess had the widest audience. They all wrote well-accepted books, but Burgess was in newspapers all over the country, day in and day out, albeit with a different audience. He realized that his books and stories were going to be read by adults as well as kids, and he always had a subtle message for them."

In 1919, Burgess was honored with a gold medal by the New York Zoological Society for his conservation program that led to the establishment of bird sanctuaries on more than five million acres of private land in every state in the United States and Canada. At the dawn of radio technology in the 1920s, his weekly nature program reached tens of thousands of listeners from Midwest America to Canada and

England with a wealth of natural science information and prestigious scientists as guest speakers. It was perhaps the first nature program for children on radio. In fact, Burgess' call for humane attitudes and practices toward wildlife is as critical today as when the 36-year-old widower first realized the educational potential of his work.

What can be said — and should be said — of an author whose work has sustained an active readership and commercial viability for over a century, whose books sold millions of copies to an international twentieth century market, and whose daily newspaper columns were read by additional millions of children throughout North America for nearly fifty years? Is there singular merit in the ability of a writer to draw these numbers of children to the written word? Is there cultural worth in a writer's ability to develop environment awareness?

In light of Burgess' achievements, it is surprising to discover that critical studies, anthologies, and textbooks often fail to include him among influential children's authors. In *The Natural History of Make-Believe: A Guide to the Principal Works of Britain, Europe, and America*, children's literary historian John Goldthwaite observes the conspicuous absence in literary criticism of an author "who could…lay just claim to having been for half a century the most beloved children's author in America." Goldthwaite notes, "I know of only one study of children's literature that even mentions him, and that only in passing."[5]

In the early twentieth century other authors wrote for children, but few wrote for Burgess' young audience and fewer still were nature writers. Arguably, none matched Burgess' broad representation of wildlife species and habitat. His stories are associated with familiar wild animals, such as frogs, raccoons, beavers, and deer, but Burgess also wrote about peccaries, wolverines, alligators, loons, bats, lynx, eels, osprey, snakes, spiders, and wasps. Decades before the term "ecosystem" became commonplace, Burgess depicted his characters as being interlinked components within a natural environment. In *Whitefoot the Wood Mouse*, for example, he describes the dramatic encounter of a snowy owl, a weasel, and a snowshoe hare, all with the same protective white coloration, but each with a different purpose when their paths accidentally cross on a winter day. The hare spots the owl and freezes in place, knowing it cannot be seen unless it moves. The owl is oblivious to the hare, but detects the weasel on its trail. In an instant, the weasel is transformed from predator into prey; its frenzied pursuit of meal becomes a frantic evasion of the grasping talons of an equally hungry owl while the hare bounds away to safety.[6]

Perhaps Burgess' emphasis on natural science rather than literary content influenced his legacy as a writer, and perhaps the fact that he wrote anthropomorphic animal stories for young children marred his reputation as a naturalist. Was his work somehow outside the genres and conventional standards in both fields of children's literature and natural science? Children's library science authority Margaret Bush suggests that in the final analysis Burgess may have been in his time "a voice in the wilderness."

Taking accurate measure of Thornton Burgess' accomplishments as a pioneer in the earliest days of environmental conservation, children's literature, and radio technology requires flagging four points: first, he was born, raised, and educated within a rural nineteenth century New England community and its value systems; second, he addressed an international twentieth-century audience of both children and adults as a successful writer, naturalist, early radio host, and lecturer; third, his perception of the relationship among people, wildlife, and nature is relevant to twenty-first-century interests and concerns; and fourth, the appeal of his characters, many created before World War I, has lasted for over a century. The four-part structure of this book is intended to provide context with which to consider these points.

At the heart of Burgess' work was his personal embrace of nature and children. Although he provided an inconceivable number of words for the pages of books, newspaper and magazine articles, letters of correspondence, and personal journals, their collective message was simple:

Nature is the greatest teacher.

Wildlife is the most worthy subject.

Children are the finest learners.

Nature's Ambassador is the story of a twentieth-century children's writer who blended fact and fiction, science and fable, entertainment and environmental education. In the early 1900s, he advocated for humane values and stewardship toward nature and wildlife, even requiring his Green Meadow Club and Radio Nature League members to sign a pledge to that effect. Perhaps the most subtle and important message in Burgess' work was his understanding of life as a common experience for all creatures, from insects to people. Daily existence for Burgess' wildlife characters was both enhanced and challenged, as his own had been, by the presence of friends, neighbors, and family within a community.

In the 1980s, the Thornton W. Burgess Society in Sandwich, Massachusetts, collected thousands of letters in a petition drive requesting the U.S. Postal Service to produce a stamp honoring the children's author. The application was ultimately rejected, but among its supporters were John Hoyt, President of the Humane Society, and S. Dillon Riley, Secretary of the Smithsonian Institution. At that time Dr. Theodore H. Reed, Director of the National Zoological Park, wrote:

> In the realm of wildlife conservation and natural history education, there is one name in the United States that must not be forgotten: Thornton W. Burgess. Long before the advent of national interest in the preservation of our ecological environment, Mr. Burgess launched his literary efforts to bring to the attention of the children of the US the natural history of the world in which we live. … Through books, freelance writing on natural history subjects, lectures, nature clubs he enlightened us on the ecology and behavior of animals. Within my own home, Mr. Burgess' books were considered a treasure. … As an active, early proponent

> of the necessity for public awareness of the need for conservation of our wildlife and environment, we are all indebted to him for the impetus he gave this concern we have today.[7]

This debt remains unpaid, obligating those who value children's literature, natural science, and environmental education to reassess the legacy of Thornton W. Burgess.

Christie Palmer Lowrance
Sandwich, Massachusetts

PART I: THE ORIGINS

Thornton W. Burgess as a school boy in Sandwich, Massachusetts in the early 1880s.

Chapter 1

A Cape Cod Childhood

Thornton Burgess' childhood shaped him as completely as a writer and naturalist as the winds and tides shape the contours of the long, narrow peninsula on which he was born. He emerged from that time with an indelible sense of connection, admiration, and stewardship for the natural world that would lastingly direct his productive life and successful career.

"I am a Cape Codder by birth and by inheritance through a long, unbroken line of ancestors... In this [place] there is something elementary, something of pounding surf, of shifting sands, the taste of salt on the lips, the flash of sun on distant dunes, the mingled smells of marsh muck, salt hay, and stranded fish, the mewing of gulls, the whistling of shore birds, the restless rise and fall of the tides, the silvery gleam of fresh water in emerald settings, the resinous odor of scrub pines."[1]

"In this atmosphere I was born and spent my childhood. From it I have never wholly escaped...Looking back through the years, I wonder if it was not then that the pattern of my life was set."[2]

Thornton W. Burgess, *Now I Remember*, 1960

The Age of Sail to the Space Age

Even if he had done nothing exceptional, the life of Thornton Waldo Burgess would have been remarkable for its span of ninety-one years over an extraordinary period of American history. He was born on January 14, 1874. Only nine years earlier Generals Ulysses S. Grant and Robert E. Lee rode to the Appomattox Court House to negotiate terms of surrender that would end the Civil War's ghastly carnage, a national turning point followed five days later by another: the assassination of President Abraham Lincoln.

Thornton W. Burgess died on June 5, 1965 amid the social tumult of the Vietnam War and the Women's Movement, a year after passage of the Civil Rights Act, and eighteen months after the assassination of President John F. Kennedy. "Shock follows shock," he had written in a letter to New Brunswick newspaperman Stuart Trueman in December 1963. "We have lost an able and good man, a brilliant man, who had he lived might well have become a truly great man."[3]

A witness to the impact of two World Wars, the 1929 stock market crash, and the Great Depression, Thornton Burgess saw revolutionary developments in communications, transportation, and energy, from telephones, electricity, and automobiles to radio, television, air travel, and the atomic bomb. Two events that book-ended his life illustrate the extent of change it encompassed. Five years after his birth, Burgess watched transfixed from a sand dune while the crew of a Provincetown whaling ship moored in Cape Cod Bay stripped blubber from a seventy-four-foot blue whale that had washed onto the shore.[4] Four years after his death, astronaut Neil Armstrong stepped onto the surface of the moon.

A Ninth Generation Cape Codder

Thornton W. Burgess was born in Sandwich, Massachusetts, a large, thriving Cape Cod town already 237 years old. Situated at the base of the sixty-mile-long peninsula that reaches into the Atlantic Ocean like an upraised arm, Sandwich had coastal resources on two saltwater bays and many freshwater ponds, as well as extensive agricultural, industrial, and commercial resources. It was named for an English town well-known to the seventeenth century settlers. Burgess was proud to be a direct descendant of Thomas Burgess, one of Sandwich's founders.

The only child of Caroline Hayward and Thornton Waldo Burgess, Sr. was born at home, but any other plans would doubtless have been thwarted by a severe snowstorm that winter day. According to the *Sandwich Observer*, "Down Cape, the trains on the Cape Cod branch of the Old Colony Rail Road were seriously delayed by getting off the track at W. Truro. The train for Provincetown was 18 hours late, and no one left the Cape for Boston."[5]

His parents had been married for two years and were living in a large, two-story house on School Street owned by Louisa Antoinette Hunt, wife of Captain Charles Isaac Gibbs. Inconclusive records suggest that the Gibbs' were living in Hyannis that year; however, they or others may have also lived in the house at the time of Thornton's birth. Both men were from old Sandwich families; they would have been acquaintances if not friends. Burgess, Sr., twenty-four, was in business with his father as a dry-goods merchant at C.H. Burgess & Son on Cross Street near the glass factory. The Burgesses' landlord was a Civil War naval veteran who had served as a Union officer on the *U.S.S. Sloop-of-War Richmond.* Gibbs participated in fighting at New Orleans, Vicksburg, Port Hudson, and Mobile Bay. He wrote his wife during the Blockade of the Mississippi that they had encountered the feared Confederate ram *Manassas.*[6] After the war, Gibbs built with his brother-in-law a shoe and boot store, now the Brown Jug Wine Shop.

In early 1874, within three weeks of each other, Caroline Burgess in Sandwich and Louisa Gibbs in Hyannis gave birth to sons, but, too soon, grief would replace their joy. Rufus Marmaduke Jenney, the Gibbs' youngest child, died the next year on September 4th and Caroline's husband, Thornton Waldo Burgess, Sr., died of tuberculosis within nine months of the birth of his namesake. An October 31, 1874 notice in the *Seaside Press* reported the circumstances of the young man's death, as well as the community's high regard:

> On Thursday morning the painful intelligence reached us of the death of Mr. Thornton W. Burgess of this place at Richmond, Va. wither he went some three weeks since, hoping to find relief from that terrible destroyer, Consumption. His wife and parents accompanied him and were with him at the time of his death. He was one of our most promising young men, beloved and respected by all who knew him, and he will be sadly missed in social and business circles. He leaves a wife and infant son, and a large circle of other relatives, who have the heartfelt sympathy of the public.[7]

There is no indication that the Burgesses' baby traveled with his parents to Richmond, where there were several sanatoriums; they probably left him in the care of Sandwich relatives. An obituary notice provides further detail:

> Mr. Thornton W. Burgess...arrived here by a special train from Middleboro on Sunday morning last. The funeral services on Sunday afternoon at the residence of his father, [Charles Burgess] were attended by a large concourse of friends; Rev. J. Livesey and Rev. P. Oxnard conducted the funeral services. The members of the Bay State Band acted as Pall Bearers on the occasion, he having been a member of the same and taking a great interest in the association as long as his health would allow him to do so. The body was interred at the Freeman Cemetery and was followed to the grave by a large number of carriages containing the friends of the deceased.[8]

Families Supported Families

Few families escaped tragedy and loss in those times. Burgess' mother Caroline and her sister Lucy had been orphaned at ages four and seven. The little girls were taken into the Sandwich home of their mother's brother, Charles Coatesworth Pinckney Waterman, known as C.C.P., a payroll master and clerk at the Boston & Sandwich Glass Company. Hardship again befell the sisters when their husbands died within two years of marriage, leaving both women widowed and the single parent of a young child.

Sometime after her husband's death, Caroline returned with her baby to the Waterman home on Main Street where she had lived for most of her life. Lucy, with her son William, moved three houses away to the home of her late husband's parents, Mr. and Mrs. Robert Tobey. The Watermans had nine children, most of them adult, some deceased, by the time Caroline and Thornton moved in. Burgess had a good relationship with his mother's uncle, one of his few male role models. He affectionately remembered "Grandfather," as he called Waterman, for helping remove a troublesome tooth and hanging a new swing for Burgess in a backyard apple tree.[9]

In 1880, with Charles Waterman's health failing, Burgess, then six, and his mother moved a street away to the Jarves Street home of her late husband's parents. Charles and Ann Burgess had six children, but their daughter Anna had died in 1873 and their son Thornton the following year, both of tuberculosis. When their youngest child, Willard, developed a lung condition, the Burgesses moved to Colorado to protect his health and arranged in their absence for their daughter-in-law and grandson to live in their home. Now an inn, the large house was centrally located on a street that linked the town's various businesses, shops, homes, and churches with the railroad station and the glass factory, which stretched along the edge of a seven hundred-acre salt marsh between the town and Cape Cod Bay.

Living on the busy, store-lined street would have been exciting for a youngster, especially when Jarves Street was closed off for parades and horse races. Dr. Edward Talbot, Joshua Holway, Nehemiah Packwood, and others with fast horses would challenge neighbors in nearby towns to come to Sandwich to "do a little trotting," and sleigh races often followed a new snowfall. People lined up along the quarter-mile course from Post Office Square in front of Charles Burgess' home to the railroad station, and stores and shops were opened for business.

Life in Sandwich

Growing up in the final quarter of the nineteen century gave Thornton Burgess a frame of reference unknown today.[10] "Life was simple then — no automobiles, telephones, or electric lights," he told a hometown audience as guest speaker at the 1939 Tercentennial. "We did have street lights. They burned kerosene. Many a time have I watched the lamp-lighter making his rounds." The cadence of horses' hooves on the village's dirt-packed streets and a blacksmith's metal-on-metal hammer strokes were ordinary sounds then.

Local news was published by numerous small papers that diligently reported the sinking of ships, the homecoming after years at sea of whaling captains like Sylvanus and Abraham Hoxie, drownings at sea and in ponds, new fashions such as parasols with colored whalebone, and the occasional equine accident. In 1888, the Rev. A.J. Brady was tossed from a carriage when his horse was startled by an engine releasing steam at the Sandwich depot. It was considered noteworthy that Mr. H. Dillaway's horse became frightened when it kicked the whiffle tree, a wooden bar on the harness of the sleigh it was pulling, "which caused him to run up Jarves St. throwing out Jimmy, son of Mr. James D. Lloyd, and then … continued on until he reached the passageway by the store of H.V. Spurr, where he ran in and down the steps onto Pleasant Street, where he then ran into the barn of John Miller." (The reporter determined that the accident "results from no fault in the horse, but through the carelessness of the person who harnessed the same into the sleigh.")[11]

Odd and curious matters were considered as worthy of coverage as historic ones. *The Sandwich Observer* reported that a turtle weighing twenty-nine and a half pounds was captured in the Sandwich mill pond, a one-eyed, forty-six-pound codfish was caught Down Cape in Provincetown, and Ulysses S. Grant stopped in Sandwich on August 29, 1874, the year Burgess was born. In 1879, Mr. George Alton "formerly of this place had recently accomplished the difficult task of skating 21 hours without a moments rest for a prise [*sic*] of $250 and a medal. About 100 people watched him."

At the time Thornton Burgess lived in Sandwich, Cape Cod's two largest factories were located there, as were smaller operations that manufactured tacks, tags, veneer, shoes, and braiding for silk watch fobs and eyeglasses cords. The Keith Car and Manufacturing Company in West Sandwich [now Sagamore in the Town of Bourne] had opened as a blacksmith shop in the early 1800s. It expanded with production of Conestoga wagons for westward expansion and later made wooden railroad cars. In the early 1900s, the company had 1,400 employees. On the bay side of Sandwich Village, the Boston & Sandwich Glass Company produced exquisite fine art and household stock pieces between 1825 and 1888, bringing into the town renowned European glass colorists and workers from England, Ireland, Bohemia, and Italy. Many of Burgess' relatives worked in these local industries as well as on farms outside the village.

Influence of Family and Community

In this busy coastal New England community, Thornton Burgess grew up among a large, multi-generational assortment of aunts, great-uncles, grandparents, in-laws, cousins, second-cousins, and cousins-once-removed. In the struggle to make ends meet, he and his widowed mother depended heavily on the support of this familial safety net. By Burgess' count, they lived in ten different dwellings in Sandwich. Within a few minutes' walk in the village, one passes five of Burgess' homes, as well as the street on which he was born and attended primary school. The year he graduated from high school, the Burgesses stayed at the Lake House, a boarding house that overlooked Shawme Pond. Under these difficult circumstances, they must have been most grateful for family hospitality and financial backing, but there were surely moments when Burgess was painfully aware of the contrast between their meager means and the comfort and prosperity of relatives and friends.

The integral role of extended family in Burgess' life is substantiated in the following excerpts of letters written when he was twenty years old and working in Boston: "Flora Burgess started for Colorado yesterday at 7:15 p.m. and of course I was there to see her off." ... "Do you think it would be extravagant to take Cousin Lottie some flowers? Like to show them some little attention, they have done so much for me." ... "I received a very nice letter from Grandma and with it $10. It was a godsend, for I never was so hard up in my life. Uncle Charlie also made me a present of $5 and would take no refusal...am living on faith, hope, and doughnuts."[12] In 1894, he wrote a good-natured letter to his mother about the untimely visit to his workplace of two grandparents and three aunts:

> They arrived at the store Tuesday afternoon and left in my care a big bag and some bundles. At 12 o'clock Wednesday they serenely bobbed in again with more bundles and appointed me guardian. At 3 o'clock that afternoon I beheld them darkening my horizon once more with more bundles. This time they put them down and opened and assorted the spoils. At 5 o'clock that afternoon a local store added to my collection a huge parcel of heaven knows what...But the first thing next morning comes a long clumsy bundle of curtain poles...[Later,] amidst the smiles of my fellow workers [they] wended their way out of the store en route for the sandy shores of old Cape Cod. All I could think of was a train of Rocky Mountain burros loaded with supplies.[13]

Growing up in the houses and rooms of relatives requires a child to pay close attention to the ways others occupied and shared space, and Thornton Burgess' practice of observation undoubtedly helped him later create animal characters that similarly shared space within an ecosystem. His description of Paddy and Mrs. Paddy Beaver bickering over the location of their house, Reddy Fox and Bobby Coon arguing over who suffered most in the wintertime, the jealous sparring of Grandfather Frog and Old Mr. Toad, and the snippy exchange of two cousins Madam Baldface the Wasp and Madam Dauber the Mud Dauber may have been based more on memory than imagination.

Caroline Hayward Burgess (1850-1912)

The most influential individual in Burgess' life was his mother, who, despite chronic poor health, was an inspiring, supportive presence and a strong maternal guide. Her husband had been seriously ill by the time their baby was four months old and died when Thornton was less than a year old. The burden of parenting had always been hers, creating a strong mother-son bond. A woman once asked Burgess if he had been the little boy who often walked in a Sandwich cemetery with Caroline Burgess. "Yes, I was that boy," he responded. They lacked money and a permanent home, but as a single parent Caroline Burgess provided her son with the loving support and dependable structure every child needs to thrive and grow. "She was a wonderful mother," remarked Burgess' granddaughter Frances Meigs.

Burgess credited his mother's efforts and "constant self-denial" with making their independence possible, and he willingly accepted the role of co-provider and helpmate even as a child:

> "Mother was not strong at the time, a semi-invalid. But somehow, with some help from my paternal grandparents, she managed to support us. At an early age, I learned to look on both side of a penny. … From the time I was 10, I managed to earn enough to buy most of my own clothes."[14]

In 1893, when Burgess, then nineteen, was working in Boston and earning seven dollars a week, he wrote his mother: "I enclose $10 as you say you are short. Now I want you to take this and use it, for I have no use for it at present…If you need more [I] can let you have $5 as well." He replied to her protesting thank-you note with a teasing and face-saving rebuke: "You know, my dear Mother, we are partners as it were, and although you are the senior and I but the junior, as such my advice must have weight or there will be danger of dissolution of the firm."[15]

More lasting than any new clothes or toys she might have provided was the imprint of Caroline Burgess' sense of personal integrity and faith in God. Her emphasis on self-discipline and self-control, rather than external expectations, helped make the quirks and disappointments of daily life more manageable. Years later Caroline Burgess' ideals would be encapsulated in the couplets that became a trademark of her son's books and syndicated newspaper stories:

> "Troubles come to one and all
> Be they big or be they small"
>
> "When things go bad and life is rough
> Advantage lies in being tough;"
>
> "Enough is all you'll ever need
> And taking more is simply greed"
>
> "Sticks will break and sticks will bend
> And all things bad will have an end."

"No greater joy can one attain
Than helping ease another's pain."

Burgess dedicated his first children's book *Old Mother West Wind* to his mother, "to whom I owe so much," and to his only child, Thornton Waldo Burgess III. His third book, *Mother West Wind's Animal Friends*, published in 1912, was also dedicated to Caroline Burgess the year she died: "In tender, loving reverent memory of my mother, who loved little children and was beloved of them, to whom I owe a debt of affection and gratitude beyond my power to pay."

Wildlife Whisperers

Family members in Sandwich provided Burgess with support and social experience while two "animal whisperers" instructed him in the ways of wildlife. His aunt, Arabella Eldred Burgess, and Alice Rebecca Cooke, a friend he met in his late forties, were bright, unconventional women who proved to him the individuality of animals and demonstrated methods for developing relationships with wild creatures. Arabella Burgess lived with her husband Frank, a Sandwich merchant and selectman, in a house near the Town Hall and grist mill on Shawme Pond. It now houses the Thornton W. Burgess Society Museum. Historian Russell Lovell notes in *The Cape Cod Story of Thornton W. Burgess* that Arabella taught nature classes at the local schools:

> She was…a nature-lover who grew plants in the house, bred and raised canaries, and had a number of other pets to whom she also gave free run of the house. Her lot ran down to the edge of the millpond which…was a resting place for the ducks, geese, swans, and other tame and wild fowl. … Arabella fed the pond dwellers from her wharf…and…is reported to have carried about a favorite hen to whom she talked.[16]

Arabella's nephew Thornton often fished from the dock behind her house and must have been fascinated by her unusual talents. Kneeling on the dock, she would call and wave bits of smoked herring through the water. Eels arrived, including one enormous eel that reputedly let her lift it out of the water. Burgess said he saw her summon carp, horned pout, and turtles. According to local lore, no matter who imitated her technique, only Arabella Burgess could draw wild creatures to her dock.

In adulthood, Burgess met Sandwich resident Alice Rebecca Cooke, whom he nicknamed "Aunt Sally" to protect her privacy. He marveled at her ability to attract skunks, raccoons, and woodchucks into her woodshed and onto her lap to be petted, crooned to, and fed bowls of milk and tempting snacks. One evening twenty-two raccoons crowded into the "Woodhouse Night Club." Among Cooke's favorite visitors were two woodchucks, Beauty, who visited the woodshed for thirteen consecutive years, and Polly, who came when called, tolerated wearing a bib, and climbed up on a table to partake of Alice's ninetieth birthday cake. Frances Meigs shared that special occasion with Cooke, her grandparents Thornton and Fannie, as well as others, and recalled that the woodchuck was unfazed at being the only wild creature at the party.

"As a boy I knew Miss Alice Cooke by sight," Burgess wrote in his autobiography. "I can still see her riding up to the village on her horse, sitting straight with an air of distinction, which now, looking back, seems a bit puritanical. Presumably she knew me by name at least."[17] In the 1920s, they met again when Burgess and his wife Fannie stopped at the Cooke home on Route 6A while antique hunting. Burgess was intrigued by Cooke's account of the nightly visits to her woodshed and readily accepted her invitation to come see for himself. He wrote of that evening in his autobiography:

> Presently in came a great skunk through the cat hole [in the door to the woodshed]. Without any hesitancy whatever he walked up those three steps and settled himself comfortable into Miss Cooke's lap, and began to drink milk from the pan she held. Two or three minutes later in came another big skunk, and I mean big. Again there was no hesitancy...the two [skunks] side by side drank amicably from the pan of milk while Miss Cooke stroked them and talked to them.[18]

Barbara Haines Gates, a Sandwich native, remembers attending these woodshed gatherings at which wildlife guests did not take or give offense. "It was weird, but wonderful," says Gates. "Alice Cooke would cuddle a raccoon, and the skunks would get up on her lap. Even a fox came and an opossum. I didn't dare move." In 1955, Little, Brown published *Aunt Sally's Friends in Fur*, one of Burgess' last books. His films of the woodshed visitors entertained lecture circuit audiences for decades. In one, Superior Court Judge Edward T. Broadhurst sat quietly while a raccoon and a skunk climbed into his lap for a breadcrumb snack.

The methods that Arabella Burgess and Alice Cooke used for taming wild animals with patience, gentle respect, and food were successful for Burgess too. *Country Journal* once published a full-page picture of the writer holding a pipe in his mouth with a chickadee perched on the seed-filled bowl. He conditioned birds to come through an open window by first placing bird seed on a window feeder and then near his hand beside the feeder. When they were comfortable taking seed there, he put it into his open hand, then in his hand just inside the window, and then completely inside the room. In *Happy Jack Squirrel*, Farmer Brown's Boy practices the same approach for winning a squirrel's trust.[20]

People often brought injured or displaced wild animals for Burgess to care for. He raised an osprey, a crow, and a tanager that followed him around his yard and flew to meet him when he returned home. He wrote in his 1936 journal that "Tanny appeared as soon as I stepped out this morning and allowed me to pick him up ... While I was shelling peas, he flew down on pan. Later as I lay down on hammock, he sat on the rope."

Influence of Village Life

From his family and community Burgess developed an appreciation for two aspects of village life that would play a role in his children's stories: heritage and gossip. Characters like Grandfather Frog and Mrs. Jerry Muskrat recount nostalgic stories of "great-great-ever-so-great" relatives and sternly remind young tadpoles and muskrats of the dire consequences of ignoring the advice of their elders. Journals and correspondence indicate Burgess' lifelong attention to the activities of family and friends, and his fictitious characters also relied on the proverbial grapevine. (Can anyone listening to noisy crows in a treetop doubt that they are updating the neighborhood?) Yet, his animal stories make it clear the importance of community gossip is not to satisfy nosiness, but to enhance well-being and survival.

Deer, mice, and hawks, as well as humans, benefit in knowing if someone in the community is moving or having a baby. When Blacky the Crow loudly and mischievously reveals to Green Forest residents that Peter and Mrs. Peter have a family, among those most interested, for obvious reasons, are Hooty the Owl, Old Man Coyote, and Reddy and Granny Fox. Knowledge — or lack of knowledge — about who has changed the location of their home, who has eggs and where, or who has annexed whose burrow or nest regularly play a key role in Burgess' plots. His characters work hard to escape the attention of gossips on the ground or overhead by emerging from a burrow at an unexpected time or approaching a nest from different directions.

The primary influences in Thornton Burgess' childhood were a devoted single mother, a large, supportive family, and a vital nineteenth-century New England community. However, the greatest and most lasting influence on his thought and creativity was the natural world that surrounded him. It would be his lifelong teacher, and he remained an eager student who readily shared its lessons with millions of readers young and old.

Chapter 2

Mayflowers and Water Lilies

Burgess himself questioned if his sense of mission in teaching respect and appreciation for the natural world would have been as unwavering if he had been born into luxury and advantage, protected from hard experiences necessitated by financial need. Working in boyhood to help support his mother and himself gave Burgess unique resources: solid observation skills, a core focus, powerful motivation, and writing material that fueled his imagination for a lifetime.

"I made such small contributions to our support as a healthy, willing small boy in a country village might earn."[1]

Thornton W. Burgess, *Now I Remember*, 1960

"My grandfather worked hard as a boy...and did anything he could to earn money. He was an only child, but he was a very happy child."

Frances B. Meigs, granddaughter, 1998

"It was in Sandwich that I first saw Peter Rabbit and became acquainted with Reddy Fox and met Jimmy Skunk and so many other little people of the Green Meadows and the Green Forest."[2]

Thornton W. Burgess, 1948

Working in Sandwich

Hardship may have shaped Thornton Burgess' childhood, but it certainly did not define him, and he always expressed gratitude for the perspective it provided. "It was my very good fortune to be born minus the proverbial silver spoon and to spend my formative years in a lovely, small village before the era of too much and too fast," he wrote.[3] At an early age he contributed to the family income by running errands, shoveling snow, and digging dandelion greens. He delivered milk and eggs door-to-door, herded his neighbors' cows to and from pasture, and sold his mother's popular molasses candy. Bonus prizes for selling magazine subscriptions to *Youth's Companion* provided Christmas presents for her.

Burgess earned money by picking woodland mayflowers in the spring, blueberries and blackberries in the summer, and wild grapes, beach plums, and cranberries in the fall. "Frequently I was afield a mile or two from town shortly after daybreak," he said. "Sometimes I had company, more often I went alone."[4] In his autobiography, Burgess relates one particularly frightening incident from those days, using the third-person pronoun form rather than first-person, perhaps to create dramatic effect or to emphasize distance from the memory:

> I see a lone, small boy picking berries. . .hurrying to fill his pail before a threatening storm broke. . .anxious he watched the ugly threat in the darkening sky. . .with about four quarts of berries in his pail he began to run for the nearest house, perhaps a mile away. The storm broke. The rain. . .became a wind-driven deluge. Panting, wet to the skin, his stockings coming down, still clinging to his pail and careful not to spill the precious berries, he stumbled out of the woods. When midway across a brush-grown old pasture there came a blinding flash of light and a terrific crash of thunder, as if the sky itself had split open. A terrified small boy fell flat, his pail rolling away, his berries a total loss.[5]

This was no childish exaggeration. A half-mile-wide forked bolt of lightning had straddled the village. It struck the steeple of the Congregational Church a few hundred yards from his aunt's house on Shawme Pond and blasted a hole in one of the massive glass factory chimneys.[6] Being alone outdoors in such a storm must have inspired Burgess' story "Buster Bear's Great Fright" in *At Paddy the Beaver's Pond* (1950):

> The storm was coming fast now. The lightning flashed with little time between the flashes. To Buster it seemed as if his heart jumped with every flash. He was sure it did with every terrific clap of thunder. Now he could see the tall pine tree at the very edge of the big windfall. It was the tallest pine tree anywhere around... He was almost there when the first drops of rain fell. He never did get there. Came a blinding flash of lightning and with it a crash of thunder that shook the ground under his feet. He fell heels over head, scrambled to his feet...he ran blindly, not seeing where he was going. He bumped into trees, and tumbled over logs. He was bawling with fright. He didn't know what had happened...Lightning had struck and shattered that tall tree.[7]

Burgess received seventy-five cents a week to take two herds of about a dozen cows to and from the twenty-four acres of common pastureland at Town Neck, which was bound on three sides by bay, salt marsh, and the Scusset River, now the eastern end of the Cape Cod Canal. He took the cows to pasture at 6 a.m. and returned with them around 4 p.m. Late one afternoon he discovered a cow was missing. With a thunderstorm approaching, he drove the rest of the herd home and returned to look for it as the storm broke. Finally, "wet to the skin, muddy and scared," he found the cow and its newborn calf hiding in underbrush.

On a different occasion, he watched horrified as a train was unable to avoid running down one of his cows that had gotten onto the track through a fence break. Fortunately, its owner was understanding. After having the cow butchered and dressed, he offered Burgess and his mother Caroline some choice cuts. "It was seldom that we could afford beefsteak," Burgess said. "But this wasn't beef...When you daily drive cows to and from pasture, they are your cows, regardless of who owns them. We couldn't possibly eat a mouthful of my cow." Ethics came first, and the two declined the offer.[8]

Cranberry Picking Provides Income

Another source of income was fall cranberry picking.[9] Long harvested by Native Americans for their nutritional and medicinal value, cranberries were first cultivated commercially by Henry Hall in the mid-Cape town of Dennis in the early 1800s. The crop was perfectly suited to the Cape's sandy soil and swampy areas and had become a significant agricultural product by Burgess' day. Families and neighbors worked together to harvest the tart, red berries before first frost. The opening of Sandwich schools was delayed five weeks for cranberry picking in 1885, and Burgess, then eleven, may have contributed to that year's harvest of 2,389 barrels.

Cranberry pickers spread out over acres of bogs, hand-pulling cranberries off sturdy, low-growing vines. They collected the berries in pans held between their legs and then emptied the contents into a crate at the end of rows. A picker's wage was generally ten cents per six-quart measure. Boys waxed their fingers for protection from the plants' wiry stems while girls wore gloves. "It was so hard on your hands," remembered one West Wareham cranberry picker. "It tore the skin off and got under your fingernails. And it hurt your knees to kneel there in the bogs so long." But Burgess had fond memories of the outdoor community effort:

> While fingers were busy, tongues were busy too, and village news became cranberry gossip. Oh, those picnic lunches at the nooning while backs straightened and fingers relaxed! ... There was the spice of good stories and old-time familiar songs. Then the tally at the end of the picking and the long walk or ride home, sometimes a matter of several miles, a jarring ride on boards put across the side of a blue truck wagon drawn by a plodding horse or a span that sometimes plodded and sometimes hurried with a jolting trot.[10]

Delivery Boy for Water Lily Grower

East Sandwich commercial water lily grower William Chipman cultivated the elegant pink flowers in more than a dozen spring-fed pools near the present entrance to the Burgess Society's Green Briar Nature Center. He paid Thornton Burgess to deliver and collect his mail and telegrams at the Sandwich post office in the village.[11] The three-mile, round-trip route took the boy past a small pond, upland pastures and woods, and along a country lane. Some thirty years later Burgess would name these places the Green Meadows, Green Forest, and Smiling Pool. Much of the area is now preserved as the town-owned, fifty-seven-acre Briar Patch Conservation Area.

From a wooded hillside likely on Burgess' route, Burgess Society naturalist Mary Beers looked down at the spring-fed pond below. "There's the 'smile' of Thornton Burgess' Smiling Pool," she said, pointing out the crescent-shape of the southern end of the freshwater pond behind Green Briar's historic jam kitchen. The dense patches of thorny briars that Burgess describes in the opening passage of *The Dear Old Briar-patch* (1947) are also here, still part of the East Sandwich landscape he knew:

> The dear old Briar-patch is an island of safety on the far side of the Green Meadows. As a Rabbit runs it is only a little way from the edge of the Old Pasture. The ground rises a little there so that it is just enough above the level of the Green Meadows for those who live in it to look out over the latter to see who comes and who may go and be they friend or be they foe.
>
> Bushes and young trees of many kinds, some bearing fruit in season, some with thorny stems clutching at those who rudely brush against them, crowd parts of the Old Briar-patch. In other parts tangled masses of greenbriar have left no room for other growth. Here and there small trees thrust their way above, inviting feathered folk to make a friendly call and rest a bit. Vines of several kinds creep and climb this way and that. Some lie in wait for careless feet. Others with hooked claws reach

for and hold back those who are not welcome here. In early spring violets and shy anemones bloom just within, and in early summer wild roses along the edge are a joy to all who pass this way.

Within are many little paths. They cross and recross. Some lead into the thickest bramble tangles where they become tunnels through which none bigger than those who made them may pass, secret places wherein to hide in time of danger...In the middle is an old house, an underground house. It was dug by Johnny Chuck's grandfather before there was a briar patch there. The seeds of the bushes and young trees and vines and brambles had not then been dropped there by the feathered folk, or blown there by the Merry Little Breezes.[12]

Mayflowers a Favorite Flower

As lovely as Chipman's water lilies were, it was the wild mayflowers, or trailing arbutus, that most delighted Burgess. He and other Sandwich residents earned money gathering the sweet-smelling blossoms in April or May. "They had a glorious fragrance, distinctive as lily-of-the-valley," says Sandwich native Barbara Bassett, who grew up near Gully Lane and Alice Cooke's house below the pastures Burgess crossed as a boy. She remembers collecting mayflowers in the same general area Burgess frequented, cutting them carefully with scissors to avoid disturbing the roots. When Burgess was ten, the *Sandwich Observer* reported that within two weeks nearly 1,322 ounces of the blossoms had been shipped for commercial sale; local schools gathered and boxed twenty-five bunches of mayflowers for a children's hospital in Boston.[13]

In 1902, Burgess was working as an editor for *Good Housekeeping* in Springfield, Massachusetts, when he wrote the following letter to George Haines, thanking him profusely for sending a cherished reminder of their boyhood days together:

My Dear George,

All the day my desk has been filled with the delicious fragrance of arbutus, such arbutus as I am fain to think grows only on Old Cape Cod. In truth I have been breathing the very atmosphere of Sandwich and the dear old haunts...All day my thoughts have been wandering home by the sea and every whiff of the pink beauties has been a whiff from old days. I want to thank you very heartily and that you should know how much pleasure the flowers have given and are giving me. A week ago Sunday I went up into the mountains after some, but for color they could not compare with these I have from you.

I have bragged a whole lot about the deep color of Cape Cod arbutus telling people here that they do not know what pink ones are. Today I have been running around showing them that I can make good my boasts. No other arbutus ever has or ever can seem quite the same as those from home.

Should like a word from you, old man, when you can spare so much time. Am driven to death myself. Have a contract with a New York magazine for a three or four thousand (word) article every month which pays me good money on the outside. They have asked me to write for them until Dec. 1902. Have an order from

Everybody's magazine for a 3,500-word article which I have not had time to touch yet...Remember me to the friends. Write a feller.

Sincerely yours,
Thornton[14]

Recreation and Friends

Not all of Burgess' boyhood outdoor activities were related to earning money. He spent countless hours hiking, fishing, camping, and hunting with his friend Ernest Woodwell. The *Sandwich Observer* reported that the two boys caught three young eagles that "weighed about five pounds each." A memoir by Woodwell's younger brother William provides a glimpse of the places Burgess frequented:

> The natural advantages of [Sandwich] for a growing boy can hardly be surpassed. There was a lower pond, irregular in shape, with a dam near the church. Between it and the upper pond was a higher dam, which furnished power for a tack factory and later a silk mill. The upper pond was an oval and fed by cold springs of water. A creek meandered from the lower pond through the salt marshes, for more than a mile, to Cape Cod Bay. There were beaches, sand dunes, and sand bars. At the extreme high tide the marshes were frequently flooded. There were a number of swimming places at both ponds and along the creek, but the ocean water was too cold to be endured.
>
> A semi-circle of hills enclosed the town on the land side, which extended across the Cape for eighteen miles. They were covered with pine, scrub, oak, and other trees, and held rabbits, squirrels, skunks, foxes, and occasionally a deer might be seen. Arbutus, which we called "May-flower," was abundant, and blueberries, blackberries, raspberries, and wild grapes all thrived in season.
>
> Carrying a frying pan and potatoes, we would catch a few freshwater fish and dine by the lakeside, or have a clambake on the beach. We built wigwams in the deep woods and hunted for bird's eggs, animals, and wild flowers.[15]

Ernest Woodwell gave the name "Thornton" to his first child who was born on Burgess' January 14th birthday. According to William Woodwell, his brother Ernest was Burgess' first illustrator, having provided pen-and-ink drawings for work that appeared in a "hunting and fishing magazine." Ernest was also the friend who adamantly counseled Burgess to raise the fee for his first commercial assignment from five to fifteen dollars. The unexpected death at sixty-two of his childhood friend was a permanent loss to Burgess, who made the following journal entry while traveling by steamer in the Caribbean:

> River muddy. Both shores jungle swamp with trees along shore mostly mangroves. Saw several herons, white and blue, and a few swallows following ship.

> Only twice in whole distance did we see human beings…aboard all day, reading *The Trees* by Conrad Richter. … Ernest would have been seventy-eight this day. Thought of him as I watched work on dock.[16]

Burgess was a deeply loyal friend, to a fault some said, a man who made and kept countless social, personal, and professional relationships over his lifetime. He regularly sent Christmas cards to Sandwich friends Alice Cooke, Ida Putnam and her brother John, Ida French, Elizabeth Clark, and Nina and George Sutton. Barbara Gates grew up next-door to Burgess' friend Lizzy Burbank, head librarian at the Sandwich Public Library and an avid birder. "They were great friends, and he always came to visit her," said Gates, who remembers the writer as "very tall and talkative":

> When [Burbank] banded birds for the government, I'd have to make sure my cats were in. The big blue jays would lay still in her hands, scared to death, but the little ones were feisty. She would take them into her house, with everything laid out on the table. I don't know how she got that little band around their legs so quickly. Thornton Burgess would ask her all kinds of questions about the best way to catch them. He was fascinated by the way she did it.

Gates' great-aunt, Lillie Haines Tangney, was another cherished friend of Burgess'. In high school, he wrote a playful poem to "Tiger Lil," signing it with the nickname he acquired as the boy who sat behind her and pulled her hair in school:

> A girl to Latin not inclined
> To the Pedagogue at once did go
> Saying, "To study this I've not the mind,"
> He answer made, "T'is true, I know
> A mind you have, but little in it
> And if this study you do drop
> For a three year course you'll get the credit
> Allow it, therefore, I shall not."
>
> Tease, Torment & Co.

Burgess continued to visit and correspond with Tangney throughout their lives, sending her affectionate, upbeat postcards on life and aging from Tobago, the Caribbean Island where he wintered after his second wife Fannie died in 1950:

> Time isn't fooled and now decrees
> I'm 81 in both my knees.
>
> There's glory in the setting sun
> In growing old there can be fun.

Blue sky flecked with white clouds, blue sea flecked with white surf, featherduster palms sweeping the sky, coconuts dropping with a thud now and then. … My love to you, T.W.B.

Now my love and every good wish for this year and many more. Let's live to be 100. TT&Co

In 1964, Lillie Tangney was ninety-two years old and residing at a nursing home in Buzzards Bay, Massachusetts. Thornton Burgess, ninety, was recovering from a stroke at the Mary Lyon Nursing Home in Hampden, Massachusetts when he received the following spirited letter from his old friend:

Dear TT & Co.,

Home is home. I want to get back. I must have someone to stay nights with me as the Dr. says I mustn't stay alone – we'll see about that…Excuse pencil as I have no ink – and these new-fangled pens are no good.

So long,

Tiger Lillie[17]

"In a sense, I have never left it …"

When Alice Cooke tipped off Thornton Burgess that planners of Sandwich's 1939 Tercentennial celebration intended to invite him to be the keynote speaker, he resisted the suggestion: "What they need for an event such as this is an orator. I am nothing of the kind." A modest man who disapproved of excessive pride, Burgess worried about being perceived by townsfolk as self-impressed with his own celebrity and considered it embarrassing to be in the spotlight at the celebration. Nevertheless, he accepted and must have been pleased by the recognition.

Carolyn Crowell, whose family still operates an orchard and farm stand where Burgess used to stop, recalls riding her bicycle up School Street just as Thornton Burgess was talking. He had been given a rousing welcome by the large audience seated at tables on the grounds of the Casino where forty-eight years earlier he had received a high school diploma. Burgess addressed the crowd as a fellow townsman, congratulating those gathered for preserving the town's historic inheritance for future generations "despite the loss of industries, despite the depression, despite the pinch of hard times." He concluded his speech saying, "May this lovely old town which you …and I love have many more Tercentenaries, always as beautiful in the hearts of her children as in our hearts today.[18]

On that historic occasion Burgess read "Gully Lane," a nostalgic poem of unexpected ambiguity he composed in 1936. The verses recalled the country lane he walked regularly as a boy delivering mail to and from William Chipman's office and the Sandwich Post Office in the village. His route likely took him across open cow pastures and hay fields above the Smiling Pool and then through a gate that opened onto Gully Lane. From there he probably turned down Gully Lane, which descends steeply to the Old King's Highway, now Route 6A, and walked on into the village.

In the late 1800s, Burgess would have shared the ancient highway with horses and oxen, wagons and carriages, pedestrians and bicycles, so "Gully Lane" preserved memories of the more peaceful portion of his route:

If I should walk in Gully Lane
Think you that I would find
The boyhood lost so long ago
The youth I left behind?

Are still the days so carefree there?
So filled with simple joy?
So heedless of the march of time
As when I was a boy.

Would clutching hands of bramble bush
Still reach to hold me fast
Or would they treat me as a ghost –
A vision from the past?

Would summer berries taste as sweet?
The wild grape spice the air
With quite the winey fragrance that
In memory haunts me there?

Ah me! So many years have fled
And mingled joy with pain
I fear to seek the boy who once
Did walk in Gully Lane.[19]

If financial need required Burgess to labor as a boy and deprived him of a college education, it gave him its equivalent in field observation and naturalistic inquiry. His most famous character, the endlessly curious, skeptical, and often misinformed Peter Rabbit, would model for young readers the benefits of seeking information about nature. Thornton Burgess left Sandwich for Boston in 1892, and several years later moved permanently to Western Massachusetts. However, the knowledge and values he gained on Cape Cod appeared for more than fifty years in the books, newspaper stories, radio scripts, and lectures he wrote for children as fascinated by nature's ways as he was.

Chapter 3

A Place in the World At Large

Thornton Burgess was eighteen years old when he moved first to Boston and then to Springfield, Massachusetts. More than a dozen years passed before his first children's book, Old Mother West Wind, *was published. In those intervening years Burgess discovered his professional calling, faced personal adversity, and transitioned from an uncertain, directionless youth into a mature, confident journalist. His major work as a writer, however, would still lie ahead.*

"I knew beyond any doubt what I didn't want to do, but got no glimmer at all of what I might like to do. All through the years since, I have had a deep and understanding sympathy for the boy who has not yet found himself when he starts out in the world."[1]

Thornton W. Burgess
Now I Remember, 1960

Leaving Sandwich

In May 1891, Thornton Burgess graduated from Sandwich Academy in a class of nine. He was bitterly disappointed that his mother's poor health prevented her from attending the ceremony at the Casino, a large community building on School Street. As class orator, Burgess gave a speech titled "Time, Not Popular Clamor, Establishes Human Greatness." He longed to attend college, but that was financially impossible. While close friends would go on to attend college — Ernest Woodwell to the Massachusetts Institute of Technology and Jackie Leonard to Harvard — Burgess stayed in Sandwich to work at a grocery store, probably his grandfather's business on Jarves Street. The next summer he rented a horse and wagon to peddle fruit for a Boston wholesaler, but it was not a profitable enterprise for the self-described shy boy who was "not a go-getter. At last Burgess and his mother acknowledged that a career in Sandwich was unlikely: "I had to face the hard fact that I must find a place for myself in the world at large."[2]

His only option for advancement was the offer of his practical grandfather Charles Burgess to pay for a year of bookkeeping courses. Burgess never had an aptitude for business or math, but he accepted, stoically, one senses, and enrolled at Comer's Commercial College at 666 Washington Street in Boston. In order to consolidate housing expenses, he and his mother moved from Cape Cod to a small apartment in Somerville, not far from her Cambridge birthplace. He commuted to school via horsecar and joined the Boston YMCA, which he described in the following letter to his friend George Haines. (His teenage enthusiasm for hunting would later be replaced by passionate opposition to the practices that supplied the game he mentions, probably at Boston's famed Quincy Market):

> Three dollars admits one to all privileges except gymnasium. There are classes in various studies every evening and I am taking German and shorthand...A splendid library, reading room, and parlors make it very nice. I see a good deal of [Ernest] Woodwell...Tonight I am going to see the big Republican parade in Cambridge. Have heard some fine speeches this fall...I would give a good deal for one day's good shooting. I am planning to come down to S- the Tuesday before Thanksgiving and stay until the next Monday. Shall hunt; hunt; hunt. Save a little game for me.
>
> Went down through the market the other day and the game set me wild. Deer, duck, partridge, quail, woodcock, snipe, rabbits, and squirrels in any amount. ...

> Our house is situated fine. Electrics go right past the door. Two depots on Boston Maine R.R. within three minutes walk. Library, High-school and City Hall within three minutes walk. Fire engine house about one block from us, so we see all that is going on. I take train at 8:02 in the morning and in ten minutes am in Boston. Get home anywhere from three to five in the afternoon.[3]

Burgess managed to pass his bookkeeping and accounting courses, and took a job as cashier and assistant bookkeeper with James & Knowles, a well-known Boston shoe company at 15 Winter Street. "I doubt if in the two years of my employment there I knew a single happy day," he confessed in an article for *The American*. "Each day but added to my knowledge that I was not cut out for a business career. I worried over mistakes and took them home with me. I hated figures only less than I hated barter and sale."[4] Nevertheless, his salary provided a stable, basic living.

One special challenge to Burgess' accounting skills was the light-fingered approach of bosses who regularly helped themselves to the business' proceeds to pay admission to local baseball games, probably the Beaneaters, a local team that would become the Boston Red Sox. When his mother's deteriorating health forced her to move in with her remarried sister Lucy in Springfield two hours away, Burgess took a small hall bedroom in Somerville. He later described those times as "lean days, lonesome days, and to a considerable degree dark days."

In the fall of 1893, James & Knowles laid him off. The mixed blessing meant release from disagreeable employment, but also loss of income at a time when ten cents paid for one or two meals a day. Subsequently he found work as a bookkeeper for a German fur and dress trimming merchant. Although Burgess occasionally put together poems and rhymes as a pleasant pastime, "adopting the writer's craft as a profession never entered my mind." When several of his creative efforts were accepted for publication, he was surprised and delighted.[5]

Thornton Burgess' first published work was "An Old Story: Dedicated to a Four-Pound Trout." The six-stanza poem written "for my own amusement" appeared in the June 8, 1895 issue of *Forest and Stream* magazine.[6] It contained the blend of naturalistic and human elements that would later characterize Burgess' writing. (The poem also suggests that fifteen years before *Old Mother West Wind* appeared on book shelves, Burgess' Merry Little Breezes, as well as a four-pound trout, were lurking in the recesses of his imagination.)

This poem was attributed to "Waldo." It was a pseudonym Burgess later used frequently, but this instance is curious. Burgess wrote for nearly forty magazines in the first decade of his career as a journalist/editor, and often used pseudonyms to disguise the fact that he had numerous articles in single magazine issues or had articles in multiple publications. He wrote as "W.B. Thornton," for example, for the prestigious *Country Life* magazine while he was an editor at Phelps Publishing Company in Springfield.[7] When "An Old Story" was published, however, Burgess was twenty-one, not yet employed as a writer, and anxious to earn money. Why would he pass up this opportunity for recognition? A comment in his autobiography suggests that in fact his own name did appear on the poem:

> Now in these days of floundering uncertainty I found a form of relief in… seeking self-expression in verse. *Forest and Stream*, a well-known sporting periodical, published some verses of mine to a four-pound trout that I had yet to catch…the honorarium was a complimentary copy of the magazine. But that was compensation enough – it was recognition; I saw my name in type as an accredited author.[8]

Burgess researcher Peter Oehlkers, a Salem State University communications professor, speculates that Burgess modestly viewed it as the unaccomplished work of an amateur, not worthy of attribution, or perhaps in writing his autobiography fifty years later he simply forgot he had used a pseudonym. Regardless of his motive for choosing anonymity, publication in a national magazine reinforced Burgess' self-confidence and attraction to writing, if not his solvency. On impulse, he placed a small paid advertisement for his writing services in *Brains*, a Boston advertiser:

> Get a good man
> That can yield a good pen
> Let him advertise for you
> Tho' it cost you a ten.
> Try the new writer,
> He's clever and bright
> His name is T. Burgess,
> And his ads are alright.[9]

Immediately, Burgess received a response from an advertising agency whose client, the Miles Standish Spring Water Company, wanted a twenty-verse parody of Henry Wadsworth Longfellow's narrative poem, "The Courtship of Miles Standish." Burgess contemplated charging five dollars for the finished piece, which he considered an exorbitant fee for a few hours work. At the urging of his pal Ernest Woodwell, he asked for and, to his astonishment, readily received fifteen dollars in payment. Another twenty-verse advertisement (for which he charged twenty dollars) and more commercial writing assignments followed. He wrote a packaged cereal insert for the Shredded Wheat Company and sport-themed ads that emphasized golfing, skiing, and baseball for the American Optical Company.

Burgess called this time in the Boston area "the two years of maladjustment," but he appreciated the insights those rocky times provided and the exposure to professional writing. "I knew beyond all doubt what I wanted to do in life. I had found myself even though I had not as yet found a place for myself…It was something to know what I wanted to do. Now I had something definite to watch for, an opening, be it ever so small."[10]

A Fateful Decision

That opening may have been considerably smaller than he anticipated. In late fall 1895, while recovering from malaria and working as a bookkeeper in Boston, Burgess received an unexpected special delivery letter from his mother in Springfield.

A neighbor there was editor-in-chief of Phelps Publishing, a large company that produced *Springfield Homestead*, a semi-weekly urban newspaper that featured social news, articles, and photographs. Phelps was associated with the nationally-distributed Orange Judd Company, which published agricultural periodicals, including *Farm and Home*, *American Agriculturalist*, *Orange Judd Farmer*, and *New England Homestead*. Together the two companies had over a quarter-million subscribers. When Caroline Burgess learned that Phelps needed an office boy, she perceived it as a golden opportunity in the field her son was drawn to and urged him to apply immediately.

Ostensibly, the job offered little in exchange for full-time employment as a bookkeeper with a reputable Boston company. Burgess would be sweeping floors, dusting desks, emptying wastebaskets, sharpening pencils, and collecting mail for seven editors. His pay would drop from $8 to $5 per week. Relocation meant leaving good friends and family in the Boston area. Furthermore, the decision and the move had to be made at once, so there would be no time to give his employer proper notice.

> I didn't want to leave Boston. I dreaded to start anew amid strangers and in a strange place. I confess that also there was a slight feeling of humiliation at the thought of being a mere office boy at my age [22].[11]

Burgess' autobiography recalls his turmoil in making this critical decision, but does not mention the passionate desire to attend college expressed in the following letter to his mother:

> My Dear Little Mother,
>
> I am coming though it breaks me all up to say so. I will mail this special so that will give you time to find me a boarding place, as I did not receive your yesterday special until this A.M...Feel so bad I don't know what to do at leaving Boston. Will be in some time Sunday, though can't say now what train. Went yesterday to say farewell to the colleges, and, Mother, I think I would give two years off of my life to go to college...Hope you can find me a good place somewhere near. Sample the cooking. Am glad you sent the money as I shall get me some clothes.
>
> Love to all. Hastily, Thornton[12]

The Right Decision

Lowly and poor-paying as it was, the job with Phelps Publishing suited him perfectly, from the hectic hubbub of newsrooms to the smell of printer's ink in the production department. Before long he received small assignments and eventually became a reporter with his own desk. "That desk was a throne to me," Burgess recalled. He began regularly contributing verse, children's stories, and short articles for the household sections of the farm papers. His pay increased to fifteen dollars a week and occasionally his work appeared on the front page. He humorously remarked that his feet were on the lowest rung of the employment ladder, "but they were firmly planted there." In time, he became sports editor for the *Springfield Homestead*, reporting on amateur and professional bicycle racing championships, Eastern League baseball games, and other sports, as well as covering news in railroad shops and fraternal organizations, and writing obituaries.[13]

Springfield, Massachusetts was a bustling city where exciting new developments in automotive technology were taking place. Brothers Frank and Charles Duryea of East Springfield had constructed the first gasoline-powered "motor wagon." In 1895, the year Burgess moved to Springfield, the Duryea brothers won the first U.S. car race; the next year they won the first automobile race in England and all prizes for gasoline cars at the world's first track race in Providence, Rhode Island. Between 1895 and 1898, the brothers commercially produced thirteen of their two-cylinder, five horsepower Runabouts. Burgess interviewed at least one of the brothers and speculated that his 1898 automobile column for Phelps Publishing may have been the first one in the country.[14]

In 1902, Burgess accepted a challenging assignment for *Country Life*, the highly regarded pictorial magazine, providing seasonal information about gardening, agriculture, outdoor recreation, and nature for its monthly calendar. The following excerpt from his autobiography shows the rigor of his research, as well as his interaction with prominent natural scientists nearly a decade before publication of his children's books:

> [The assignment] means seemingly endless hours of research, of checking and rechecking. In its field *Country Life* was authoritative. There could be no slips. All my bird work would pass under the critical eyes of Dr. Frank Chapman, world-famous ornithologist of the American Museum of Natural History. All my botanical and horticultural work would have to survive the scrutiny of Dr. Liberty Bailey of Cornell University.[15]

Working As a Writer

Between 1895 and 1911, Burgess worked for Phelps Publishing as a reporter, photographer, and managing editor; a literary and household editor for *Orange Judd*; and an associate editor for *Good Housekeeping*, which was owned by Phelps. In these various capacities, he researched and wrote full-length articles, filler pieces, news snippets, and advertising copy. He also reviewed query letters, made production decisions about use of advertising or editorial copy, and fielded communication with readers and writers.

His 1907 and 1908 letters to one prospective *Orange Judd* contributor, William W. Christman of Delanson, New York, indicate Burgess' editorial responsibilities and reveal his early interest in advocating for wildlife conservation:

> 1/28/1907: I have found two papers of yours on the "Chipping Sparrow." I think these must be the ones to which you referred in your last letter to me. I hope to be able to use at least part of these to promote interest among our young people in bird life and protection.

> 4/21/1908: I regret my inability to use this article on the hammer stone. My space is so crowded and I have so much that I want to use that I feel obliged to use

> articles of a more general nature than this is. This interests you, and interests me personally, for I have spent many a pleasant hour tramping over the plowed fields on this same quest, however, there are more people who would not understand the charm of it all. I therefore feel that I had best return it to you that you may dispose of it elsewhere, if possible.
>
> 2/17/1909: The great mass of material which I have on hand crowded out your little nature story during the holidays, but I am going to try to use it right away...the trouble with the editorial business is that we never know until we start to make up the paper just how much space is going to be allowed us. Thus it happens that things we plan to use get crowded out by advertising at the last moment.[16]

As an associate editor of the popular household magazine *Good Housekeeping*, Burgess wrote poems, children's stories, advice, and general interest features such as "Dogs for the Home, "An Old Aunt's Gift," "Cape Cod Turkey," "The Germ in the Refrigerator," "A Neighborhood Cow," and "A Ballad of Christmas Toys." His Cape Cod background was useful in writing articles about selecting and preparing lobsters, fresh fish, and oysters.[17]

In 1905, Phelps published a collection of Burgess' breezy *Good Housekeeping* verses in a book titled *The Bride's Primer.* The light-hearted spoof on "the ways of brides and their misadventures" described such domestic catastrophes as exploding homemade ketchup, jelly-making, wallpaper hanging, the bride's poor choice of a bathrobe, and the groom's inability to keep a fire going.

Marriage and Home

With his career thriving, Burgess, twenty-nine, became engaged to Nina Elvira Osborne, twenty-two, a popular young West Springfield woman active in local charities. Burgess' numerous photographs of Nina convey his infatuation and their mutual love of the outdoors. Four hundred guests attended the June 29, 1905 wedding ceremony at the Park Street Congregational Church, with almost half that number attending a reception and wedding supper at the Osborne home. The *Springfield Daily News* commented on the ceremony's abundant use of natural decorations:

> The altar of the church was handsomely decorated with palms, ferns, and daisies. Immediately in front of the pulpit and at the end of the center aisle was erected a beautiful arch of mountain laurel and daisies. After the guests were seated a chain of daisies closed the entrances to the pews on the heads of which were bunches of daisies and ferns...The ceremony was performed with a ring service, the party standing under the floral bower. At intervals during the service Miss Lulu Sackett sang two selections.[18]

The couple spent their honeymoon canoeing and camping in the Adirondacks, and returned to the three-story house Burgess had purchased earlier that year at 61 Jackson Street, later renamed Washington Road. The spacious home abutted Springfield's lovely Forest Park (but its eighty-foot driveway and frequent snow shoveling receive considerably more mention in Burgess' journals).

A Child's Birth, A Mother's Death

As his mother's happiness in marriage had been short-lived, so, tragically, was Thornton Burgess'. He and Nina had been married eleven months when she went into labor on May 17, 1906. Their son Thornton Waldo Burgess III was born the next day. Burgess had called a doctor, but Nina died of complications later that night. The notice of her death in the *Springfield Daily News* read:

> The sympathy of many friends will be extended to Thornton W. Burgess of the Phelps Publishing Company, in the death of his wife, Mrs. Nina Osborne Burgess, at her home, 61 Jackson Street, a son born yesterday surviving her. Mrs. Burgess was well-known in this city and West Springfield and was esteemed by all who knew her.[19]

The Rev. Dr. W. H. Webb, who had presided over the couple's wedding only months earlier, conducted the funeral service at the Washington Road home. Overcome by shock and grief, Burgess was unable to attend. To help with the baby and the household, Nina's mother, Mary Osborne, moved in with Burgess and his mother Caroline, whose sister Lucy also lived in the city and undoubtedly helped out. Burgess' personal writings eight months after his wife's death reveal the totality and duration of his sorrow, and the sustaining strength he found in work:

> 1/1/1907: I have scattered a few flowers on the grave of Her who was the light of my life and who only a year ago so bravely and cheerfully looked forward to her hour of traivel [*sic*]...I shall try to at least be cheerful. I owe it to my friends. But O I am so lonely...And still day by day the conviction grows that She is waiting for me, trusting me to absolutely not fail her...so I would go step by step the best I can.

> 1/4/1907: It is thirty-three weeks tonight since my little girl entered the larger life and still I cannot reconcile myself. Still I cry "Why? Why? Why? Why is faith so poor a comforter?"

> 1/6/1907: Took baby for a long walk in the park. He saw his first birds (pigeons) and his first deer and elk. Not the least afraid. He is very, very like his Mother at times. As he lay in my arms, she...she looked out from his eyes.

> 2/2/1907: Worked till 11 p.m. Blessed is work; it holds the thought and heart aches and sorrows are for the moment forced aside.

2/6/1907: Thirty-eight weeks ago tonight that my little girl was taken ill. I've lived years. I wonder when and where I shall meet her. God help me to guide her boy right.[20]

Unforeseen Changes

On April 30, 1911, Burgess, then thirty-seven, married Fannie Phillips Johnson in Ithaca, New York after a two-year courtship. She was the widow of entomologist Willis Grant Johnson, Burgess' friend and colleague at *Orange Judd*. Fannie, thirty-nine, and her two children, Helen, twelve, and Chester, seventeen, moved to the Springfield home with Burgess, his five-year-old son Thornton, and his mother Caroline, sixty-one. It was evidently a stressful adjustment for all as the two women tried to run the household and raise the children together.[21] To make matters worse, only a few months after remarrying, Burgess learned that *Good Housekeeping* had been sold and the offices would be moving to New York. The following Monday morning, he found a terse note on his desk: "T.W.B. Two weeks from date your services will be dispensed with." He recalled those desperate times in his autobiography:

> Had I been single, or had I possessed an adequate reserve fund, the situation would have been less drastic. I had long wanted to break loose on my own to see what I could do as a free-lance writer, but with those dependent on me I had not dared make the attempt. Now I was out, with the long wanted freedom, but afraid of it just then. It was swim or sink...I had wanted independence. Now I had it, with all its uncertainties. No salary. No fixed income of any kind. No adequate reserve.[22]

"The period that followed was difficult for the entire family," observed Burgess' granddaughter Frances Meigs. "One week there might be twenty-five dollars from the sale of a story, the next week nothing."[23] Burgess credited Fannie with her support of his determination to continue to write for a living. His experience with *Orange Judd's* agricultural publications helped secure work as a copywriter/ photographer for J.H. McFarland Company in Harrisburg, Pennsylvania, one of the first garden catalogue publishers to use color photographs.[24]

Although he was faced with nearly overwhelming financial pressure and professional uncertainty, Burgess had learned to watch for and trust in small opportunities, for a menial office boy's job had provided unimaginable fulfillment of his dreams. Once again, doors opened slightly in an unfamiliar field. With the modest success of *Old Mother West Wind* in 1910 and a weekly contract to write a children's newspaper column in 1911, he perceived that there was potential to earn a living by writing children's books and stories.

By 1913, Thornton Burgess left journalism and advertising permanently. He was on the right path, but there was certainly no indication that he would achieve national recognition as a writer, the personal friend of eminent scientists, or a board member of esteemed institutions. When international success and celebrity eventually came, he would credit a handful of bedtime stories written to comfort his young son Thornton as the catalyst.

The Origins: Photos

Thornton W. Burgess, Sr. (1850-1874) died of tuberculosis in Richmond, Virginia the year his son was born. (Photo circa early 1870s)

Caroline Hayward Burgess (1850-1912), wife of Thornton W. Burgess, Sr., mother of Thornton W. Burgess II. She is buried in Springfield, Massachusetts. Photo circa 1910.

Charles Coatesworth Pinckney (known as C.C.P.) Waterman, a payroll master and clerk at the Boston & Sandwich Glass Company, was the uncle of Caroline Burgess. She and Thornton lived with him after her husband died.

Charles and Mary Burgess, parents of Thornton Burgess' father, Thornton Sr. Their daughter-in-law, Caroline, and grandson, Thornton II, lived in their house on Jarves Street in the 1880s.

Burgess was close to his cousin William "Will" Hayward Tobey.

Flora Burgess, one of many cousins Thornton Burgess grew up with in Sandwich.

Arabella Eldred Burgess, Thornton's aunt, was well known as a nature lover and an "animal whisperer." She's shown here with a pet hen. Burgess often fished in Shawme Pond from the dock behind her house.

School Street scene showing Burgess' birthplace (second house on right with porch). The Casino and Burgess' elementary school are further up on the opposite side of the street.

Cars and horses share Jarves Street in this turn-of-the-century scene. The post office is at the right and just beyond it is Charles and Mary Burgess' house, now an inn, where Burgess and his mother lived.

This Sandwich postcard shows Post Office Square with the Burgess home to the left and the post office building in the middle of the picture.

This charming picture shows three boys on elm-lined Main Street. To the right of the post office (left side of photo) is another home where Burgess and his mother Caroline lived with relatives.

First Congregational Church, which Burgess and his mother Caroline attended.

Greek Revival-style Sandwich Town Hall, built in 1835 at the head of Shawme Pond.

Early nineteenth century view of Sandwich Grist Mill.

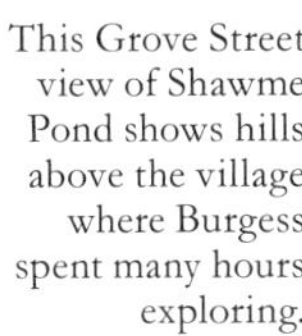

This Grove Street view of Shawme Pond shows hills above the village where Burgess spent many hours exploring.

Thornton Burgess at 17.

High on Academy Road was the high school Burgess attended. It overlooked the village, a broad salt marsh, and Cape Cod Bay

The Lake House was a popular boardinghouse on Shawme Pond where Burgess and his mother Caroline lived in the early 1890s.

Like many Cape Cod children, Thornton Burgess picked cranberries in the fall to earn money.

When Burgess was a boy he earned money by taking cows to graze for the day at the town's common land on Town Neck, a few miles from this pastoral East Sandwich scene.

This view from an East Sandwich meadow looking towards Cape Cod Bay was probably familiar to Burgess as a boy.

This view of a boy fishing on Shawme Pond shows the town's ancient cemetery to the left.

Fishing and boating were popular on Shawme Pond in Burgess' day.

When he was five, Burgess walked with his cousin Will and grandfather across this boardwalk to see a harpooned whale on the beach. *Courtesy of Sandwich Town Archives and Research Center.*

View of Boston and Sandwich Glass Factory circa 1888-1896. *Courtesy of the Sandwich Historical Society/Sandwich Glass Museum.*

Burgess in 1905, the year he married Nina Osborne.

Nina Osborne, Burgess' fiancé.

Nina Burgess at home playing the piano.

Burgess was a skilled professional photographer, as this picture of Nina demonstrates.

Nina Burgess seated in a chair.

The newlyweds on a camping trip in the Adirondacks, circa 1905.

Thornton W. Burgess III at two years, the only child of Thornton and Nina Burgess, circa 1907.

...at age 3.

...in the garden.

...at the family's home on Washington Road in Springfield, Massachusetts.

Young Thornton W. Burgess III in the lap of his grandmother Caroline.

This photo of a family meal shows four women and three young children, including Caroline Burgess and her grandson Thornton III (at left).

In 1911, Burgess married Fannie Johnson of Ithaca, New York.

Fannie Burgess with furry friends at Alice Cooke's woodshed.

Burgess with his dear friend Alice Cooke, whom he nicknamed "Aunt Sally." His book on the wildlife visitors to her woodshed was published by Little, Brown in 1955.

PART II: THE WRITER

Professional portrait of Thornton W. Burgess, 1898.

Chapter 4

A Writer Becomes an Author

"The writing of a book is but a beginning," Thornton Burgess once commented. He referenced both the unexpected directions that his work took him and the constant, endless necessity of selling it. This chapter describes the start and development of his literary career, as well as factors that help sustain it for more than fifty years.

"Was he ever *not* writing?"

John Richmond, marketing manager
Thornton W. Burgess Society

"I began writing the West Wind and Bedtime Stories with two distinct objects in mind, namely the teaching of the facts of natural history and the teaching of moral lessons. It was a theory of mine which the succeeding years have convinced me was correct, that the young child is best and easiest educated by indirect methods and that the logical vehicle for this kind of instruction is the animal story.[1]

Thornton W. Burgess, 1919

"He has a rare gift of making nature study a delight for little people by his genius of impersonating all sorts of animals in very human situations."[2]

Journal of Education, 1913

Origin of *Old Mother West Wind*

In November 1909, Burgess' three-and-a-half year-old son Thornton and one of his grandmothers took a month-long trip to Chicago.[3] The two-fold purpose of the trip was to visit family and give the widowed writer a solitary stretch of time to concentrate on work. Accustomed to reading stories together at bedtime, Burgess composed and mailed the boy daily bedtime tales or verses to compensate for the separation. He added copies of the letters to his stockpile of material for potential articles. A few months later, he found a use for them in Phelps Publishing Company's *Good Housekeeping* magazine, where he was an associate editor. "How Reddy Fox Was Surprised" was published in the April 1910 issue, and other stories ran in the June and July issues. When an editorial representative from Boston publisher Little, Brown and Company stopped by the Phelps offices that summer, a senior editor mentioned these children's stories to him. As related by Burgess, the next moment was the stuff of any writer's fantasies:

> The visitor came over to my desk, introduced himself, and asked to see the stories. He read one or two, asked how many I had, then urged me to get them together and send them to Little, Brown for consideration as a possible book.[4]

Little, Brown editors liked his work, but wanted to see more stories. For the next two nights, Burgess returned to his office to put new material onto the office Dictaphone for transcription the next day:

> When these were mailed…I told my home folks that I had written every last animal story I knew, that I was written out…Somewhat to my astonishment, within

a week or two the unbelievable had happened – I had signed a contract that would make me a bona fide author. It was for *Old Mother West Wind.*

A Syndicated Columnist

Initially, Burgess' first children's book was a serendipitous opportunity to explore another market for his writing, but when he lost his job the year after *Old Mother West Wind* was published, it became a key to financial survival. Burgess was seeking additional sources of income when he spotted a syndicated column of children's stories in a local newspaper:

> They were pleasantly wholesome entertainment, nothing more. Why not equally entertaining stories with an educational value as well? Why not amusing entertaining short stories of our friendly neighbors in fur and feathers that would at the same time open for young readers the beautiful wonder world of Mother Nature?[5]

Burgess submitted a half-dozen sample stories to the George Matthew Adams Syndicate in Chicago, but it had similar material and rejected them. Unaware of any other syndicates to approach, Burgess dropped the idea. "That was that," he wrote resignedly. But later that fall he received an encouraging letter from Adams, who was organizing Associated Newspapers, a new syndication service for the *Boston Globe*, *New York Globe*, *Kansas City Star*, *Philadelphia Bulletin*, and *Chicago Daily News*. Adams had been impressed with Burgess' work and offered him a contract to write six stories a week. They would run daily except Sunday. Payment was thirty-five dollars per week for a six-month trial period. It would increase to fifty dollars per week if his work was satisfactory. Burgess gratefully accepted. "What a blessing to have a fixed sum, even so small a one, coming in every week!" he said. "It was a solid nucleus around which to build."[6]

Burgess was anxious about his ability to meet this daunting production schedule, but needn't have worried — his first syndicated column appeared on February 1, 1912 and the last one ran on January 19, 1960, five days after his eighty-sixth birthday. "It will be just short of forty-eight years," Burgess wrote his friend Stuart Trueman, editor-in-chief of *New Brunswick's Telegraph Journal.* "I wonder if that is some sort of record for continuous publication of columns."[7] At their height of popularity, his daily stories were printed in more than one hundred newspapers in the U.S., Canada, and other countries. Australian friend Andrew Knie sent clippings of them from a local newspaper and Sandwich resident Peg Pola remembers reading Burgess' stories in the *Japan Advertiser*, now the *Japan Times*, in the late 1920s when her father worked in Yokohama.

In addition to providing a base income, Burgess' syndicated columns became a significant cross-marketing tool for selling the children's books he was now regularly writing. According to veteran publisher and advertising manager Jason Rogers, author of *Newspaper Building* (1918), Burgess' stories were also extremely effective in selling newspapers:

> Realizing that the immense circulation of our Sunday newspapers as compared with their week-day issues was largely represented by the hold on the children obtained by their comic sections and such matter, we secured the service of Thornton W. Burgess in the Associated Newspapers to produce his own famous 'Bed Time Stories.' These little stories are without question the best thing of the kind produced, and are one of the very best newspaper features… In my meetings with prominent businessmen it is not unusual for me to hear the remark: "My grandson is a great admirer of your newspaper. He started us taking *The Globe* for that Bed Time Story, and now we all like it."[8]

After writing eight years for Associated Newspapers, Burgess followed the advice of his colleague H. T. Webster and switched to the *New York Herald Tribune* syndicate. To his great dismay, he discovered that the first signed contract had conferred all publishing rights rather than only first publishing rights. This wording enabled Associated Newspapers to re-publish every Burgess story written under contract with them as often as they wished without reimbursing him. He was in the painful position of having his original syndicated "Little Stories for Bedtime" compete for readers and sponsors with his new, more costly "Burgess Bedtime Stories." Self-competition was a blow to his income as well as professional pride:

> My new material would be sold to a paper at a good price. My former syndicate would offer a rival paper my old stories at a ridiculously low price. Eight years old, these were practically new to the present generation of young readers. The paper paying a good price for my new work expected, and rightly, the exclusive use of my name as author. Failing to get this, there would be immediate cancellation of the contract. Thus contract after contract was cancelled. Of course this reflected in my income. … Meanwhile my earlier work was reappearing in an increasing number of papers with no recompense to me, and there was nothing I could do about it. At one time nearly one hundred papers were printing my old stories, and I had no legal redress.[9]

To help readers distinguish stories for the *Herald Tribune* syndicate from old stories being simultaneously re-published by the Associated Newspapers syndicate, Burgess began heading the new work with a few lines of rhyme. "My plan was to drop these couplets as soon as my column had become established in my new connection. I tried it. It couldn't be done. Letters of protest were too numerous and insistent to be ignored."[10] The catchy couplets — which Burgess said sometimes took as long to write as a story — became a trademark of his books and newspaper columns.

During his early years in syndication, Burgess worked with other struggling writers and artists who also became successful, including H.T. Webster, illustrator of "Caspar Milquetoast," and Charlie Voight who drew the "Betty" cartoon. Cartoonist Jay Norwood "Ding" Darling went on to work in environmental conservation as appointed head of the U.S. Biological Survey and founder of the National Wildlife Federation. In 1957, Burgess reconnected with Darling when both were vacationing on the West Indian island of Tobago: "I had lost all track of him," he wrote in his journal. "I heard he was over at Arnos Vale [town]. So three days ago [Canadian friend Horace] Black and I drove over. Ding and I had a great pow-wow...I think Ding got as much of a kick out of the meeting as I did. Most of the associates of those old days are gone now."

Market Testing

One technique of media market testing in Burgess' day was to announce the cancellation of a regularly featured column or program and let reader or listener response determine its fate. In 1930, WBZ tested the popularity of Burgess' radio program in this manner, and the station was overwhelmed with complaints.[11] "Half the pleasure and profit of owning a radio is gone since Mr. Burgess has discontinued his talks," wrote Burt, Elsie, and Stephen Chaffee of Stafford Springs, Connecticut. "We listened to the farewell meeting with hearts full of sadness and regret." Mrs. Gertrude Titus of Swampscott, Massachusetts, declared, "What a bright spot those hours that you have talked to us has been...It was to me the best of all the week." In 1949, the *New York Herald Tribune* ran a similar cancellation test on its thirty-year-old "Burgess Bedtime Stories" column. Burgess reported the gratifying results in his journal:

> 1/28/1949: One of those who protested dropping of stories by *Tribune* sent me copy of very fine letter he had received from managing editor saying it was a test and they took pleasure in restoring them [the Bedtime Stories].
>
> 1/31/1949: Letter from Kay Phelps of *Herald Tribune* saying results of test of reader interest in my stuff were amazing, they received nearly 300 calls and letters. Gave me a very good feeling.
>
> 2/4/1949: Fine letter from managing editor of *N.Y. Herald Trib.* saying, "Never, in my newspaper experience, has a feature come through a test with such a great victory. There is no doubt at all that all our readers like the stories."

A congratulatory exchange between Burgess and his friend and illustrator Harrison Cady indicates their view of the *Tribune's* marketing ploy:

> 3/31/1949: Nice letter from Cady. He has talked with Weare of the Syndicate who says my stories are dead; children no longer interested, so Harrison much pleased by results of the *Herald Tribune* test. [We] Have long suspected lack of interest by new manager of syndicate. [Harrison] thinks he knows little about either art or literature.

BURGESS BOOKS PROLIFERATE

After releasing *Old Mother West Wind*, Little, Brown requested a second book and published *Mother West Wind's Children* in 1911. "Then I felt beyond all question I was an author," Burgess said.[12] In 1912, he wrote *Old Mother West Wind's Animal Friends* for Little, Brown and *The Boy Scouts of Woodcraft Camp*, the first novel in a series of four for Penn Publishing Company in Philadelphia. A 1915 trade advertisement declared that "for children 6 to 11 ...Mr. Burgess is becoming more popular every day... Nearly 100,000 copies of his books have already been sold."[13]

Between 1910 and 1918, Burgess delivered eight books in the *Mother West Wind* series, completed the four-book *Boy Scouts* series, and wrote most of his twenty *Bedtime Stories* books, of which *The Adventures of Reddy Fox* (1913) was the first. Like many Burgess characters, Granny Fox's misbehaving grandson Reddy was introduced in newspaper stories.

Packaging previously published stories together in a book was a common practice. "As Burgess mastered the technique of coalescing separate articles into a single book, the contextual flow and development of his plot and characters improved," says Burgess bibliographer Wayne Wright. "He hit his stride with the start of The Bedtime Story-Books series in 1913. To me, those books about individual animals created from his newspaper columns are his best work and his legacy to children's literature. Even though they centered on one animal, the other characters also appear in each book, so the same loved characters appear over and over."

Emphasis on Nature and Wildlife

From the start of his literary career, Burgess' fictitious books featured nature and wildlife, but as his personal commitment to conservation and environmental education strengthened, so did the incorporation of environmental information into his writing. The first full-scale book in which natural science dominated the storyline was *The Burgess Bird Book for Children* (1919), gorgeously illustrated by the prestigious ornithological artist Louis Agassiz Fuertes. The Massachusetts Audubon Society's *Bulletin* called it "the bird book of the year for children."[14] Nearly one hundred years later favorable reviews of the *Burgess Bird Book for Children* continue to appear, now on the internet. *Burgess' Books of Nature Stories* series (1944 to 1950) distinctly concentrated on environmental detail. *The Crooked Little Path* (1946), for example, does not open with a character or storyline, but with a description of a woodland path:[15]

> The Crooked Little Path begins at the edge of the woods and winds among the trees far into the Green Forest to the Great Mountain. It makes sudden bends this way and that. It twists and turns around stumps and big rocks. It climbs little hills and runs down the other sides. It clamors over old logs and fallen trees. It loafs along the bank of Laughing Brook, then skips across on steppingstones.

Next, Burgess invites young readers to imagine how the path was created:

> Many feet have made and are still making the Crooked Little Path. Some are big feet. Some are not so big. Some are tiny. Some are padded and soft. Some are hard, sharp edged, and without toes. Some are horny, having wide-spreading toes.

> Some have long sharp claws. Some have short, stout claws. Some are shod with leather, for the Crooked Little Path is sometimes used by Man.

When Buster Bear comes wandering along this path looking for a winter home, he initiates a discussion with Flathorns the Moose about the advantages and disadvantages of hibernation. Within the book's first ten pages, young readers learn that bears feed in the summer, eat berries, acorns, and beechnuts, do not have a permanent den, and may travel considerable distances, but do not migrate as birds do, to different regions. Burgess also uses his storyline to discuss forest vegetation, noting that not all the young, green hemlock trees in a thicket will survive: "As they grew some would be crowded to death by stronger neighbors until at last only a few of the strongest would be left to keep on growing."

Burgess' method of packaging ecological fact within fiction was highly effective, says Mark Wilson, a *New York Times* and *Boston Globe* staff photographer who, with his wife Marcia, a naturalist/educator, gives live owl education programs. The Wilsons' both read Burgess' books as children, and Mark particularly remembers reading when he was nine years old *The Burgess Book of Nature Lore*:

> It hit a chord with me. It seemed very much alive. It got me thinking about things I was seeing, great blue herons stalking in the marsh, wood turtles, and owls. I lived in woodlands on a meandering meadow river in Tewksbury, the Shawsheen, where I spent a lot of time looking for turtles and frogs. I would find American bitterns, pileated woodpeckers, great horned owls, skunks and raccoons. As a kid it was great to read a book that described the real creatures I was discovering. The way he developed the world was the world I was learning about as a kid. It really encouraged me to get out and explore.

"They weren't like other folk stories," agrees birder and naturalist Ed Hands, president of the Natural Resources Trust in Easton, Massachusetts, who attributes his lifelong interest in nature to reading Burgess' stories. "His animals talked, but they acted like animals you would see in the woods. I knew about muskrats because of Jerry Muskrat. The stories rang true, they brought you outside. And when Burgess talked about animals that you saw, like a rabbit, he made you want to find the ones you didn't see."

Wartime Contributions

Throughout his writing career, Thornton Burgess used Peter Rabbit as a naïve foil whose curiosity and ignorance about nature revealed new information to young readers. During World War I, the author enlisted Happy Jack Squirrel to assist the war effort. When the U.S. Treasury Department's program for selling twenty-cent thrift stamps failed to stimulate interest among school children, the chairman of the Springfield [Massachusetts] War Savings Committee sought Burgess' help. The author agreed to write five newspaper stories on thrift and patriotism that could be used by grade school teachers.

Burgess was confident stories about the thrifty habits of his popular gray squirrel character would appeal to children, but felt something extra was needed to focus their interest on purchasing savings stamps. He suggested creating a Happy Jack Thrift Club that offered membership certificates, buttons, and prizes of story booklets for those who filled a stamp book. "The results were immediate and astonishing," Burgess said. Stamp sales soared, and other communities and states adopted his idea. President Woodrow Wilson was among the prominent officials who wore a red Happy Jack Thrift Club button. Burgess marveled at the proliferation of Happy Jack plays, parties, and parades, but he believed there was a simple explanation:

> Happy Jack took thrift out of the abstract, endowing it with life and exciting interest, and made the meaning of it so clear that a small child could understand it and the reason for it. The wisdom of it became at once fully apparent. No child would admit that a squirrel was or could be wiser than he or she. I realized as never before the educational value of animal characters in storytelling...These experiences brought home to me the power of the written word for both good and evil. It can be as destructive as atomic energy, and equally constructive.[16]

Twenty-five years later, the Writers' War Board asked Burgess to assist in World War II fund-raising efforts. Conceived by U.S. Secretary of the Treasury Henry Morgenthau, Jr. and headed by author Rex Stout, the Writers' War Board solicited contributions of domestic propaganda from well-known artists, communication specialists, and writers like Thornton Burgess and E.B. White in order to motivate public support and financial contributions to efforts such as the Seventh War Loan drive.[17] In Burgess' wartime journal, ominous and catastrophic historic events mingle with his routine reports on daily life and work:

> 3/15/1945: Nice note from Julian Street Jr. of War Finance Division of Treasury Dept including sheet with bond-selling blurbs from 15 famous writers, artists with insert cut of each. Was included and found myself in fast company. It was sent to 12,000 newspapers. Gives me a feeling I am doing a little something for the war effort.
>
> 3/23/1945: Snow of last evening about gone this morning. Patton's 3rd Army is across the Rhine...Trying to get some propaganda for 7th War Loan drive into my stories for May and June.
>
> 3/24/1945: Looks as if the final push is on. The Rhine has been crossed in several places. God grant that the end to the war in Europe is as near as it seems.
>
> 3/28/1945: Worked mostly on 7th War Loan messages...M. Hanson phoned asking if I will get on radio program at Boston Sat. P.M. April 14 for S.P.C.A.
>
> 3/29/1945: Got off 7th War Loan material...then to see National Velvet, a wonderful picture in color...also war pictures that brought home the fearfulness of the conflict

in the Pacific. Find that even with a hearing aid I cannot get speech from the screen. Plenty loud but fail to get articulation.

4/2/1945: Nice note from Rex Stout of Writers' War Board thanking me for 7th War Loan messages and congratulating me on their quality.

4/14/1945: Made electrical transcription with Miss Kerns at Sta. WHDH instead of going on air as planned. This because of it being a day of national mourning for Roosevelt [President Franklin D. Roosevelt died of cerebral hemorrhage on April 12, 1945]. Funeral service at Washington. Made another transcription at WBZ with Carl deSuze, interview without notes. Quiet evening at hotel. All stores closed all day.[18]

Book Signings

A successful author was expected to help promote books. Burgess regularly attended book signings in Detroit, Chicago, New York, Rochester, and other major cities. At fifty-two, he autographed books in Hartford, Connecticut, for five hours and got a 9:30 p.m. train back to Springfield. He joined novelists Ben Ames Williams and Kenneth Roberts, poet Robert Frost, explorer Admiral Byrd, and author Carl Van Doren at the 1938 Boston Herald Book Fair.[19] His journal describes a major book signing in Ohio:[20]

10/26/1934: Did not sleep well. Reached Cleveland at 6:45. Went to Statler Hotel, shaved and had breakfast. Then to Hallett Bros store across street and found a splendid display of books for Authors' Week. Met Talbot Mundy and had pleasant chat. Started in at once autographing books, a great stock of them. Marjory Flack (Mrs. Larrson) friend of the Cadys and of John Leonard [probably his Sandwich relative], at next table autographing and making drawings. Beyond her, Kurt Weise doing likewise. Three of us spoke in store auditorium. To lunch at Rowfant Club, a most delightful gathering, but had to rush away to broadcast at Station WGAR at Statler Hotel. Found Marie Peary (Snow baby) splitting half hour program with me. She was a wonder, speaking without notes, without the least hesitancy. Back to store to autograph all afternoon with a few minutes for tea. Jolly cocktail party at hotel and then Weise, Miss Flack, and I left at 7:40 for Pittsburg, dining on train and reaching there at 10:40.

10/27/1934: Weise, Miss F., and I breakfasted together then went over to the Horne Store where we promptly started in on the autograph business...Had been a good advance sale of my books. Autographed steadily until noon when we lunched at store restaurant...Autographed steadily all afternoon to closing time save for time out to speak. All of us very tired. Rain made it a poor day for children to get out. Same party to dinner. Very jolly. [William] Heylinger [author of boys' adventure books] and I got the 9:45 for New York and had a grand talkfest.

Busy Lecturer and Photographer

Until deafness made public speaking impossible, Burgess actively lectured for thirty years, speaking on Sunday for the Humane Society at the Boston Public Library, for example, and the following Tuesday in Fitchburg at the Teachers College and the Rotary Club. His record of speaking engagements and reimbursement between 1921 and 1939 shows that he traveled to Albany, New York ($500); Allentown, Pennsylvania ($125); Augusta, Maine ($150); Baltimore, Maryland ($125); Brunswick, Maine ($100); Elmira, New York ($200); Huntington, West Virginia ($100); Nashua, New Hampshire ($100); Rochester, New York (six times between 1921 and 1927); St. Paul, Minnesota ($200); and Washington, D.C. ($125).[21]

When Burgess started writing children's books, his experience as a photojournalist proved useful in publishing *Mother Nature's News* and other publications he distributed to schools. His wildlife movies were often the basis of lectures. He undoubtedly drew laughter with his footage of raccoons trying to extract fish from a fishbowl and his own futile effort to get two young owls to release their hold on a tree limb. In 1954, at the age of eighty, he entertained a New Brunswick audience of one thousand school children with films of skunks and raccoons vying for snacks in the lap of his friend Alice Cooke.

Under the auspices of the National Research Council, Burgess accompanied ornithologist Dr. Alfred O. Gross of Bowdoin College on a 1927 trip to document and film tropical wildlife on Barro Colorado Island in Gatun Lake in Panama. The two men also made a photographic record in the early 1930s of the now-extinct heath hen, a subspecies of the prairie chicken. Burgess' film of the last known heath hen has been produced for distribution as a DVD by the U.S. Division of Fish and Wildlife.

Correspondence an Inspiration

Not all Burgess' writing was for publication. He devoted countless hours to correspondence with fans young and old who wrote to share their thoughts on his work and to question him about wildlife and nature. Burgess' response was typically informative and encouraging, as the following 1951 letter indicates:[22]

> Dear Dana,
>
> No, Grandfather Frog has no gills. He lost those long ago when he grew up. Curiously enough when he is in the water he breathes through his skin, instead of through his gills. I think that is a handy sort of skin, don't you? The principle reason for not putting a frog in the aquarium is because the frog is likely to eat all the others in the aquarium smaller than himself.
>
> Your story friend,
> Thornton W. Burgess

Judging from one polite, carefully handwritten letter, Burgess also inspired literary effort. A boy, whose father worked in Pyinmana, Burma [Myanmar], sent a sample of his own creative work. The elaborate story about Burmese wildlife included "one big female elephant that eats you alive."[23] Burgess explained the inspiration he derived from his correspondents, particularly children, in an article on the accomplishment of writing one thousand stories:

> From all parts of America, and even from as far away as Tokyo, Japan have come letters from little children, and from big children, from parents and grandparents and each one of these letters is an inspiration for further endeavor. A little boy from Japan writes me that Blacky the Crow speaks the same language there that he does here in America. From Northern Quebec an old trapper writes that all the little wild folks are called by names where he lives. From Chicago comes a letter from a woman who writes to thank me for the influence the daily stories are having on the molding of her little five-year-old's character. A blind grandmother of St. Louis dictates a letter to express the pleasure she finds the green meadows and green forests of childhood through the medium of the stories. Boys write me that they have given up their traps, and instead of killing are doing what they can to make life easier for their little wild neighbors. School teachers take the time to send a word of appreciation of the help in nature study they find through the medium of these stories.
>
> And the children! God bless the little folks. Their letters come from every state in the Union, written in sprawling hand, printed and sometimes written for them but these letters alone would suffice if there were no other stimulus to keep the work going. … The writing of a thousand stories has not been a task but a pleasure.[24]

Burgess was particularly touched by the letters he received from two World War II servicemen, one in Europe and one in the Pacific. They had read the 1944 *Life* article that celebrated Burgess' ten-thousandth syndicated story and wrote to congratulate him. An Army captain "Somewhere in Eastern France" asked a specific favor: Would Burgess write a Peter Rabbit story for his five children for Christmas since he would not be home with them? [See Chapter 16] And a young sailor from "Somewhere in the Pacific" wrote the following:

> I cannot tell you to what depths my morale had dropped…nor can I say the reason for the low spirits. Then I saw your article in *Life*, which set many long-forgotten memories in motion, memories of animated wood folk who came to life…and spoke; told me of their joy and happiness in living, gave me little bits of philosophy that even today I remember. ... I was a little boy again, propped up with one of your books and at peace with the world. I just had to sit down and humbly write my great appreciation and many thanks…For myself, I am Eddie Hardy, 21, aboard one of Uncle Sam's destroyers, seeing to it that more people like you can write for more people like me.[25]

In Burgess' last years, he dictated letters three days a week to his secretary Ernestine Johnson. When newspapers reported his 1963 stroke in Hampden, Massachusetts, he was inundated with cards from concerned well-wishers. "He got more mail than the rest of the town put together," says David Cesan, Johnson's son.

Writing a Lifetime Habit

"He was such a hard worker," said Burgess' granddaughter Frances Meigs. "He'd come down to the house to get lunch, and he'd be reading something, then go back up to his studio. Morning, noon, and night, he was constantly reading or writing." Burgess once told a reporter he planned to stop working when he was sixty-five, but found he had too much to do at that age, and decided to continue writing until he was seventy. When he reached that milestone, he declared, "I have more irons than ever in the fire at seventy and so I have decided to keep going until I am one hundred."

Burgess' journals document his sustained, unwavering focus on work. In November 1926, he was preoccupied with the financial debts of his son and step-children, beset by physical ailments, and devastated by the defeat of the Massachusetts anti-trapping bill. He had campaigned hard for votes to outlaw use of the steel leg-hold trap, which he considered viciously cruel. With these concerns on his mind, he journaled on November 7: "Humane trapping act lost. ... I am as discouraged as ever I have been in all my life...[sent a] set of stories off to Cady," and a week later wrote, "Work today, but a heavy heart...stories dragged somewhat."

By all accounts, the total number of books Burgess wrote is impressive, but often confusing. Some sources cite seventy books and others 170. In his descriptive bibliography of Burgess' works, Wayne Wright delineates the difference between Burgess' full-scale chapter books (70) and single-issue picture books, booklets, and folded cards (144). "Particularly with the *Mother West Wind* series of eight volumes and *The Bedtime Story-Books* of twenty volumes," Wright says, "many other picture books and booklets were produced that related to them textually and bibliographically, such as books by the Eggers Company, Samuel Lowe Company, Wonder Books, Grosset & Dunlap, Whitman Publishing Company and Toy Works Press.

"In the bibliography I didn't include publications that only used Burgess' name and characters without an actual text," he says. "It's hard to count items that were reissued with multiple titles or the picture books that were first published as single stories in other books. I treated those as separate books unless they were different titles of the same book." *The Wishing Stone* series provides a good example of the difficulty in numbering Burgess' books, Wright says: "It was first published in *St. Nicholas* magazine from November 1914 to October 1915, and subsequently as a hard cover book by the Century Company. Then Little, Brown and Company later published it as three separate books."

Wright's personal interest in Thornton Burgess traces back to hearing stories read from his mother's collection when he was a boy. He conducted research on the children's author for graduate studies in library science. When Wright was hired by the Thornton W. Burgess Society to catalogue Burgess' library in Hampden, Massachusetts, then owned by the Massachusetts Audubon Society, he discovered books inscribed by renowned scientists and conservationists. The National Museum of Natural History's renowned taxidermist Dr. Carl E. Akeley, author of *In Brightest Africa*, wrote: "To Thornton Burgess, a friend of wildlife who gets results. God bless him." Massachusetts Audubon Society executive director Russell Mason had signed his 1962 book, *Picture Primer of Attracting Birds*: "With the highest regards for a great naturalist and a real educator." Dr. William Hornaday, first director of the New York Zoological Society, had inscribed his book *Thirty Years War for Wildlife* (1931) with a complimentary note to Burgess: "To my esteemed friend, Thornton W. Burgess, Purveyor of good animal love, beloved by millions of American boys and girls, and others, with the compliments of the Author. W. T. Hornaday."

The bibliographer suspects that other reminders of Burgess' role in twentieth century literature and natural science are still hidden away in attics and archives. "One collection we received was from Floyd Armstrong, an old farmer from West Winfield, New York," Wright says. "It included a picture of him as a boy with his father reading a book to him. When I got out a magnifying glass, I could see it was *The Burgess Flower Book for Children*." A similar discovery was made by historian Julie Arrison, who manages a twenty-room Salem mansion for Historic New England: "I found a letter written by Stephen Phillips, the boy who grew up in the house," she says. "He was writing to Santa Claus around 1914 asking for two Thornton Burgess books for Christmas."

Chapter 5

Publishers, Markets, & Illustrators

Asked what sells a book, Thornton Burgess replied, "Youngsters demand the truth in their stories. If they find that, books will popularize themselves." Since most of his books were still in print when he died in 1965, many after fifty years, Burgess clearly understood the interests and expectations of his audience. Literary success would never have occurred, however, without the publishers, markets, and illustrators who supported his creative work.

"Your books have [the] distinction of being the dirtiest books in the library."

Librarian's comment to Burgess

"Dear Sirs,

I am a third grader. Your books are very good. I especially liked your Prickly Porky book. Your books are 69 years old and still in good shape. I liked the pictures because they are black and white. Your books are interesting. I liked Reddy Fox because he never got scared. I liked the books because they didn't give the answers right away...I liked Grandfather Frog the most of all. But I liked all of your characters too. Your books are puzzling."

Jenni Carson, Student, Oct. 2, 1985
Letter to Thornton W. Burgess Society

"Why were his characters never caught? These were bedtime stories — you wouldn't want to put children to bed just after reading that Peter Rabbit got eaten by Reddy Fox!"

Chuck Roth, former Education Director
Massachusetts Audubon Society, 2010

Two First Books

As a seasoned editor/journalist, Thornton Burgess had seen his byline on thousands of newspaper and magazine articles by the time his first book, *The Bride's Primer*, was published in 1905. Printed in both standard and deluxe editions by Phelps Publishing Company, *Primer* contained a collection of Burgess' humorous verses, an essay by Tom Masson, and twenty-four full-page illustrations by F. [Frederick] Strothmann, the popular commercial artist who illustrated national magazines as well as books by Mark Twain and Ring Lardner.[1] However exciting, publication of this handsome book did not compare to the thrill Burgess experienced five years later when he held *Old Mother West Wind*, his first children's book:

> I leafed through my first copy from cover to cover; put it down only to pick it up again and do it all over. How eagerly I looked for the illustrations. I looked through that little volume the first thing in the morning and the last thing at night. That book was mine, my very own, every line of it. It was the child of my brain. I was an author accepted as such. Not only had I written a book, but it was published by one of the most famous publishing houses in America. It was a small volume, but there it was in my hands, visible, tangible evidence of a dream come true.[2]

With modest sales of two thousand copies and royalties of $210, *Old Mother West Wind* was the inauspicious beginning of an international literary career and a fifty-five-year relationship with respected Boston publisher Little, Brown and Company.

Little, Brown and Company

A pre-Civil War trade publisher, Little, Brown and Company had expanded into mainstream publishing with such successful books as Admiral Alfred Thayer Mahan's *Influence of Sea Power upon History* and *Fanny Farmer's Boston Cooking-School Cook Book*. In 1898, it acquired Roberts Brothers, a company publishing literary works by Emily Dickinson, Christina Rossetti, and George Sand; however, the prize among Roberts' writers was Louisa May Alcott. The acclaimed author of *Little Women* enabled Little, Brown to move into the increasingly competitive children's book market.[3] *One Hundred and Fifty Years of Publishing*, Little, Brown's 1987 corporate history, describes the publishing arena Thornton Burgess entered in 1910:

> The first decade of the twentieth century saw a tremendous upsurge in the publishing of books for children; publishers, authors, and titles were plentiful. Series books had a great appeal and favorite authors were encouraged to produce at least a book a year. [Note: Burgess wrote sixteen books for Little, Brown between 1914 and 1916.] Among the most popular and productive authors were Susan Coolidge, Lily F. Wesselhoeft, A.G. Plympton, and Mary P. Wells Smith, and of course the books by Louisa May Alcott continued to lead the field…By far the most prolific author to publish with Little, Brown was Thornton W. Burgess."[4]

Former Little, Brown president Arthur Thornhill, Jr. has fond memories of the children's writer. "Thornton Burgess had a magic touch," Thornhill recalled in a 2010 telephone interview. "Everyone loved him, adults as well as children. Before my father [Arthur Thornhill, Sr.] became president of Little, Brown, he was in sales and used to go around with Thornton Burgess to lectures and book signings. That was a long and amiable relationship. Helen Jones was the company's children's editor for many years and would have been the one who worked on his books." By the end of the 1920s, Little, Brown had published eight of Burgess' book series, including all the Mother West Wind and Adventure books. Its last series book, *The Burgess Seashore Book for Children*, was released in 1929. Between *Old Mother West Wind* in 1910 and *The Burgess Book of Nature Lore* in 1965, Little, Brown published sixty books by Thornton Burgess.

"We don't have actual dates that the Little, Brown' series books went out of print, but most of them were not being published in the 1940s," says Burgess authority Wayne Wright. "That's when Grosset & Dunlap began issuing them with permission from Little, Brown." But Little, Brown continued to publish important new books by Burgess, including his outstanding natural science series, *Books of Nature Stories* (1944 to 1950); a Golden Anniversary edition of *Old Mother West Wind* (1960); and his autobiography, *Now I Remember* (1960). "Technically, Little, Brown published Burgess books the longest," says Wright.

In 1945, Burgess met with Angus Cameron, Little, Brown's editor-in-chief, to discuss the autobiography that Arthur Thornhill, Sr. pressed him to submit, but Burgess was not convinced of the project's merit. "Who am I and what have I done that my biography is of sufficient interest to others to warrant its publication?" he protested. "It's difficult to believe." Cameron persisted, however, and finally prevailed. In 1949, Burgess wrote in his journal: "Received, signed, and returned to L.B. and CO contract for 'The Autobiography of an Amateur Naturalist' to be in publisher's hands by Jan. 1, 1950. It is another milestone."[5] Apparently, neither publisher nor author were concerned about meeting the deadline; over the next decade Burgess's autobiographical chapters appeared sporadically as articles in the *Cape Cod Compass*, providing a leisurely trial run and additional income. Finally, nine years after he signed the Little, Brown contract, Burgess wrote a letter updating companions Kathy and Frank Jones:

> I am mailing today the sixteen chapters of the biography to Thornhill to find out if it is the stuff they want...Have eight more chapters written, but not yet typed. If the report from Thornhill is good, I'll get busy again and push the work through.[6]

With Little, Brown's 1960 release of both *Now I Remember* and the fiftieth anniversary edition of *Old Mother West Wind*, Burgess was deluged with fan mail, interview requests, and media attention. His fifteenth-thousandth syndicated column also ran that year. "To have written all that time was very remarkable," observed Arthur Thornhill, Jr. "Most authors don't write that long and that successfully. Even now, there are younger people who still tell me that they remember reading Thornton Burgess' books. In my experience I can't think of anyone at that time, maybe J.D. Salinger, who sold in [Burgess'] numbers."

Other Burgess Publishers

Another early publisher of Burgess' work was the John Eggers Company in New York.[7] In 1914, Eggers mass-produced thirty-two miniature books illustrated by Harrison Cady and copyrighted by JM Cole. They were used to advertise at least twenty products and businesses, including the American National Insurance Company, Anderson Candy Company, the Providence Baker, the *Hartford Courant*, and the Saltine Company. Eggers put out a set of larger books in 1922, as well as new sets of six titles each in 1924 and 1928.

The printing plates that Eggers Company used for color separation of Harrison Cady's artwork were willed by John Eggers to his graphic art department director. In the 1990s, the director, then quite elderly, became increasingly worried about the condition and safety of the plates. She contacted the Thornton W. Burgess Society, but before arrangements could be made to transfer the metal plates and prints of Cady's artwork to the organization, the woman was beaten and robbed in her Brooklyn home and died soon afterwards. The nephew who inherited the plates subsequently died, but his widow knew of the Burgess Society's interest and contacted them. "It was quite a difficult process [to organize the plates]," says Wayne Wright, who assisted in the acquisition. "Different plates would print red or yellow or blue, and then, using those plates, Eggers made browns and greens. Many of the plates were in decent condition, but it took a lot of studying to figure out what color each one was meant to print."

Whitman Books, Platt & Munk, and Wonder Books also printed Burgess books, but Grosset & Dunlap was the only publisher to rival Little, Brown's production. Between 1940 and 1959, Grosset & Dunlap brought out seven of Burgess' eight book series, excluding the *Boy Scout Series*, and continued publishing Burgess titles in various bindings throughout the 1970s. Although Grosset & Dunlap's Burgess titles went out of print in the 1980s, the company had actively published his work for over four decades. A 1950s Grosset & Dunlap trade flyer for book sellers proclaimed Burgess books to be "the finest nature stories ever written for children":

> Burgess had the genius of depicting authentic animal life in all his stories because…1) He creates a realistic picture of animal life by telling how the beaver nibbles and fells trees for his home. He shows them gathering food and at fun and play. He also relates quite vividly most of the tricks used by animals for self-protection; 2) He shows the circumstances of daily animal life that are similar to our own human existence, thus helping to prepare children for the future; 3) He counters unfortunate stereotypes. Most adults for example feel that toads are ugly. But Burgess teaches children that the toad's big, bulging eyes, legs, and webbed feet have a beauty born of purpose, that all in nature must be looked upon in this way; 4) He makes the changing seasons clear to children; 5) He instills in children a sense of sympathy for animals, so by the time they are older they understand that animals do not exist solely to be hunted and killed.[8]

Penn Publishing Company

The Boy Scouts of America was founded in 1910, the year *Old Mother West Wind* was published. It was a measure of Burgess' rapid acceptance as a children's author that he was hired two years later by Penn Publishing in Philadelphia to write a juvenile reader about Boy Scouts. According to senior archivist Steven Price at the Boy Scout Museum in Irving, Texas, Burgess worked closely with the Boy Scouts' chief librarian Franklin K. Mathiews. The series did not have the longevity of other Burgess books, but it remained popular into the 1930s and was recommended by the editors of *The Horn Book*, a highly regarded children's book publication.

Burgess was anxious about the writing assignment with Penn Publishing, his first juvenile novel, but he was pleased to contribute to the fledgling organization he believed in. "The Boy Scout movement has appealed to me from the very first as a long step in the right direction," he said in the introduction of *The Boy Scouts of Woodcraft Camp*. His 1914 *Good Housekeeping* article on Boy Scouting, "Making Men of Them," explains his ideas on the importance of "the inner boy" and "the two natural cravings of boy nature," namely "hero worship" and "gang membership."[9] [Burgess' terminology was ordinary usage in his day; in context he obviously refers to the well-recognized need of children for strong role models and positive peer groups.]

> Unfortunately, however, a great majority of fathers are not available to their sons at this time when they are most needed. They are chained to business through the hours when their boys are free of the restraint of school, which is just the time when they most need wise guidance in finding a proper outlet for their accumulated energy and surcharged spirits. So the boy seeks some other man to tell him things and show him things, for at this age a boy is naturally inquisitive and wonderfully acquisitive.
>
> All too often this other "man" is not a man at all save in the eyes of his young admirer. He is simply an older boy, himself in need of wise direction. He is the leader of the gang — though the word here is not meant necessarily to imply badness or even mischievousness; merely a loosely bound group of boys playing and acting together in the strong loyalty of youth which is their code, and which passes among them for honor...It is just here that the Boy Scout movement comes to your aid as a powerful ally. It takes up and applies to the life of your boys beyond the home the very precepts you have sought to inculcate in the home.[10]

His article was addressed to mothers, a familiar audience for the former *Good Housekeeping* editor. Burgess spoke as a trusted friend or relative offering counsel on the importance of male companionship and guidance. The endorsement of the Boy Scout organization as parental support would become increasingly meaningful as World War I took men from families and society. Whether consciously or not, Burgess' words applied to his own son Thornton, then eight years old, for, by the writer's own admission, he had often been unavailable as a father. His viewpoint may have also reflected his own fatherless boyhood.

In "Making Men of Them," Burgess mentions a correction to *The Boy Scouts of Woodcraft Camp* that Boy Scout administrators requested when Penn Publishing Company submitted his text to them for fact-checking. He had described a fictitious example of Boy Scouts assisting a New York police officer at a street accident by grasping their staffs at the ends to form a circle around an injured man and hold back the gathering crowd:

> It was diplomatically suggested to me that I did not know city crowds, and that while the incident was very interesting, it was best not to have boys in fiction do things that boys in real life could not do. Accordingly, I cut out this part of the incident. And then, even before the proofs were read, occurred the famous suffragette parade in Washington, at which Boy Scouts put the police to shame by doing the very thing I had described, holding back a turbulent crowd when the police failed to do so. [11]

Burgess Books in Braille

In September 1949, Burgess received a letter from Mrs. Johnson of Templeton, Massachusetts, who enclosed a letter in Braille from her ten-year-old son Scott. He had attended the Perkins Institute for the Blind, where he "read and loved my books in Braille." According to Jan Seymour-Ford, research librarian at the Perkins School for the Blind in Watertown, Massachusetts, three Burgess books — *Old Mother West Wind*, *Burgess Nature Stories*, and *The Burgess Bird Book for Children* — were listed in the school's 1941 library inventory catalogue. The listing indicates they were transcribed into Braille between 1916 and 1941, says Seymour-Ford. Since the Perkins School published and sold Braille books, it was possible they printed the Burgess titles for sale and/or distribution, but Seymour-Ford thinks it more likely they were single library copies. "Probably one person sat down with a mechanical brailler or a stylus and made one copy," the librarian said.

Old Mother West Wind would have been among the very few fiction selections in Braille for young children prior to World War II. "The 1941 catalog books in the Perkins circulating library probably contained just about everything available in Braille at the time," Seymour-Ford says. "There were only about 150 fiction titles for the youngest Braille readers and between 900 to 1,000 fiction books for older children and adults. The two other Burgess books would have been in the latter category. *The Burgess Bird Book for Children* was probably popular. Bird watching was a popular activity for [Perkins] students, since birds can be identified by sound."

In his autobiography, Burgess described the heightened appreciation of nature he derived from two visually-impaired women who were regular listeners of his Springfield-based Radio Nature League program. Miss V was a student at the Perkins School and Mrs. W was a music teacher who exchanged lessons for reading sessions of Burgess stories. (He must have been intrigued to learn from Mrs. W. that the highest note of a chirping cricket was F sharp and the lowest was G.) It is possible Miss V was responsible for Burgess' presentation at the Perkins School, of which he says: "I left the platform with the feeling I had been granted a great privilege; that I had received more than I had given."[12]

Canadian Markets and Readers

Canadian publishers McClellan & Stewart, Ltd., Oxford University Press, and Grolier's released both English and French editions of Burgess books, and numerous Canadian newspapers carried his syndicated column, some for more than forty years.[13] He joked with editor Stuart Trueman that he had been associated with the *New Brunswick Telegraph Journal* so long he felt like a staff member.

Among Burgess' Canadian readers is retired librarian Peggy Hamilton who grew up in rural Nova Scotia in the 1950s and '60s. "My father used to travel in his work and brought my sister and me a new book as often as he could," she says. "He read the stories to us and then took us into the woods and fields in our neighborhood to show us the homes, tracks — and sometimes the animals themselves — that were in the stories":

> The characters became very real to us and helped build lasting respect for animal life and the world in which we all live together. I regretted deeply that all the animals did not live in our area. … I re-read some of the stories recently to see if they were different through older eyes. I did not realize how exactly he had the essence of his characters and how much of a conservationist he was.

Toronto native and travel industry executive Rob Rankin also has fond childhood memories of reading Burgess books at his family's cottage on Georgian Bay:

> We probably had 40 or so of the books there. A friend down at the beach also had a decent collection, and we used to play a game where we listed every character we could think of. Once you start reading the "Mother West Wind" stories, the list quickly gets very long. Our books ranged from newer ones to a very old copy of Granny Fox that was given by my mother's grandmother to my mother's aunt in 1920. My mom Nancy Rankin can't remember how she got it, but it's a much-loved hardcover that has now been enjoyed by generations. The color illustrations are faded, but still lovely.

The Rankin family found additional Burgess books at the Midland Library and listened to *Peter Cottontail* on cassette during car trips. "I think we viewed the stories as entertainment and as lessons on human nature or proper behavior more than as natural history," says Rankin. "The talking and clothes made the characters seem more like little people than animals. Furthermore, there always seemed to be a lesson that was being imparted. The folly of vanity was a pretty common theme. Often there were little rhymes woven into the story that explicitly stated the particular lesson that the story was illustrating. When I read them to my daughter now, I realize how much of the time the animals spend playing tricks on one another. [They] act almost like children."

"How many people remember the very first book they read on their own?" asks Nova Scotian Margaret Boylen, who grew up with Burgess' Bedtime Story-Books, starting with *The Adventures of Reddy Fox*. "I thought each chapter was an individual story, and I started in the middle of the book and then went back to the beginning to finish it." She is now reading to her grandchildren the same Burgess books she once read to her own seven children: "Now I make up stories about Buster Bear and include them." In 1999, New Brunswick veterinarian Nelson Poirier wrote a column for the *New Brunswick Times* on what incites a naturalist's interest in nature:

> Before I was able to read for myself, my mother started to read me the series of animal stories by Burgess. Night after night, my mother would mete out one or, if I begged enough, two chapters of the hilarious adventures of Reddy the Fox, Paddy the Beaver, Jimmy Skunk, Old Mr. Toad, Johnny Chuck, Peter Rabbit, and all those other wonderful critters that would gather together at the Smiling Pool. I now realize the impact these books had, as I can still recall those adventures many years later. Mr. Burgess had written these books more than 30 years before I was born. They certainly stood the test of time as 25 years after my mother read them to me I read them to my own children, and now 25 years later, they can still recite those tales. I have no doubt that my mother and Mr. Burgess were the sparks that led me at a very young age to have the desire to work with animals later in life as a veterinarian.[14]

Poirier was surprised by the number of letters he received about his article. "One was from a lady...that wanted me to have the letter she received as a child from Mr. Burgess in 1926," he says.

Beginning in the 1920s, Burgess made annual fishing trips and visits to New Brunswick and Nova Scotia and built a camp on an island in Bolton Lake, New Brunswick. While vacationing on Tobago in the 1950s, he became friends with New Brunswick editor Stuart Trueman and his wife Mildred who later visited Burgess in western Massachusetts. New Brunswick Telephone Company general manager Horace Black was another Canadian friend Burgess especially valued. He wrote heartfelt news of Black on the final page that concluded his decades of journaling: "Wire in evening from Saint John saying Horace Black died suddenly yesterday. A rare friend gone. A shock though I knew he had heart trouble. I shall miss him greatly."[15]

Japan and "Yama Nezumi Rocky Chuck"

Far from the Green Forest and Smiling Pool, an astonishingly strong market for Thornton W. Burgess stories developed in Japan. In 1932, Heibonsha Publishers brought out the first Burgess translation, *Kitsune no Konta* (*The Adventures of Reddy Fox*). The entire twenty-volume Bedtime Stories series was later released in Japan by Kinnohoshisha Publishers between 1960 and 1972, with translations and illustrations by various individuals.[16]

The popularity of the *Bedtime Story-Books* translations resulted in production of a fifty-two-episode anime that aired on the Fuji Television Network from January to December 1973. Despite visual and linguistic differences, *Yama Nezumi Rokkiy Chakku* [*Rocky Chuck*] retained the spirit, message, and camaraderie of Burgess' tales. The Anime News Network website provides detailed information about the cartoon's production and a summary of the series' plot: "Based on the books of Thornton W. Burgess, the animals of the Green Forest live together and stay away from predators and humans. They have to find food, shelter, and deal with new animals that are passing through or decide to stay."[17] Ziv International released the anime series as *Fables of the Green Forest* in Canada and many other countries in 1978 [see Chapter 6].

Since North America's woodchuck does not have a counterpart in Japan, Burgess' title character became "Rocky Chuck the Mountain Rat," or a marmot. Interviewed in 2010 by e-mail, Sachiko Azuma of Tokyo fondly remembers watching *Yama Nezumi Rocky Chuck*. She suggests a plausible explanation for the translation of Johnny Chuck's name: "Maybe because then, for the Japanese, Rocky Mountains were synonymous with American beautiful nature and wildlife." Azuma adds:

> Regrettably, Japanese versions of Thornton Burgess books are unavailable now, so I feel people are forgetting his work in Japan, but some people love "Yama Nezumi Rocky Chuck" even now. I watched this animation series every week when I was at kindergarten. It was popular for little children. I remember that all the animal characters except dogs are afraid of, or kept a safe distance from, human beings or traps. It had left a strong impression on my mind. In my childhood I

felt that animals are not only lovely, but something great, a part of nature. Is it a message from Mr. Burgess? I hope so.

Cape Cod-based musician and instructor Misao Koyama grew up in Tokyo and also remembers watching *Rocky Chuck* on television when she was five years old. "I think it was on Sundays," she says. "My brother and I watched it together on the floor eating snacks. I never sing, but when the song came on, I was singing it. I saw it recently on YouTube and it brought back such memories. I liked the program because the animals were talking. They would be having problems, and every time, at the end of the show, they would say to each other, 'we are friends — I will help you.' There weren't many channels back then, maybe four or five, so those programs were very precious."

Other Foreign Editions

Between 1931 and 1971, forty-five Burgess books were published in England by Bodley Head, MacDonald & Company, and Tom Stacy. A 1931 Bodley Head advertisement in the *Publishers Circular and Booksellers' Record* stated:

> Ten million children love the Thornton Burgess books — for years Canadian and American children have read them, listened to their author in his weekly broadcast talks, and followed the adventures of Peter Cottontail and his friends in magazines and journals. Now for the first time, British children are to have an opportunity of making friends with Reddy Fox.[18]

French editions for Europe and Canada were published by Editions de la Paix in Paris and Brussels in 1941 and 1944. The titles included *Les Aventures de Grand-pere Grenouille* (*Grandfather Frog*), *Guillaume la Skonks* (*Jimmy Skunk*), *Bruin L'ours* (*Buster Bear*), *Dodo la Marmotte* (*Johnny Chuck*), and *Roux le Reynard* (*Reddy Fox*). Single books were translated and published in Swedish and Norwegian.[19] Little, Brown informed Burgess that contracts had been signed with Dutch and German publishers, and that requests for permission to publish had been received from the National Library for the Blind in London. Bibliographer Wayne Wright says there is no evidence that those books were produced.

Perhaps Burgess' most unusual foreign language edition was a Chinese version of *Mother West Wind's Animal Friends.* Translated by K.E. Wood, this edition was printed in 1921 by Kway Hsuch Publishing House in Shanghai. An American nurse in Hangchow, China, had requested permission to translate it. She hoped reading it would encourage Chinese children she knew to appreciate an animal's viewpoint. Receiving an author's copy was a special experience for Burgess:

> In the course of time, there arrives in a woven straw container a paperbound volume…I merely turned the pages from back to front, scanning them up and down instead of across from left to right…wondering if it could be possible that I was, in a way of speaking, truly in those strange black characters, and with me Peter Rabbit and his friends.[20]

According to Thornton W. Burgess Society executive director Gene Schott, collectors consider the rarest Burgess work to be *Wah Wah Taysee, a Native American Tale* published in 1935 with illustrations by Jack Canning. This commercial project was written and printed for Mohawk Beverages in Pittsfield, Massachusetts.

Current Publication of Burgess Books

Print-on-demand copies of *Now I Remember* and *My Grandfather, Thornton W. Burgess* are available, but the only current standard publisher of the naturalist's books is Dover Publishing of Mineola, New York. As copyright protection expired, Dover began to acquire publishing rights to Burgess titles in 1991. With thirty-two titles now in print, Dover offers nearly half of Burgess' total book list. "We see it as preservationist publishing," says Dover children's book manager, Jason Schneider, adding:

> It is important material to have out there. His name still carries weight. Being a naturalist, he places the animals in the story as they would actually be, among certain animals that are natural enemies. There are morals in the stories without being didactic; there is a lesson to learn, but it doesn't attack you. It is done sweetly. I absolutely think his anthropomorphized characters have an everlasting appeal.

Dover's top Burgess sellers are *Old Mother West Wind*, *Grandfather Frog*, and *Peter Cottontail*, the latter of which has sold over 100,000 copies since Dover first issued it. Schneider attributes continued interest in Burgess to an engaging style that is easy for children to read with their parents. "The books have a certain moral quality that parents like to pass on to their children, and kids like talking animals." Schneider says. "There are hundreds of thousands of books that go in and out of print, but these books have staying power."

Illustrators

Many illustrators worked with Burgess, but several were particularly important to his long literary career.

George F. Kerr

The first illustrator to create a visual representation of Burgess' animal characters was George F. Kerr.[21] He provided artwork for three Burgess stories in *Good Housekeeping* and the first four books in the *Old Mother West Wind* series. A well-known cartoonist and illustrator for the *New York Herald* and *American Weekly*, Kerr also worked with Frank Baum, author of the *Wizard of Oz* books. It was Kerr who first depicted the clothing that Burgess' animal characters wore.

W. Harrison Cady

"There is a well-known quote of Thornton Burgess saying 'I created the characters, but it was Harrison Cady with his gifted pen that made them come alive,'" says Gene Schott, executive director of the Thornton W. Burgess Society. "Without a doubt, Cady made many Burgess characters famous by creating the images that appeared in the minds of children as they read the stories. If you look at the earlier illustrations, Peter Rabbit was thin and lean, but it was Cady who gave him a more friendly, roly-poly look."

Schott points out that in later works more realistic artists like Phoebe Erickson and Lemuel Palmer were employed to represent Burgess' characters, but the whimsical, colorful illustrations of Harrison Cady have remained the ones most associated with Burgess' books. The two men had an unusually long, pleasurable, and productive working relationship. They were great friends from the beginning of their fifty-year professional collaboration to the end of their lives when both were widowers. Burgess died in 1965 at ninety-one, Cady in 1970 at ninety-three.

Cady' artistic rendering of Burgess' stories first appeared in the June, August, and October 1911 issues of *People's Home Journal*. Burgess was delighted with the interpretation of his characters and honored to be associated with such a highly-regarded artist. A staff writer with *Life*, Cady's work appeared in thirty magazines, including *American Boy*, *Harper's Bazaar*, *Country Gentleman*, *Ladies' Home Journal*, and *St. Nicholas*.[22] In 1913, Little, Brown hired Cady to create artwork for *The Adventures of Reddy Fox* and *The Adventures of Johnny Chuck*, the first books in Burgess' Bedtime Story-Book series.

Like Burgess, Cady was Massachusetts-born, a native of Gardner who lived in the coastal town of Rockport. In *O Rare Harrison Cady*, a book of Cady's reflections, he remarked:

> Thornton Burgess and I had a close, pleasant relationship that lasted a generation. We became collaborators through the good offices of Little, Brown and Company, the old Boston publishing firm. He had been managing editor of *Good Housekeeping*, then published by Amos Judd in Springfield. Previously he had worked for a couple of advertising agencies, supplementing his income by producing six nature stories a week for a newspaper syndicate. The syndicate, in the market for an illustrator for this increasingly popular feature — certainly one of the most widely read in the history of American journalism — tried several artists but none proved quite satisfactory. Then someone at Little Brown, which was interested in Thornton's work, said "There's a man drawing for *Life* magazine named Cady. He has a good many animal characters including a lively rabbit. Why not try him?"
>
> Thornton warmly appreciated my contribution to his delightful stories and the long succession of his Nature books...The stories had a tremendous appeal, and still do, selling some eight million copies before I lost count...Our collaboration possibly set a record for longevity and meeting of two minds in the world of fine arts.[23]

Independent of Burgess, Cady developed a Sunday cartoon in 1920 titled "Peter Rabbit," which is described at length in Michael Dowhan's comprehensive bibliography of Burgess and Cady's book, magazine, and newspaper work:

> Cady borrowed Peter Rabbit's name and appearance, developed his own storyline, and launched a full-pace Sunday comic strip in the *Tribune* on August 15, 1920. The first two episodes were unsigned, but, on August 29, Harrison Cady's name, in its familiar printed style, appeared under the title. … While Peter Rabbit's name and appearance were identical to that of Burgess' favorite foil, the similarity ended there and Cady's debt to Burgess thereafter was minimal…Burgess endeavored to have his characters only act and talk as animals would in their natural environment of the Green Meadows and Smiling Pool. Cady's Peter was urbanized and involved in many affairs of a middle-class householder."[24]

There was clearly little resemblance between Burgess' wild Peter Rabbit who eludes coyotes and hunts for clover patches and Cady's urban cartoon character who drives a car, attends concerts, entertains celebrity friends, and employs a maid. The comic strip showcased Cady's playful sense of humor as well as his artistry. In forays into the country, however, Cady's Peter occasionally encountered such Burgess characters as Buster Bear, Johnny Chuck, and Danny Meadow Mouse. In one strip, he introduces himself as a tour guide named Harrison Cady to Peter Rabbit's two sons. According to Dowhan, the "Peter Rabbit" strip ran for twenty-eight years with 1,459 multi-frame episodes.

A self-taught artist, Cady painted artistically complex pieces as well as conventional illustrations and continues to be a collectible artist.[25] Through purchases and donations, the Thornton W. Burgess Society in Sandwich has obtained over four hundred pieces of original Cady artwork.

Louis Agassiz Fuertes

Harrison Cady was the best known Burgess artist, but the most prestigious was Louis Agassiz Fuertes. Born in Ithaca, New York the same year as Burgess, Fuertes was a brilliant artistic prodigy. His talent as a teenager impressed distinguished ornithologists who praised his work for its technical accuracy and representation of the attitude and expressiveness of species.[26] Fuertes illustrated leading bird books published from 1896 until 1927 when he was killed at the age of fifty-two after a train struck his car at a railroad crossing. Fuertes' work illustrates five Burgess books, including *The Burgess Bird Book for Children* (1919), *The Burgess Animal Book for Children* (1920); *Birds You Should Know* (1933), *The Little Burgess Bird Book for Children* (1941), and *The Little Burgess Animal Book for Children* (1941).

Robert McCracken Peck, senior fellow at the Academy of Natural Sciences in Philadelphia and author of the distinguished 1982 biography *A Celebration of Birds: The Life and Art of Louis Agassiz Fuertes*, says that the revered ornithological artist would have found nothing demeaning or stigmatizing about working on Burgess' children's books. "One of his first books was Marian Bailey's book for children, *Birding on a Bronco*," says Peck. "He was a great believer in children's education and worked closely with children through the Ithaca Bird Club. I think the Burgess books would have interested him greatly as a way of getting children excited about birds and animals at a young age and bringing them to a new level of understanding about nature. The point was to do the best painting he could to make the birds alive and interesting."

Given Burgess' and Fuertes' family ties in Ithaca, common interest in the early Boy Scout movement, and professional work for agricultural/farming publications and *St. Nicholas* children's magazine, they may have been acquainted prior to working together on *The Burgess Bird Book for Children* or perhaps Fuertes' two children introduced their father to his stories. According to Peck, Fuertes was being courted by many magazines and book publishers and would consider each offer on its own merit. "It would have been his decision to work with Burgess on the bird and animal books," Peck says. "I'm sure the invitation to illustrate them was welcomed by Fuertes."

In *A Celebration of Birds*, Peck says that *The Burgess Bird Book* and *The Burgess Animal Book* were more personally and professionally satisfying to Fuertes than other projects he was working on at the time, such as bird portraits for trading cards for the Church & Dwight Company, best known for its Arm & Hammer consumer products.[27] "Although he appreciated that the cards were helping popularize nature, the work may have been a little embarrassing because it was so obviously commercial," the biographer said in a 2011 telephone interview. "He was grinding out the work, he wasn't particularly happy about it."

"Fuertes was sometimes working on a tight budget and might receive ten dollars for a painting," says Peck. "Fortunately he was very prolific and in such demand that people had to wait in line for him. He would take any interesting commission his time would allow, as long as it was in good taste and reputable. But he was selective in the commissions he took and once turned down a job for *National Geographic* because it didn't interest him and because he didn't feel suited to it." Peck speculates that the idea for Fuertes to illustrate the children's books came from Burgess' publisher Little, Brown.

"Fuertes worked closely with authors, and he probably corresponded and met with Thornton Burgess to discuss the illustrations," says Peck. "The fact that Burgess had written dozens of books with a natural history theme, was interested in serious science, and worked on conservation with William Hornaday would have appealed to Fuertes very much. And they had mutual friends and acquaintances. (John Burroughs, Frank Chapman, William Beebe, Anna Comstock, and Edward Howe Forbush also sought out Fuertes to illustrate their work.)[28] Illustrating books that were educational with someone like Thornton Burgess would have been an attractive and dignified, even exciting, activity," Peck remarked. "Fuertes would have felt he was working with a peer and a kindred spirit."

Later Illustrators

In mid-twentieth century, anthropomorphism was drawing fire from natural science educators, so Grosset & Dunlap hired illustrator Phoebe Erickson to give a more natural, realistic look to Burgess' animal characters. Winner of numerous awards, including the 1968 Dorothy Canfield Fisher Children's Book Award, Erickson illustrated five Burgess books: *Baby Animal Stories and The Nature Almanac* (Grosset & Dunlap, 1949); *Stories Around the Year* (Grosset & Dunlap, 1955); *Little Peter Cottontail*

(Wonder Books, 1955); and *The Adventures of Peter Cottontail* (abridged, Grosset & Dunlap, 1958).

Massachusetts Audubon Society education director Chuck Roth knew Erickson personally as his mentor and a noted illustrator who had worked as a Disney animator. "Erickson adored Burgess," Roth says. "She loved him to death, and was so proud he had chosen her to do some of his books." He remembers Erickson describing a visit she and husband Arthur Blair made to Burgess' Hampden home. A fly was annoying the group, but when Erikson's husband finally swatted it, Burgess amused the couple by dramatically exclaiming, "You've killed my fly!"

Michael Hague of Colorado Springs, Colorado, is credited with being the only Burgess illustrator to depict the Merry Little Breezes. A prominent illustrator of such classics as *The Velveteen Rabbit*, *The Teddy Bears Picnic*, and *The Wizard of Oz*, Hague provided artwork for the eightieth anniversary edition of *Old Mother West Wind*, which Henry Holt and Company released in 1990. "I was thrilled to do something that is a true American classic," said Hague in a 2011 telephone interview. "There are not that many American folk tales. The anthropomorphic animals were right up my alley."

At the beginning of his career Hague prepared for work as a children's book illustrator by reading a broad selection of children's books, including Thornton Burgess'. "So I had read his stories long before the assignment," says Hague. "I love them. I think they were told with a unique simplicity and directness that readers could identify with, even if there was a complicated philosophy in them. I was often surprised at how well they read, how well they stood up. Some things don't translate over time, and others do." Illustrations for the Holt anniversary edition took Hague about six months to complete.

Book Sales and Readership

Burgess' total mid-twentieth century book sales were reported by some sources to be as high as eleven million, but reliable figures are difficult to obtain. More than fifty years have passed since he wrote his last book and more than one hundred years have elapsed since his earliest books were published. Corporate mergers and lack of early record-keeping make even rough estimates questionable. However, a few established facts are available:

- In an October 4, 1954 journal entry, Burgess recorded the following sales summary he received from Little, Brown president Arthur Thornhill, Sr.: "Sale of books 1910 to Sept. 1 '54 by Little, Brown 5,027,611; to June 1954 by Grosset & Dunlap, 2, 414,617; Book-of-Month Club 30,750 sets of 2 each. Total 7,503,500."[29] This 1954 figure of 7,503,500 does not include sales from three major books that Little, Brown published between 1960 and 1965: *Now I Remember*, *Old Mother West Wind Golden Anniversary Edition*, and *The Burgess Book of Nature Lore*. A total of seventeen other Burgess books were released or re-released by various publishers between 1955 and 1984.

• In 1987, Little, Brown's corporate history cited the same 7.5 million book sales figure that Arthur Thornhill, Sr. quoted to Burgess in 1954[30], meaning that the 1987 figure does not include more than thirty years of sales (1954 to 1987) by both Little, Brown and Grosset & Dunlap.

• In addition, Thornhill's 1987 figure of 7.5 million books presumably does not include more than seventy-five years of book sales (1910 to 1987) by other domestic publishers such as Wonder Books, Golden Books, Eggers Publishing, and Penn Publishing, or sales by international publishers such as Bodley Head, McClellan & Stewart, Ltd., Oxford University Press, Heibonsha and Kinnohoshisha Publishers.

• In a 1964 interview, newspaper editor Stuart Trueman, who knew Burgess personally, stated that his book sales to date were eight million.[31]

• A 1967 *Reader's Digest* article on Thornton Burgess written by Louis Levine, who also knew Burgess well, stated that his books "have reached a staggering sale of 8,500,000 copies in the United States, plus countless more in Europe and China."[32] This statement suggests that the forty-five titles in England and twenty titles in Japan, for instance, are not included in that figure.

Since single books purchased by libraries, schools, and families were shared among multiple readers, the total readership of books in Thornton Burgess' lifetime was substantially larger than any estimate of his book sales. In addition, his syndicated stories were read over a forty-eight-year period by another audience of countless millions of newspaper readers.

Chapter 6

New Directions

Burgess was a dedicated and focused writer, but he was also a risk-taking entrepreneur, ready to explore technologies and ventures that could maximize the reach, impact, and financial return of his creative work. He was not ambitious for prestige in the usual sense, but professional recognition was extremely important to him. So was money. Despite his success, the weight of family obligation and financial need that shaped his childhood remained with Burgess throughout his life. He was both a dreamer and a realist. When undertaking a new endeavor, he often commented in his journals: "Doubt anything will come of it." From experience he knew that professional failure was not the worst that could happen, nor was professional success the best.

"New recognition in Coronet article, We the People program, making of records, approaches from agents in fields of movies and radio, etc. … What will the New Year hold?[1]

Thornton W. Burgess, 1947

"Letter from Program Productions, New York, asking if I would be interested in discussing use of Nature Stories in television. Wrote them 'Of course.'"[2]

Thornton W. Burgess, 1948

"What is perhaps most pioneering about Mr. Burgess is his use of new technology to reach his audience."

Bethany Rutledge, archivist, 2009

"Have got to get some extra income in some way."[3]

Thornton W. Burgess, 1936

An Unlikely Businessman

Although Thornton Burgess actively pursued commercial offshoots of his literary career, some fruitful, some not, he was the first to admit that business did not suit him. "I disliked selling as much as I did trying to get the same answer twice to a column of figures," he said of his work as a young bookkeeper/salesman in Boston. "I was a misfit in the business world."[4] At Phelps Publishing, however, he developed a skill in marketing and promotion, but he was motivated by opportunity more than competition. His modest, down-to-earth, unassertive nature remained unmodified by eventual prominence as a children's writer. Hal Borland, the *New York Times* reviewer of *Now I Remember*, wrote: "Mr. Burgess never became sophisticated, which is perhaps the key to his stories…he is still in awe of what happened to him, boyish in appreciation of praise and approbation…The Burgess style was as simple and homely as the tastes of his young audience."[5]

Close friends and family commented that ingrained naiveté may have served Burgess' creativity, but at times it blinded him to the self-serving motives of people he trusted in business and personal matters. "He was taken in by a lot of people, financially and emotionally," remarked granddaughter Frances Meigs. In 1912, for example, he made a professionally disastrous mistake in relying on a verbal understanding that resulted in losing eight years of publishing rights to his work. Burgess spelled out the consequences in the following excerpt from an affidavit:

> Over a long period of years, the Tribune Syndicate (which later became the *Herald Tribune*) has experienced cancellations by subscribers to my new stories, due to the competition of the old stories offered by the Associated Newspapers. In some cases, after cancellation of the new stories, newspapers have subscribed the old ones at much reduced price, none of which of course came back to me. I have never, since the expiration of my agreement with the Associated Newspapers, received one cent in return for the frequent and continued republication of these old stories.[6]

Burgess Characters as Products

English author Beatrix Potter's 1903 Peter Rabbit doll is generally considered the first patented product based on a literary character. As their literary characters became popular, American authors Howard Garis (*Uncle Wiggily's Adventures*), Frank Baum (*The Wonderful Wizard of Oz*), and Thornton Burgess (*Old Mother West Wind*) also explored commercial markets. Burgess had written twenty-four books by 1915 when he signed a contract with Kansas City toy manufacturer Henry J. Sieben, president of Sieben Novelty Co., so there was no shortage of wildlife characters to select from. The newly created Quaddy Playthings Manufacturing Company would "produce a line of children's toys and related merchandise bearing the configuration of Thornton Burgess creations."[7] ("Quaddy" was short for quadruped.) The extensive product line included puzzles, card games, pull toys, cloth and paper dolls, greeting cards, figurines, lamps, high-chair trays, coloring books, door stops, buttons, lunch boxes, plates, cups, and banks.

One of the earliest Burgess products was a Peter Rabbit board game called "Hunting in the Meadow." Harrison Cady provided artwork for the box, game, and advertising, and also illustrated a series of ten Quaddy postcards that featured Peter Rabbit, Happy Jack Squirrel, Hooty the Owl, and other Burgess characters. Sieben Novelty Company and Quaddy Playthings closed in 1920, but Burgess continued to use the Quaddy logo.[8]

In 1915, Burgess negotiated a two-year contract with Paye & Baker Manufacturing Company of Attleboro, Massachusetts, for production of jewelry and metalware items, which were marketed nationally through catalogue sales. Two years later Daniel Low & Company of Salem, Massachusetts, began producing and selling Burgess character-based pins, pendants, brooches, infant bib holders, as well as other items, while French & Ward Woolen Mills in New York obtained the manufacturing rights to depict Burgess' various Quaddy animal characters on woolen materials.

Tinware products that featured Burgess' designs were made by TINDECO [Tin Decorating Company], a successful manufacturer in Baltimore, Maryland. In 1916, the *Kansas City Star* capitalized on the writer's popularity by printing a Burgess quilt pattern designed by artist Ruby Short McKim. Directions required tracing the newspaper's pattern pieces onto carbon paper, which would then be used to cut out 10" x 10" blocks of muslin.[9]

Song Writing and Records

While Burgess was working as a journalist in Springfield, a pianist asked him to put words to a tune he had composed, stipulating that the song be titled "Eva."

The piece was published and became a familiar vaudeville hit "played on every street piano." Unfortunately, he and his collaborator elected to receive three hundred dollars for all rights rather than to collect royalties.[10]

In 1938, Burgess wrote stories and lyrics for *Mother Nature's Song and Story Book*, for which Rebecca Richards composed music and Lemuel Palmer and Henry Johnson provided illustrations. Although promising negotiations with Decca Records fell through because of a pending strike, Burgess secured a contract with Adventure Company, which specialized in children's records. Within two weeks, he prepared material for recordings of his stories and went to New York. In his journal, he noted:

> 11/12/1939: Pucinato [agent], Goodman [Adventure Company owner], and Uncle Henry [recording artist] came to my room and we went over stories until 1:30. Then to studio from 2 to 4 where I made three records, two with story on both sides and two with complete story on each side. Goodman eager to have everything just as I want it. All enthusiastic…"
>
> 12/10/1939: Good letter from Pucinato including check for $250 advance royalty from records."

Burgess' recording work with Adventure was documented in a 1953 news item in *The Billboard*, an entertainment industry weekly newspaper: "Gotham Records this week acquired the Adventure kiddie label from Sol Goodman. The deal was an outright purchase and includes the masters [master tapes] as well as the right to use the name. The transaction included sixty 78rpm masters, four LP's, and eight 45's. Included are masters of such artists as Lanny Ross, Uncle Henry and Thornton Burgess…"[11]

The indefatigable Burgess made a record with Pathways of Sound in Cambridge, Massachusetts in 1964: "Mother West Wind's Thornton W. Burgess Reads to You" was produced and directed by Joe Berk. The record jacket read: "Happy Birthday to Mr. Burgess! And we are delighted that this Grand Old Gentleman of children's literature has chosen to celebrate his ninetieth birthday by making a record for us. Parenthetically, Mr. Burgess remarked not too long ago that it seemed to him that making a record at his age was something of a record in itself. … The recording session took place in Mr. Burgess' barn studio, and if one listens closely, the many animal friends of this gentle and sensitive man can sometimes be heard in the background voicing their enthusiasm."[12]

A New Nature Magazine for Children

In 1937, Burgess interested magazine publisher Moody Gates in the idea of incorporating and publishing a children's nature magazine with him. Trade opinions they solicited supported their belief that *The Burgess Story Magazine* had great potential. The following excerpts from Burgess' 1940 journal show the effort he put into this new project over four months, as well as the diversity of his professional activities:

1/23: Got four stories off to Munk [& Platt publishers]. … Letter from Gates. He is about to show dummy of magazine and enthusiastic as ever. Hope his judgment is not at fault.

1/24: Check from *Tribune* only $572.45, next to lowest so far. If the magazine goes across will be great relief.

1/25: Gates phoned in evening that he had seen someone in News Co and they thought we should have more pictures and less text, citing comics and their big sales. Evidently hasn't yet got our idea. Suggested I come down and talk it over, so I'll go down [to New York] next week.

2/2: 7:18 train for N.Y. Gates met me at station. Very satisfactory interview at Am. News Co. … Laid out plans for magazine.

2/4: Worked on stories for Platt & Munk. Understand Cady is to illustrate them.

2/7: Request from *New Yorker* for interview.

2/8: Down to get prices on cuts for magazine. To S.P.C.A. Auxiliary meeting to hear Sec. [Russell] Mason on Mass. Aud. [Audubon] Society.

2/19: Lem [Lemuel Palmer, book illustrator] over for me to look at his drawing for 15 characters of a book he is to illustrate.

2/22: Worked on a film and did two stories in forenoon.

2/23: Interview with Mr. Cook of New Yorker.

2/24: Out to museum [American Museum of Natural History] at 9:45…Introduced by Dr. [James] Chapin [research associate, president of American Ornithological Union]. Full house, mobbed afterward for autographs.

4/13: Attended NY meeting of the National Life Conservation Society. Nearly 500 there. Was first speaker.

4/14: On air at 1:45, interview with Dr. [Francis] Rowley [president of Massachusetts Society for Prevention of Cruelty to Animals], Mr. Noble with him. Every seat taken for 4th consecutive Humane Society lecture at [Boston] Public Library.

4/18: Got proofs of [magazine] cover and am much pleased with them. Hope MB [Moody Gates] will be. All plates now made and last of copy sent. Will the magazine be a success? I wonder.[13]

On May 9, 1940, he worriedly wrote Gates: "I am perfectly willing to gamble my material and the necessary work and time. I confess that as the test approaches I get a bit all gone at the pit of my stomach...Still I have yet to mention the matter to those in the publishing business and not be told 'You've got something there.'" He and Gates printed 50,000 copies of the first issue in the summer of 1940, and professional colleagues and contacts were "enthusiastically receptive":

> Your new magazine looks as if it should be a best seller for the youngsters, and I will discuss selling it at our Information Desk sometime today with Mrs. Sloan who is in charge of that part of the Museum. ... I am very sorry you cannot be with us at the Executive Committee meeting on May 28th.[14]
>
> Bradford Washburn, executive director
> Boston Museum of Science

> I was much interested to receive in the mail yesterday the first copy of your new *Story Magazine.* We are making mention of this new magazine in the June *Bulletin* which goes to press this week...in the meantime, may we have ten copies of the first number to have here on hand, so that our members and customers may become acquainted with it.[15]
>
> Russell Mason, Secretary-Treasurer
> Massachusetts Audubon Society

> We were very pleased with the *Burgess Story Magazine.* It is a fine piece of work and we hope it goes and goes well. The five hundred copies have arrived here...[16]
>
> William H. Carr, associate curator
> American Museum of Natural History

> I was delighted to receive the first number of the *Burgess Story Magazine.* Thank you very much! Also hearty congratulations! I think it is fine and should have a very wide sale. I think you have worked it out splendidly to keep the interest of a wide reading audience, both adult and juvenile. And the format is great. It is all most refreshing in this mad, war-torn world. I hope it will meet with great success.[17]
>
> Hazel L. Muller, programs supervisor
> American Museum of Natural History

> I have read with much interest the first issue of the *Burgess Story Magazine* with *Mother Nature's News.* It is charmingly written and I have tried it out on some grand nieces and nephews. We are discussing a broad program of education for the American Wildlife Federation to be undertaken by Marts and Lundy with some professional help from the schools. Education must be the backbone of any program of conservation, and I am certain that your efforts in this direction will be of tremendous value.[18]
>
> F. C. Walcott, president
> American Wildlife Federation

The magazine contained Thornton Burgess stories interspersed with articles about wildlife and nature, a format Burgess had used successfully before. It was favorably reviewed in the Boston periodical *Books of the Week*:

> Thornton Burgess, America's most beloved writer of children's stories, has just fathered an entirely new magazine to be called 'The Burgess Story Magazine.' Its chief purpose is to supply wholesome reading matter for children, at a low enough price to bring it within reach of practically all. Such a magazine deserves immediate and whole-hearted support.[19]

Despite the warm reception, Burgess commented guardedly in his journal: "Now for the opinion of the public, which is what really counts." He was right to be cautious. The times were volatile and public needs and tastes were changing. With sales of only twenty percent, the magazine was quickly judged a commercial failure. No other issues were produced. A newsy letter to Burgess from Austin Clark, his longtime friend at the Smithsonian Institution, may have unintentionally identified the cause of the magazine's demise:

> Recently I have been attached to the Eighth American Scientific Congress as Press Relations officer, and during the week of the meeting of the congress I had with me here a number of the members of the National Association of Science Writers. But the invasion of The Netherland, Belgium and Luxembourg took place on the very first day of the meeting, and after that it was impossible to get any newspaper space for the proceedings of the Congress.[20]

With the public's anxious attention riveted on Europe, 1940 was a poor time to introduce a gently written, child-centered nature magazine. Even as the failure of his new publication became evident, however, Burgess was considering new proposals from several publishing houses.

Television

Thornton Burgess typically had many irons in the fire. In one week in 1948, he was working on books for Grosset & Dunlap, negotiating a contract for his autobiography with Little, Brown, considering a Boston revival of his Radio Nature League program, and negotiating with film companies in New York and New Jersey. In November 1947, he had accepted an invitation to appear on *We The People*, a popular CBS television program that featured individual speakers with inspirational stories, and forwarded the requested script. He caught the 7:40 a.m. train to New York and arrived at the theater for a rehearsal. "Found my script not to be used and my part short due to crowded program," he groused. "Frank Sinatra on among others."[21]

Burgess was eager to explore opportunities in television. While he could address thousands in a lecture hall and tens of thousands in a radio studio, this new medium offered limitless exposure for his stories and nature education messages. Burgess' hopes were high after New York agent Muriel Lawrence contacted him to say that the Fletcher Smith Film Studio in New York was interested in televising his stories. In 1946, this studio had been among the first to produce animated television advertisements promoting Sunbeam Bread, Mott's Apple Juice, and Pickwick Ale. Later it produced "Ivanhoe" and other full-length animated cartoons, and created background action scenes for Hollywood movies. When Burgess received Mrs. Lawrence's enthusiastic letter about Fletcher Smith Studio's interest, he replied he needed more information about the company and their proposal. He wrote in his journal: "Think I will have to go to N.Y. and talk over this television business. Can't afford to go into it blindly." After scheduling Monday and Tuesday appointments in New York, he noted: "Doubt anything will come of it, but at least will find out what can and cannot be done":

> Met Mrs. Lawrence at N.B.C. Nice visit with Bill Pooler at studio where he was working. Mrs. L...had made appointment for us with Fletcher Smith studio, [and] Princeton Film Center, Mr. [Gordon] Knox being our man there. Liked both Smith and Knox. Both good types and both interested in seeing what can be done with my stuff in television. Mrs. L. had a lot of enthusiasm. May something work out. Think I met the right people.[22]

Between January and March 1949, Burgess and Lawrence worked hard to secure a commitment from either of the two companies. Fletcher Smith Studio's corporate experience with commercial projects for children seemed a more appropriate match for Burgess, but the Princeton Film Center in Princeton, New Jersey, appeared more interested in his work. Burgess may have been swayed by Lawrence's salesmanship when he observed: "[She] Has thoroughly interested Princeton Film Center...Are putting up million dollar studio. Have big outlet for educational films and home entertainment...would have three outlets, schools, home and television for my stuff. Looks good."

In April 1949, he met Lawrence and Knox to discuss a plan for approaching manufacturing companies such as General Mills about using Burgess stories to sell their products. The next month Burgess approved an AP press release on Princeton Film Center's option of his work. The following announcement appeared in Atlantic City and Newark newspapers on June 3, 1949:

> The Princeton Film Center of Princeton, N.J. announced today it will film for television the children's stories of Thornton W. Burgess. The Film Center described the series as a "combination of live action sequences and animation techniques, executed in an entirely new format. 'Mr. Burgess will personally appear in many of the films to enact the role of the old story-teller,'" the company said. ... Commenting on his work, Burgess said he points his moral lessons for children at animals rather than at his readers.

> Children hate to be lectured, but even the youngest child feels instinctively that he is superior to the animal characters. No matter how much he loves them, he doesn't mind the animal being taught a little lesson...The Princeton Film Center has specialized in producing documentary and educational films. The contract with Burgess marks the Center's debut in the television field.[23]

Burgess was pleased with the prospect of working with Gordon Knox, founder in 1941 of the Princeton Film Center. A native of Greenville, Texas, Knox produced hundreds of documentaries for private industry and government agencies, including the State Department and the Air Force, and had worked with Warner Brothers, the American Film Center, Boeing, and Venezuelan oil companies. But what most impressed Burgess was the company's plan to develop a state-of-the-art production facility with a theater, a 5,000-square-foot sound stage, a film library, and a distribution department.[24]

In late October 1949, after nearly a year of negotiation, Burgess received a disappointing letter from Muriel Lawrence and wrote in his journal: "She has heard from Knox that they [Princeton Film Center] are dropping television project. What we had expected of late. Doubt that I will ever see Peter on television or hear him on radio." With three decades in the public eye, Burgess' folksy persona and familiar animal stories seem an unrealistic vehicle for an established film company's entry into the new medium of television. A pilot television program on Peter Rabbit aired in 1957, but did not lead to further contracts. The following excerpts of letters to Kathy and Frank Jones, caretakers of his Hampden home, were written while Burgess was wintering in Tobago that year:

> 4/14/1957: Had a copy of the note from Epstein [an agent] saying the pilot film was slated for television yesterday morning. So Peter has hit the screen at long last. Hope it may lead to something good.
>
> 4/18/1957: Am wondering if you saw Peter Rabbit on TV Saturday morning. Will be a bit curious as to results. It can be the key of something good or it can be the burial of the whole TV idea. I have reached the point where I am immune to any feeling of elation on the one hand or disappointment on the other.[25]

Influence on Children

Intrigued as he was by television's exciting potential to expand the audience for his work, Burgess had far-sighted concerns about its influence on children. In the following excerpt from "Can Your Child Read?", an undated article likely written in the mid-1950s, Burgess cautioned parents and teachers about the new medium:

> The television picture is rubber stamped on the adolescent mind. It lacks the depth etched by mental cooperative effort to make a lasting impression. It is a lazy method of obtaining without effort temporary entertainment or presentation of news items and facts. Educationally it is all too often a short cut. Like many short cuts it is often abortive.

> Visual education unquestionably has a place in school curriculum today, but that place should not usurp the place of reading as I fear is too often the case. The boy or girl who has not been taught to read, how to read, the love of reading, has been, or is being cheated, to his or her own personal loss, and to the loss of society as a whole. The well-read man or woman always is an efficient member of society.[26]

"Fables of the Green Forest"

Less than ten years after his death in 1965, Thornton Burgess' most wildly extravagant dreams for television exposure were surpassed by the international success of an anime (stylized cartoon) series that originated in Japan. Based with appreciable accuracy on his books, the fifty-two-episode television cartoon was developed by Zuiyo Eizo Animation studio, a predecessor of Nippon Animation. It aired in Japan in 1973 as *Yama Nezumi Rokkiy Chukku* or *Rocky Chuck the Mountain Rat.*

In 1978, the anime series was produced for an international audience by I. Holender and M.J. Ruderian and distributed worldwide by Ziv International. It was known as "Fables of the Green Forest" in Canada; "Chuck, der Biber" in Austria; "Dieren Verhalen van het Groene Woud" in The Netherlands; "Fables de la Foret Verte" in France; "Fábulas del Bosque Verde" in Spain and Mexico; "Le Favole Della Foresta" in Italy; "Os Bichos da Floresta Verde" in Portugal; "Povestiri din Padurea Verde" in Romania; "Rocky und seine Freunde" in Germany; "Сказки Зелёного Леса" in Russia; and "ءارضخلا ةباغلا" in Saudi Arabia.[27]

Originally sung by Mituko Horie and Chataraazu, the catchy Rocky Chuck theme song was enjoyable in any language[28], but translation added a unique flavor to the Burgess stories. Among the fifty-two episodes listed by Anime News Network are "Chatterer the Chatty Squirrel," "Buster Bear the Scatterbrain," "Peter Rabbit of Briar Forest," "The Monster of Poplar Hill," "Bobby Beaver's Blunder," and "Mrs. Quack the Goose."[29] Today "Fables of the Green Forest" has a Facebook page, and YouTube downloads have had hundreds of thousands of hits. Comments such as the following indicate the anime is fondly remembered:

> "This show rocked when I was a kid."
>
> "My childhood! Today I am 44. When I was a kid and my mom was calling me indoors because Green Forest was beginning."
>
> "I liked the Old Man Coyote episode, I liked his books the most of the Green Forest books."
>
> "As a kid I tried to eat a raw egg like Uncle Billy did in the episode where he was trapped in the henhouse. Just say it didn't go down as smooth as Uncle Billy made it look. On top of that, I'm still grossed out by raw eggs."
>
> "What memories! When I was about 5, I ran away with a boy to find the Green Forest."

"I used to watch this show when I was a little kid and still remember how that opening theme song went…a part of my childhood."

"I remember this on TV Ontario. Then in the '90s they resurrected it on YTV as 'Friends of the Forest.'"

"I never thought I would hear or see Green Forest again. Such great memories as I was a child watching this on my old living room floor."

"Great. I've been searching for this for a long time. I used to watch it in Romania back in the 1980s, but could only remember the title in Romanian 'Povestiridin padurea Verde.' Now if I could just get a copy of it to be able to re-watch it."

Other Options

In October 1947, Little, Brown informed Burgess that a California movie agent wanted a one-hundred-twenty-day option for use of *Old Mother West Wind* characters for cartoon animation. It sounded promising. The agent had a contract with an RKO movie producer, was "in" with a CBS vice-president, and had "a toy idea." Burgess' journal cautiously indicated his low expectations, but he couldn't resist making the pleased observation: "First direct contact with Hollywood." He granted a ninety-day option to the filmmaker with sixty days renewable, and wrote in his journal: "Have my fingers crossed…it is all very interesting."[30]

Nearly a year later, he noted, without detail, that he had responded to a "letter regarding use of my stuff in television. No longer have any hope of radio, movies, or television programs format." Within three weeks, though, he received additional requests from New York for an option on television rights and two requests from California and Chicago for radio rights options. As late as 1961, at 87, Burgess and his lawyer Louis Doherty were negotiating with New World Productions for television and motion picture rights to Burgess' stories. In February, the company said they had unsuccessfully made every effort to develop a series and a month later informed Burgess there was serious interest in a five-minute pilot film based on his characters.

Thornton Burgess also corresponded with the Walt Disney Studio, but nothing came of it. [Ironically, while Burgess wintered on Tobago in 1960, Walt Disney, Inc. filmed *Swiss Family Robinson* there.] Ultimately, the break into television and cinema he hoped for never materialized, but whatever regret or disappointment he felt must have been diminished by the satisfaction of other events. His long-awaited autobiography *Now I Remember* and the fiftieth anniversary edition of *Old Mother West Wind* were released in 1960. He described a hectic two-day schedule of events in his journal:

9/19: Off by train at 7 o'clock. Met at Back Bay by Hobson of Little, Brown. To 34 Beacon and autographed i00 [*sic*, 100] books. To lunch at Union Club with officers and heads of company. With Houghton to Jordan Marsh big book department to autograph nearly one hundred books.

> 9/20: Publication Day for autobiography and Golden Anniversary edition of *Old Mother West Wind.* Raining hard. Hobson came for me and we taxied to office. To Ritz for lunch for press and libray [sic] folk arranged by Helen Jones. (James) Sherman presided. Cady there and everyone enjoyed him. Margery Mills and Alice Dixon Bond among guests. Had met both years ago. At 3 o'clock went to W.B.Z. for tape recorded interview with Mr. Nelson. Had chat with Gordon Swan [WBZ radio program manager]. My room at 5:30 to stay. Again no dinner. Not hungry.[31]

Publication that year of his fifteen thousandth syndicated story also brought acclaim, including an eight-page article in *Life.* He wrote Canadian editor Stuart Trueman about the media attention:

> There has been a succession of newspaper men and photographers here at my home including a staff writer from Life who spent a couple hours a day with me for six consecutive days. By the time he was through I was in a mental vacuum. And Life's photographer is due any day now for pictures to go with the article.
>
> The AP photographer was here all one afternoon. … I was in Boston for three strenuous days on two TV shows and one radio, lunches, interviews and autographing books. Last week I had two days of same in New York. Getting about was rather tough on my bum legs. … On my return I found a letter from the Canadian Broadcasting Corporation saying they would like to arrange for a TV interview here at my home…very flattering and at times embarrassing. And this after 50 years. I am amazed. As a result, both books seem to be going very well.[32]

Chapter 7

The Writer's Craft

In 1919, the eminent conservationist Dr. William T. Hornaday introduced Thornton Burgess to the annual meeting of the New York Zoological Society as "a genius" who found his way "into the hearts of a million children." "He was a magic man," says Manomet Bird Sanctuary founder and naturalist Betty Anderson who listened avidly to Burgess stories while sitting on her father's lap. In fact, Burgess was a gifted story-teller with a passion for nature who wrote for the sharp eyes and attentive ears of children. A fourth grader explained to New York Public Library superintendent Anne Carroll Moore why he treasured Thornton Burgess' books: "He sees what I see and I understand his language."[1] *This chapter examines the process, technique, and perspective of the writer.*

"How many authors can cater to three- and four-year-olds, and twelve- and thirteen-year-olds? How many can weave a story that is compelling to children, but is interesting to adults? It is the web of relationships his stories have that gives them authenticity."

Julie Arrison, historian
Historical New England, 2011

"As a child, I identified with Thornton Burgess characters, never realizing I was also learning facts gleaned from the author's close observation of nature, a habit sorely needed today. After hearing red squirrels, I realized that Chatterer could have no other name."

Pat Rogers, artist/curator, 2011
Thorton W. Burgess Society

"I've always believed that a writer's creative ability is like a pool of spring water – the water level may occasionally recede, but the spring will always fill up again with fresh ideas. At least that's the way the business of writing has worked for me."[2]

Thornton W. Burgess, 1959

Qualities as a Writer

Thornton Burgess never formally studied journalism, marketing, children's fiction, or nature writing, but he had strengths that accounted for his accomplishment in those areas. He was a natural and effective writer who had an exceptional understanding of his young readers. He wrote about what he knew best and loved most in a style appropriate to his audience, whether children or adults, and to his purpose, whether advertising copy or bedtime stories. In addition, Burgess had a powerful work ethic and an unbreakable focus that enabled him to work through professional adversity, poor health, financial woes, wartime, and loss of loved ones.

He was a wordsmith, clearly comfortable with the demands of professional writing: endless blank pages to fill, editorial deadlines to meet, and the physical necessity of sitting at a table or desk composing for hours a day, year after year, decade after decade. He had tremendous discipline. "Stories are not born of inspiration," Burgess remarked. "They are the result of methodical, sometimes irritating work."[3] Initially he was appalled at his own audacity in signing a contract that would commit him to write six syndicated newspaper stories a week for six months, but his confidence, shored up by financial need, was justified: one thousand articles appeared, then five thousand, then ten thousand...Each milestone was celebrated by the media and his fans. One suspects Burgess himself became curious to see how many stories he was capable of producing. In 1960, at eighty-six, his fifteen thousandth syndicated story ran. Five years later he concluded his writing career with the publication of a new children's book by Little, Brown. "I rather like the idea of having a book out when

I am ninety," he confided to Stuart Trueman. "Makes me feel very good; not on the shelf yet...Sort of rounds out life."[4]

Burgess generally composed rapidly and revised little. Some six- or seven hundred-word stories were written in an hour, a pace of production he established as a young journalist racing to meet deadlines. Old, yellowed papers, now brittle with age, show a minimal number of corrections lined out with pencil on the double-spaced first drafts and carbon copies he made on his manual Remington typewriter. He eventually turned to dictation and made corrections on the proofs. Burgess likened his writing process to the act of unwinding a ball of twine: "I begin with the title and unwind. There isn't any plot yet. That develops for me as I go along just as it will for the reader...and there can be no skipping ahead to find out." Refining a plot "gets in my way" and "trips me up," he commented in his autobiography, "or it is lost sight of and I have to go back and find it."[5] He told a reporter, "My writing is spontaneous. Usually when I start a story, I haven't any idea at all how it's going to end."

There was nothing arrogant or lazy in his approach. He was well aware it was technically questionable, even unacceptable by some standards, but he also knew it was "peculiarly my own." "This does not mean I think a story so good it could not be improved," Burgess admitted. "A more gifted writer might rewrite it to its decided betterment. But...I know that it is the best of which I am capable; that reading it over a year hence I would at most change no more than a word or two here and there."[6] He trusted the creativity of his subconscious, which he felt was at work when his conscious mind was not, a process he explained in *Now I Remember*:

> The subconscious mind files and stores away for possible future use all the facts that come through to it from the conscious mind. There they are held, even though that part of the mind we call memory fails to retain even the faintest impression of them. If and when the time comes for use of this forgotten knowledge, perhaps in a wholly new way, the subconscious returns such facts as are needed for the completion of the work at hand, and in such manner that they can be applied to the problem of the moment. So the work goes forward smoothly.[7]

Asked if he wrote only when he was in the mood, Burgess bluntly replied, "Why not ask the carpenter if he works only when he feels like it or the accountant if he balances his books only when the spirit moves. ... When a columnist has to meet daily a deadline, mood has no place whatsoever. How one does or does not feel doesn't enter into the situation. If I waited to feel in the mood, most of my more than 15,000 stories would not have been written."[8]

Although Burgess considered himself a procrastinator, he apparently met deadlines without difficulty and prepared his syndicated material weeks or months in advance, even while he was vacationing. At eighty-four, he sent a batch of stories to his secretary in March, saying it "puts me ahead until September." He kept regular writing hours and preferred to start early in the morning, but could work "any hour of the twenty-four if I must." There is no evidence he labored over his work, but he occasionally noted in his journal that the writing was coming slowly: "Could not get underway on stories. Like a car stalled in the snow with wheels going round and round getting nowhere."[9]

Understanding his Audience

Working as a journalist, editor, and advertising specialist, Burgess had diverse assignments that required him to tailor his writing to the interests and tastes of farmers, athletes, businessmen, horticulturalists, parents, homemakers, nursing mothers, hunters, builders, conservationists, as well as to young children. As a result he developed control, speed, and confidence in his writing, but, most importantly, he perfected the ability to write for a specific audience.

It is clear from Burgess' journals, interviews, and personal letters that he had a natural rapport with children. He was comfortable being around them and talking with them, and they were comfortable with him. Children throughout the U.S. and around the world mailed him drawings, original stories, lists of their favorite characters, and requests for his books. They described their encounters with woodchucks, beetles, and turtles, sent him holiday greetings, get-well wishes, and thank-you notes, and sought his opinion while at the same time offering theirs. In 1959, for example, he received the following letter from a teenage fan:

> Though I am fourteen years old I still enjoy the adventures of Peter Rabbit, Johnny Chuck, Jerry Muskrat, Little Joe Otter, and all the rest. ... Giving these animals the characteristics of people not only pleases little children but in a simple way that a young mind can understand, tells them where these animals live, what each is afraid of, and all the ways that each one has. And for people my age, it is much more fun to read your stories when I wish to know about animal life, that to read from some dull, boring encyclopedia...Thank you very much for writing all these wonderful stories for me and the millions of children who enjoy your stories so well.
>
> WALTER MITCHELL
> ORISKANY, NEW YORK[10]

Burgess was genuinely interested in how children thought and how they saw things, not as an analyst, but as an equal, albeit an older, more experienced equal. He wrote to the perspective of the learning child, not the informed adult. "His books lack the condescension you find in some early literature," observed Thornton W. Burgess Society archivist Bethany Rutledge. "There is something very trusting in the way he relates information about nature to children, as if he is fully confident they'll know what to do with it."

Burgess maintained that children would accept lessons modeled by animals because they feel innately superior to them, in the same way adults feel superior to children. He often related the story of a mother who wrote to say her son resisted keeping a window open at night until she read him the story of Jerry Muskrat who built his home specifically to supply it with fresh air. Burgess explained his understanding of "the child mind" in a 1924 article in *Nature* and in his autobiography:

People's Home Journal cover, March 1927. Original Harrison Cady illustration.

HARRISON

Original Harrison Cady illustration of Peter Rabbit and friends, published in 1922.
Courtesy of the Thornton W. Burgess Society.

Illustration by Michael Hague, for *Old Mother West Wind*, 80th anniversary edition, published by Henry Holt and Company, New York, 1990.

Happy Jack Squirrel and the Merry Little Breezes. Michael Hague was the only Burgess illustrator to depict the Merry Little Breezes, shown here with Happy Jack Squirrel. Since Happy Jack was a gray squirrel, this would appear to be, despite the label, Chatterer the Red Squirrel. However, Burgess bibliographer Wayne Wright notes that illustrators often make their own decisions about how to interpret a character.

Harrison Cady's illustration of Grandfather Frog and Buster Bear characters for a set of Burgess books published by John H. Eggers Company in 1922.

Painted by the acclaimed ornithological artist Louis Agassiz Fuertes, this jubilant meadowlark was selected as the cover of the Burgess Bird Book for Children which has continued to be bought and read since it was first published by Little, Brown and Company in 1919.

Sunshine the Yellow Warbler, the one bird who is all yellow. Zee-Zee the Redstart, dressed chiefly in black and orange.

Ornithological artist Louise Agassiz Fuertes was famous at a young age for his ability to represent not just the appearance but the attitude of birds he painted. His renderings of a yellow warbler, redstart, redheaded woodpecker, downy woodpecker, a redwing blackbird, and a starling appeared in the classic *Burgess Bird Book for Children* (1919).

Creaker the Purple Grackle. At a distance he appears black and is called Crow Blackbird. The Male Cowbird. You may know him by his coffee-brown head.

HARRISON CADY

Original Harrison Cady illustration "Grandfather frog stays in the smiling pool," published by John Eggers 1922. *Courtesy of the Thornton W. Burgess Society.*

Original Harrison Cady illustration: "Billy Possum has a friend."
Courtesy of the Thornton W. Burgess Society.

A Harrison Cady illustration of a Thornton Burgess story. Publishing date unknown.

This is a typical Harrison Cady depiction of Jimmy Skunk published in *On the Green Meadows* in 1944 by Little, Brown and Company.

The work of brilliant wildlife artist Louis Agassiz Fuertes illustrates five books by Thornton W. Burgess. This picture of Jimmy Skunk appeared in the *Burgess Animal Book for Children*, first published by Little, Brown and Company in 1920.

This version of Jimmy the Skunk is a realistic rendering of wildlife by Lemuel Palmer, a talented young artist Burgess worked with. It first appeared in *While the Story-Log Burns* published by Little, Brown and Company in 1938.

Phoebe Erickson, one of Thornton Burgess' favorite illustrators, provided a more realistic look for his Peter Rabbit.

This exquisite artwork provides the cover of the Japanese translation of *The Adventures of Danny Meadow Mouse*, first published by Kin-no-Hoshi-sha Publishers in 1969. The book appeared as one of a twenty-volume set of Burgess' Bedtime Story-Books. In the 1970s, the complete set was given to Penelope and Russell Lovell as a gift by a Japanese friend, and they subsequently donated it to the Thornton W. Burgess Society.

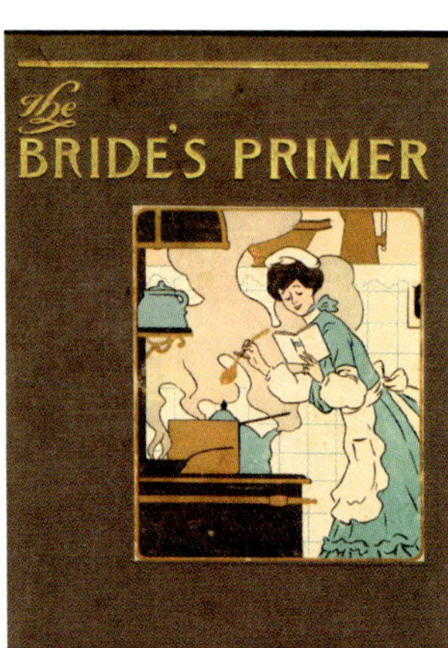

Published in 1905 by Phelps Publishing, *The Bride's Primer* was illustrated by well-known artist F. Strothmann. A light-hearted spoof at the misadventures of brides, it contained Thornton Burgess' essays, articles, and poems.

Thornton Burgess books were translated into numerous languages. This French edition shows that "Patteroose le Reynard" can look quite different from the familiar Reddy Fox drawn by Harrison Cady.

Published in 1929 by Little, Brown & Co., this introduction to seashore life was illustrated by W.H. Southwick and George Sutton with photographs provided by the American Museum of Natural History.

> The child mind is colorful. Dry facts make no impression. The young mind cannot retain that in which it has no interest. Present facts in such a way that the imagination may seize upon them and they will be impressed upon the memory forever. Nature presents an interest which is inherent. It remains but to capitalize this by presenting that which it is desired to impart in such form that the imagination becomes but a setting for the truth.[11]
>
> I am convinced that failure on the part of parents, teachers, and others having to do with the guidance of the young to appreciate how extremely plastic is the child mind, how deep and lasting are the impressions for good or ill made therein by events and surroundings of daily life, is often at the root of many of the youth problems of today. [Children's impressions] are not to be ignored, denied or laughed away.[12]

Veteran children's bookseller Carol Chittenden feels that Burgess' appreciation for the child reader's emerging self is "an absolutely key factor" in his enduring popularity. "The relationship of child to adult is small to large and weak to strong," she says. "Kids look for ways to equalize that. Nature is available to us all, so even if you're small, you can see the bug crawling across the floor and the squirrel going up and down the tree. Animals are small too."

Predators and prey

Literary practicality and respect for children explain why Burgess' predator characters like Reddy and Granny Fox, Old Man Coyote, Hooty the Owl, and Redtail the Hawk never caught and killed his prey characters. Questioned — and regularly criticized — about this unlikely scenario, he explained simply: "Children learn soon enough the hardship of life." He also observed that he would run out of characters if the predators were successful. When he declared that Reddy Fox would never catch Peter Rabbit, it got press coverage. Despite protests at his lack of realism, Burgess continued to write for his young readers, not his critics.[13]

Susan Fisher Curtis, a retired social worker in Cleveland, sees clinical benefit in the author's philosophy. "I heartily agree with Burgess' protective approach," she says. "Children are exposed to way too much reality, and to too many dark stories. They don't have the brain development, the experience, or the context to take in and make useful much of this information. So they grow up, [absorbing] trauma after trauma until they become adults." Several decades ago, Curtis related, some children came to her practice for counseling for apparent sexual abuse. "We would set up a play situation to enable them to reveal their secret, but there was no secret. It turned out they weren't being abused in their house — they were just watching too much violence and sex on television. I am all in favor of protecting children so they can find their own paths."

In her own childhood, Curtis's father read to her the "Uncle Remus" stories (with an accent), while her mother read Thornton Burgess' stories and shared his belief in nature as an endless source of wisdom and recreation. "I think Burgess' stories are wonderful little teaching tales for children," Curtis says. "I see in him a person who had to figure out his way through life, and so do his animal characters."

The mortality rate may have been low on the Green Meadows, but the struggle for survival was constant as animals sought food, shelter, and safety. Young readers did not need to learn that Burgess' beloved characters were seized, killed, and consumed to comprehend the essence of predation, for it is unmistakable in such passages as the following description of a coyote's pursuit of a rabbit in *The Adventures of Old Man Coyote* (1916):[14]

> (Peter) began to hurry, and the nearer he got to the Old Briar-patch, the faster he hurried. He would run a little way as fast as he could, lipperty-lipperty-lip, and then stop and look and listen nervously. Then he would do it all over again. It was one of these times that he was listening that Peter thought he heard a soft footstep behind him. It sounded very much like the footstep of Reddy Fox. Peter crouched down very low and sat perfectly still, holding his breath and straining his ears. There it was again, pit-a-pat, pit-a-pat, very soft and coming nearer. Peter waited no longer. He sprang forward with a great leap and started for the dear Old Briar-patch as fast as he could go, which, you know, is very fast indeed. As he ran, he saw behind him a fierce, grinning face. It was very much like the face of Reddy Fox, only larger and fiercer and gray instead of red.
>
> Never in all his life had Peter run as he did now, for he knew he was running for his life. It seemed as if those long legs of his hardly touched the ground. Peter began to breathe hard. It seemed to him he could feel the hot breath of the fierce stranger...Snap! That was a pair of cruel jaws right at his very heels. It gave Peter new strength and he made longer jumps than before. The dear old Briar-patch, the safe old Briar-patch, was just ahead. With three mighty jumps, Peter reached the opening of one of his own private little paths and dived in under a bramble bush. And even as he did so, he heard the clash of sharp teeth and felt some hair pulled from his tail. And then, outside the Old Briar-patch, broke forth the same terrible voice Peter had heard in the night. ... Peter...hurried to the very middle of the Old Briar-Patch and there he stretched out at full length and panted and panted for breath.

Realism Geared to Children

Although Burgess' first children's book, *Old Mother West Wind*, was originally written for his child, not an international reading audience, it contained all the characteristic elements of the dozens of books that followed — the fictitious plot, entertaining animal characters, story-telling style, scientific fact, poetic imagery, and moral observations. It also contained within the opening paragraphs one aspect of nature that Burgess consistently depicted throughout fifty-five years of writing for children: the constant threat of danger to wildlife.

> Old Mother West Wind came down from the Purple Hills in the golden light of the early morning. Over her shoulders was slung a bag — a great big bag — and in the bag were all of Old Mother West Wind's children, the Merry Little Breezes.

> ... When she reached the Green Meadows, Old Mother West Wind opened her bag, turned it upside down and shook it. Out tumbled all the Merry Little Breezes and began to spin round and round for very joy. ... First they raced to see Johnny Chuck...And if they teased Johnny Chuck, they were good to him, too. When they saw Farmer Brown coming across the Green Meadows with a gun, one of them would dance over to Johnny Chuck and whisper to him that Farmer Brown was coming, and then Johnny Chuck would hide away, deep down in his snug little house underground, and Farmer Brown would wonder and wonder why it was that he never, never could get near enough to shoot Johnny Chuck. But he never, never could."[15]

Burgess' ability as a writer to balance nature's realities with the limitations of a child's life experiences must explain to a significant degree his credibility with children and the longevity of his appeal. Consider his gentle and masterful handling of such a potentially disturbing topic as a father bear attempting to kill its own offspring:

> Now when Buster Bear saw those cubs, not knowing they were his own, he was filled with sudden anger. He didn't want any more Bears in the Green Forest. He wanted the Green Forest just for himself and Mrs. Bear. Those young Bears were likely to make a great deal of trouble...so after the first surprised stare Buster growled. It was a grumbly-rumbly growl deep down in his throat. The twins heard it as they started to run, and it was the most awful sound they ever had heard.
>
> "They look good enough to eat," thought Buster. "I can do two things at once, rid the Green Forest of a pair of troublesome youngsters...and get a good dinner." Of course this was very dreadful, but you know Buster Bear didn't know that those cubs were his own. They meant no more to him than Peter Rabbit, and you know he wouldn't have hesitated an instant to gobble up Peter if he had had the chance.
>
> Now little bears are much like little boys and girls in very many ways, and one of these is their faith in mother. Another is that when they are frightened or in trouble they cry and yell for mother. ... The instant they saw Buster, they began to whimper and cry softly...But when they saw Buster Bear climbing up after them, they simply opened their mouths and bawled."[16]

The confrontation becomes comprehensible and less fearsome through Burgess' explanation of the perspective of the male bear as well as of the cubs. He often encouraged young readers to appreciate and sympathize with both sides of survival and predation, pointing out that Hooty the Owl looks for food for his babies and Reddy and Granny Fox seek food to relieve their hunger[17]:

> They were very hungry indeed, and they could not eat bark like Peter Rabbit, or buds like Mrs. Grouse, or seeds like Whitefoot the Woodmouse. Their teeth and stomachs are not made for such food...It was hard going for Granny and Reddy

Fox. The snow was soft and deep in many places, and they had to keep pretty close to those places where rough Brother North Wind had blown away enough of the snow to make walking fairly easy. They soon found that their hope that they would find some of their neighbors too weak to escape was quite in vain. When jolly, round red Mr. Sun dropped behind the Purple Hills to go to bed, their stomachs were quite as empty as when they had started out.

Nature in a Social Context

Burgess' anthropomorphic depiction of wildlife within a social context enabled children to identify with his characters through their own experiences of so wanting to tell a secret or hating to share food or special objects, feeling unsafe or afraid of being alone, angry at a relative, or overpowered by a bully. As Burgess knew personally, children also experience the ecological stress on his animal characters who had to adjust to the proximity of others, whether friend, family, or enemy. When Old Man Coyote suddenly moves into the neighborhood, Peter is so upset by the strange, frightening nighttime howling that he loses his appetite. But Peter's enemies Reddy and Granny Fox are also disturbed by this menacing newcomer, and respond by moving away. As in human families, parent animals in Burgess' stories work to feed and instruct their young. A mother quail explains the facts of bird life to her covey of fifteen babies in *The Adventures of Bob White*:[18]

> "You see, my dears," explained Mrs. Bob, as they nestled under her wings, "the Great World is full of dangers, especially for little Bob Whites, and so if you want to grow up to be as handsome and smart as your father, you must mind instantly when we speak to you." ... While they were in the dear Old Briar-patch they were quite safe, but just the same, every little while Mrs. Bob would give the danger signal, which meant to squat and keep perfectly still, or another call that meant to come running to her as fast as ever they could.
>
> There was danger from the air where old Redtail the Hawk sailed round and round, watching below for heedless and careless little folks. There was danger from Reddy and Granny Fox and Old Man Coyote, prowling about with sharp eyes and keen ears and wonderful noses, all the time hunting for heedless little people. And there was danger from Mr. Blacksnake and his cousins slipping silently through the grass.

Human Impact on Wildlife

Burgess' stories also enable children to realize the human impact on wildlife, for in addition to finding food and a safe place to sleep, his characters must elude people, especially those with weapons. Lightfoot the Deer, the Bob Whites, and Mr. and Mr. Quack are relentlessly pursued by men trying to kill them with "terrible guns" while Blacky the Crow flees before a frustrated hunter takes aim at him. In *The Adventures of Jerry Muskrat*, Burgess graphically describes how a hunter's baited trap works:[19]

> After awhile...his tail dropped down in the water where it covered the lower part of that old log. Snap! With a squeal of pain and fright, Jerry jumped right up in

> the air. He lost his balance and fell off the old log. Then he tried to scramble away. He couldn't. Something was holding him by his tail and pinching it most dreadfully. Jerry was too frightened to think. He couldn't imagine what dreadful thing had got him. He pulled and pulled until it seemed to him he must pull his tail out by the roots. Finally he twisted around to see what held him. It was a trap! The stout, cruel jaws of it were gripping his tail about an inch from the end.
>
> ...So when that cruel, steel trap caught him by the tail in its wicked jaws, Jerry plunged back off the old log into the water and tried to swim away. If he had only known it, this was just what the trapper had expected him to do and had hoped he would do. That trap had been fastened in such a way that Jerry could get into deep water. You see, the trapper hoped that Jerry would drown himself, and Jerry did come pretty near doing just that thing.

More than one hunter had to face his horrified children after they learned about such practices in their bedtime stories. In fact, Burgess did not oppose hunting, but he was actively opposed to what he considered unfair, excessive, and cruel hunting practices. In 1926, he worked actively for passage of state legislation to outlaw steel traps and was devastated when it failed. Thirty years later he shared those memories with his friend Aida Flemming, founder of the International Kindness Clubs and wife of New Brunswick premier Hugh John Flemming:

> "Years ago we had a bitter fight here in Massachusetts to outlaw the steel trap and finally succeeded. It was a state law. Then the trappers and so-called sportsmen nullified by getting it modified to allow the towns to decide if steel traps should or should not be used within the town's limits. I still hope for the day when the only legal traps will be of the humane type. Meanwhile we must rely on educating the public, especially the children."[20]

Knowledge of Subject Matter

An interviewer once asked Burgess where he got his material. "In the field and by constant study," he replied. Frances Meigs verified that her grandfather constantly read nature books, even during lunch breaks. Walks with him invariably turned into nature lessons, she said: "He always saw things I didn't see." Field observation was a lifelong practice for Burgess, whose journals were filled with daily reports of the number, kind, and activity of wildlife, especially birds, that he saw. On July 20, 1937, he reported, "Saw two male Tanagers today back of bungalow and later one in front. Saw Humming bird do the pendulum swing. Also saw one sitting in oak tree. From window beside my machine [typewriter] saw flickers, hairy woodpecker, nuthatches, bluebirds, tanagers, humming bird, wren, black-and-white warbler."

Burgess regularly conversed with and consulted natural science experts such as Smithsonian curator Austin Clark and Bowdoin College ornithologist Dr. Alfred Gross, and he often incorporated their information into his storylines. The following 1925 correspondence between Clark and Burgess indicates the depth and caliber of factual information behind Burgess' animal stories:

Dear Mr. Clark:

What has happened to the enclosed leaf? Under separate cover I am sending a chrysalid which a small boy says was darker green and with a gold line instead of black when found. The shape is that of Anosia plexipuss but the markings are not like those shown in the plate I have. With the chrysalid I am inclosing the remains of a big spider. The woman's letter is herewith. ... Another seeker wants to know how the great tan and white spiders with the orange banded legs stretch their webs from bushes as much as five feet apart since the spiders can neither jump nor fly across the space. This same party has observed certain wasps cutting the grass about their holes and asks what kind they are and why they do it.[21]

Clark responded:

The large tan and white spider with the banded legs is **Epeira trifolium**. These so-called orb spinners sit on some exposed position and give out a compound thread, or several slender threads more or less entangled. These are carried by the wind and catch on some object often quite a distance away, giving the spider a tight rope from which the [sic] begin operations...Only two of our wasps have the grass cutting habit. The one you refer to is undoubtedly **Ammobia tibialis** which lines its burrows with cut grass leaves and packs them with paralyzed crickets."[22]

Nearly two decades later, a talented web-spinner named Madame Orb the Spider appeared in Burgess' *On the Green Meadows* (1944). Children's historian John Goldthwaite suggests in *The Natural History of Make-Believe* that Burgess' book may have influenced E.B. White's depiction of the spider heroine in his beloved classic *Charlotte's Web* (1954).[23]

Burgess may not have had his Aunt Arabella's gift of communicating with eels and turtles, but he had a special rapport with animals that enabled him to make close observation of their appearance and behaviors. To gain a wild creature's trust, he used patience, slow movements, and bribery with food. People regularly stopped at his house with baby rabbits or injured birds that needed care. The Springfield Society for the Prevention of Cruelty to Animals often asked him to take in wild animals, and reciprocated when he was unable to help a wild creature. Burgess' fondness for skunks was well-known. (He maintained they should be the national symbol, not the eagle, because they employed defense before offense.) When he took in a baby skunk for the Springfield SPCA, he wrote in his journal: "Cutest little rascal. Eyes not yet open. Yet he is lively." Two days later he accepted a second one: "Bigger than the other. Cute. Does a lot of stamping, but friendly. Other has both eyes open, but not widely yet. ... Latter played around on porch. Finally as I sat on upper step one crept into each hand and went to sleep."[24]

Style Suited to Children

Burgess wrote steadily in the first two decades of his career, creating thirty-two books as well as his daily syndicated columns between 1910 and the late 1920s. As his sense of plot and character evolved, so did his content development and style, but the focus of his work remained the reading or listening child. He explained in the preface of *The Burgess Bird Book for Children* that he had avoided technical terms and formal description "so that there may be nothing to confuse the young mind." Clarity and simplicity, he said, were his stylistic objectives. Although literary specialists have criticized Burgess' repetitive and basic language, historian John Goldthwaite suggests that Burgess' approach was intended to accommodate, not limit, his young audience:

> What Burgess is doing here is extending a courtesy to his five- or seven-year-old listener. He is saying four times in succession that Billy Mink has woken up, thus giving the child a moment to absorb what is happening and the time to realize that something else is about to happen. His assumption is that prose may run along quicker than a child can follow — a truth that might be profitably be attached as a rider to every law proscribing writing down to children. There is a simple power to [Burgess' stories] that may be inaccessible to adults...These are warm stories but not whimsical ones. The creatures do not play at forest games, or attend birthday parties, or cozy up to cottage fires with hot cocoa as they do in so many works of this nature. Burgess seems to have been about some other business, honoring some unspoken contract, as it were, to care for this make-believe preserve."[25]

The extent to which Burgess' young audience defined his style — and set him apart as a nature writer — becomes apparent by comparing an excerpt from one of his stories with the work of two other respected nature writers of his day:

> Walking through the early October woods one day, I came upon a place where the ground was thickly strewn with very large, unopened chestnut burrs. On examination I found that every burr had been cut square off with about an inch of stem adhering, and not one had been left on the tree. It was not accident then, but design. Whose design? A squirrel's.
>
> The fruit was the finest I had ever seen in the woods, and so the wise squirrel had marked it for his own. The burrs were ripe, and had just begun to divide. The squirrel that had taken all these pains, had evidently reasoned with himself thus: now these are extremely fine chestnuts and I want them. If I wait until they fall, the crows and jays will be sure to carry off a great many of the nuts before the fall. Then after the wind has rattled out what remain, the mice, the chipmunks, the red squirrels, the raccoons, and the grouse, to say nothing of the boys and the pigs that come in for their share. So I will forestall events a little.[26]
>
> JOHN BURROUGHS
> *SQUIRRELS AND OTHER FUR-BEARERS* (1875)

> For the first time in his life Peter was watching one of Madame Orb's [spider] nets being made...Madame Orb had fastened a new line to one of the spokes as far out as she could easily reach from the hub. She carried it across to another spoke and fastened it, then did the same thing to the next. So she went round and round

in a spiral, spinning a line and fastening it to each of the radii, the spokes of her silken wheel…When she reached the outer frame, she stopped.

"It looks finished to me now," said Peter.

"Well, it isn't. How do you think it will catch flies and other insects when there isn't a sticky line in it?" retorted Madame Orb.

"Do you have two kinds of silk?" [Peter] asked.

"Of course," replied Madame Orb impatiently. "Of course I have two kinds of silk. How in the world do you suppose I could make a successful net if I didn't have. Without a sticky kind, few insects would get tangled in my net, and if all my net was sticky I never could have made what you see here."

Peter Rabbit looked at Madame Orb with such respect as he never had dreamed he would have for a Spider. With every shimmering line of silk that she spun and added to her net Peter's wonder grew…Everything about that net was wonderful, the plan of it, the way in which it was made, the beauty of it, and wonder of wonders, the use of two kinds of silk, both spun from Madame Orb's own body.[27]

Thornton W. Burgess
50 Favorite Burgess Stories (1944 and 1946)

Next morning, I sallied forth to inspect the traps, and there, oh, joy! were the tracks of the pack, and the place where the beef-head and its traps had been was empty. A hasty study of the trail showed that Lobo had kept the pack from approaching the meat, but one, a small wolf, had evidently gone on to examine the head as it lay apart and had walked right into one of the traps.

We set out on the trail, and within a mile discovered that the hapless wolf was Blanca. Away she went, however, at a gallop, and although encumbered by the beef-head, which weighed over fifty pounds, she speedily distanced my companion, who was on foot. But we overtook her when she reached the rocks, for the horns of the cow's head became caught and held her fast. She was the handsomest wolf I had ever seen. Her coat was in perfect condition and nearly white.

She turned to fight, and, raising her voice in the rallying cry of her race, sent a long howl rolling over the canyon. From far away upon the mesa came a deep response, the cry of Old Lobo. That was her last call, for now we had closed in on her, and all her energy and breath were devoted to combat.

Then followed the inevitable tragedy, the idea of which I shrank from afterward more than at the time. We each threw a lasso over the neck of the doomed wolf, and strained our horses in opposite directions until the blood burst from her mouth, her eyes glazed, her limbs stiffened and then fell limp. Homeward then we rode, carrying the dead wolf, and exulting over this, the first death-blow we had been able to inflict on the Currumpaw pack.[28]

Ernest Thompson Seton
Wild Animals I Have Known (1898)

Use of Language

A creative body of work produced over a lifetime will inevitably change, whether from the artist's aging or his or her desire to experiment or diversify. Michael Hague says that considering the length of Burgess' career and the duration of his book sales, he is surprised at how well the children's writer's material has generally held up. Certain usage and references show their age, however. His "yes, sirs!" can get tedious, and the regional vernacular in language and the social and racial stereotypes in characterization that were considered praiseworthy innovation in the early twentieth century can seem awkward or offensive to today's readers.

Burgess was dubbed "the new Uncle Remus" early in his career, but apparently not lastingly, perhaps because his work became more associated with natural science than story-telling. The comparison would have been commercially valuable, however, for Joel Chandler Harris' celebrated "Uncle Remus" stories were widely acclaimed. In addition, Burgess may have recognized an opportunity to expand and diversify his own stories with Southern characters and their distinctive speech. Unc' Billy Possum, Mr. Mocker the Mockingbird, and Ol' Mistah Buzzard who migrated from the South up to New England exemplified regional differences in nature. Young readers learned from their conversations that wild animals, like people, sometimes leave their homes, move about permanently or temporarily, and encounter others that sound, look, and act differently than expected. In Chapter IV of "A Funny Dispute," in *The Adventures of Ol' Mistah Buzzard*, Old Mother West Wind delays her return home to the Purple Hills to settle a testy argument about differences:[29]

> "Ah'm very fond of Brer Gopher," replied Ol' Mistah Buzzard. "Do yo' know him?"
>
> "Do I know him! I should say I do!" exclaimed Digger the Badger, who, you know, came out of the Great West. "Why, when I was a little fellow Mr. Gopher and I used to have digging matches, and he surely can dig. But I didn't know that he had moved down South."
>
> "Why, what are you talking about, Brer Badger? He and his family have always lived down Souf!" exclaimed Ol' Mistah Buzzard.
>
> Now Digger the Badger is quick-tempered. "You're wrong!" he shouted. "Mr. Gopher and his family have always lived out West!"
>
> When she had heard all about it, [Old Mother West Wind] began to laugh. "You are both right and both wrong," said she. "Mr. Gopher who lives way down South does wear a shell coat, and he is cousin to Spotty the Turtle, but lives on the land and digs holes in the ground. Mr. Gopher whom Digger the Badger knows does wear a coat of hair, and he is a distant relative of Striped Chipmunk. And the two Mr. Gophers are not related at all. Now make up." And Ol' Mistah Buzzard and Digger the Badger did.

Literary Recognition Not A Career Objective

Although financial security was extremely important to Burgess, celebrity was never his objective or interest as a writer. He enjoyed professional accolades and the camaraderie of fellow writers, but he most relished the company of knowledgeable nature lovers. His joy and pleasure was in photographing birds from a cold, windy blind on Martha's Vineyard with an ornithologist, observing the mysteries of caterpillars with a lepidopterist, or chatting with a game warden about the local deer population.

"He wasn't the literary stereotype," observes historian Julie Arrison. "I think that makes him more real. He surrounded himself with people of scientific interest he could learn about nature from. He strikes me as a strong character, somebody who wrote as he wanted to write and lived as he wanted to live."

Chapter 8

LITERARY PERSPECTIVE: "THIS APPEAL OF THORNTON BURGESS"

Widely respected children's book reviewer Eden Ross Lipson considered a classic book one that children enjoy enough to read to their own children. In her 2000 revision of The New York Times Parents' Guide to Best Books for Children, *Lipson recommended Thornton Burgess'* Old Mother West Wind, *a ninety-year-old book passed on by four generations of readers. More than thirty of his other books remain in print. Despite the endurance of his work, however, Burgess' contributions are often missing from anthologies, texts, and studies that review the canon of children's literature in America. This chapter offers a perspective on issues that might have impacted his literary legacy, specifically the source of Peter Rabbit's name (Thornton Burgess or Beatrix Potter), book series and serialization, didacticism, and critical appraisal. It will also examine the reader appeal of Burgess' books, which appears to transcend critical opinion and mere nostalgia.*

"The first story teller was the first educator, and the greatest educators of all times have been the greatest story tellers...Toys in this age of mechanical perfection leave little or nothing for the imagination. They serve only to amuse for a little while, and are cast aside. Books on the other hand, are living things. They become companions, ever ready to lead to fields of romance, adventure, new scenes, new experiences and joyous hours of delight. No child can have too many books of the right kind."[1]

Thornton Burgess
"The Gift of Gifts for a Child," 1923

"When you're listening to a young child talk, it's direct, ingenuous. That's the way he or she approaches children's literature. We have buried under today's sexualized, merchandised, consumerized model, the model of what children should be and are, which is the pure way they encounter life. I think that's Burgess' genius: he is the master story-teller who sees through a child's eyes, through the lens of childhood wonder."

Nancy Rubin Stuart
historian, author
Defiant Brides

"Burgess writes about how a kid's world functions. There is hiding and teasing and running and jumping around, and scary things. Animals live with a sense of danger and so do children. Kids admire the courage and cunning of these little animals. If he had written these stories about a cast of human characters, I don't think they would have lasted."

Carolyn Lesser, author
Great Crystal Bear

"*Old Mother West Wind*: This delightful collection of short, easy-to-read stories about Reddy Fox, Peter Rabbit, Danny Meadow Mouse, and the other creatures of the meadow and woods has been a favorite for generations and with good reason. The type is large and clear; the illustrations are old-fashioned and simple. Good for reading aloud to younger children. If you love it, then find *Old Mother West Wind's Children*."[2]

Eden Ross Lipson, literary critic
New York Times Parents' Guide to Best Books for Children (2000)

Fiction or Non-fiction?

Evaluating the written work of children's author Thornton Burgess is not simple. Was he a non-fiction nature writer or a children's fiction writer? Although his work was admired for the factual accuracy of his representation of wildlife and habitat, many of his earlier stories are written in the Aesopian fable tradition. The following excerpt from *Mother West Wind "Where" Stories*, for instance, explains how Thunderhoof the Bison acquired a hump as a result of his pride and arrogance:

> Mother Nature picked up her staff and with it struck Thunderhoof on the neck, so that his head was brought low, and in fear of another blow, he humped his shoulders up. 'Thus shall you be, still big, still strong, but hump shouldered and carrying your head low in shame, no longer Lord of the Prairies…' said she, and turned her back on him.[3]

Burgess' books were written over a fifty-five-year period, so it is necessary to consider his work from various decades to understand his direction and purpose. Apparently influenced by his autobiographical reminiscences, one critic described the "enchanted atmosphere" that pervades Burgess' works, declaring that "the reader enters a lost Arcadia." The writer would surely have been amused by this thought, as would anyone who has read, for example, *The Adventures of Bowser the Hound* (1920), Burgess' story of a farm dog that becomes hurt, nearly drowned, and miserably lost after Old Man Coyote deliberately lures him over a riverbank far from home:

> "For a few minutes he stood shivering, shaking and whimpering, not knowing which way to turn. Then he started down the river on the ice, for he knew he would freeze if he continued to stand. He limped badly because one leg had been hurt in his fall. After a while he came to a place where he could get up on the bank…Which way should he turn? Where should he go? Night was coming on; he was wet, cold and hungry, and as utterly lost as ever a dog was. Poor Bowser!"[4]

Burgess wrote fables, creation stories, explanatory tales, and cautionary tales, but the progressive development of his dedication to factual natural science is evident in passages such as the following from *At Paddy the Beaver's Pond* (1950):

> Deep in the Green Forest, at the foot of the Great Mountain, a new home was being built by two busy workers. And how they worked. The time was short before Jack Frost would interfere and there still so much, so very much to be done… there was a dam to build to make a pond. There was a house to build. There was a winter supply of food logs to be cut and stored. And they had only a few weeks in which to do all this.
>
> Down at the bottom of the pond they were digging and cutting an underwater passage right into that island they had first built for a foundation. That passage was planned with care. It led in and up until it opened on what would have been

> the surface of the island before roof and walls were begun. Before beginning the latter they had built a mound of mud on the middle of the island. On this they had leaned long poles, the rafters of the roof. Now from below they dug away all that mound of mud, taking it out through the new hall. When all was out a nice dry room was left where the mound had been. It could be reached only from underwater...
>
> Only a few nights later Paddy was cutting down a tree. He had it cut half through, prying out big chips with his great orange-colored cutting teeth. There was a sound much like the report of a gun. Paddy didn't even turn his head to look around. He scrambled for the water and plunged in...That report had been made by Mrs. Paddy's broad, thick tail slapping the water hard. It meant danger...Then Paddy saw Puma. He fears no one more than he does the big Mountain Lion. Puma rose slowly to his feet. He drew back his lips with a snarl. He walked to the edge of the water, lashing his tail. He was in a rage with disappointment.[5]

Lucien L. Agosta's biographical section on Thornton Burgess in *Twentieth Century Children's Writers* (1983) suggests that Burgess' method of integrating fiction and non-fiction is a function of his multiple objectives:

> His animal stories belong to a genre which includes, at one extreme, stories featuring animals which are actually humans masquerading in feathers or fur, and, at the other, stories presenting the cycles of animal life with strict and often brutal realism. Burgess' animal stories fall somewhere around the middle of this generic continuum. His bestiary is made up of anthropomorphic creatures which reason, converse, and gossip. They do not, however, ride bicycles, snooze in armchairs or sew the clothes they are always depicted as wearing...Burgess animals are hybrids; they operate in a realm at once natural and yet infused with a human moral code. This accommodation between the human and the bestial allowed Burgess to entertain his youthful readers while offering them moral guidance and teaching them nature lore. These three intentions inform nearly all of Burgess' works.[6]

Two Standards for Evaluation

Evaluation of Burgess' accomplishment is complicated by the fact his work was held to critical standards in two fields: one a literary art and one a science. Librarians might fault the proliferation of his book series but accept their anthropomorphism, for example, while natural scientists, indifferent to the number of book series he wrote, increasingly considered unacceptable the clothed and talking animal characters constantly learning life lessons, no matter how accurately their habitat was portrayed. As the twentieth century progressed, Burgess' emphasis on moral values tended to ruffle the professional feathers of both literary and natural science interests, although, as Burgess pointed out, young readers and their parents generally did not object. If literary critics were reluctant to credit Burgess' work on the merits of its science, natural scientists were equally challenged to embrace as one of their own a man celebrated for writing bedtime stories for young children. It is telling that the most prestigious awards given to the author of seventy children's books came from the New York Zoological Society, the National Life Conservation Society, and the Boston Museum of Science.

Early Years of Children's Literature

When *Old Mother West Wind* was published in 1910, the fields related to children's literature, including publishing, writing, and library science, were just beginning to forge an identity separate from adult literature. It would be six years before Bertha Mahony opened the first bookstore for children in Boston and nine years before Macmillan Publishing hired Louise Seaman as the first juvenile department head in book publishing. New York Public Library's legendary supervisor Anne Carroll Moore had not yet begun writing her ground-breaking literary reviews of children's books for *The Bookman*, the *New York Herald Tribune*, and *The Horn Book*. "When you see some of the old photographs of public libraries around 1912, you realize how young children's services were," says children's library science authority Margaret Bush, whose fifty-year career began at the New York Public Library. "When we go back to the early 1900s we have to think about the percentage of families who could read and how few children actually went to school. The numbers of children in the workforce were tremendous."

While Thornton Burgess and others were writing books for children, an alliance of professionally trained librarians, editors, and booksellers stepped forward as leaders in shaping the new literary field, including Mahony, Seaman, Moore, Connecticut librarian Caroline Hewins, and Boston Public Library librarian Alice Jordan. These bookwomen would become friends, collaborators, and colleagues in mobilizing public resources, stimulating readership, identifying methodology, and implementing and upholding critical standards in children's literature.[7] One important service they provided was developing book recommendations for schools, libraries, and parents. Margaret Bush points out in a comprehensive article on "New England Book Women" in *Library Trends* (1996) that Bertha Mahony relied heavily on the book lists of librarians Caroline Hewins and Clara Whitehill Hunt in stocking her new bookstore for children. "From the outset, Bertha Mahony was determined that the shop would carry and promote only books of literary and artistic quality," says Bush. She notes that Mahony developed her own influential booklist, "Books for Boys and Girls: A Suggestive Purchase List," to assist customers and publicize her new bookstore.[8] Reflecting the burgeoning interest in children's books, Mahony's list evolved after five revisions into a massive eight-hundred-page compendium. Titled *Realms of Gold in Children's Books*, it was published in 1929 by Doubleday, Doran & Company.

Realms of Gold Recommendation

Realms of Gold listed fifteen books by Thornton Burgess, including seven of his eight volumes in the *Mother West Wind* series, *The Christmas Reindeer*, and the four-book Boy Scout series.[9] It also mentioned Burgess' well-received *Bird*, *Animal*, and *Flower* books [1919, 1920, and 1923], but *Realms of Gold* editors qualified their recommendation by saying: "The chief value of these three books lies in their pictures [two illustrated by ornithological artist Louis Agassiz Fuertes], and in their possibilities for arousing interest in very young children." The editors added the superfluous comment that "a seven- or eight-year-old who has a real interest will need other books."

It is worth noting that Thornton Burgess had published fifty-nine books by 1929 when *Realms of Gold* was released, and among them his four-book Boy Scout series (1912-1915) seems a misguided choice for Mahony and Whitney's prestigious recommendation. *The Boy Scouts of Woodcraft Camp* was Burgess' first effort at writing juvenile novels, and, while popular into the 1930s, the series is generally considered his least successful for reasons that must have been obvious in literary circles fifteen years after their publication. Considerably different in style, tone, and structure from the Mother West Wind books he was writing at the same time, the Boy Scout series featured "all the stereotypes and stock situations of the worst of the popular boys' literature of its day," commented literary biographer Lucien Agosta. Perhaps *Realms* editors were influenced by the fact that the books had been reviewed and approved by Boy Scout librarian Franklin L. Mathiews, who worked with Anne Carroll Moore to initiate Children's Book Week.

Beatrix Potter, Thornton Burgess, and Peter Rabbit

One of the characters Burgess used in the story-letters that would become *Old Mother West Wind* was a rabbit whose insatiable curiosity and gullibility would make him the most popular among the hundreds of animal characters Burgess created, and whose name made him the most controversial.

Confusion and criticism still persist regarding the origin of Peter Rabbit's name. Some readers attribute it to Thornton Burgess while others believe he plagiarized it. Burgess himself unfailingly credited English author, illustrator, and conservationist Beatrix Potter with the first literary use of the name "Peter Rabbit" and himself with development of an American character named "Peter Rabbit" to please his young son who had read Potter's books. Burgess explained in his autobiography that "Beatrix Potter of England named Peter Rabbit when she found him in Mr. McGregor's garden. With fascinating text and talented brush, she made a classic of the event in the delightful little volume children everywhere know and love...When I began writing stories for my own small boy, a rabbit was already named Peter and there was no changing the name."[10]

In 1901, Potter's *The Tale of Peter Rabbit* first introduced the English rabbit with his mother and siblings Flopsy, Mopsy, and Cottontail. Nearly a decade later, in 1910, Burgess' *Old Mother West Wind* introduced the American Peter Rabbit along with his friends Bobby Coon, Happy Jack Squirrel, Grandfather Frog, Mrs. Redwing, and numerous other animal characters. Both books were originally written as story-letters intended to bring comfort to a child: Burgess' for three-and a half-year-old son Thornton, who was away from home for a month, and Potter's for Noel, the ailing five-year-old son of her former governess Annie Moore.

Potter decided to put her story-letter and charming illustrations into a book, and when several publishers turned it down, she self-published *The Tale of Peter Rabbit.* Appreciative of the book's instant popularity, Frederick Warne & Co. reconsidered its earlier rejection and accepted the book for publication in 1902, issuing three printings in as many months.[11] Both Potter and Burgess would learn painful lessons about copyright law early in their careers. Burgess unintentionally relinquished publishing rights to his daily syndicated columns while Potter's publisher failed to register an American copyright for *The Tale of Peter Rabbit.* "The result was that in 1904 a pirated edition was published by Henry Altemus & Co," stated Potter biographer Leslie Linder. "It was the same format as the Warne edition, and the pictures and text were copied from the fourth printing in 1903. There was nothing more Warnes do about it."[12]

By the time *Old Mother West Wind* was published by Little, Brown and Company, English and American versions of Potter's book and Peter Rabbit's name were well-known in the U.S. According to historian Ralph Lutts, nature writer William J. Long used "Peter Rabbit" as his pen name in 1905 for a series of socio-political articles titled "Brier-Patch Philosophy" that appeared in *Harper's Monthly.*[13] Lutts commented, "Long's Peter Rabbit essays presented a rabbit's point of view of the human condition, animal intelligence, and the sham natural history controversy [known as "nature faking," see Chapter 14]. … The collected essays were published in 1906 as *Brier-Patch Philosophy* and the book included this dedication: 'To those who have found Their Own World to be something of a brier-patch, the Rabbit dedicates his little book of Cheerful Philosophy.'"

Origin of Thornton Burgess' Peter Rabbit

When Thornton Burgess' wife died after delivering their first child, he became simultaneously an anguished widower and the single parent of a newborn baby. As a jack-of-all-trades editor for *Good Housekeeping* and several agricultural publications, he had constant deadlines to meet, so help with childcare and running the household was essential. In November 1909, his son Thornton traveled with a grandmother to visit family in Chicago. "Every night after dinner I wrote a story or some verse and mailed them to him," Burgess said. "Later two or three of these stories were published in *Good Housekeeping.*"[14] Burgess' first story-letter to his son was a moral tale titled "How the Frog Lost His Tail," which began: "Once upon a time, Mr. Frog had a tail, a nice long tail of which he was very, very proud. Now it isn't well to be proud, for sometimes something happens to humble proud folks." It tenderly concludes, "Good night Boy. Sleep tight."

For the rabbit character in his story-letters, Burgess used the name "Peter" that Thornton was familiar with, and he retained it in the manuscript submitted the next year to Little, Brown and Company. Although he explored revising the name in "Peter Cottontail Changes his Name," it was not a satisfactory transition and was abandoned. Opinion varies on Burgess' use of the name "Peter Rabbit." In a 2010 telephone interview, Margaret Bush, former president of the Association for Library Services for Children, said, "I think we would look at it today as plagiarism, but you have another way to look at it. People could say on the one hand he was paying tribute to [Potter], and, on the other hand, that it was a commercial ploy to take something well-known and borrow it. Publishers would never allow it to happen today."

David Mitchell is a former children's literature history professor at the University of New York at Albany and at present is curator pro bono at the university's Miriam Snow Mathes Historical Children's Literature Collection. He sees the name usage as a matter of influence typical of the period, not plagiarism. "Given the popularity and the warm critical reception in America of Potter's Peter Rabbit, I expect that a rabbit character named Peter was a popular marketing advantage, but Burgess didn't borrow anything but the name," Mitchell says. "The character was different, the stories were different, the pictorial representation was different. The Burgess Peter Rabbit shows up first as just one of the animals in *Old Mother West Wind* and is not the center of attention. He doesn't get his own book until 1914 in volume three of the Bedtime Story-Books."

Joel Chandler Harris

A significant influence for both Burgess and Beatrix Potter was American author Joel Chandler Harris, a native of Georgia who, like Burgess, was raised by a single mother without financial means. In the early 1900s, Burgess' fables and stories won him comparisons to Harris' famous story-teller Uncle Remus; however, it was Harris' innovative use of regional dialect, language, and characters that most inspired Burgess in creating the distinct personalities and speech of his Ol' Mistah Buzzard and Unc' Billy Possum characters. Linda Lear states in her acclaimed 2007 biography of *Beatrix Potter: A Life in Nature*, that the English author was also a great admirer of Harris:[15]

> Creatively Beatrix was always moved to interpret a familiar story in her own way. In 1893, the same year as her picture letter to Noel Moore about her rabbit Peter, she began a series of eight illustrations of Joel Chandler Harris' Uncle Remus stories, finishing the last one in 1896. The adventures of that trickster Brer Rabbit had been family favorites and it was a natural text for her to choose.
>
> The impact of Harris' talking animals on contemporary writers both in Britain and America was enormous, not only because of his cunning but likeable rabbit protagonist, but also because of the cadence and virtuosity of the colloquial dialect, the pacing of the stories and his subversive humour. *Uncle Remus* proved to be 'the great bridging gap between the beast fable and the animal fantasy.' Like her contemporaries Rudyard Kipling, Kenneth Grahame, and A. A. Milne, Beatrix was enthralled by these apparently naïve animal fables set in the context of everyday life... Beatrix was fascinated by the language of *Uncle Remus*. Such words as "rabbit tobacco," "puddle-ducks," and "Cottontail" found their way into her vocabulary. So did the adapted cadences such as "lippity-lippity," a subdued version of Harris's "lippity-clippity, clippity-lippity." ... When she came to write and illustrate her own tales, *Uncle Remus* was her reference point in the creation of a world where animals and humans overlap."
>
> *[Note: Harris' Southern rabbit generally ran "lippity-clippity, clippity-lippity"; Potter's English rabbit ran "lippity, lippity"; and Burgess' New England rabbit ran "lipperty, lipperty, lip."]*

Common Ground[16]

Although Burgess and Potter had dissimilar backgrounds, they shared common ground. They were born eight years apart, Potter in 1866 in London, England, and Burgess in 1874 in a rural New England town named for Sandwich, England. Potter grew up in the affluent home of a barrister; she was well-educated, but socially isolated. Burgess and his widowed mother struggled to make ends meet in the thick of family and a close-knit community. Both writers found great comfort and inspiration in the outdoors, and developed their skill in field observation as children. In *Now I Remember*, Burgess writes vividly of his memory as a five-year-old of seeing a gigantic blue whale washed up in shallows off the Sandwich barrier beach and hearing the mingled cries of seabirds and shouts of whalers stripping off its flesh.

While much of Burgess' boyhood in the fields and woods of his native Cape Cod was spent collecting berries, herding cows, gathering mayflowers, and doing other work to supplement the family income, Potter's family annually left London to vacation for three months in Scotland or the Lake District. There she practiced sketching nature scenes and became sufficiently expert in mycology, the study of fungi, to submit her work to the Royal Academy of Science.

In June 1905, Burgess married his sweetheart Nina Osborne. That same month and year, Beatrix Potter accepted the marriage proposal of her editor, confidant, and friend Norman Warne. Within two months, Warne died of leukemia, and within ten months, Nina Burgess died following childbirth. Potter and Burgess, then in their thirties, immersed themselves in work, finding in writing the solace and sense of order and control that life denied them.

Both writers commercialized their animal characters. Potter's 1903 Peter Rabbit doll had brush bristles for whiskers and lead shot to weight the feet, and she developed Peter Rabbit wallpaper and board games and used other characters as themes for clothing, accessories, and housewares. Burgess copyrighted "Quaddies" as the name for his product design characters for tinware, jewelry, textiles, and pottery. Potter used her royalties to fund purchase of conservation land in the Lake District for the National Trust while Burgess used his books to support wildlife education, anti-hunting laws, and conservation legislation, such as the 1918 Migratory Bird Treaty Act.

Books Series and Serialization

To sustain the attention of the public and the commitment of publishers, Burgess and other authors often developed a book series, which is a collection of sequential books with the same or related characters and themes. Burgess wrote nine series, including Mother West Wind, Boy Scouts, Bedtime Story-Books, The Wishing Stone, Green Meadow, Natural History Books for Children, Green Forest, Smiling Pool, and Books of Nature Stories. The Mother West Wind series was written between 1910 and 1918. His most popular series is the twenty-volume Bedtime Story-Books written between 1913 and 1918, but the six Books of Nature Stories (1944-1950) are probably his best and most compelling work.

At the time Burgess began writing children's books, publishers and an eager public pressured authors to deliver books rapidly, without regard for quality. The Stratemeyer Literary Syndicate, for example, put out inexpensive books within a month. Edward Stratemeyer provided writers, many of them journalists, with an outline of stock characters and plots to develop and perpetuate a book series, among them the Bobbsey Twins, Nancy Drew, the Rover Boys, and the Hardy Boys. Stratemeyer developed dozens of series and wrote under dozens of pseudonyms. Howard Garis, author of *Uncle Wiggly*, wrote for the Stratemeyer syndicate, but Burgess did not.

Librarians and literary specialists concerned with the quality of children's books especially opposed the proliferation of book series. "Libraries certainly had series books, but the aversion to some of the series was always that it was formulaic writing," says Bush. "Many series chugged out book after book." In 1929, librarian Mary E. S. Root attempted to eliminate all series books she considered inferior literature by compiling and distributing a list that named "books in series not circulated by standardized libraries." Root's list was published in *The Wilson Bulletin*, a professional journal for librarians. It included the works of over sixty authors.[17]

"It was a concerted effort to not circulate, and by implication to not acquire," says children's literature historian David Mitchell. "The arguments for doing so in Root's article do not really apply to the Burgess books, but all series came to be tarred with the 'do not circulate' brush. I have seen mimeographed lists [of books to be excluded] from state library agencies that were circulated to public and school librarians that do include the Oz books and the Burgess Bedtime books." Christine Jenkins, an assistant professor at the University of Illinois at Urbana-Champaign, suggests in an academic paper on "The Cycle of Story" another motive for librarians to discourage book series:[18]

> The series' lack of literary qualities is the reason usually cited for librarians' negative view of series books, but along with that has been children's librarians' traditional rejection of story as commodity, of made-to-order texts for children marketed as 'product.' This division is not limited to children's publishing, but is found throughout the book industry in the ongoing tension between culture and commerce, between texts as literature and texts as product.

Jenkins adds:

> At the same time, the demand is certainly there. And reading research consistently identifies a strong positive correlation between children's series book reading and their later development into fluent adult readers...And yet...the idea that a children's story is simply one more saleable commodity continues to disturb those who are concerned with preservation and perpetuation of story. And not just any story, but good stories, worthwhile stories, authentic stories...stories that nourish children's hearts and inspire their imaginations.

In addition to his numerous book series, Burgess' syndicated newspaper column of children's stories came out six times a week. These pre-published serialized stories were often gathered into a collection that focused on one character or habitat and published as a book. "[Serialization] is an old process," observes Nikki Giovanni, an acclaimed poet and English professor at Virginia Tech who avidly read Burgess books as a child. "Charles Dickens was a serial writer whose stories came out once a week in the newspaper, and [Herman] Melville published in magazines once a month. *Rolling Stone* published twenty-seven serial chapters of Tom Wolfe's *Bonfire of the Vanities*. He and Burgess were doing what their contemporaries and forefathers were doing, and what has been done since."

While the early twentieth century bookwomen were generally more opposed to book series than to the serialized newspaper stories Burgess produced, they undoubtedly disapproved of both practices. "It seems to me the idea of material being serialized and then put in a book relates to the idea of literature versus commodity," remarks Bush. "The daily press would have been seen as commodity and [those serialized stories and subsequent books] would have been seen as being created more crudely in chunks. They would have not been considered as literary as other work."

Morality and Education

Thornton Burgess wrote in an era when instruction and a moral purpose were valued and expected in children's books. Since this perspective was ingrained in Burgess since childhood, incorporating morality as a literary element into his animal stories was natural. Even the story-letters for his young son Thornton, which were essentially first drafts of *Old Mother West Wind*, had been written in hope of correcting "little flaws" in the child's character. Many of his chapters and stories opened with a catchy two- or four-line rhyme that offered a bit of moral advice and forecast the story, such as those in *The Adventures of Little Joe Otter*: "The heedless young who disobey/Will for their folly have to pay;" "If there are things you would find out, Just use your eyes and look about;" "By sitting still may much be learned, And thus be useful knowledge earned."[19] Burgess' sense of morality also extended to the ethical treatment of wildlife and responsible attitudes toward nature [see Chapter 14].

He was not a story-teller by default. Burgess' belief in the importance of children's education was coupled with the belief that children are instinctively attracted to stories, which guarantees their attention and interest: "To try to cram a child's mind with dry facts is as useless as for a farmer to sow his wheat on unbroken ground," he said. "But present those facts in such form as to arouse interest and at once the imagination is stimulated to seize and feed upon them and they become as difficult to remove from the memory as before they were difficult to implant." He considered animal stories a particularly effective vehicle for conveying life lessons:

> The success in conveying moral lessons has proven greater than I ever dared to dream it would. As everyone knows a child resents being preached to; so does the adult for that matter...I have found that the moral aimed at one of the characters is

> wholly another matter...during the last half dozen years I've come to the conclusion that the attitude of the average child toward the animal character is practically the attitude of the adult toward the child.
>
> As the adult looks down to the level of the child and in the superiority of greater wisdom guides and corrects the child, so in turn the child looks down from the height of superiority to the level of Peter Rabbit and Johnny Chuck. Not only is the child not offended by the moral pointed at Peter or Johnny, but very thoroughly and consistently approves of it, quite unconscious that it is being applied and absorbed in his own case. The moral lesson is never pointed at the reader but always at the characters. The result is that I have had scores of letters from parents thanking me for the moral lessons which their children have absorbed. It is an interesting bit of psychology.[20]

However, Burgess' approach became less popular in the middle of the twentieth century. Children's literature was changing. Books advocated by those within the field increasingly offered a view of life that depicted realistic experiences and choices involving death and loss without overt moral implications.

"He Sees What I See"

While the height of Burgess' literary popularity occurred in the first half of the twentieth century, his books continued to be published, bought, and read. One explanation for the durability of his appeal was inadvertently provided by literary critic Anne Carroll Moore. Seeking a child's perspective for her article on Christmas gift book recommendations, she invited Edouard, a "bright and inquisitive" fourth grade New York Public Library patron, to her office. But Moore may have been taken aback by the boy's response, which she relates in *Roads to Childhood* (1920):

> The sight of books piled high in unfamiliar surroundings did not daze him nor did it call forth...a speech yielding...clever quotations from his favorite authors. He paid no attention to literary tradition. He surveyed the array calmly and then spoke: "Is there a book here by Thornton Burgess?"
>
> Without waiting for an answer, he instinctively put his hand under a great pile of Boy Scout and war books and drew forth "Mother West Wind Where Stories" and clasped it to his heart.
>
> "If I had a million dollars I would engage Thornton Burgess to write all the stories I could read." Then followed a declaration of Edouard's passionate love for "Danny Meadow Mouse" and all his associates. If he could live always in the country as "Danny Meadow Mouse," he would almost be willing to change his own being; but if he must continue his existence as a boy he believed he would rather live in New York where he could see *Twenty Thousand Leagues Under the Sea* in the movies, read of the little people of the meadow and forest in winter, and watch their life in the long summer vacation spent in the country.
>
> "Are there no other books which tell of the country, of birds, of animals, in a way you like?"

> "Thornton Burgess can put it all over the others," was his reply, "because he sees what I see, and I understand his language."
>
> I shall not attempt to analyze or explain this appeal of Thornton Burgess nor answer the question sometimes raised as to whether he is not writing too many books of a kind in a manner monotonous to older readers. For thousands of boys younger and older than Edouard he has lifted the curse from nature study by putting them in touch with life as they see it.[21]

Nearly twenty years later, Burgess' journal notes that he and Moore sat side-by-side as fellow participants at the 1939 Book Fair at the Boston Public Garden. His amiable journal description is disappointingly brief: "About 2,000 in audience...Miss Moore of N.Y. Pub. Library next to me. A pleasure to meet her again."[22]

If Moore took the opportunity to share with Burgess the story of Edouard's blazing admiration, it seems likely he would have recorded it, but possibly not, for he was long-accustomed to the candid praise of children. [But the event undoubtedly enabled the estimable librarian to see firsthand that girls as well as boys enjoyed nature books that put them "in touch with life as they see it."]

Reader Appeal

With packed lecture halls and signings, and book sales that some sources stated were as high as eleven million by the time of his death in 1965, Burgess' books obviously resonated with children. Noted *New York Times* book reviewer Orville Prescott was among those who savored Burgess' books as a child. In Prescott's autobiography, *The Five-Dollar Gold Piece*, he describes earning the gold coin his grandmother promised when he learned to read: "Charmed by my newly acquired reading skill...I asked for a set of books. Mother responded by giving me the first three volumes of Thornton W. Burgess' animal stories for children. The adventures of Johnny Chuck, Jimmy Skunk, and Peter Rabbit delighted me and lured me on."[23]

An intrinsic poetic quality makes his stories particularly likeable as read-alouds, says children's librarian Ellen Bump in Hampden, Massachusetts, who notes: "When we read them here, the children are captivated." Patricia Rogers, former director of exhibits at the Thornton W. Burgess Society, points out that many books in Burgess' day were not written specifically for children. "Even Heidi would be hard for younger children to read," she says. "Burgess brought the text down to a child's level. He repeats so much because he knew that's how children learn. But because he told real facts, adults enjoyed the stories too. To me, his legacy is the accessibility of his stories."

To Cape Cod bookseller Carol Chittenden, structure and subject matter help explain Burgess' appeal: "His stories are just about the right length, and each one is complete in itself," she says. "They are short, engaging anecdotes that work so well with children between the ages of six and nine who are practicing reading. The stories are interesting and entertaining enough for them to stick with it. I think children will always warm to animals, and now there is even more value in using animals as characters because it gets around the problem of using different social and economic and ethnic variations."

When author Nancy Rubin Stuart was seven years old, she began reading Burgess' books. "Children are drawn to things they don't see every day on the screen or on the page," she says. "They're fascinated by something simple more than something complex. With Burgess, a child can understand and relate to his stories, and they have gentle morals. I think his books have enormous application to today."

What second grade teacher Judy Saunders sees in her students listening to Burgess' stories is a response to his mix of suspense, humor, and good will. "There is excitement in the books," she says. "We were reading *Lightfoot the Deer* and they begged me not to stop." The stories stimulate classroom discussion about her students' personal experiences, Saunders says, mentioning an incident in *The Adventures of Buster Bear*: "The bear caught a fish, put it down, and left to catch more, but trouble ensued when his friend Little Joe Otter wandered over and took it. At the second grade level, what's yours and how other people know it's yours is so important." Saunders finds the scarcity of illustration in Burgess stories helpful for emphasizing comprehension skills and descriptive writing with students, while words like *soberly*, *cleverly*, or *disguise* provide an opportunity for vocabulary development.

"Children just connect with animals, they seem to have a special curiosity about them," Saunders notes. "Mr. Burgess took it to another level by giving his animals that 'voice,' which we suspect lives within each creature of the forest, but we have never before heard it spoken so eloquently. And Mr. Burgess has also given each character a darker side. Children love when animals sometimes misbehave and cause problems. I think children can see themselves in similar situations and can laugh."

Critical Appraisal

While extensive research has produced no concrete evidence of factors that may have undermined the respectability of Burgess' work or brought prejudice to his reputation, the literary establishment of his day had concerns. Was he "not writing too many books of a kind in a manner monotonous to older readers?" Anne Carroll Moore had pointedly asked her readers. And in the first half of the twentieth century, "No one wielded more power in the field of children's literature than Moore," observed Harvard professor Jill Lepore in a 2008 *New Yorker* article.[24]

Some literary critics objected to Burgess' stylistic use of repetition and simple plots with sunny endings. Although respected children's literary authority Charlotte Huck praised these particular characteristics as appropriate for younger readers in her classic text *Children's Literature for the Elementary School*, she omitted Burgess while mentioning the work of numerous contemporaries. Zena Sutherland and May Hill Arbuthnot's classic text *Children and Books* also omitted commentary on the Burgess books, and while *The St. James Reader* provides a complete listing of Burgess' works, it offers little information other than basic biographical detail.

Perhaps his numerous book series, commercial work, and emphasis on natural science and moral lessons rather than artistic development discouraged Moore, her literary contemporaries, and those who followed them from including Burgess in the record of significant twentieth century children's authors. And possibly a more subtle factor shaded early critical estimation of Burgess' work.

In 1921, Anne Carroll Moore visited Beatrix Potter at her home in Sawrey, England. Lunch extended into tea and an invitation to spend the night as the two delved into mutual literary interests and concerns. When Bertha Mahony contacted Potter with a request for biographical information, the English author was intrigued to learn about her pioneering bookstore and *The Horn Book*, the first critical publication devoted exclusively to children's literature.[25] Potter's relationship with the American women who were shaping early twentieth century children's literature was mutually valued and long-lasting. It is a reasonable matter for conjecture that Thornton Burgess' use of the name of Potter's most famous character was seen as an infringement that affected to at least some degree the opinion of a highly influential group of literary critics who deeply admired the English author.

Jacalyn Eddy's 2006 book *Creating an Empire in Children's Book Publishing, 1919-1939* includes the comment that in 1919 the concepts that had shaped children's literature "represented one way in which America's more affluent citizens articulated their vision of the world...Bookwomen were part of the advance guard of the crusade to ensure that children received what they regarded as the best reading material possible, affirmed in their efforts by both personal conviction and discursive communities within their institutions. So affirmed, bookwomen engaged in a variety of activities that exerted substantial influence over the institutions in which they worked and the book-buying public."[26]

Margaret Bush's comprehensive article on American bookwomen in the formative years of children's literature concludes with a discussion between *The Horn Book* editor Paul Heins and children's book writer and critic John Rowe Townsend as they consider the field of children's literature and the industry it produced. Townsend said:

> The children's book world, the children's literature industry, surely was the creation of not writers or publishers but of the band of American ladies in the late nineteenth and early twentieth centuries who built up library worlds with children and started a mission that was to extend itself into the education and publishing fields...For many years it has been possible for books to do well on the children's list which are not strikingly popular with children and which are ploddingly worthy rather than vital or perceptive.[27]

"The discussion comes back around to those lists of books," remarked Bush. "How many of the books lauded by librarians, critics, awards committees, *The Horn Book*, are truly read and loved by children?"

In a biographical essay on Thornton W. Burgess in *The Guide to Literary Masters and Their Works* (2007), Elizabeth D. Schafer neatly lays out the divergence of opinion about Burgess: "Critics disliked Burgess's writing for its didactic tendencies, its stereotypes, and its recycled plots," she says. "Readers, however, enjoyed his stories and bought approximately eight million of Burgess's books. Burgess had a global impact, and he helped many people to respect and value the environment and its inhabitants and to comprehend how each animal and plant influences the ecosystem."[28]

Critics, not young children, however, influence literary historians, which could explain why Burgess' place in the record of twentieth-century children's literature is faint and relatively undistinguished. But is it accurate? The most relevant question in assessing the work of Thornton W. Burgess may be not what did he accomplish, but who determined the merit of his accomplishment?

The Writer: Photos

Thornton W. Burgess at his desk.

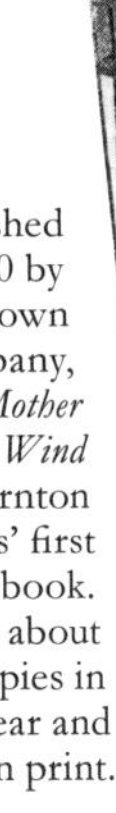

Published in 1910 by Little,Brown and Company, *Old Mother West Wind* was Thornton Burgess' first children's book. It sold about 2,000 copies in its first year and is still in print.

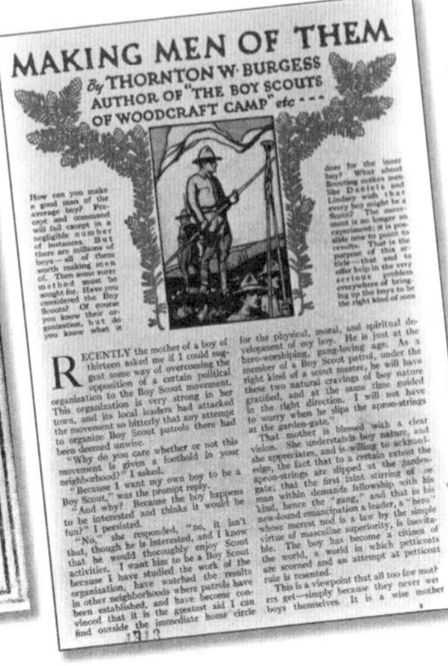

MAKING MEN OF THEM

By THORNTON W. BURGESS
AUTHOR OF "THE BOY SCOUTS OF WOODCRAFT CAMP" etc

How can you make a good man of the average boy? Precept and command will fail except in a negligible number of instances. But there are millions of boys—all of them worth making men of. Then some surer method must be sought for. Have you considered the Boy Scouts? Of course you know their organization, but do you know what it does for the inner boy? What about Scouting makes men like Daniels and Lindsey wish that every boy might be a Scout? The movement is no longer an experiment; it is possible now to point to results. That is the purpose of this article—that and to offer help in the very serious problem everywhere of bringing up the boys to be the right kind of men

RECENTLY the mother of a boy of thirteen asked me if I could suggest some way of overcoming the opposition of a certain political organization to the Boy Scout movement. This organization is very strong in her town, and its local leaders had attacked the movement so bitterly that any attempt to organize Boy Scout patrols there had been deemed unwise.

"Why do you care whether or not this movement is given a foothold in your neighborhood?" I asked.

"Because I want my own boy to be a Boy Scout," was the prompt reply.

"And why? Because the boy happens to be interested and thinks it would be fun?" I persisted.

"No," she responded, "no, it isn't that, though he is interested, and I know that he would thoroughly enjoy Scout activities. I want him to be a Boy Scout because I have studied the work of the organization, have watched the results in other neighborhoods where patrols have been established, and have become convinced that it is the greatest aid I can find outside the immediate home circle for the physical, moral, and spiritual development of my boy. He is just at the hero-worshiping, gang-loving age. As a member of a Boy Scout patrol, under the right kind of a scout master, he will have these two natural cravings of boy nature gratified, and at the same time guided in the right direction. I will not have to worry when he slips the apron-strings at the garden-gate."

That mother is blessed with a clear vision. She understands boy nature, and she appreciates, and is willing to acknowledge, the fact that to a certain extent the apron-strings are slipped at the garden-gate; that the first faint stirring of the man within demands fellowship with his kind, hence the "gang," and that in his new-found emancipation a leader, a "hero" whose merest nod is a law by the simple virtue of masculine superiority, is inevitable. The boy has become a citizen of the world, a world in which petticoats are scorned and an attempt at petticoat rule is resented.

This is a viewpoint that all too few mothers get—simply because they never were boys themselves. It is a wise mother

"Making Men of Them" — 1914 Good Housekeeping article on the Boy Scouts.

Harrison Cady and Burgess at work outdoors.

Burgess watching Cady at work.

Cady and Burgess seated on wharf, undated.

Harrison Cady illustration of Reddy Fox.

A Harrison Cady illustration of Peter and Mrs. Peter Rabbit.

Harrison Cady illustration of Peter Rabbit.

PETER RABBIT

A PORTRAIT

This little chap through briar-patch
Can come and go without a scratch.

Where others fear to poke a nose
He freely comes and freely goes.

He's long of leg and long of ear,
But empty-headed too, I fear.

His enemies are many and
They lie in wait on every hand.

Too often you will chance to see
Him where he really shouldn't be.

He fears the fox and hawk and gun,
And from them he can only run

Or, swallowing a bunny's pride,
In hole or hollow log may hide.

He has no sense yet somehow he
Survives, and we admit that we

Find patience growing rather short
With those who shoot at him for sport.

His curiosity is great,
And mischief seems to be his fate,

Yet I would scarce know what to do
Without the little scamp. Would you?

Full-page illustration by Phoebe Erickson, one of Thornton Burgess' favorite illustrators, shows the interest of publishers in real-life representation of his characters. Image from unidentified source.

Harrison Cady was the best known of Thornton Burgess' numerous illustrators.

Thornton W. Burgess book covers.

Burgess, wife Fannie, and one of his favorite illustrators, Phoebe Erickson, at Laughing Brook.

Burgess dictating stories to his secretary.

Thornton, Fannie Burgess, Harrison and Melinna Cady picnicking, date unknown.

School children listen to Burgess presentation circa 1950s.

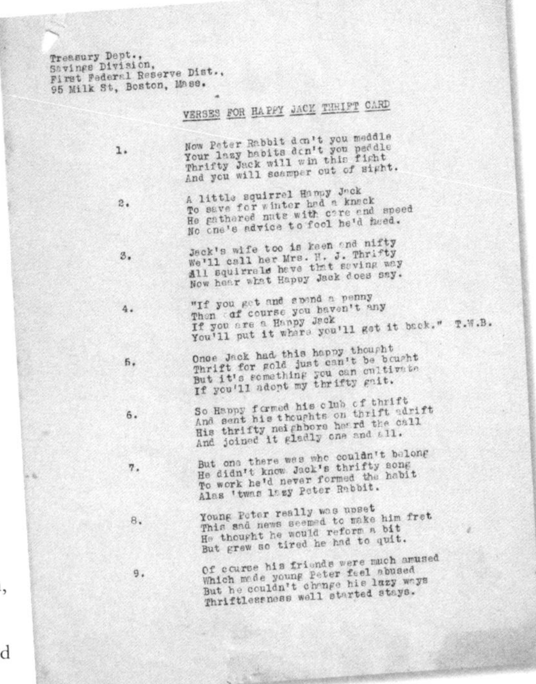

Treasury Dept.,
Savings Division,
First Federal Reserve Dist.,
95 Milk St, Boston, Mass.

<u>VERSES FOR HAPPY JACK THRIFT CARD</u>

1. Now Peter Rabbit don't you meddle
Your lazy habits don't you peddle
Thrifty Jack will win this fight
And you will scamper out of sight.

2. A little squirrel Happy Jack
To save for winter had a knack
He gathered nuts with care and speed
No one's advice to fool he'd heed.

3. Jack's wife too is keen and nifty
We'll call her Mrs. H. J. Thrifty
All squirrels have that saving way
Now hear what Happy Jack does say.

4. "If you get and spend a penny
Then of course you haven't any
If you are a Happy Jack
You'll put it where you'll get it back." T.W.B.

5. Once Jack had this happy thought
Thrift for gold just can't be bought
But it's something you can cultivate
If you'll adopt my thrifty gait.

6. So Happy formed his club of thrift
And sent his thoughts on thrift adrift
His thrifty neighbors heard the call
And joined it gladly one and all.

7. But one there was who couldn't belong
He didn't know Jack's thrifty song
To work he'd never formed the habit
Alas 'twas lazy Peter Rabbit.

8. Young Peter really was upset
This sad news seemed to make him fret
He thought he would reform a bit
But grew so tired he had to quit.

9. Of course his friends were much amused
Which made young Peter feel abused
But he couldn't change his lazy ways
Thriftlessness well started stays.

When Thornton Burgess was asked to help promote savings stamp sales among children, he wrote stories and rhymes based on his characters that emphasized thrift that led to popular Happy Jack Squirrel Thrift Clubs and other activities.

Thornton Burgess with his friends Melinna and Harrison Cady, circa early 1960s.

Melinna Cady and Fannie Burgess, unknown location.

Author Thornton Burgess and illustrator Harrison Cady were friends and collaborators for over fifty years, and they both worked professionally well into their 80s. Left: This image is probably a professional picture taken for an article. Right: The two friends at Laughing Brook.

Thornton and Fannie Burgess in his office.

Burgess in Springfield, Massachusetts.

Professional portrait of Thornton W. Burgess by Bachrach.

Original figurines of Burgess characters by Sandwich jeweler Nina Sutton.

Burgess coming down the hill from working at his writing studio perched on top of the small hill behind his house.

Burgess is shown on the set of early 1950s television programs.

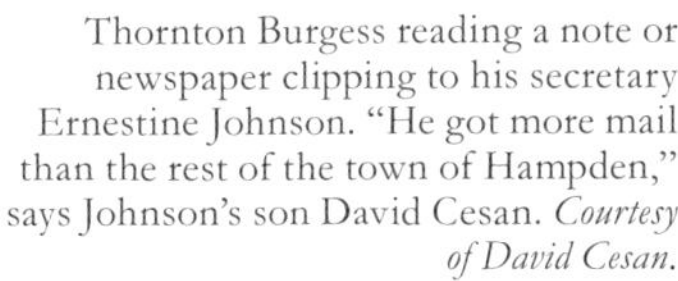

Thornton Burgess reading a note or newspaper clipping to his secretary Ernestine Johnson. "He got more mail than the rest of the town of Hampden," says Johnson's son David Cesan. *Courtesy of David Cesan.*

Thornton Burgess in his office at Laughing Brook, circa late 1950s.

Burgess relaxing.

Burgess in his office at typewriter.

Burgess with book, circa 1940s.

PART III: THE NATURALIST

Burgess in forest.

Chapter 9

The Green Meadow Club and Bird Sanctuaries Program

Public sentiment and support were increasingly important to the vested interests that sought control over natural resources, particularly wildlife, in the early twentieth century. For environmentalists, children's author and naturalist Thornton W. Burgess was a uniquely valuable ally. He offered access to a massive audience, regular media exposure, and credibility with children and adults. While light-hearted and entertaining, his animal stories and nature clubs introduced readers of all ages to the concept of stewardship to nature, and the public's response was remarkable. Burgess' Green Meadow Nature Club and Bedtime Story Clubs attracted hundreds of thousands of participants. In 1925, the Christian Science Monitor *reported that within its first three weeks his* Radio *Nature League enrolled 20,000 members who pledged to "assist in the preservation and conservation of all desirable wildlife in America." His bird sanctuaries program proposal led to the dedication to conservation of millions of acres of private land in the U.S. and Canada. In promoting environmental values for children and adults, Thornton W. Burgess may have more effective than anyone else in the early twentieth century.*

"Nature was the first teacher and still is the universal teacher."[1]

Thornton W. Burgess, 1922

"You have surely done more for wild life and for arousing sympathy for the wild creatures about us, and taught people more about them than anyone I know of."[2]

Dr. Willard Gibbs Van Name
Emeritus associate curator
American Museum of Natural History, 1944

"I think we really grasped the fact that the late Thornton Burgess was a powerful writer when our daughter May was six and had pneumonia…We had rushed her to the hospital the night before with no time to pack even a single doll for comfort. 'What would you like us to bring you from home?' we asked. 'The Burgess Bird Book' was her answer. It was almost the only thing she asked for during her 10 days in the hospital."

Jean Caldwell, journalist
September 17, 1967

"Little Stories for Bedtime"

Before the inventions of radio and television found a permanent place in twentieth-century American homes, newspapers were the primary source of news, general information, advertising, and entertainment. For millions of children in the U.S. and Canada, Thornton Burgess' syndicated stories were an integral part of daily life.

"When I was a small child, in the late 1920s, we got the old *Boston Post*," remembers naturalist Betty Anderson, founder of the Manomet Center for Conservation Sciences (originally the Manomet Bird Observatory). "It had the Thornton Burgess stories and Daddy would read them every night. When I was seven or eight, I used to cut the stories out of the paper and kept a scrap book of them."

At the height of Burgess' fame, the "Little Stories for Bedtime" and later "Burgess Bedtime Stories" columns were carried six days a week, sometimes seven, by more than one hundred newspapers in North America. To capitalize on the popularity of its Burgess column, the *Kansas City Star* announced an add-on feature: free membership in a Bedtime Story Club and a red Peter Rabbit button for readers who registered. An instant success, the new *Kansas City Star* club had 50,000 members at the end of three weeks. The unanticipated extra cost for buttons, certificates, and additional clerical help ran into "four figures," according to Burgess.[3] Bedtime Story Clubs quickly caught on at other newspapers. In Jason Rogers' 1918 book *Newspaper Building*, the publisher describes the phenomenal response of his *New York Globe* readers to the Bedtime Story Club:

> Following the lead of the *Kansas City Star*, which organized a Bedtime Story Club with a red "Peter Rabbitt" [sic] button as a club emblem, we stuck to the job until we had 198,000 children enrolled as members of The Globe's Bedtime Story Club. This meant that a large part of these 198,000 children 'cried for *The Globe*' every night. We carried the idea to the extent of monster meetings of the Bedtime Story Club in the public parks, where we brought out 15,000 to 20,000 at a gathering. We had a 'Peter Rabbitt Show' at one of New York's largest theaters for a full week to crowded houses. The members of our 'Bedtime Story Club' have done really wonderful things in the way of co-operative effort to raise small funds for charitable purposes. We regularly hold sewing, composition, drawing, and other contests to keep them interested.
>
> This huge children's organization, the largest of its kind in any city in the country, is a deep-rooted, far-reaching affair. It works its way into all sorts and conditions of households. Children of the richest and most exclusive families in New York and vicinity are just as much interested as others.[4]

Burgess's animal stories about Bobby Coon, Whitefoot the Deer, Happy Jack Squirrel, and their friends were published Monday through Saturday, but in 1915 he wrote a personal letter for the Sunday edition of newspapers that offered Bedtime Story Clubs. In the *Milwaukee Journal's* October 3rd issue of that year, Burgess' letter column reported on the enthusiastic proliferation of Bedtime Story Clubs, and, ever a promoter of environmental education, he suggested Club members try to learn more about wildlife through reading and firsthand experience:

> This is a big club right in and around your own home city, but there are many other cities with Bedtime Story Clubs, too, so that, taken altogether we are already a tremendous big organization. The last I heard Kansas City had the biggest club, over 50,000 members, but Cincinnati was not far behind with over 40,000 members... The New York Club is planning a big meeting of all its members at the famous park, where they can all get acquainted with one another and with the little meadow and forest people who are there.
>
> Of course those of you who live in the city do not have the same chance to do this as those of you who live in the country. But...the more you learn by reading about the ways of the little wild people the easier it will be to get acquainted with them when you do have the chance. And the more you learn about them, the more you will love them. Once you love them you will see exciting ways in which to help them.[5]

People's Home Journal

Shortly before Burgess' "Little Stories for Bedtime" syndicated column debuted in 1912, he also found a magazine outlet for his work. He had sent three stories to a New York literary agency, which sold them to *People's Home Journal*, a popular monthly magazine that advertised its circulation as 900,000. The size of his check was disappointing (he learned later the agency had doubled its commission), but "this was forgotten in my pleasure with the illustrations...by Harrison Cady."[6]

The talented, successful staff artist at *Life*, Cady "had arrived," said Burgess, while he himself "was still trying for a foothold." Cady's first illustration of Burgess' stories appeared in the June 1911 *People's Home Journal*. When Burgess sent an appreciative note, Cady responded with the suggestion they meet in New York. Lunch at the Salmagundi Club was the beginning of their close friendship and working partnership. The two men had in common a modest, self-deprecating personal style, a strong work ethic, sense of humor, professional pride, and love of nature acquired growing up in rural New England. Cady advised Burgess to call on *People's Home Journal* publisher Moody Gates about buying more of his animal stories. "They like them," he urged. The next morning, after a two-hour wait, Burgess met with Gates, "a rather short man with a smooth, smiling face." Finding him receptive, Burgess decided to pitch a series, rather than just a handful of stories.[7]

Inspiration of the Green Meadow Club

As Gates quizzed him, however, another idea took shape, "complete to the last detail." Without any forethought, Burgess spontaneously outlined a new *People's Home Journal* children's feature: the Green Meadow Club. Its focus would be a monthly story about a wildlife character:

> These stories will be educational as well as entertaining. With each story you will offer prizes for the best letters from children between certain age limits about the...chief character of the story. They will tell of its habits, appearance, and points of interest. Membership in the club will be open to any boy or girl who will promise to be kind to birds and animals and protect them from their enemies.[8]

Impressed, Gates offered the writer a one-year contract. Years later, Burgess noted that during the twelve years his Green Meadow Club feature ran in *People's Home Journal*, he had written one hundred forty-four stories instead of the two or three he had first hoped to sell. Even if Gates and Burgess intuitively sensed the potential appeal of the Green Meadow Club at their brainstorming session, they could never have anticipated it would launch a nation-wide conservation drive and earn praise from U.S. leaders in government and science. Gates introduced the Green Meadow Club in the magazine's January 1914 issue, describing it as "a society for the prevention of cruelty to animals among the children in the homes of the subscribers of *The People's Home Journal*." Children joined by submitting a signed pledge form that stated:

> I promise to learn all I can about the little wild people about me; to try to make them my friends; never to believe ill of them until I am sure of it; never to harm or frighten them needlessly; to do all I can to protect our song and insectivorous birds; to be gentle and merciful to all animals.[9]

The simple words were intended for children, but the pledge articulated Burgess' strongest beliefs as a naturalist. Wild creatures were worthy of respect and consideration. People must avoid misleading or prejudicial information about them.

Wildlife needed and deserved protection against the harm that adults and children can intentionally inflict. ("Why do they do it?" Burgess lamented after a neighbor brought him two baby birds that survived deliberate destruction of a nest of six.) At face value, the Green Meadow Club pledge was only a child's agreement to good intentions. As a statement of personal commitment, however, it was embraced by the tens of thousands of *People's Home Journal* readers throughout the U.S. and Canada who became Green Meadow Club members.

Mother Nature News

In 1917, Burgess began editing *Mother Nature News*, a nature study supplement to the magazine's monthly Green Meadow Club feature. Made available to schools as well as newspaper readers, the newsletter included a story, an animal fact sheet, and a nature Q & A. In the May 1917 newsletter, for example, Burgess described the diet, range, and physical features of the fox family, noting that black- and silver-furred foxes can be born to red-furred parents. Promotional advertising described it as "the only paper of its kind." Written in Burgess' personable, interactive style, *Mother Nature News* drew on current factual natural science information from state and federal regulatory agencies and other research-gathering sources:

> "Isn't it interesting that the oldest living things in America are trees? ... That the Department of Agriculture estimates that homely Old Mr. Toad is worth at least $19.50 in a garden because of the tremendous number of harmful bugs and worms which he destroys? ... That every tree has within a record of its age, having a clearly marked ring for every year it has lived. ... That birds are more closely related to the reptile than to any other life."[10]

Additionally, did readers know, Burgess might ask, that a chickadee could hang upside down on a twig or a chipping sparrow could sing in mid-flight? Could they identify a meadow lark, a bobolink, an indigo bunting, or a kingbird? Whether addressing a radio audience, a reading audience, or a live audience, Burgess actively encouraged questions about nature, and children readily responded. When Green Meadow Club members quizzed him on the frequency of a snake shedding its skin, the distance a hummingbird can fly, or whether or not porcupines can throw their quills, Burgess' answers often appeared in an upcoming edition of *Mother Nature News*.

Bird Sanctuary Program

With his strong advertising background, Burgess was skilled in cross-marketing and persuasive appeals to "join the cause" and "involve your friends." The friendly competition of a children's writing contest with a prize helped sell a reading club, which helped sell a newspaper, which helped sell books. As a resourceful writer, he constantly recycled old creative ideas and developed new ones. Perhaps the most successful example of this was the bird sanctuary program Burgess initiated and coordinated through *People's Home Journal* from 1917 to 1924.

In 1904, as children's editor for *New England Homestead*, Burgess had written an article that called on young readers to "band together as Friends of Our Native Birds," advocating not only appreciation of birds, but empathy and personal involvement in their welfare:

> All you have to do is to put out food for the birds and then drop a card to the Young Folks' Editor, this office, telling what you have done. Your name will then be added to the roll and published. This is for older folks as well as boys and girls.
>
> Who will be first from his or her county to be enrolled? Think of the suffering you can relieve at no trouble to yourself. ... Don't delay, girls and boys! Did you ever have the cold nip your fingers and toes until you cried? Then think of the little birds who cannot help themselves. If they have enough to eat they will keep warm. Won't you help in this great work? ... Get all of your friends to do likewise. Let us see what town will lead in this good work.[11]

More than a decade later, international concern about food supplies prompted interest in the critical role birds played in crop productivity. The U.S. Department of Agriculture distributed estimates of the annual crop damage caused by insects, citing $60 million to cotton, $53 million to hay, and $120 million to cereal grains. Citizens were entreated to "think of feeding nearly $3,000,000 worth of good food every day to mere insects...without adequate bird defense, how could the nation's increased crops be made safe for a hungry world?"[12]

Burgess recognized the opportunity to promote a worthy conservation effort by pairing it with the proven popularity of the Green Meadow Club's nature-based magazine forum. Reconfiguring his "Plea for Our Feathered Friends" call for boys and girls to "think of the little birds," he proposed that *People's Home Journal* and its Green Meadow Club sponsor a bird sanctuary drive. Green Meadow Club members, he said, would collect written pledges for posting of private lands on which hunting would be prohibited and "reasonable vigilance" would be used to support bird life. These sanctuaries would be "patriotically dedicated to the cause of conservation and the best friends of our food crops — the birds." Moody Gates endorsed the idea, and he and Burgess challenged their readers with the goal of five million acres of bird sanctuaries.

The idea of wildlife sanctuaries was not new. Conservationists, naturalists, scientists, politicians, regulatory officials, and organizations like the Audubon Society were interested in developing protected land areas for wildlife, but the voluntary, unregulated commitment of private land for a national citizen-led conservation program was unique. "I don't know anything like it," remarked Kurk Dorsey, environmental history professor at the University of New Hampshire and author of the *Dawn of Conservation Diplomacy*. The origin of the Green Meadow Club bird sanctuary program was described by Dr. William Hornaday in his 1920 report for the Permanent Wild Life Protection Fund:

> In a particularly felicitous moment Mr. Thornton W. Burgess...proposed to the editors of the *People's Home Journal* the idea of a contest in making game sanctuaries. At once Mr. Moody B. Gates, the editor, saw the point; and without loss of time a workable plan was wrought out, the executive machinery was constructed, the button pressed, and the wheels set in motion. It was decided to ask men and women, boys and girls, to take blank pledges, go to owners of lands, point out the great necessity of providing protected sanctuaries for our harassed birds and quadrupeds, then ask for signatures pledging the signers to make of their property an all-wool, yard-wide haven of refuge, in which no killing of any wild thing save predatory and intolerable wild life destroyers would be permitted. Prizes were offered for those who achieved the greatest success in obtaining signatures, and both the number of sanctuaries made and the total number of acres they contained, would carefully be taken into account.[13]

The concept was the essence of simplicity. There were no applications, permits, qualifications, restrictions, regulations, or inspectors. Signs provided by the magazine to post on designated property read: "Green Meadow Club Bird Sanctuary, Hunting on these premises forbidden under penalty of law. Any person molesting birds or nests on this property will be prosecuted. Birds are our best friends."[14] (Dorsey suggests that enforcement probably took the form of a landowner making a trespass complaint to a local law enforcement agency.) The *People's Home Journal* publicized the program in most of its issues. When the magazine was honored for its conservation work by the Permanent Wildlife Protection Fund of the New York Zoological Society, managing agent William Hornaday pointed out that the *Journal* gave considerable advertising space for ads such as the following:

> "If you have an acre of land in the village or country, pledge it as a Green Meadow Club Bird Sanctuary. And send that pledge to the Sanctuary editor today. Do more than that! Get as many of your neighbors as you can to do the same thing... every acre counts and we have set the mark to be reached at 5,000,000 acres. It is a great big, patriotic, splendid movement and it is attracting nation-wide attention. ... More birds mean more food for humanity, and more food means reduced cost of living and increased prosperity."[15]

The Green Meadow Club bird sanctuary program attracted high-level attention (some undoubtedly solicited by Burgess and Gates). T. Gilbert Pearson, president of the Audubon Society, wrote to request the program's circulars and commented: "I am greatly interested in what you tell me of your work in the establishment of sanctuaries, and am astounded to learn of its extent." A *People's Home Journal* pamphlet on its bird sanctuary program, "A Conspicuous National Service," contained the following endorsements:[16]

> *Herbert Hoover, National Food Administrator:* "I have noted with much satisfaction the good work your *Journal* is doing for the protection and encouragement of

insectivorous and migratory birds. It should bring about important results for the welfare of the entire country in making the people realize how closely related to the whole question of food conservation is the matter of bird protection."

T. S. Palmer, assistant chief, Bureau of Biological Survey: "I am very glad to learn of the good work you are doing in establishing bird sanctuaries through the medium of the Green Meadow Club. Sanctuaries furnish one of the best means of increasing the numbers of some of our common birds, and are especially important in the more thickly settled States. The value is not measured by size but by the opportunities which they afford birds to escape pursuit and to find proper food and nesting sites."

Lucia Additon, president, Oregon Women's Press Club: "I am exceedingly interested in the work of your Green Meadow Club for Bird Sanctuaries and Bird Mess Halls. It is a capital movement and I would like to develop it in this State...we are intending to print some leaflets on the subject for distribution amongst some thousands of children to push along the Sanctuary idea."

John Burroughs, author and naturalist: "Your scheme for bird sanctuaries throughout the country seems to be a good move. I heartily approve of any plan which has for its object the protection of our birds."

Remarkable Results

As a grass-roots conservation effort in the early twentieth century, the Green Meadow Club's bird sanctuary program launched by Burgess and Gates in the *People's Home Journal* produced stunning results. In November 1917, *People's Home Journal* announced that 1,314 individual bird sanctuaries on 163,000 acres had been pledged in the program's first year. In its second year, 2,604 sanctuaries were pledged on 770,329 acres of land. "No sooner was the work of 1918 disposed of and the awards distributed than Mr. Gates announced his intention to repeat the effort in 1919," wrote William Hornaday in the *Statement of the Permanent Wild Life Protection Fund (1917-1919)*. "The returns came in December 1919, and were fully as gratifying as before. Altogether the number of sanctuaries (3,131) was well above the figure for 1918 and the total acreage dedicated was fifty percent higher, reaching the admirable figure of 1,520,668."[17]

According to Hornaday's records, children and adults established 6,468 bird sanctuaries on 2,454,259 acres between 1917 and 1919. In the next year, 3,929 additional new sanctuaries were created on 800,469 aces. Over four years, the Green Meadow Club bird sanctuaries program established 3,254,720 acres of land posted for the protection of birds and other wildlife in North America.[18] Forty-two states in every region of the United States and some Canadian provinces were participating. In 1918, for example, in New Mexico, twenty-eight sanctuaries were established on 16,429 acres; in Montana, 113 sanctuaries on 66,771 acres; in Nebraska, forty-five sanctuaries on 20,091 acres; in Pennsylvania, 192 sanctuaries on 83,714 acres; and in Texas, ninety-six sanctuaries on 97,249 acres. In Canada, 119 sanctuaries were created on 53,695 acres.[19]

Teenagers Mira Hunt and Marjorie Lloyd together contributed more than two hundred sanctuaries with more than 60,000 acres pledged for conservation. In a detailed statement about her work for the bird sanctuaries, Hunt, then fourteen, of King, Montana, describes the purposefulness and dedication the Green Meadow Club program inspired:

> "I live on a homestead one mile from Canada, between the Milk River and the Sweet Grass Hills, part of the Rockies. As the people out here live quite a distance apart, I traveled over a great many miles to get my pledges signed. I went horseback to the Milk River Valley to get signers. Then papa took me to the Sweet Grass Hills in the car, which was about eighty miles the round trip. I also went to several farmers' meetings and the Red Cross. Almost every person was willing to sign, and some were anxious to when they knew what the pledges were for. But a few objected. One man in particular would not sign because the birds ate his berries one year. He had only a few, but the birds got them, and he is still grieving about it. I talked and explained for half an hour, but couldn't convince him it was for the best. I could have gotten several more ranch signers if it had not been for our school in the summer. As a member of the Green Meadow Club I was anxious to do my part in this valuable wartime work for our country, to help feed our Allies."[20]

In High Point, Saskatchewan, where game hunting was popular, George L.L. de St. Remy became a staunch advocate of the Green Meadow Club's conservation program. A ranchman who lived twenty-five miles from the nearest town, St. Remy identified 52,425 acres of land for the bird sanctuary program. He reported the following:

> During my campaign I traveled many hundreds of miles and addressed many gatherings of farmers while they ate their meals in restaurants and hotels. I examined the soil in many places, and where the land was a heavy clay, I found that the cutworm and wireworm caused enormous loss in a wet, late spring by attacking the germinating seeds. If the farmer had to sow his crop twice on this account, he was pretty sure to sign up for a Sanctuary when the facts were pointed out to him.
>
> Some signers had bitter experience with the Hessian fly, and were delighted to know that the Green Meadow Club was taking active steps to eradicate this pest. I found many owners of the ranch areas bitterly antagonistic. Having no crops at stake they invited shooting and hunting by city folk who came out for the sport, and they were against Sanctuaries. Great help is given by the propaganda of the Green Meadow Club, and I wish I were financially able to devote my whole time to your noble enterprise as no better work can be undertaken in a new country where most people are not educated to the necessity of protecting the birds — their best friends — in the absence of sufficient legislation.[21]

The Permanent Wildlife Protection Fund of the New York Zoological Society supported the *People's Home Journal* conservation effort with additional awards of gold medals, cash, and natural history books. The following schools and individuals were among those honored in 1918:[22]

- Rev. Harold E. Mouse, Elkins, West Virginia: 128 sanctuaries on 65,268 acres
- Rev. J. J. Resh, Freeland, Pennsylvania: 87 sanctuaries on 72,932 acres
- Flora Whitfield, Raton, New Mexico: 24 sanctuaries on 139,090 acres
- Marjorie Lloyd, Antigo, Wisconsin: 100 sanctuaries on 9, 391 acres
- George Stevens, Ogema, Wisconsin: 66 sanctuaries on 7,204 acres
- Cantrall School, Cantrall, Illinois: 54 sanctuaries on 14,402 acres
- George Horton, Dwight, Illinois: 87 sanctuaries on 13,820 acres
- Joe B. Woodward, Brownfield, Texas: 14 sanctuaries on 53,017 acres
- Sixteen Acres Elementary School, Springfield, Massachusetts: 109 sanctuaries on 16,011 acres

"No lover of birds needs to be told what this great array of fully protected sanctuaries means to our birds," declared Hornaday. "The work of the *People's Home Journal* has been a conspicuous achievement for conservation."[23] [Of Hornaday's involvement, biographer Gregory Dehler remarked, "If you read any Hornaday book closely, what he really wants is individuals to take an active interest in conservation. There was no reason to wait for a law to tell one to do the right thing or to rely on the government to do everything. The *People's Home Journal* campaign fit well into his thinking."]

Some sanctuaries were comparatively small, but the commitment to support wildlife was still significant. Dr. R. D. Woodmansee of Columbus, Ohio, for example, posted twenty-five acres of land that he had previously planted with 25,000 catalpa trees and installed one hundred birdhouses and feeding stations among them.[24] A four-acre sanctuary was posted in Kent Cliffs, Putnam County, New York, by none other than William Hornaday, which he described in a July 25, 1917 letter to Burgess: "If it were not really a very fine place for birds, and very much frequented by birds, I would not mention so small a sanctuary; but the fact of the matter is, it is surrounded on three sides by a large tract of forest (which also is a sanctuary, although I am not permitted to enter it as such.)"

The true purpose of his short letter is revealed when Hornaday recommends that Burgess, not he, personally invite the owner of the abutting seventy-acre forest, Miss Clara L. Stevens, to establish it as a bird sanctuary. Hornaday's confrontational manner was apparently less effective with neighbors than legislators and politicians: "It would be best not to mention my name because the lady is slightly 'disaffected' toward me, although it is not at all serious," he explained with unexpected delicacy.[25]

The tremendous response to Burgess' and Gates' bird sanctuary program was due in part to timing. The warnings of conservationists and political activists had alerted the American public to the consequences of ignoring the needs of wildlife, and they had directly linked protecting birds to preserving the all-critical food supply. At a time when wartime news of destruction and catastrophe was inescapable, the Green Meadows Club bird sanctuary program offered something meaningful, something positive that ordinary people, even children, could do to benefit the national welfare, as the following excerpt from Burgess' *Mother Nature News* newsletter explains:

> The birds are universally recognized to-day by scientists and agriculturalists as a sort of aerial police force, protecting our food crops against man's most relentless living enemies — the insect hordes which destroy annually nearly two thirds of the world field and orchard products. *The People's Home Journal* bird sanctuary campaign has been the one constructive effort in this country to check bird extermination to establish recruiting stations for nature's feathered anti-insect armies.[26]

Within seven years, the bird sanctuary program originated by Burgess and implemented by Gates achieved the pledging of more than five million acres of private land for support and protection of birds and other wildlife. According to results announced by *People's Home Journal*, in addition to the previously mentioned figures for 1917 through 1920, the Green Meadow Club established 2,908 sanctuaries on 1,398,709 acres in 1921, and the following year, 1922, established 1,378 sanctuaries on 336,268 acres. The Green Meadow Club program officially passed its goal of five million acres in 1923.[27] In those years of war and recovery, William Hornaday may have been correct when he declared, "The bird sanctuaries program exceeded anything accomplished along these lines of conservation by any organization in the world." But momentum for the program faded as wartime needs receded, and the conservation drive ended in 1924.

Whether or not the Green Meadow Club bird sanctuary program had legal status that enabled property owners to prosecute violators, as stated on the signage, was irrelevant compared to its overall accomplishment: nearly one hundred years ago, a children's magazine club introduced tens of thousands of individuals — and their families, friends, and communities — to environmental activism. The Green Meadow Club bird sanctuary program engaged children and adults, landowners, and interested citizens, both American and Canadian, in a common effort to preserve and protect nature.

Was the bird sanctuary program simply a "feel-good" diversion for a nation at war? It was apparently taken seriously by public officials like Herbert Hoover and T. S. Palmer, conservationists like John Burroughs and T. Gilbert Pearson, and political activists like William Hornaday and William Finley. Its ecological impact on wildlife is, of course, unknowable, as is its sustained impact on environmental values. However, there can be no question that Thornton Burgess' Green Meadow Club bird sanctuary program helped support North American wildlife at a critical time, and, more significantly, it helped lay a foundation for the environmental movement that would come decades later.

Chapter 10

Dr. William T. Hornaday, the Permanent Wildlife Protection Fund, and the Migratory Bird Treaty Act

In promoting the People's Home Journal *bird sanctuary program, Thornton Burgess developed a unique friendship with one of the most dynamic figures of the early twentieth century conservation movement: Dr. William Temple Hornaday, director of the New York Zoological Society. At first glance, the modest, self-effacing author of* Old Mother West Wind *and* The Adventures of Johnny Chuck *had little in common with the abrasive, brilliant, controversial strategist for U.S. environmental reform. But their mutual fervent commitment to wildlife conservation and environmental education — as well as self-interested appreciation for the other's effectiveness in advancing these objectives — provided a basis for political alliance and a lasting relationship.*

"The wild things of this earth are not ours to do with as we please. They have been given us in trust, and we must account for them to the generation which will come after us and audit our accounts."[1]

DR. WILLIAM T. HORNADAY, 1913

"I rejoice when I reflect upon the amount of good work that your stories are accomplishing for the maintenance of the migratory bird law and the treaty."[2]

DR. WILLIAM T. HORNADAY, 1916

"Spoke at Am. Museum of Nat. History — introduced by Dr. James Chapin, illustrator who went on Congo expedition, research associate at museum, and president of American Ornithological Union. Full house, mobbed afterward for autographs."[3]

THORNTON W. BURGESS, 1940

BEGINNING OF A VALUABLE FRIENDSHIP

The first meeting of Thornton Burgess and Dr. William Hornaday did not go well. Burgess had called on the director of the New York Zoological Society in hopes of soliciting an endorsement of his Green Meadow Club's bird sanctuary program. The distinguished conservationist was preoccupied with guests, however, and a long wait preceded Burgess' short interview. It was immediately obvious Hornaday knew nothing of his books, syndicated columns, or the *People's Home Journal's* new conservation club. The administrator was "glad I was trying to interest children in Nature...and trying to protect the birds," Burgess wryly noted in his autobiography, but would recommend nothing without thorough investigation, which at present he had no time to undertake:

> It was painfully plain that he was not at all interested and in five minutes I was on my way with nothing to show for my trip to the Park. I was chagrined, yet...I laughed to myself as I thought over the smooth finality with which the good doctor had disposed of another pest.
>
> Little did I dream then that the next time I saw him it would be as his guest at lunch, and that for the whole afternoon he would conduct me on a tour of the Park, cementing a treasured friendship that lasted through the years until his death and that to this day is an inspirational memory.[4]

Their second encounter was more productive. Hornaday had recently endorsed a conservation society formed by New York teachers. The *New York Globe's* Bedtime Story Club, a 200,000-member group based on Burgess' syndicated newspaper column, had also offered the group its support. Burgess was irked, however, that promotions implied his widely popular readers clubs were exclusive to the *Globe*. He seized the opportunity to introduce Hornaday to his work with a perhaps-you'd-be-interested-to-know letter detailing the impressive size of clubs in other metropolitan newspapers and the success of the *Kansas City Star* in initiating the idea. Hornaday's reply was warm, interested, and apologetic, and the two men began to exchange letters:

> January 25, 1916
> My Dear Mr. Burgess,
> I am sorry that I have been so ignorant of the details of your work, but I am glad from the bottom of my heart to learn that you have so diligently been teaching the ethics of wildlife protection to the members of the Bedtime Stories Clubs. Your work and influence constitute a force to be taken into account when we reckon up the strength of the "Army of the Defenses." I shall make due note of it in compiling the chronology for my next issue of the *Statement of the Wildlife Protection Fund.*
> To this end I would be glad if you would give me now the number of newspapers in which your Bedtime Stories appear, and the various states represented in the distribution. Of course it is impossible to compute the number of readers, but you can undoubtedly make a fairly good guess at the total.
> You will be interested in knowing that Prof. Hugh P. Baker, Dean of the New York State College of Forestry at the Syracuse University, contemplates forming a strong organization of school children throughout the state of New York, devoted to the conservation of forests and wildlife, and an increase in the chances of the remnants of wild creatures for further survival. A great interest is being taken in schools here and there in the making of bird boxes, and the feeding of birds. We have made here in the Zoological Park a rather extensive exhibit of bird houses and bird-feeding appliances, and it has attracted a great deal of attention.
> Unfortunately, however, the enemies of wildlife are increasing almost as rapidly as the defenders increase. I am going to send you by this mail a copy of my *Bulletin No. 2*, in which I invite your attention to an article on page 51 by Mr. Madison Grant, and another on page 36, by the undersigned, on conditions of wild life west of the great plains. These two impressions will give you an idea how things look in the far West and Northwest. In some places it is horribly discouraging, but we cannot stop on account of that.
> Yours very sincerely,
> W.T. Hornaday[5]

> Feb. 2, 1916
> Dear Mr. Burgess:
> Your letter of January 27 is a revelation of important activities in behalf of wild life. I had no idea that the Bedtime Stories Clubs extended as far. Truly you have in your hands tremendous power, and it is delightful to know that you are utilizing it for good on a grand scale. Henceforth I will look upon you as one of

the great forces for the betterment of conditions affecting our distressed and harassed wildlife; and although you do not seem to need it, I wish you more power to your elbow!

Meanwhile, the rest of us are doing work of a different kind which will supplement yours. We are striving for better laws, for better enforcement of laws, and the creation of a great number of wildlife sanctuaries. Our bill in Congress is making friends rapidly, and if it is not completely crowded out of sight by the turmoil over national preparedness and revenue measures, it will surely be passed by both houses at this session. Actually we are doing our level best to have it favorably reported on by the committees to which it has been referred and brought to a vote.

When you come to New York and can make it possible, do come up and see me, and if you can come at lunch time and have luncheon with me at our restaurant, I will like it all the better.

Yours very sincerely,
W.T. Hornaday[6]

Mutual Benefits

A few weeks later, the proffered lunch and a leisurely tour of the Zoological Society facilities gave the two men an opportunity to discuss their work and common interests, such as nature education for children and the new Boy Scout movement. Burgess had written a major article on scouting for *Good Housekeeping* and just completed his four-book "Boy Scout" series while Hornaday had recently proposed to provide medals to Scouts for distinguished conservation service. [The Hornaday Award for achievement in conservation is still given by the Boy Scouts of America.]

For Burgess, then forty-one years old, recognition as a successful children's author had been achieved, but full recognition as a naturalist had not. He initially sought an endorsement for his work from Hornaday, knowing that his own reputation would be enhanced by connection with the esteemed conservationist. Widely credited with saving the American bison from extinction, Hornaday was a Congressional lobbyist, acting agent for a national conservation fund, author of definitive books on global wildlife, and overseer of the largest municipal zoo in the country.

Burgess was a family man who wrote stories for young children while Hornaday, twenty years his senior, was an international figure who moved in elite circles. Close association with Theodore Roosevelt, Andrew Carnegie, Henry Ford, George Eastman, and Margaret Olivia Sage, who was then considered the wealthiest woman in America, provided him with ample access to political and financial resources, but few in any field had Thornton Burgess' access to the public, a pivotal factor in Hornaday's political agenda. Millions of adults and children — voters and the next generation of voters — avidly bought Burgess' books, regularly read his newspaper columns, flocked to his lectures, joined his Bedtime Story and Green Meadow Clubs, and, most importantly, believed what he said. The source of Hornaday's initial interest in Burgess was undoubtedly summed up in one sentence in his correspondence: "Truly you have in your hands tremendous power."

Power was not a term Burgess would have liked, though he probably wouldn't have disagreed with Hornaday's assessment. To the writer, power meant rallying children and adults to participate in an awards contest for creating bird sanctuaries. To the conservationist, power meant amassing Congressional votes to more tightly regulate the hunting of migratory birds, disabling a political opponent, or running full-page ads intended to shame hunting interests with statistics, scathing words, and photographs of grinning gunners holding armfuls of dead birds. "He gave no quarter and asked none," Burgess said of Hornaday.[7]

To defend the interests of wildlife, many early conservationists like Hornaday struggled against public apathy, economic opposition, and political resistance. "[Conservationists] gradually came to understand they needed more than their own view of birds to make their cause truly popular and politically viable," explains University of New Hampshire professor and environmental historian Kurk Dorsey in his book *The Dawn of Conservation Diplomacy*. "They needed to sell bird protection to the vast majority of citizens who did not share their attitudes."[8] If public sentiment was critical to "mobilizing the rank and file of the conservation movement and the general public," as Dorsey notes, positive public relations, economic justification, and sentimental rationale were needed.[9] Although Burgess urged families to "be a friend to wildlife" and Hornaday built a case for legal protection of wildlife with horrific details of brutality and slaughter, both men passionately served the same cause with the same fundamental convictions. When Burgess offered Hornaday the benefit of his popularity and credibility, as well as his heart for wildlife, Hornaday couldn't have been more pleased:

> I am delighted by the fact that you desire to enter into the very serious business of promoting the protection and increase of the wild life of our country. Goodness knows, you are needed badly. You have it in your power to influence the minds of millions of children, saying nothing of grown-ups, and you can easily turn that into a valuable asset of the protection of birds and animals...As an educator, you have a larger audience than any other teacher of the young.[10]

Permanent Wild Life Protection Fund

The sources of Burgess' and Hornaday's influence were as different as their application of it. Burgess had a direct, personal link with the American public through his writing, lecturing, and nature organizations. To a great extent, Hornaday's financial and political leverage derived from his virtual autonomy as Campaigning Trustee, or managing agent, of the privately endowed Permanent Wild Life Protection Fund. This position was and is less-known than his thirty-year tenure as director of the New York Zoological Society and founder of the Washington Zoo. His work through the Permanent Wild Life Protection Fund reveals the global scope of Hornaday's conservation ambitions and explains how a children's author could play a role in a critical era in American environmental history.

According to Gregory Dehler, author of *William Temple Hornaday: An American Crusader for Wildlife*, the zoologist had accepted the position of director of the New York Zoological Society in 1896, expecting it would become a leading conservation organization. Corporate goals, however, focused on establishing the world's largest zoo within ten years, which did occur under Hornaday's directorship. However, to fund such conservation objectives as the Flathead Bison Preserve, Hornaday pursued traditional fund-raising. "He said it almost killed him to go through this arduous process," Dehler remarked. Hornaday resolved the issue by creating a substantial endowment fund, the Permanent Wild Life Protection Fund, and named himself its acting officer, or Campaigning Trustee.

"He decided to set a seed amount of $100,000 and asked for contributions from his wealthy friends and acquaintances," Dehler explained. "On the one hand, he was protecting the New York Zoological Society and on the other he was buying his own freedom from them. Hornaday was someone who waged a battle to keep science and natural history ideas relevant in popular culture at a time when scientists were going into the 'ivory tower,' getting out of the field, looking at things with microscopes, and using language internally. For him it was important to look at animals wholly in habitat. If you looked at them outside of habitat, he thought that was losing the wonderment of nature, which was to see birds flying, not how their stomachs worked."

As an independent advocate for wildlife conservation, Hornaday held a glaring spotlight on environmental issues ranging from the practice of hunting from automobiles to the rapid-fire capability of automatic and pump guns to the present and future conditions for game in Africa and Asia, as well as the international millinery trade's destructive use of wild bird plumage. In his remarkable 1913 book, *Our Vanishing Wild Life*, Hornaday used field information provided by T. Gilbert Pearson, William Brewster, J.P. Wharton, and hundreds of others to report wildlife extinction and near-extinction statistics in all forty-eight states. In North Carolina, for example, the species he listed as completely exterminated included the ivory-billed woodpecker, parakeet, pigeon, roseate spoonbill, long-billed curlew, Eskimo curlew, bison, elk, gray wolf, puma, and beaver.[11]

Beyond North America, Hornaday announced conservation successes and failures in England, France, Italy, and South and Central America. On behalf of the Wildlife Protection Fund, he made a $500 contribution to the Ligue Francaise pour la Protection des Oiseaux in Paris and noted:

> At the present moment our Fund is in a position to render great aid in the organization and promotion, in France, of a great national movement for the increase and protection of the wild bird life of that nation. There never was a time when crop-protecting birds were so much needed in France as now, and the need to promote the protection of these birds is imperative as a protective measure for the field industries of France.
>
> We are already in close touch with the bird protectors of France, and particularly the Ligue Francaise pour la Protection des Oiseaux, having its headquarters in Paris and existing as a branch society of the French National

> Society d'Acclimatation. A comparatively small amount of financial help from the Permanent Wild Life Protection Fund, subscribed annually for the next three years, would greatly assist the League, not only in the actual payment of the costs of propaganda, but also in encouraging the bird protectionists of France through the helping hand of America.
>
> It is entirely possible that ere long it will be found desirable to extend aid to Italy of a similar kind, and for similar purposes. The American people do not need to be told that the people of France and England now have mighty little money to spend on such causes as the protection and increase of bird life; nor is it necessary to point out further that the successful protection of birds means a corresponding increase in the food supply of nations.[12]

While sympathetic to European circumstances, the Wild Life Protection Fund's acting agent had only scorn for American special interests and citizens who refused to recognize that, in Hornaday's opinion, extinction of species was imminent, not theoretical:

> If the people of the United States lazily and wickedly permit all the game of the nation save rabbits to be exterminated, then will they richly deserve a gameless, lifeless, insect-ridden, devastated and eroded continent, and when they get it, it will serve them right...No good citizen can sit or stand idly by and see our priceless national wildlife assets annihilated.[13]

In addition to lobbying for the Wild Life Protection Fund and working in his full-time capacity as the Zoological Society's director, Hornaday wrote twelve books; *Our Vanishing Wild Life* was based on a decade of national wildlife data collection. He was often accused of embellishing and manipulating information, but the conservationist had no need to exaggerate his account of extermination of sweeping herds of bison and endless flocks of passenger pigeons. In *Our Vanishing Wild Life*, he says of the passenger pigeon:

> There is no doubt about where those millions have gone. They (passenger pigeons) went down and out by systematic wholesale slaughter for the market and the pot, before the shotguns, clubs and nets of the earliest American pothunters. Wherever they nested they were slaughtered. It is a long and shameful story, but the grisly skeleton of its Michigan chapter can be set forth in a few words. In 1869, from the town of Hartford Michigan, three car loads of dead pigeons were shipped to market each day for forty days, making a total of 11,880,000. It is recorded that another Michigan town marketed 15,840,000 in two years.[14]

Our Vanishing Wild Life is impressive for its early use of photography and charts, but more so for its pre-World War I mapping of known and threatened wildlife extinctions and their cause — from market hunters and game hogs to plume and tusk hunters to devastating predation by domestic cats. Hornaday also outlined the immediate need for protective legislation. "It is one of the great environmental books," says Dehler. "Hornaday was trying to get people to feel ownership in nature. Basically his idea was to reform people's behavior. In that, Hornaday and Burgess were kindred spirits."

Poor Mrs. Quack

Within weeks of their first meeting at the Zoological Society's Park, now the Bronx Zoo, Hornaday and Burgess were swapping ideas and resources. Burgess asked the zoologist for information on the sage grouse while Hornaday suggested that Burgess develop a storyline in his syndicated newspaper column that would depict the plight of migratory birds.

> Dear Mr. Burgess,
>
> I must bestir myself about materials on the sage grouse, and I will do my best to provide something that will be useful. At this very moment a lot of gunners in Illinois, above and below Bloomington, are out in force, banging from shore to shore in regular battle style, killing ducks that are going north to breed. This warfare is being carried on contrary to the regulations of the federal migratory bird law, but, as the gunners say, in accordance with the rotten laws of the state of Illinois which permits spring shooting when not otherwise prevented.
>
> I think that you can score a good point by describing "The Gauntlet of the Guns" that a wild duck runs when spring shooting is in vogue, all the way from the Gulf to Canada. In the days of spring shooting I often wonder how a duck could get through alive, and how any duck could find feed and get a little rest on the journey without being killed. The picture of Mrs. Duck running the "Gauntlet of the Guns" rather appeals to my imagination.[15]

It appealed to Burgess too. Between March and May of 1916, his syndicated stories described the severe hardship experienced by migratory ducks during hunting season. In 1917, Little, Brown published *The Adventures of Poor Mrs. Quack*, a collection of the stories Burgess wrote specifically for emotional appeal and political effect, as well as for environmental education. As Peter Rabbit and Jerry Muskrat listen to Mrs. Quack's sad account of losing her mate and children, she describes her flock's diet, bathing habits, mating patterns, and preferred feeding grounds, even explaining to the ever-inquisitive Peter what a marsh is. She also tells her new friends about the process of migration, an unfamiliar experience for the wild rabbit and muskrat:

> You folks who don't have to leave your homes every year don't know how well off you are or how much you have to be thankful for...We don't leave because we want to, but because we have to. … Jack Frost freezes everything tight up there where my home is...He comes earlier up there and stays twice as long as he does here, and makes ten times as much snow and ice. We get most of our food in the water or in the mud under the water, as of course you know, and when the water is frozen, there isn't a scrap of anything we can get to eat. We just have to come south.[16]

In *The Adventures of Poor Mrs. Quack*, Burgess strategically utilized the arguments bird protectionists used for game limits, hunting seasons, and fair hunting practices, but he presented them sympathetically from the perspective of a wild duck, not an outraged conservationist. Mrs. Quack gives a personal account, so to speak, of encountering armed hunters who lured ducks within shooting range by using decoys, feed, duck calls, even captive live ducks, and who could kill scores of unsuspecting ducks with a single long-distance shot:

> For awhile we had nothing much to fear. We would fly by day and at night rest in some quiet lake or pond or on some river, with the Great Woods all about us or some great marshes. ... Then as we flew we began to see the homes of these terrible, two-legged creatures called men, and from that time on we never knew a minute of peace, excepting when we were flying high in the air or far out over the water. If we could have just kept flying all the time or never had to go near the shore, we would have been all right. But we had to eat.
>
> And to eat we had to go in close to shore where the water was not at all deep, because it is only in such places that we can get food...It takes a lot of strength to fly as we fly, and strength requires plenty of food...But for all our watchfulness, we could never be sure, absolutely sure, that all was safe. Sometimes those terrible two-legged creatures would be hiding in the very middle of the wildest, most lonely looking marshes. They would be covered with grass so that we couldn't see them. Then, as we flew over them, would come the bang, bang, bang, bang of terrible guns, and always some of our flock would drop. We would have to leave them behind, for we knew if we wanted to live we must get beyond the reach of those terrible guns.
>
> Sometimes we would have to try three or four feeding-places before we found one where there were no terrible guns. And when we did find one, we would be so tired and frightened that we couldn't enjoy our food, and we didn't dare sleep without someone on the watch all the time. It was like that every day. The farther we got, the worse it got. Our flock grew smaller and smaller. Those who escaped the terrible guns would be so frightened that they would forget to follow their leader and would fly in different directions and later perhaps join other flocks. So it was that when at last we reached the sunny Southland for which we had started, Mr. Quack and I were alone. What became of our twelve children I don't know.
>
> "Is the journey back as bad as the journey down?" asked Peter.
>
> "Worse, very much worse," replied Mrs. Quack sadly.[17]

Burgess repeatedly used animal characters like Mrs. Quack to articulate the conservationist's argument against limitless killing by so-called game hogs, contrasting human greed with the natural need of predatory animals to kill for sustenance:

> It wouldn't be so bad if a hunter would be satisfied to kill just one duck, just as Reddy Fox is, but he seems to want to kill every Duck. Foxes and Hawks and

Owls catch a good many young Ducks, just as they do young Rabbits, but you know how we feel about that. They only hunt when they are hungry and they hunt fairly. When they have enough to make a dinner, they stop. … If we do not keep out of their way, it is our own fault. I guess it is Old Mother Nature's way of keeping us wide-awake and sharpening our wits, and making us better fitted to live.

With these two legged creatures with terrible guns, it is all different. We don't have any chance at all…their terrible guns kill when we are a long way off and there isn't any way for us to know of the danger…and they often simply break the wings or otherwise terribly hurt the ones they shoot at, and then leave them to suffer, unable to take care of themselves. Oh, dear, I'm afraid that is what has happened to Mr. Quack.[18]

Colin Rowat of London, England, remembers his father, Dr. Bruce Rowat, reading Burgess' books to him as a boy. In looking over them again after many years, he noticed that the story of Mrs. Quack seemed noticeably different. "Having re-read the Burgess books now as an adult, I'm struck by the uncustomarily dark tone of *The Adventures of Poor Mrs. Quack*," said Rowat. "I can't help but wonder if the great guns scything down the ducks aren't reflective of the War." Burgess' tone indeed reflected war — in Congress, however, not Europe — as Dr. Hornaday relates in the following triumphant letter:

My Dear Mr. Burgess,

I have been so horribly busy with my various campaigns that I have not kept in touch with you as I should, but I am glad that you feel that I am with you in spirit for all that. I noted with great pleasure your treatment of Mrs. Quack, and her troubles; and I rejoice when I reflect upon the amount of good work that your stories are accomplishing for the maintenance of the migratory bird law and the treaty.

Like a great deal of my work and that of the Audubon Society and other organizations, your work has gone into the general fund of public sentiment for the protection of birds; and the result was overwhelmingly manifested two months ago when we had a show-down in the United States Senate with the enemies of the migratory law. They put up a great fight. They spent a lot of money and a lot of effort in lobbying at Washington and in their public campaigns, but we smote them hip and thigh and gave them the worst licking that any bunch of enemies of wildlife ever received. They were beaten in the Senate in their efforts to destroy the migratory bird law appropriations by a vote of 52 to 8, which was a decrease of more than 50% from their provisos showing of strength in that body.

But the crowning triumph was the Senate's treatment of the international treaty with Canada for the protection of all the migratory birds north of Mexico, clear to the Arctic Ocean. The attitude of the Senate was of course clearly foreshadowed in the vote to sustain the migratory bird law; but even with all that we were not prepared for the lightning stroke of progress which set the treaty triumphantly through the Senate in four days! Naturally we expected that a fight would be put up by the Missouri contingent; but we were informed by grapevine telephone that in the executive session of the senate, when Senator Reed of Missouri arose to make a great long speech of denunciation in his usual style, a southern senator went over to him and thrice over commanded him to "sit down and keep still" — which Reed finally did. The treaty was ratified by a practically unanimous vote; and whether the federal law is sustained by the supreme court or not, the treaty will stand.[19]

The Migratory Bird Treaty and Act

Hornaday had speculated whether the Migratory Bird Treaty Act would survive an inevitable legal challenge, and was probably not surprised that it came from the state of Missouri. When U.S. game warden Ray Holland caught hunters shooting ducks out of season at a club in Neosho, Missouri, he arrested them. The group included two bankers, an insurance executive, a Democratic committeeman, and the state's attorney general Frank McAllister. At his arraignment, McAllister ordered the local sheriff to arrest Holland instead — for having ducks in his possession without a license. The case was ultimately tried by the U.S. Supreme Court. In an opinion by Justice Oliver Wendell Holmes, Jr., the court ruled on April 19, 1920, that the Migratory Bird Treaty of 1916 and the Migratory Bird Treaty Act of 1918 were constitutional. Holmes wrote:

> To put the claim of the State upon title is to lean against a slender reed. Wild birds are not in the possession of anyone; and possession is the beginning of ownership. The whole foundation of the states' rights is the presence within their jurisdiction of birds that yesterday had not arrived, tomorrow may be in another state and in a week a thousand miles away.[20]

"You can always have the satisfaction of knowing that you have contributed substantially to these grand results," Hornaday had written to Burgess on the passage of the 1918 Migratory Bird Treaty Act between the U.S. and England representing Canada. The legislation prohibits taking, killing, or possessing a migratory bird or taking parts of a migratory bird, such as eggs, feathers, or nests, except for instances of Native American use, research, or permitted hunting.[21] One of the earliest U.S. environmental laws, the Migratory Bird Treaty Act is still highly relevant today. It is one of three U.S. statutes, for instance, capable of establishing liability in a case such as British Petroleum's 2010 Deepwater Horizon oil spill in the Gulf of Mexico.

"Without [the act], all the birds that died would not be a legal concern of the federal government," says Dr. Tom French, assistant director for the Natural Heritage and Endangered Species Program of the Massachusetts Division of Fisheries and Wildlife. "The act has no allowance for 'incidental take,' a legal term for accidental deaths. There is no excuse that you 'didn't mean to kill' a brown pelican. Every single protected migratory bird that dies is a violation."

There were other issues at stake for the early conservationist, French explained:

> Today, if you go to Harvard University's Museum of Comparative Zoology and look at their collection of extinct Eskimo Curlews, the tag on the last bird which was collected in 1902 says 'Boston Market.' That means it was shot for sale in the food markets of Boston. Before the Migratory Bird Treaty Act, there were no seasons, and the hunters used small boat-borne cannons that could kill a hundred ducks at a time as they sat in a tight flock on the water. A hunter could shoot ducks and geese at night, and they kept resident geese as captive decoys to call in migrating geese. The early bird watchers and Audubon Society members were particularly concerned about the unregulated killing of egrets, terns, and other birds for their feathers to be used in women's fashions, especially on hats.

The Migratory Bird Treaty Act eventually included agreements with Japan, Russia, and Mexico. Veteran U.S. Fish and Wildlife ornithologist Chandler "Chan" Robbins was on the American negotiating team that worked with the Soviet Union. He still has a photograph of participants standing on the wide front steps of a modern cinderblock building. "The negotiating was done at Voronezh," recalled Robbins in a 2010 telephone interview. "There was a committee of three people from our country and three from theirs and two interpreters. We were there approximately a week. We met with Russian ornithologists who had the same concerns about migratory birds. The Soviets were very happy to include habitat as well as species that moved from the United States to the Soviet Union and back. There were probably over fifty species. The legislation was extremely effective because the U.S. Fish and Wildlife Service had responsibility for enforcing it."[22]

Other Burgess Books Focus on Conservation Issues

In addition to *The Adventures of Poor Mrs. Quack*, Burgess wrote other books that specifically supported the early conservation movement. *Lightfoot the Deer* (1921) was dedicated to "the most beautiful of our four-footed friends in the Green Forest with the hope that this little volume may in some degree aid in the protection of the innocent and helpless." Like *Mrs. Quack*, it reflects the perspective of a hunted wild animal, in this case a mammal, not a migrant bird, as well as of a hunter. Burgess' broad understanding as a naturalist and a former hunter is utilized in one dramatic scene during which a fox stalks ducks being watched by a hunter being watched by a nosy blue jay, a beaver, and the whitetail deer that the hunter is pursuing. With six wild animals and one armed human in close proximity, none are injured or killed, but Burgess doesn't pass up the opportunity to reinforce conservation values:

> Now when you come to think of it, it would have been a far greater shame for the hunter to have killed Mr. and Mrs. Quack than for Reddy Fox to have done so. Reddy was hunting them because he was hungry. The hunter would have shot them for sport. He didn't need them. He had plenty of other food. Reddy Fox doesn't kill just for the pleasure of killing.[23]

Lightfoot is a full-grown stag, well able to look out for himself. As the story develops, the deer and hunter engage in a fair contest based on mutual skill in tracking and evasion. Burgess disturbs that tenuous balance by introducing free-running hunting dogs, and delivers another conservation message about fairness:

> The ground was damp and scent always lies best on damp ground. This made it easy for the hounds to follow him with their wonderful noses. Lightfoot tried every trick he could think of to make those hounds lose the scent. "If only I could make them lose it long enough for me to get a little rest, it would help," panted Lightfoot as he paused for just an instant to listen to the baying of the hounds. But he couldn't...He was becoming very, very tired. He could no longer bound lightly over fallen logs or brush as he had done at first. His lungs ached as he panted for breath. He realized that even though he should escape the hunters he would meet an even more terrible death unless he could get rid of those hounds.[24]

In *The Adventures of Bob White* (1919), Burgess' readers can also compare the experience of both the hunter and the hunted, but this book is an unmistakable vehicle for environmental education, even providing a math lesson in calculating the number of caterpillars a family of quail might eat in a month:

> One day Bob White ate twelve caterpillars while Farmer Brown's Boy was watching him. He got out a stubby pencil and a scrap of paper. "If every one of these Bob Whites eats twelve of those horrid worms at one meal that would be — let me see." He wrinkled his brows. "There are Bob and Mrs. Bob and fifteen young Bobs...That makes 204 caterpillars for one meal," he muttered, "and in one month of thirty days they would eat 6,120 if they only ate one meal a day. But they eat ever so many meals a day and that means —" He stopped to stare at the figures on the bit of paper with eyes round with wonder. "No wonder I've got a good garden when those fellows are at work on it!" he exclaimed.[25]

Burgess highlights the agricultural benefit of supporting insectivorous birds like quail that eat cucumber beetles, cinch bugs, grasshoppers, and weed seeds, but his human protagonist, Farmer Brown's Boy, gets to the heart of the conservationists' argument for protection when he says, "Why those little brown birds are actually making money for us and we never guessed it."[26]

With the possible exception of Farmer Brown's Boy Tommy and his later counterpart in *The Burgess Book of Nature Lore*, Burgess' few human characters are intruders in the wildlife community who generally serve to exemplify conservation dos and don'ts. When Farmer Brown suggests in *Bob White* (1919) having "broiled Bob White on toast, his son Tommy indignantly replies that he wouldn't shoot them "for anything in the world." He tells his father, "I did like to hunt with my gun once, but that was when I didn't know as much as I know now. It was exciting to try to find the birds and then see if I could hit them. I just thought of them as wild things good to eat...I never thought of them as having any feelings...I wouldn't have anything happen to them for the world."[27] In a conversation obviously intended to promote Burgess' Green Meadows Club bird sanctuary program, Farmer Brown and his son discuss posting their property to prohibit hunting and convincing their neighbors to do the same.

A Price to Pay

Conservation politics in the early twentieth century was not a place for fragile souls. The value of the life of a domestic animal was low and a wild animal's even lower. Hornaday's *Our Vanishing Wild Life* grimly describes birds' eyes being sewn open and horses being blinded before being led away to be bear bait. There could be a price to pay for opposing commercial and hunting interests. Although many were involved in the early conservation movement, Burgess saw Hornaday as "Almost alone against the vast and constantly growing army of gunners who were truly blind to, or refused to read, the writing on the wall…he battled for protective legislation in behalf of the ducks, a shortened open season and reduced daily and seasonal bags."[28] As a result of his stance, life-long friends turned against Hornaday, Burgess noted, "among them leaders in the field of natural science, men who were supposed to be working for the preservation of natural resources, naturalists of note, museum heads."[29]

Burgess, too, lost good friends over his conservation position. When Hornaday formed the Committee of One Hundred to at least symbolically demonstrate support for his conservation positions, he included Burgess. "I felt honored to be included on that committee," Burgess wrote. "I was bitterly assailed for so doing. Men whom I had long looked up to, and whose regard and good opinion I cherished, turned against me. Pressure was brought in many ways. It was an unpleasant business all the way."[30] Hornaday echoed Burgess' observation in his 1920 *Statement of the Permanent Wildlife Protection Fund*, even injecting a bit of humor:

> To the wild life protector who endeavors to do his whole duty and hew to the line, life is not all a bed of mountain roses, nor even of lilies of the valley. Sometimes he is compelled to thwart the purpose of his own friends who persist in trying to go wrong; and in warfare for the success of his causes he makes enemies in direct proportion to the extent of his activities. The more he succeeds, the greater the number of those who hate him for his success; and he who takes up the sword of Protection may bid farewell to all dreams of "popularity."[31]

In general, Burgess' support of early conservation efforts with his bird sanctuary program and children's books and daily newspaper stories has gone unnoticed. As Hornaday predicted, it anonymously entered "the general fund of public sentiment." That was undoubtedly sufficient for Burgess, but Hornaday's personal recognition of his "valuable service to the migratory birds" must have been especially meaningful:

> I am delighted to find that you and your publishers have put Mrs. Quack in a book…at this point I wish particularly to thank you for your valuable service to the migratory birds in the production of this series for your great multitude of

> readers. … I thank you also for "Paddy the Beaver" in book form. "Paddy" is a James Dandy, and it worthwhile to have him between covers. If these two books do not please the great American Boy and Girl, then no books ever will.[32]

When Burgess completed *Happy Jack Squirrel*, his 1918 book about a gray squirrel, he dedicated it to the conservationist: "To Dr. William T. Hornaday, to whom posterity will owe a debt of gratitude for his valiant fight to preserve American wild life, who has been a lifelong champion of Happy Jack Squirrel, and to whom the author is deeply indebted for encouragement and assistance, this book is gratefully dedicated."

Hornaday's unrestrained delight at having a 204-page children's book dedicated to him — "thank you a thousand times for this honor" — suggests several things: Perhaps the fire-breathing conservationist was unaccustomed to personal thank-yous and public acknowledgement of his tireless efforts, or perhaps he was just immensely pleased that this was an accolade he could share with his grandchildren at bedtime:

> My Dear Thornton Burgess:
>
> Out of a much of wearisome and worrisome things, with few compensations, there has swept upon us like a mountain breeze your "Happy Jack" book, with its wonderful dedication to me. It has been gloated over, with many gloats, by the entire family, each member of which is proud with the Pride of Proprietorship.
>
> Some men of Science (of whom W.T.H. is not one) have mice and rats, and skunks and bats, and fishes and bugs of sort "named in their honor (?)" And they can take those things and keep them! Give me, instead, a fine book, by a genius friend, which goes to the hearts of the boys and girls of America, and will LIVE!!
>
> Thank you a thousand times for this honor. I am conservedly proud of it, and appreciate it more than would any other fellow you could have picked out.
>
> And how my grandchildren will revel in these breezy chapters! At this moment they and their Mother have a hard and fast alliance with a real, live sleek Happy Jack who came over a ___ that I put up to ___ Chamber window to be fed. I gave up a whole handful of real chestnuts only last night. That squirrel has survived on this ridge for 3 years, in spite of dogs + cats innumerable. He is a Wise Guy, or he couldn't save his bacon the way he does!
>
> The volume came today, the handsomest of all your books that I have seen, and tomorrow the reading sessions begin. Incidentally its larger type and small words will encourage Loraine to read these stories herself. Long life and prosperity to Happy Jack with the Silver Tail.
>
> Faithfully yours,
>
> W. T. Hornaday[33]

Distinguished Service Award

In 1919, Thornton Burgess received the greatest professional honor of his life when the Permanent Wildlife Protection Fund conferred on him its gold medal award for distinguished service to wildlife conservation. Philanthropist Margaret Olivia

Sage, founder of the 76,000-acre Marsh Island Wildlife Sanctuary in Louisiana, was the first recipient of the annual award in 1915, and conservationist Aldo Leopold was the second in 1916. Hornaday introduced Burgess with a reference to his vast audience of book and newspaper readers before handing him the medal and citation, which read:

> Thornton W. Burgess, Author of Bird and Animal Stories — In acknowledgment of distinguished services rendered to the wild life of America, and the children of America, in opening the eyes of the latter to the most interesting features of wild life, and at all times insisting upon its humane and thorough preservation.
>
> As the author of 2,500 "Bedtime Stories," and 27 books of stories about birds and mammals, Mr. Burgess has spoken long and well to an audience of millions of American boys and girls. His conscientious and correct presentations, his inspiring love for the wild creatures, and his sane and logical treatment of the sport question called for the highest honor that it was within the power of the Trustees of the Fund to bestow.[34]

According to Burgess, his friendship with Hornaday "lasted through the years until his death." His journal records the invitation to be a board member of a Hornaday museum. In *Now I Remember*, Burgess commented on one special letter from Hornaday:

> Among letters I greatly cherish is one that starts thus: "My dear Thornton: When I call a grown man by his first name it is a sign that in my affections and esteem he has been given a front row in the orchestra apart from the common herd.[35]

Hornaday biographer Gregory Dehler has read thousands of the conservationist's letters and concurs that his familiar use of first names was quite rare. "He had so many correspondents it is hard to pick out his friends, and only a few were true friends," says Dehler. "There are just a handful of people he addressed by their first name — George Shields was one, his brothers, John Phillips, the Pennsylvania game warden, and Edmund Seymour, president of the American Bison Society.

"He was close to Roosevelt, but I don't think he'd call him anything but 'My dear Colonel,' and he was close to Carnegie, but he would never call him 'Andrew,'" Dehler says. "If he referred to Burgess as 'Thornton,' it is a sure sign they were friends."

Chapter 11

Austin H. Clark and the Radio Nature League

In the early 1920s, Thornton Burgess again ventured into unfamiliar territory. Sitting awkwardly before a table microphone in the WBZ radio broadcasting studio in Springfield, Massachusetts, he read one of his syndicated stories to a preoccupied announcer in an otherwise empty room. It was the inception of one of the earliest children's radio programs, possibly the first to focus on nature. In 1925, he introduced the Radio Nature League, a weekly program that offered the equivalent of today's interactive exchange of talk radio, the child-centered approach of television's "Mr. Rogers' Neighborhood" and the educational focus of a PBS "Nature" program. With Smithsonian scientist Austin Hobart Clark, he explored the potential of radio to popularize science and educate the public. By using airwaves to bring issues, information, and the living voices of natural scientists into American homes in the 1920s and 1930s, Burgess contributed to two factors that increasingly defined the second half of the twentieth century: environmental awareness and the incorporation of science into daily life.

"The possibilities of radio as a direct and practical aid to science have been demonstrated during the last year by Thornton W. Burgess, author and naturalist."[1]

THE WASHINGTON POST, JAN. 31, 1926

"I am getting so now that when anything [for research] is wanted, I say, 'Just go ask for it on the radio.'"[2]

THORNTON W. BURGESS, 1926

"The power of the radio in promoting conservation and for the scientific education of our people cannot be overestimated. It reaches scores of thousands who seldom or never read the printed page but whose thirst for accurate information is insatiable."[3]

AUSTIN H. CLARK, CURATOR
SMITHSONIAN INSTITUTION, 1926

"My dear sir: I wonder if you can begin to realize what a feeling of gloom and sorrow [at cancellation of the Radio Nature League] you cast over the thousands of your Radio friends who you have taught so well to love and care for all the wildlife that formerly that cared so little for. ... Please for the sake of all wildlife as well as the pleasure and profit we derived from your most interesting talks don't give up for a longtime yet."[4]

BENJAMIN BEARDSLEY, M.D.
HARTFORD, CONNECTICUT, UNDATED

RADIO BEGINNINGS

In the spring of 1922, Burgess' popular syndicated column in the *New York Tribune* attracted unexpected attention. Charles Popence, manager of the Westinghouse Electric and Manufacturing Company in Newark, New Jersey, wrote to inquire about the writer's interest in reading his children's stories to a group that Burgess, for all his experience as a public speaker, had never addressed: a radio audience. "You no doubt are aware of the strides that the Wireless Telephone has made during the past few months," Popence said, adding that his company's Radiophone Broadcasting Station had already acquired 200,000 listeners "scattered all over the United States."[5]

Programming in the earliest days of radio was generally limited to a few evening hours. Westinghouse's Saturday night slots were already filled by Harper Brothers Publishing, the Century Club, *New York Telegraph*, *New York Mail*, and Howard Garis, author of the *Uncle Wiggily* books and syndicated stories, Popence said. Friday night slots were available, however, and Burgess was definitely interested. By July his Bedtime Stories were read at 7:00 p.m. over the Westinghouse station WJZ in Newark.

Popence had mentioned that Westinghouse's affiliate station in East Springfield, Massachusetts, might also be interested. Burgess contacted them, and readily accepted the invitation "to tell one of his stories" on the air. At that time, WBZ-Springfield was located a few miles from Burgess' home. A driver would pick him up and deliver him home. There was no payment, but Burgess recognized the value of a learning experience and a new source of exposure. In *Now I Remember*, Burgess described his introduction to the WBZ radio studio:

> I was completely ignorant of what lay ahead of me. I never had seen a receiving set, not even a crystal set. I never had seen a microphone. I was taken to the great Westinghouse plant in East Springfield and there guided through one of the big buildings to the top floor. There, in what I may call an embryo studio that contained all the transmitting equipment, I made myself known to the lone operator. He was also the announcer. He was too busy to talk and left me to stare at this gadget and that and wonder what they were for.[6]

Eventually the station operator/announcer sat down in front of a table microphone, introduced Burgess, motioned for him to come replace him, then stood up and turned away to other tasks. A seasoned lecturer, Burgess was comfortable addressing large, responsive, live audiences of several thousand people. Reading his stories in the silent isolation of a small radio studio, however, was initially unnerving. "The temptation to shout was almost irresistible," he said. "I kept my voice down, trying to speak slowly and distinctly. Fortunately I had previously made some phonograph records. That experience helped me now."

> Had I been in a vacuum talking to a blank wall, it could hardly have seemed flatter...the longer I talked, the more silly I felt...I did not have stage fright for there was no visible audience to cause it, and at that time my ignorance of radio prevented imagination from visualizing the vast body of listeners that later would become familiar to me.[7]

Convinced he had made a fool of himself, Burgess was vastly relieved the next morning when a fellow passenger on the Springfield train to Boston declared, "We could hear you as if you were right in the room." The stories read by either Burgess or trained readers became so popular on WBZ's daily hour of children's programming that he was asked to give a brief nature talk afterwards. In response to enthusiastic letters from listeners, these talks became a regular ten-minute feature that was eventually extended to a half-hour.

The Radio Nature League

Motivated by the positive reception to his nature talks — and perhaps by the recent conclusion of the *People's Home Journal* bird sanctuary drive — Burgess introduced the concept of a radio nature group in early December 1924, something "[I] had in my mind for a long time," he later told a friend. He outlined the proposal on New Year's Day 1925 and asked listeners for a convincing show of interest in order to implement it. Within a week, letters and telegrams from ten states and three Canadian provinces arrived, the first from the Secretary of the Massachusetts Fish and Game Protective Association who considered it "a great idea." The Radio Nature League became official on January 7, 1925, and by the next program 2,690 people had joined.[8]

Like Burgess' Green Meadow Club, the Radio Nature League was a loosely structured free affiliation based on appreciation and concern for nature; that it was a "league" implied a more serious purpose than a "club." Members would be "bound together through radio by a common interest in Nature."[9]

From the start, Burgess used his radio program as a podium from which to build support for the environmental values and causes he believed in. Membership simply required a good-faith pledge as stated on his WBZ letterhead: "To do everything possible to preserve and conserve all desirable American Wild Life, including birds, animals, flowers, trees, and other living things; also the natural beauty spots and scenic wonders of all America." The program was instantly embraced by the public. On January 21, 1925, Burgess announced:

> The League is three weeks old tonight. ... Already it stretches from coast to coast, from Northern Quebec to Florida and by way of Bermuda across the Atlantic ocean to England. The present membership is just under 4,500...From a little village down in Connecticut, Fabyan, Mrs. Fred Parker has sent a list of 49 members. It includes nearly all the kiddies in town and this past week they started in feeding the birds, becoming Silver Star members. I understand there are but three homes in the village which have radios and each Wednesday might these three homes are open to the children that they may attend the weekly meeting of the Radio Nature League. Aren't you proud of that little village in the Nutmeg state? I feel like shouting "Hurrah for Fabyan." It not only is doing something practical for its wild life but it is doing something even finer for its children.[10]

Blue Whales and Shrews

Shortly after launching the Radio Nature League, Burgess posed a math question to listeners: If a blue whale was the largest mammal at roughly 150 tons and a shrew the smallest at 40 grains (0.09 ounces or 2.6 grams), how many shrews would it take to equal the weight of one blue whale? When the answer of fifty-two and a half million shrews (then judged to be accurate and later corrected by Smithsonian marine scientist Austin Clark) arrived by cable the next day, Burgess was stunned — not because it was so prompt, but because the respondent Cory Withington lived in Manchester, England. Burgess wrote in his autobiography, "My voice had crossed the Atlantic! What a thrill. Bear in mind this was before short wave. It brought me letters from all over England."[11] Burgess proudly announced that before the League was two weeks old, it had enrolled four members "from across the ocean."

Dr. William Hornaday, Austin Clark, Dr. Harry Oberholser, a biologist with the U.S. Biological Survey, and other friends in the scientific community joined Burgess' radio organization. Oregon conservation official and acclaimed photographer William L. Finley wired Burgess: "The Radio Nature League is the child of a big idea. It will encourage greater love and interest in the out-of-doors. Please enroll our family of four. We want to join and listen in."[12]

In mid-February, the *Christian Science Monitor* reported:

> In less than three weeks radio has enlisted more than 20,000 members in a radio nature league whose sole aim is to assist in the preservation and conservation of all desirable wildlife in America. This humanitarian idea first came to Thornton W. Burgess, nationally famous naturalist, lecturer and writer of stories for children, who enlisted the services of Westinghouse Station WBZ...Five thousand letters have been received by Mr. Burgess, whole families pledging themselves to the league in one letter...Mr. Burgess, whose life has been devoted to the writing of child stories and the study of animal life, foresaw the possibilities of using the long arm of radio for this excellent purpose. [13]

Building Membership

The immediate popularity of the Radio Nature League could be partially attributed to the novelty of having the vocal presence of a celebrity or prominent person in one's living room. Utilizing his marketing background and folksy charisma, Burgess cultivated a sense of community by reminding listeners of their "common desire and purpose to do all we can do to preserve the beautiful, wonderful wild life still remaining, but which will not long remain unless we, you and I, do all we can to save it."[14] His emphasis on shared responsibility and credit for the program's growth, as well as his sense of its value, was evident in an early script written by Burgess and read in his absence that week by Fannie Burgess whom he cast in the role of bemused wife:

> For two weeks now I have had to live with the Radio Nature League. I have had it for breakfast, lunch, dinner and between meals. Mr. Burgess is an enthusiastic man. When he goes into a thing, he goes in "all over," as they say. In all the years I have lived with him I have never seen him as intensely interested in anything as he is in this Radio Nature League. He talks about it by day and I am quite sure he dreams about it by night. And it is because he believes in it, believes in it with heart and soul that it offers a wonderful opportunity to do something worth while in a big way to save the wild life he loves so intensely; to preserve the beauty spots, both small and great, of his beloved America for the joy and well being of the children of today and the children of tomorrow.
>
> Last week Wednesday night he came home from the WBZ studio as delighted as any small boy I have ever seen on a Christmas morning. He had received two telephone calls and 19 telegrams from outside the state of Massachusetts asking for enrollment in the League.[15]

Membership numbers were personal for Burgess. "You will never know how delighted I was when in response to my request for a thousand members by my birthday [January 14] you gave me nearly 3,000," he said, noting that equal numbers of adults and children had enrolled. Nature and birding clubs, Boy and Girl Scout troops, and sportsmen and game protection organizations were all invited to take part, however, Burgess stressed that his main focus was "the home folk, the boys and girls and fathers and mothers and all the other folk in every household where there is a radio."

Recognition Develops Commitment

Burgess knew well the commercial value of member recognition and made good use of listeners' letters. His radio scripts were crammed with names of individual League members who posed an observant question, discovered odd-looking wildlife specimens, reported unexplained wildlife behavior, became a state's first member, or simply invited others into their home to listen to the Radio Nature League. The following items were excerpted from a seven-page radio script, which mentioned the names of sixty-five individuals:[16]

> My, how little folks can ask questions! Little William Shockley of Harrington, Delaware, wants to know if a tadpole will grow legs and become a Frog. That depends, William, on the kind of tadpole it is. Legs it certainly will grow sooner or later, the hind ones first, and it certainly will lose its tail, but it may not become a frog because — why because it may become a toad. Both Frog and Toad babies are tadpoles.
>
> Cecelia Stuart of Milford, Massachusetts, has been feeding some birds which are black with purple and green backs and wants to know what kind they are. They are Starlings, Cecelia, and are naturalized citizens all through the east now and rapidly spreading. They belong in Europe. Some bird students are beginning to suspect it would be better if they had remained there.
>
> Richard Price of Northampton, Massachusetts, has noticed little tracks in the snow around piles of cornstalks and wonders if they are made by mice and wants to know if Mice live under piles of cornstalks all winter.

Burgess developed Price's question into an educational discussion, offering a broad answer suitable for various ages and interest levels:

> Probably those are the tracks of Danny and Nanny Meadow Mouse. Medow [sic] Mice, also called Field Mice, often make their nests in or under piles of cornstalks and pass the winter there very comfortably. A shock of corn is a regular castle for Danny and Nanny…There is plenty to eat, material for a comfortable nest and best of all, safety. Shadow the Weasel is about the only one who can get at them there.

> Mr. Vernon Bailey of the Biological Survey of the United States Department of Agriculture has been making a long and careful study of Meadow or Field Mice. One pair that he had in captivity had 17 families, a total of 85 children, in twelve months, and he figured it out that if nothing happened to any of these or to their children for a period of one year at the end of that time their [*sic*] would be one million mice descended from that single pair.

Burgess further utilized Price's questions by linking them to ecology and conservation:

> So you can see what would happen if the mice had no enemies to keep them in check. You see for yourselves in just this one matter the answer to a question I have had asked of me — "Of what good are Hawks, owls, and Foxes?" They help in very large measure to keep the earth from being overrun with Mice. They are in the Green Forest and on the Green Meadows by right and for a purpose — to help maintain the balance of Nature.

Another method Burgess used to highlight individual listeners and emphasize conservation was to maintain lists of members who fed wildlife (silver stars), put up birdhouses (red stars), or created bird sanctuaries (gold stars).[17] In reading the names of these members, he created a primitive form of social networking that encouraged participation among friends and neighbors who tuned in. But in Burgess' opinion, the explosion of interest in the Radio Nature League was not caused by excitement in a new technology, the momentary thrill of hearing one's name or question read aloud, or his skill as a radio host. He attributed its success to the "open meeting" presentation and the instinctive, universal love of and curiosity about nature.

> I early discovered that interest in some form of nature lore is practically universal. Laborers on the street would stop to tell me how they would split a headset so that two members of the family might listen. As the membership continued to grow, a cross section showed farmers, day laborers, businessmen, doctors, lawyers, clergymen, teachers, members of other professions, college students and children of all ages in my audience. Housewives on distant lone farms enrolled. My mail became something of a burden, but was interesting in the extreme. Some letters asked for information while others volunteered it. Gradually I realized that I had in my charge an instrument for education with undreamed of potentialities.[18]

When Martha Conture of Granby, Massachusetts, wondered about the color of goldfinch eggs, Burgess informed her and his radio audience that they are "pale bluish white."[19] Frank Comstock of Meriden, Connecticut, spotted a rattlesnake in a tree and asked Burgess if this was unusual. Burgess explained that rattlesnakes, unlike black snakes, are not tree climbers, and suggested that if this one was motivated by a nest of baby birds or other prey, it may have found a means of access, such as a nearby low building, into the tree. Another reader sought Burgess' opinion of the bizarre behavior of a catbird that had begun to mimic distress in an unmistakable effort to draw human attention to a crow that had fallen into a nearby pond. Was it calling for help? No, Burgess said, the catbird's effort to attract attention to the plight of its natural enemy was undoubtedly opportunistic, not altruistic.

Jane Wood from Elkington, Connecticut, observed the sudden appearance of countless tiny toads or frogs: Which were they? Where had they come from? Where were they going? Burgess, ever the storyteller, explained that these were toads, not frogs, "on their way to seek their fortune in the Great World." Some would become meals for other creatures such as snakes, crows, hawks, owls, ducks, and hens, and some would be the casualty of a human encounter, he said. But many would find their way to a garden to eat insects. "There is really nothing mysterious about," said Burgess. "Mother Nature has whispered to each of these tiny little fellows that it is time to leave the water and dwell henceforth on the land. They will hide from the sun beneath rocks or leaves, and shed their skin, then dispose of it by eating it."

Occasionally radio listeners' anecdotal evidence conflicted with science, but Burgess was tactfully respectful of both positions. A persistent challenge to his neutrality, however, was the subjects of hoop snakes and protective mother snakes that reportedly swallowed and then released their young. He read letters from various League members who staunchly asserted they had witnessed baby-swallowing-and-releasing snakes and snakes that took their tails in their mouths and rolled away. Burgess duly noted that these stories came from all sections of the country and "always the story is the same," but he gave his listeners a perspective to consider:

> No scientist or student of snakes has ever seen one...Unquestionably people have seen snakes do something which has led them to believe they were rolling like hoops. Their eyes have been deceived just as the magician on the stage deceives the watching eyes. The interesting thing to learn is just what happened...Science would like to see a hoop snake. It does not laugh at people who say they have seen a hoop snake because science knows only too well how easily the eye is deceived.[20]

The Meanest Animal

Announcer Gordon Swan said letters from listeners would occasionally elicit a chuckle from Burgess, such as the housewife in Geneva, New York who wrote him about a skunk that wandered into her kitchen and seemed disinclined to leave. Having few options, the woman cautiously went about her business. Although she set tempting food outdoors, the skunk preferred to stay in her house, napping comfortably beneath the sofa. After several days, the wild creature departed through the open door it had entered. Referencing Burgess' well-known affection for skunks, another listener teasingly asked if he considered it incorrect to say someone was "mean as a skunk," and if so what was the meanest creature? Burgess' blunt answer may have surprised his radio listeners:

> Unfortunately, the meanest animal in the world is man himself when he sets out to be mean. There is no other animal to compare him with. As an illustration

> of this, last spring there appeared in the newspapers an account of a fight that took place between a dog and a woodchuck in the town of Leominster, Massachusetts, and which was watched by a crowd of people. Automobiles drew up to watch. Finally the dog was whipped and limped away, then that woodchuck that had bravely fought for life and liberty was stoned to death by two bystanders, and no one interfered. Poor brave Johnny Chuck…a mean man is the meanest animal in the world.[21]

Burgess shared his personal opinions on conservation issues and would counter arguments for bounties on hawks by pointing out the good they did in controlling rodent populations: "Man sees a hawk take a chicken, but he doesn't see that hawk take the rat which has killed ten chickens." He spoke against irresponsible hunting and the purposeless, indifferent, or misguided killing of wildlife: "I know of nothing as wholly disgusting as the sight of a man or boy beating to death a little helpless, harmless striped garter snake or green snake, solely because it is a snake," he said. Typically, his solution to such destructive behavior was to educate listeners with useful information:

> I want all of you to get firmly fixed in your minds the one important fact that there are only four kinds of poisonous snakes in all the United States, and that all others are harmless. Of the four dangerous serpents, two are in the north, and these are the Rattlesnake and Copperhead. In the south are the Rattlesnake, the Cottonmouth Moccasin, and the rather uncommon small Coral Snake…No matter what people may tell you the bite of any other of our American Snakes is harmless.
>
> If you learn to know these snakes…you will never fear any of the others. The Rattlesnake is an honest snake. It has but one desire, and that is to be let alone. This is why it always gives warning with the curious rattle on the end of the tail.[22]

In the Studio

As a child, Frances Meigs appeared with her siblings on radio with their famous grandfather. "I remember the studio as a small room, dreary and dark, and very sparsely furnished," Meigs recalled. "It wasn't like studios today, run by people with buttons. We were supposed to say something, but we were so in awe and timid. My voice was like a whisper." In a 1988 interview, WBZ program director Gordon Swan recalled Burgess as "tall and thin, a little gaunt…a loveable character, a nasal New England grandfather."

According to Swan, Burgess never ad-libbed, but always typed out a script for the entire program, complete with occasional sound effects by Swan or birdsong imitator Edward Avis. After placing his mail on one side of a small table, he then spoke into a standing carbon microphone:

> He'd always start out, "Good evening, Neighbors, hello, Boys and Girls." He was never nervous, and always wore a bow tie, a suit coat and glasses. When he found out I had a cottage in Sandwich, we had something in common, and he drove me out to see his new house in Hampden. I got to know him as a friend…

> In 1927 he got into daytime radio broadcasting, and his program reached almost all of New England. There was a friendly feeling between people on the air and the audience. His audience was very loyal. He probably did more for conservation than anyone else.

A Radio Nature League Fan

One avid young Radio Nature League listener in the 1930s was Chandler "Chan" Robbins. A revered U.S. Fish and Wildlife ornithologist now in his nineties and "mostly retired," Robbins worked with conservationist Rachael Carson and ornithologist Frank Chapman. "I enjoyed the Radio Nature League, and was a big reader of all Thornton Burgess' children's books," Robbins said in a 2010 telephone interview. "I particularly liked *The Burgess Bird Book for Children*. I think at the time he was really about the only person who wrote primarily for the benefit of children. This was a need to be filled, and he filled it admirably."

Robbins and his brothers once won the children's division of a Radio Nature League contest to identify ten birdsongs that were duplicated on radio by Edward Avis, a birdsong expert who appeared regularly on Burgess' program.[23] The winner was to receive an autographed copy of a Burgess book, but to Robbins' lasting disappointment, "instead of sending three copies of the same thing, he sent two autographed copies of his book to my brothers, but he sent me a copy of *Reid's Field Guide*."

As a child growing up in Belmont, Massachusetts, Robbins enjoyed listening to Burgess' guest scientists and experts from the Smithsonian Institution, National Museum of Natural History, and the Boston Society of Natural Science. "I don't think the talks were over the heads of children," Robbins says. "Thornton Burgess was about the only one on the radio in those days who had a program for children. Kids were really interested in anything he brought up. He wasn't condescending. He was speaking as an adult giving information that was interesting to both adults and children. I never met him in person, which I regret."

Friendly and Accessible Style

Salem State University communications professor Peter Oehlkers says Burgess instinctively used the correct approach for radio media: "There are two secrets to radio success: One, it is about the hosts, so he became "Neighbor Burgess," and two, get audience participation, which is what the Radio Nature League did," says Oehlkers, who maintains the Thornton W. Burgess Research League weblog. "You wouldn't think he was an engaging host because many of the scripts are dry, but I guess he had a very appealing direct address to the audience, a kind of informality."

A genial style came naturally to the veteran journalist/public speaker, who was long accustomed, from thousands of interviews and hundreds of lectures, to putting people at ease. He was "Neighbor Burgess," just as Fred Rogers was "Mister Rogers" of the 1950s children's television program. The concept came, Burgess said, from a letter he received from an elderly couple who lived on an isolated Midwest farm. "Once a week I was a good neighbor who dropped in and sat with them beside the fire, telling them of things in which they had been interested all their lives. After that, when I was at the microphone I often kept before me a mental picture of the dear old couple to whom I was a neighbor. People who wouldn't dream of reporting to an institution an unusual experience or observation would write to 'Neighbor Burgess' at considerable length. Thus I accumulated a mass of interesting and valuable material, some of which I turned over to museums or individuals who could make good use of it."[24]

The Living and the Dead

The WBZ staff was occasionally alarmed by the contents of the daily mail, for Burgess' radio listeners sent him all manner of life forms for identification, from large spiders and beetles to a dead iguana. He was asked to identify a live duck with long, pink legs, later determined to be a displaced South American tree duck. One listener sent a deceased flea with a request for Burgess to identify it as a dog, cat, or human flea. A lively garter snake mailed to the radio station earned the nickname "Houdini" by repeatedly escaping from a tightly secured box. Young Frances Meigs was in the studio the day the snake was first discovered missing, and recalled that a panicked Gordon Swan leapt out of the room while her grandfather went looking for it.

Burgess also received a dead moth with the following message from the U.S. Fisheries research vessel *Albatross II*, then working on Georges Bank:

> Dear Mr. Burgess,
>
> Enclosed is a moth in paper. Haven't the slightest idea what he is, but last night at about 10 PM June 28, Saturday, a swarm came aboard. We are 180 miles SE of Boston Light ship, quite a way out from Cape Cod. We passed through a cloud of them Wed. night midnight, 8th June about 20 miles off Cape Cod...Saw a story in paper about hornets six miles off Cape Cod. Guess this has that beat. Thought you would be interested in the moths being way out here, Wind has been SW, strong fog. Will have the pleasure of listening to you out here the rest of the summer... wishing you luck.
>
> Harry R. Chutham
>
> P.S. Had a moth saved here to send you but I guess he escaped. The whole crew, skipper and all will testify to the swarm of moths aboard here.[25]

"Like A Row of Little Soldiers"

It is testimony to Burgess' status as a radio host that people were willing to purchase a set to listen to his program — some even wrote to apologize for not getting one sooner. The letter of Ivan A. Baylry, a migratory bird warden in North Sydney, Nova Scotia, proves that Burgess' program was taken seriously, beyond entertainment, as a supportive agency for wildlife interests:

> I have thought it might interest you to hear of two islands locally called Bird Islands near Sydney. A lighthouse is on the outside island. I visited these islands last June and counted twenty two species of birds there. For ages it has

been a breeding place for two kinds of cormorants, two kinds of Terns, puffins, murres, razorbills, Black Guillemots, Leitches Petrel, and several other species. The Skags, the Puffins and Auks can be seen sitting up like a row of little soldiers along the edges of the cliff all through the summer. The tops of the islands are covered with fine turf, and the petrels and puffins burrow in this for their nests, while the terns nest on top...These are wonderful little islands, the two forming a group over a mile long.

I have arranged with the Canadian National Parks Branch to have these set aside as a Bird Sanctuary. The lightkeep, Thomas Stephenson, a returned soldier with his wife, baby and an assistant, are the only inhabitants living on the outside island. I have sworn him in for a special migratory bird warden for these islands, he using his own gasoline boat for patrol work when necessary. I proposed to the Department a salary of $100 to be added to his regular lightkeeper salary, but you know what so often happens to bird-protection funds. Our funds have run short, and it looks as if this additional expenditure cannot be made.

It has occurred to me that some of the interested bird lovers of the Radio Nature League might like to aid in keeping this light keeper for the protection of these valuable breeding islands.[26]

Thornton W. Burgess and Austin H. Clark: Kindred Spirits

Although the Radio Nature League was possibly the first nature program for children on radio, Burgess was not the only one interested in promoting conservation and natural science on the air. Other science- or nature-based programs were being broadcast in New York by the Museum of Natural History and the New York Aquarium, and in Washington, D.C. by the Smithsonian Institution. Within six months of initiating his program, Burgess met a kindred spirit who would give his Radio Nature League free access to the nation's top scientists.

Austin Hobart Clark was a Smithsonian Institution biologist whose early experience and fascination with radio's potential to popularize science matched Burgess'.[27] In 1923, the marine science curator, also an acclaimed lepidopterist, had been intrigued by his first appearance on station WRC in Washington, D.C. and readily agreed to schedule experts from various departments for more Smithsonian Radio Talks. Unlike the Radio Nature League's informal, sociable format, these programs were similar to an academic science lecture, but also found an interested audience.

When Clark invited Burgess to deliver a fifteen-minute radio talk for a new Smithsonian series, he was unaware of the writer's considerable experience. Accustomed to cajoling resistant senior scientists to step up to a microphone, Clark took a persuasive approach in his first letter to Burgess: "Everyone at all interested in nature knows your work — all my five children are enthusiastic about it — and everyone professionally occupied with natural history knows how accurate all your statements are."[28]

Burgess' prompt acceptance letter informed Clark that he was a seasoned radio host who had been giving weekly nature talks for the past seven months and was committed to exploring the new medium: "I am convinced that in radio lies the most effective means of saving our vanishing wild life and the natural beauty in America, and I am gladly giving much time and effort to this end." It was the beginning of an intense, energized dialogue between two radio pioneers eager to tap into each other's professional expertise, undoubtedly glad for the company on an untraveled road. Clark responded to Burgess:

> Your cordial letter of 27th May contained much of the greatest interest to me. The radio offers a wonderful opportunity for getting the real facts of science to the mass of the people, especially the somewhat numerous class who read only with difficulty and thus never get beyond the newspaper headlines. We have in the radio therefore a most useful instrumentality for correcting various popular misconceptions some of which are distinctly harmful.[29]

Burgess readily replied:

> Your letter and the four talks arrived this afternoon. Of course the letter was read immediately and I have already held up productive work long enough to read the talk "What Other Peoples Eat." I assure you there is no possible chance that these talks will bore me. ... As a matter of fact, if it can be arranged without too much inconvenience to you, I shall ask you to give one of these talks at some weekly meeting of the Radio Nature League. You could broadcast from Boston...I am sending you herewith two or three of my own talks...I believe that we can work together splendidly.[30]

"Austin Clark and Thornton Burgess were early adopters of radio," says Smithsonian researcher Marcel LaFollette, whose 2008 book *Science on the Air* examines the unique role of early radio and television technology in popularizing science. "They were experimenting with it. The first people who went on the air didn't know how loud to speak." LaFollette's research utilized a twenty-year correspondence, archived at the Smithsonian and the National Museum of Natural History, that illuminates Burgess's and Clark's collaboration and friendship.

"The thing I found intriguing was their grasp of a new communication technology," she commented in a 2011 telephone interview. "They turned out to be kindred souls, sharing similar political values, a fascination with natural history, and the enthusiasm of adventurers in unexplored territory. They were also experimenting with content, with what the audience would like to hear. Burgess had this extraordinary intuition for what people were going to be interested in."

Mutual Interest in Radio

In an almost daily exchange of letters, the writer and the biologist shared experiences, data, literature, opinions, and aggravations. Burgess believed a radio presentation required more than information. "The radio audience is not as other audiences," he told Clark. "To reach it properly you have to yourself get out on the air, just the same as from the platform you must put your personality out over the footlights."[31]

In an undated article for *Popular Radio* magazine, Burgess referenced a skeptical opinion, no doubt Clark's, of radio audiences: "A scientist of long experience on the lecture platform, but at that time none before the microphone, to whom I had outlined my plan for a national radio organization...replied, 'I have no faith in an invisible audience.'"[32] Burgess, on the other hand, said he had more confidence in that audience than the live ones he spoke before so frequently because a radio audience was exclusively focused on his words and ideas. He explained to Clark why his programs covered so many topics, unlike Clark's thematic programming: "When you are talking to people of all classes and all tastes, a hodgepodge is necessary... and as much personality is needed as there is on the stage, it is not sufficient to have first class material. There must be personality with that material."[33]

Within weeks, the two men had exchanged copies of their radio scripts, proposed expanding the Radio Nature League to Washington, D.C., made plans for Clark to give a talk in Boston, discussed problems with speakers and "semi-ignorant sentimentalists," and extended warm invitations to visit each other, as Clark would be vacationing with his family in Manchester, Massachusetts, during the summer. When Clark sent a copy of his talk on "Giants of the Animal World," Burgess was not hesitant in questioning the Smithsonian curator about the twenty-three-foot length Clark attributed to a monitor lizard: "Is this correct or is it a slip of the typewriter? I had always supposed that somewhere between four and five feet was the maximum length of lizards of all kinds."[34] Several days later Clark responded: "The huge monitor I mentioned is Varanus komodoensis (see Ouwens, Bull. Jardin bot. Buitenzorg, Java, ser. 2, vol. 6, 1912, p.1, pls. 1-3), which is known to reach seven meters and is said to grow much larger."[35]

The directness of Burgess' question and the technicality of Clark's answer make it clear they understood each other well. Clark offered Burgess extraordinary access to scientific resources and contacts by virtue of his connections at Harvard University, the Smithsonian Institution, the National Museum of Natural History, the Museum of Comparative Zoology at Harvard, and other institutions. He provided the writer with research books and a list of prominent scientists to use as Radio Nature League speakers, including Dr. Glover M. Allen, his Harvard roommate.

Burgess, on the other hand, had a decade of experience in popularizing natural science through books, newspaper and magazine articles, and lectures. He offered a proven, successful model for accomplishing what Clark envisioned: bringing science and the public together via radio. Clark was impressed with Burgess' ability to motivate a radio audience to collect specimens and field data for research, unquestionable proof of radio's potential benefit to science. The Smithsonian curator told wildlife biologist and conservationist John C. Phillips: "The maintenance of the prestige of science before the general public, which means the supervision by competent men of the channels of popularization, is one of the most important problems today. … Burgess who, because of his great popularity, can do more than all of us together to keep popular science within safe bounds."[36]

As collaborators, Clark and Burgess had personal and intellectual compatibility that enabled them to pool diverse resources, apparently unhampered by competition or rivalry, in order to explore a common interest. Burgess' broader objective in radio was to change through education the way people perceived nature and science and, therefore, the way they acted. Clark's aim was to educate the public in order to reinforce the authority of science and its institutions, without primary regard for the public's interests and concerns.[37] Clark suggested Burgess write an article on "The Radio as an Adjunct to Ornithology" for *The Auk*, the American Ornithologists' Union's journal, and Burgess urged Clark to write a scientific book on caterpillars. ("I have fifty caterpillars to one moth," he said, referring to his Radio Nature League correspondence.) From her analysis of the Clark-Burgess correspondence, Marcel LaFollette observed:

> Burgess embraced more cosmopolitan, democratic, and pragmatic attitudes towards popularization. He assumed the public was eager to learn about science and nature and that radio could assist that quest for understanding, and he was not adverse to employing entertainment to enliven his presentations. He had considerable respect for scientists, but did not regard them as the sole proprietors of scientific knowledge. Although Burgess exploited radio to promote his books and to reach out to faithful readers, he also had a passionate commitment in using broadcasting to encourage environmental conservation, at a time when those concerns were emerging in the public consciousness.[38]

"Almost Like an Encyclopedia"

Clark offered what Burgess most prized: pristine scientific information. "He used Austin Clark almost like an encyclopedia," LaFollette commented. "Listeners would write in to him with dead bugs or seashells, and he would send them to Clark who would answer their questions or get other scientists at the Museum of Natural History or the Smithsonian." The following letters provide insight into the dynamics of the friendship between the children's author and the scientist:

> Dear Mr. Clark:
>
> The following has me somewhat puzzled. A Mrs. Prescott of Manchester, NH, writes: "Two years ago my husband put the trunk of a birch tree in the shed. Last fall a fungus appeared in several places, each a little larger than a hen's egg. Two weeks ago…we found them all perforated where the moths had emerged. We are curious to know what kind they were. They were a bit larger than the destructive house moth, a little darker, and the wings seemed to be somewhat checked."
>
> Does this mean anything to you? … I am also enclosing a newspaper clipping which was sent to me. Can you name the fish?[39]

Dear Mr. Burgess,

The fish referred to in the clipping is evidently the stone-roller or black sucker (Hypentelium nigricans), also known as the hammer-head sucker on account of its broad head. ... The moth to which you refer is undoubtedly the common fungus moth, for which Mr. Carl Heinrich, of the Bureau of Entomology, tells me the name is Tinea rileyi. ... I am continually hoping that you will stroll down this way so that we may have some more discussions.[40]

Dear Mr. Burgess,

The little bug just received this morning is the chrysomelid beetle Chirida guttata. It is very pretty when alive, but soon fades after death. The small coiled object is a seed pod of Medicago hispida, the toothed medico, a leguminous plant closely related to alfalfa. The plants of this genus have the pods coiled in a more or less tight spiral, which gives them a curious appearance. The species was determined for me by Mr. Ellsworth P. Killip of the National Herbarium.[41]

Dear Mr. Clark,

Thank you for your good letter. ... The yellow caterpillar I thought you might be familiar with, because it was so rather distinctive, being all hairy and all yellow, with simply two tufts at the forward end. ... Within the last ten days I have had three specimens of the Monkey slug, or Hag-moth larva, brought to me. One was from a plum tree, one from a rose-bush and one from an apple-tree. They were entirely new to me and cannot be called common around this section...Certainly they are the most curious looking creatures I have ever seen...I always feel a little bit guilty troubling you with them, but know your appreciation of the fact that it is all in a good cause in the dissemination of knowledge and so continue to inflict them on you.[42]

DR. WILLIAM MAXON, CURATOR OF PLANTS
U.S. NATIONAL MUSEUM

Dear Maxon,

The inquiries enclosed were sent to me by Thornton W. Burgess, 61 Washington Rd., Springfield, Mass. Myxomycetes are too much for me, and I wrote him that I had turned these over to you. Could you help him out?[43]

Dear Mr. Clark,

Under separate cover I am sending you a little box containing a wasp and a chrysalis, which I should like to have identified. The nearest thing that I can find to the wasp is in the *Field Book of Insects* by Lutz, labeled Chlorion ichneumonea. However, as Lutz does not give enough of a description I am not sure. I am simply guessing from the plate...I am also sending along a beetle whose identity puzzles me. Is it male or female, and what is it? Please return these specimens at your convenience.[44]

Dear Mr. Burgess:

The material just received consists of the following:

Chrysalis of Papilio Troilus.

The beetle is Xyloryctes satyrus (female); the (male) has a conspicuous horn just above the head. … You were correct in identifying the wasp as Ammobia (Chlorion) ichneumonea…There is an excellent account of its activities in *Wasp Studies Afield* by Phil Rau and Nellie Rau, Princeton University Press, 1918, p. 193.[45]

Dear Mr. Expert:

A woman has sent me the enclosed photograph sent her by her son who is a radio operator on a ship plying between Texas and the Atlantic Seaboard cities. This fish flew on the deck. It was white, according to the letter. The operator thought it was unusual because of the four wings…I have a picture of one drawn by Helen Tee-Van. This is the Cypselurus furcatus. This one, however, has a blue back.[46]

Dear Mr. Burgess,

The picture seems to represent Cypselurus furcatus, which is generally common in all warm seas and on our eastern coast extends as far north as Cape Cod. It is a small fish, growing to a length of 6 inches. In color they are mostly silvery white, with the back shading into a more or less deep blue; I could very well imagine they could be described as white, especially little ones.[47]

Dear Mr. Burgess,

The object referred to in yours of 20th March has just arrived. It is the hinder portion of the skull of a cat. Skulls are queer things. With very little mutilation a skull may become a most deceptive thing…I'll keep you posted on everything concerning my radio series.[48]

Thanks to Austin Clark, information about the identity of plants, length of lizards, natural range of flying fish, and habits of squeaking butterflies were Burgess' for the asking. He was always apologetic for the imposition and grateful for Clark's help with time-consuming questions, well aware of the beneficial effect on his all-important credibility as a nature writer and naturalist. [Burgess once refused to submit an article until he could authoritatively state the color of a heron's eyes, and for lack of first-hand information he perseverated for several years about whether or not a sliding otter's front legs were positioned forward or backward. The matter was finally settled by an old Michigan trapper who told Burgess' friend, biologist Vernon Bailey, that he had personally witnessed an otter sliding with paws "always back."]

Common Interest in Science

Early twentieth century scientists were usually reluctant to accept the non-specialist who had experience without education and training, LaFollette says, but Burgess' lack of academic credentials and affiliations did not thwart his exploration of radio technology and nature with Clark. She attributes this in part to Burgess' compulsive curiosity about the natural world, which permeates his letters to Clark: "[It] is no different than the kind of thing you read in the correspondence of scientists at the time. He is an amateur, he is not trained as a scientist, but he had many of the same traits, the same reverence, the same love of going deeper, for finding evidence, and for accuracy. It was a type of curiosity that was very familiar to the biologists like Clark and natural historians with whom he was corresponding. It was the same kind of thing that would lead the Harvard Biologist E. O. Wilson, when he is walking along, to lean down and look at an ant. The same [curiosity] we think of as infusing the work of the great scientists is the kind of thing you see in Burgess' letters."[49]

In fact, LaFollette suggests that Burgess' lack of academic credentials may have contributed to the strength of his relationship with Clark. who had a biology degree from Harvard University, but no advanced degrees like many of his colleagues, something he was sensitive about. "Maybe one reason they were kindred spirits was that they both perceived themselves as outsiders," she remarked.

Given their rapport, it is easy to envision an incident Burgess shared with his Radio Nature League audience. He and Clark were driving together by car when Clark spotted a white, mold-like patch on an alder tree, and they stopped to inspect it. The lepidopterist showed Burgess that the patch was comprised of hundreds of aphids feeding on tree sap. Then he took out a knife and exposed a small gray caterpillar beneath the aphids, the only known predatory caterpillar, he said, which was feasting on the insects feasting on the sap. "Think of all that was happening on that alder close by the roadside," Burgess later told his radio audience. "Yet thousands of people passed this summer without the least idea that anything interesting or unusual or wonderful was going on almost within arms' reach as they passed. It's a wonderful world if we have eyes that see."[50]

William L. Finley and Lower Klamath Lake

Although much of the Radio Nature League program concerned traits, identification, and care of wildlife, Burgess did not avoid the political aspects of conservation. On January 27, 1926, he invited his friend, wildlife photographer William Lovell Finley, then State Game Commissioner of Oregon, to appear on the program to talk about the ecological damage caused by the U.S. Department of the Interior's drainage of Lower Klamath Lake. The 85,000-acre wetland area had been an important breeding ground for resident birds and wildlife and a sheltering ground for migratory birds until it was drained to create irrigation for local agriculture. After Finley's talk, Burgess suggested concerned radio listeners sign and send to him a petition opposing the action, which he promised to forward to the Secretary of the Interior. In a letter to Bowdoin College professor Dr. Alfred Gross, he described the response of Radio Nature League members:

> Any time that I can aid you in any of your investigations by asking for information on the air, please do not hesitate to write me. The radio audience is very responsive. A week ago Finley was here and I had him tell his Klamath Lake story on the air. I followed it by the statement that I was going to send a petition to the Secretary of the Interior, asking him to turn the water back into Klamath Lake. I invited those who were listening in, who felt that this was the thing to do, to send in their names to be added to that petition. They have poured in so fast I have not had a chance to count them. I know that I already have between two and three thousands, if not more.[51]

Months later he told Austin Clark he was still receiving and forwarding petitions for Klamath Lake reclamation, including one from a woman with one thousand names on it. [Two years later, in 1928, President Calvin Coolidge authorized reflooding a portion of the wetlands and established the presently named Tule Lake National Wildlife Refuge.][52]

Burgess and Finley knew each other professionally and personally before the conservationist's appearance on the Radio Nature League. It is most likely they met in the late 1910s when Finley was a featured speaker at the Massachusetts Audubon Society's Tremont Temple lecture series in Boston or when Burgess was publicizing the *People's Home Journal's* bird sanctuary program. They were both listed on the masthead of the January 1924 issue of *Nature Magazine*, which included Burgess' article "Nature Study Key to Knowledge" and listed Finley as "Western Field Representative."

In 1924, Burgess and Finley were collaborating on a children's book that would combine Finley's wildlife photography with Burgess' written text. The plot involved a boy named Laurie who visits southern California, learns about indigenous Western wildlife, and helps prevent a condor egg theft. The following letter from Finley to Burgess outlined their plan:

> The idea of a condor series could be worked out much as we did it, making a number of different trips into the mountains, as both the egg and the young bird would be of considerable value from a collector's standpoint. The interest in the story, as you suggested, would carry in fine shape if you could bring in some collector who was trying to find the condors' home. Eagle nests are generally robbed in that part of the country. We had such an experience when we were in southern California in 1921–22.[53]

Condor photographs were readily available, since Finley and his partner Herman Bohlman had made one of the most complete photographic records known of the species. In his letter, Finley informed Burgess that photographs would also be available of the Pacific horned owl, roadrunner, Nutall's woodpecker, black phoebe, brewer blackbird, least vireo, water ouzel, striped skunk, bobcat, and jack rabbit. Author Worth Mathewson mentions in his biography *William L. Finley, Pioneer Wildlife Photographer* that Finley told a newspaper reporter in the early 1920s that he would "soon write a book on the California condor."[54] However, Oregon State University reports that the William L. Finley archival collection contains no evidence that the collaboration with Thornton Burgess was ever published.

Burgess regularly used Finley's photographs in his Radio Nature League newsletters. He facilitated the introduction of his friend Dr. Alfred Gross to Finley, who was interested in making a trip to Barro Colorado, a Panamanian wildlife refuge Gross had visited several times. Over the years Burgess kept in touch with Finley and his wife Irene, also a noted photographer. In 1946, he received a letter from her saying, "Since he suffered a shock six years ago, Bill has lost memory." Burgess had noted in his journal: "So sorry."[55]

Billboards, Litter, and Mosquitoes

In the mid-1920s, Burgess used his radio program to endorse Maine's effort to eliminate roadside billboard advertising, predicting, "Someday these huge signs are going to go everywhere. A beautiful view is a public possession," he told his listening audience. "It is intangible, but nonetheless real, personal property of everyone who passes that way...The right of the public in a beautiful view is just as real as its right in a highway."[56]

Burgess' awareness of the issue would have been heightened by frequent long-distance road trips he and his wife Fannie made to New Brunswick and Nova Scotia. On these Canadian trips and meandering five-hundred-mile jaunts around New England to visit friends and family, Burgess saw the extent and impact of roadside littering and lectured his listeners on it:

> And you will remember that if you are motoring not to scatter papers and luncheon debris around eating places or by the roadside. Sometimes when I see the condition in which erstwhile beautiful spots are left by thoughtless picnickers, I am tempted to urge all manufacturers of automobiles to fit out each machine with a wastebasket and garbage pail.[57]

When Mrs. F. A. Lusk of Avon, Connecticut, wrote him to decry the stripping of mountain laurel from roadsides, Burgess wholeheartedly agreed. "The laurel is a slow-growing shrub that may take three years to regenerate broken branches," he told radio listeners. "These exquisite blossoms are not for home decoration. They fade and fall too quickly. Their beauty is in the natural environment where the Creator meant them to be. Who breaks the laurel from the roadside, cheats himself and robs his fellow man. It is just thoughtlessness."

Burgess spoke for protection of other wildflowers too: "The beautiful lady slippers! Pink, white, yellow, and variegated. We are losing them. You know they are orchids. A big bunch of lady slippers is not beautiful. This flower is beautiful only when it stands singly, stands alone, springing from between its two broad leaves. Then it is exquisite."

In 1926, Burgess launched a radio campaign to enhance roadside beauty by eliminating tent caterpillar nests. Appealing to his audience, particularly Boy Scouts and Girl Scouts, to clear their communities of the leaf-eating larvae, he said:

"Remember that early in the morning, late in the afternoon, or on a cold dull day is the time to catch these tent caterpillars in their nests and destroy them. Do this and preserve the beauty of our roadsides." As he had with the Green Meadow Club's bird sanctuary program, Burgess provided basic information, kept records of participants, and announced the most successful individuals and organizations. The Massachusetts Department of Agriculture offered prizes for this campaign in 1926 and 1927. More than one million caterpillar masses were reportedly destroyed. The next year eager participants complained there were not enough nests to remove. Judged a success, the campaign was ended.[58]

"Of all our outdoor friends, none are more often abused and neglected than our neighbors, the trees," Burgess told his radio listeners. At a time when Japanese beetles, American chestnut blight, and general destruction by road crews installing overhead lines and wires were taking a toll on trees, Burgess often invited his friend, Connecticut tree surgeon Philip Hansling, to appear on the Radio Nature League. During a 1927 radio program, Hansling discussed historic trees, including an ancient sycamore that measured thirty-two feet in circumference in 1869 and a few surviving linden trees planted in 1745 by Col. George Watson in Plymouth, Massachusetts. Hansling also recounted finding embedded in his leafy patients hand-molded bullets, eight-inch handmade spikes, and two teeth, whether human or otherwise he did not specify.

In 1925, Burgess warned his Radio Nature League listeners about mosquitoes, informing them that a malarial mosquito has spotted wings and that the female will lay 200 to 400 eggs on stagnant water. "Never allow water to stand if you can help it," he said. "Whenever you find old cans with even a little water in them, promptly turn them bottomside up. Even rainfilled hollows of trees are breeding places."[59]

A Unique Organization

The Radio Nature League gained more than 10,000 official members within five months and had 40,000 enrolled members within two years. "Disembodied Voice Leads Multitude, Thornton W. Burgess Directs Army of Conservationists in Radio Nature League" announced the headline of a 1928 *Hartford Courant* article that heralded Burgess' brainchild as "one of the most unique organizations in the country" and "one of radio's most popular features":

> The idea of the Radio Nature League was conceived by Thornton W. Burgess, naturalist and writer. His thesis was that the majority of people are interested in some form of natural history and that they welcome an opportunity for the exchange of observations and opinions...His idea was to form an organization bound together by a common interest or specially for the observation of the vanishing wildlife and of the natural beauty spots of America.[60]

Despite Burgess' popularity, radio was increasingly becoming a marketplace for paid advertising. His lack of a permanent commercial sponsor made it difficult for a station to justify running his program, and disagreements between Burgess and WBZ management about scheduling and/or sponsorship periodically resulted in his resignation or threat of resignation. In February 8, 1935, he shared good news with Austin Clark: "For something over a year I have been back [on the air], hoping I might find a sponsor for only thus could I afford the help needed to handle the correspondence and to revive the Radio Nature League to make it a factor in conservation. I had just about decided that I would have to give up the talks again when I found a sponsor in Brewer & Company, Incorporated of Worcester, manufacturing chemists...We started the programs February 2 and are on twice a week, 8:30 Wednesday evenings and 7:30 Saturday evening, fifteen minutes each. It is a try-out for twenty-five programs over WBZ and if successful we will go on a network...So now watch out! You are likely to be pestered with questions as of old for I find the thirst for information as keen as ever."[61]

The Radio Nature League ran consistently for six years, from January 1925 to August 1930, and sporadically with different names and formats until July 4, 1939. His last radio program, the Good Neighbors Club, was sponsored for six months by the Massachusetts Society for the Prevention of Cruelty to Animals on WSPR. With an official record of 50,000 members and potentially unknown thousands more listeners, the size of his audience was never an issue. In an October 1928 article, the *Hartford Courant* reported that schools were enrolling entire student bodies or science classes: "The weekly talks have been used in schools throughout New England in their nature study work. The plan of delegating one student to listen on the night of the broadcast and report to the class the next day has been successfully worked out in many schools."[62]

Notably effective as an educational tool, Thornton Burgess' Radio Nature League was impressive for other accomplishments, as the *Hartford Courant* cited: "The organization is universally recognized as a potent force in the work of conservation... Many thousands of bird houses have been put up during the last four years solely through the efforts of the Radio Nature League, and an unquenchable interest in our feathered friends has rewarded the tireless work of the League's founder. Thousands of people who had never thought of doing such a thing before, now maintain winter feeding stations for the birds...In innumerable cases the influence of the League has been exerted with splendid results for the protection of our disappearing wild flowers. Still more concrete work has been done in the form of annual campaigns against the destructive Tent caterpillar. In a three-week campaign this last spring over 370,000 egg-masses of these Tent caterpillars were collected and burned by children under 16 years of age. Roadsides which for years had been an eyesore were this year almost entirely free from this nefarious scourge."[63]

Burgess received no pay for his years of work with the Radio Nature League, and he never fought for a salary. "I loved reading over his radio scripts," remarked Thornton W. Burgess Society archivist Bethany Rutledge. "He wasn't just reading stories, he was trying to spread information, whether it was about endangered species, invasive plants, migratory birds, or tree health. He had an incredible passion for the New England countryside, for wilderness, for habitat, for the delicate interrelations between many species."

Chapter 12

Dr. Alfred O. Gross, Labrador, and the Heath Hen Survey

First collaborators, then quickly friends, Thornton Burgess' relationship with Dr. Alfred Otto Gross was another example of his ability as an uncredentialed amateur to establish a bond with a prominent scientist. On the strength of their amiable connection and mutual interest in natural science and photography, Gross invited Burgess to join him in field research in Panama, Labrador, Maine and Massachusetts. Together they attended the historic 1931 Matamek Environmental Conference on Biological Cycles in Labrador, Gross as a speaker, Burgess as a guest reveling in the company of elite natural scientists from North America and Europe. Their most important work together was Dr. Gross's population census and photographic record of the heath hen, a sub-species of the prairie chicken, as it approached and reached extinction. According to Mark Madison, chief historian for the U.S. Fish and Wildlife Service, theirs is the only known record of an ornithological extinction observed in the wild down to the last individual member.

"I remember Thornton Burgess as a popular figure, admired for his accomplishments in educating young people about nature and conservation, and I remember him as a person, warm-hearted, entertaining and outgoing. And just as important, I remember him with everlasting gratitude for introducing me early in life to the natural world that has given me so much satisfaction ever since."[1]

Dr. Olin Sewall Pettingill, Jr.,
ornithologist, 1983

"Those powers of observation that come from time in the field are incomparable skills. One great tragedy in the ecological field is that much of what we get today is more theoretical. The kind of work Gross and Burgess did isn't being collected today. We've excised subjectivity from the scientists. Back in Burgess' day there was a demand for objectivity, but there was acknowledgement of the fascination of nature."

Tom Chase,
Massachusetts director of conservation strategies,
The Nature Conservancy, 2012

A True Friend

In childhood, when he and his mother were sustained by a network of family and friends, Thornton Burgess learned the importance of relationships. As a congenial, socially inclined adult, he kept countless numbers of people in his professional, personal, and social circles, but among them was one specially cherished friend: Dr. Alfred Otto Gross.

Born in Illinois in 1883, the ninth child of German immigrant parents, Alfred Gross was academically and professionally successful. He attended the University of Illinois and Harvard University, taught biology for forty years at Bowdoin College in Brunswick, Maine, was director of Bowdoin's Fort Kent Ornithological Research Station, and wrote two hundred sixty-five scientific books and articles.[2]

Gross and Burgess shared an uncomplicated devotion to natural science. After Burgess offered to use his Radio Nature League to help Gross obtain bird specimens, they became great personal friends who visited each other's homes, attended family weddings and professional events together, and traveled as a foursome with their wives. The teasing barbs that crop up in their correspondence and Burgess' journals suggest they relished a good joke, especially at the other's expense. "Both men thoroughly enjoyed each other's company," remarked Dr. Olin Pettingill, an ornithology student of Gross' at Bowdoin. "I rarely saw them together without hearing their mutual banter."[3] Just six months before Burgess died in 1965, Gross wrote an encouraging, affectionate letter to his old friend, then in a nursing home:

Dear Thornton,

Tomorrow is your birthday and I wish to congratulate you in reaching the 91st landmark in your illustrious life. What a satisfaction it must be to have accomplished so much for so many. You have a host of friends all over the world that wish you well in still more years to come.

Edna and I think of you so very often and wish that we could drop in to see you. We are so happy that you have received the Bradford Washburn award from the Museum of Science in Boston. It is just another of the many honors that you have received.

Edna is well and going strong. She has been having a lot of fun trying all sorts of receipts [*sic*] in the kitchen and trying them out with me as the guinea pig. The results are good, for I have gone from 120 to 134 pounds and prospects of more.

Edna and I send you our love,

Alfred[4]

Common Interest in Research

According to archival correspondence at Bowdoin College, the two men met in New York in late 1924, probably at a professional meeting they both attended. When Burgess learned that the biology professor needed specimens for a study of ruffed grouse parasites and diseases for the Massachusetts Fish and Game Protection Association, he sent Gross the first of many birds, and shortly received the following appreciative thank you note:

I received your letter and the fine specimen of Ruffed Grouse. The bird was injured by the plunge into the wires mentioned in your letter but otherwise was a perfectly normal bird. It is not uncommon for birds to be killed by such plunges into wires when frightened because the wires are not visible to the birds. But a plunge into a building is another matter and most of all such birds examined have been badly diseased. It was a great pleasure to meet you in New York and to know what Thornton Burgess looks like. My three kiddies always read your *aryicles* [sic] in the *Boston Hearld* [sic] and it was a real thrill to them when I came home and told them I saw the athur [sic] of those delightful stories. You have started a wonderful organization in your [Radio] Nature League and now that I know you it seems I hear of you at every turn.[5]

Later that year, Gross asked if Burgess would inform his radio listeners during hunting season about the need for grouse specimens shot by hunters or found dead.[6] Naturally Burgess was more than willing to help. This was exactly the sort of service he and Austin Clark hypothesized that radio could provide to scientific research. Beginning on October 14, 1925, and throughout that fall, Burgess regularly publicized Gross' request and received the following letters from the ornithologist:

My Dear Mr. Burgess,

I wish to tell you of the splendid response we are receiving from the announcements of the Ruffed Grouse Investigation over the radio. The number of specimens thus far received have greatly exceeded our expectations. Three birds came today marked "shipped as requested by Mr. Burgess." Letters received with other specimens indicate that your broadcasting has been the stimulus which prompted the sender to help us in this work. It is very evident that you are reaching many persons we would fail to get by other means of publicity.[7]

My Dear Mr. Burgess,

I received the two birds which you sent to me this week in very good condition…I have received 305 specimens of Ruffed Grouse this fall. … I regret that I am unable to give you a complete report at this time for it will be a matter of months before all of this work is complete…diseases constitute only a part of our work for we are taking advantage of this unusual mass of material to study the birds, especially the entire specimens from every angle. There are no less than six important diseases, but it is yet too early to predict which will be the most important. *Dispharynx*, the stomach worm, is undoubtedly very important in Southern New England (Mass. and Conn.)…Only one case of *Dispharynx* has come from Maine and that was from the southern part of the state, Dr. [Arthur A.] Allen [Gross' Cornell University colleague in the study] has found this parasite very common in New York and southward. What does this mean? Is it possible that the pheasant which is common in southern New England and New York where it has been introduced, is responsible? … I have sent several diseased specimens to Dr. E.E. Tyzzer of the Department of Pathology, Harvard Medical School, for determination but he does not wish any report on these birds made until he has had an opportunity to publish his material. I wish you would thank the many contributors for the excellent cooperation they are giving the Ruffed Grouse Investigation. Each contributor will receive a complete report of the investigation.[8]

Burgess also supported the study by offering a copy of Edward Howe Forbush's second volume on Massachusetts birds as a prize to the individual child and school that supplied the greatest number of grouse specimens. Some sources, including Burgess' autobiography, credit the Radio Nature League with contributing a total of two thousand grouse specimens to the study; however, given conflicting reports, it is likely the radio solicitations contributed *to* a total of two thousand specimens.[9] Regardless of the actual figure, Gross informed Burgess in 1926 that he had received many more birds than the previous year and gratefully acknowledged the impressive impact of Burgess' on-air appeals.

Constant exchanges of information between the writer and the biology professor continued through the years as both in their separate professions sought to piece together patterns and puzzles of the natural world. Burgess frequently ordered Gross' photographs to use in his syndicated work and lectures. In 1928, he ordered twenty-two wildlife pictures from Gross, sent a check for $110 for a previous order, and informed Gross he would be sending him a wood tick found on a woodcock: "Perhaps you may be able to identify this fellow and decide whether or not it is the same one that is found on young partridges. This one came from Huntington, Mass."[10]

Within a few years, they dispensed with "Dr. Gross" and "Mr. Burgess" and informally addressed each other by surnames or first names as they chatted about family activities, workloads, travels, projects, and scientific matters of mutual interest.

One issue Burgess discussed regularly with both Alfred Gross and Austin Clark was the appropriate attitude to take toward owls and hawks. Should they be considered noxious predators that took domestic fowl from farmers or beneficial predators that helped control the rodent population? He was clearly concerned about providing his readers and radio listeners with accurate, authoritative information rather than baseless opinion. He asked his radio audience to collect field information on snowy owls in particular, in order to provide scientists with data to interpret. By inviting his radio audience to participate in the debate about hawks, owls, and other predatory birds, he helped educate his tens of thousands of listeners about the function of nature as well as the methodology used by scientists and regulatory officials.

Barro Colorado, 1927

In September 1927, Burgess joined Gross for three weeks of the professor's two-month sabbatical to study life histories and behaviors of tropical wildlife at the Barro Colorado Station in the Panama Canal Zone.[11] It was one of three trips Gross made to the research facility. Approximately five miles long and four and a half miles wide, the island was artificially created when the Panama Canal was flooded, resulting in an isolated habitat for hundreds of species of trees, birds, and mammals. He and Burgess traveled there with family members who stayed in an off-island hotel, except for Gross' son Bill who joined them on Barro Colorado. Burgess described the tropical experience in several Radio Nature League newsletters:

> Recently it was my good fortune to spend some three weeks in the heart of primeval jungle in Panama for the observation of tropical wild life. To one coming directly from the North the complete change is at first somewhat overpowering. Little is familiar with the exception of a few migrants among the birds. For two or three days king birds, known in some places as bee martins, were with us. We saw the yellow or summer warbler, the alder flycatcher, the bank swallow and the night hawk en route for points still farther south. But with the passing of these, little remained of the familiar birds of the north. As for the animals, the deer and a form of red squirrel were all we saw to remind us of familiar four-footed folk of the green forest.[12]

> One of the most interesting birds to come under my observation was the motmot. Possibly some of you who have visited museums have seen mounted specimens...It is the only bird of my acquaintance which barbers itself, if I may use that expression. In other words, it deliberately trims its own tail, presumably to give an artistic effect...The bird is an exquisite creature, in size, shape, and in movements reminding me somewhat of our own cuckoo. However, instead of being somberly colored like the cuckoos, this bird is very richly dressed. The tail is of unusual length, bluish green in color. The middle pair of feathers are two

inches longer than the other feathers of the tail...Of course you know that a feather structure consists of a midrib with a vane on either side, this vane being composed of what are called "barbs."[13]

On this trip, Burgess saw and photographed sloths, anteaters, king vultures, lizards, and exquisite butterflies. When he returned, he wrote to Austin Clark: "I had a wonderful time at Barro Colorado island. I was there three weeks with Dr. Gross of Bowdoin College. We had the place to ourselves. Your friend [entomologist Dr. James] Zetek was not in Panama when I arrived, but came shortly afterward and I had a chance to get fairly well acquainted with him. He sent his very best to you."[14]

Labrador Expedition, 1931

Four years later Burgess again accompanied Gross, along with his son Bill and a Bowdoin student, on a seven-week expedition from June 10 to July 31 to Labrador. One objective of the trip was to collect and record ornithological data on Labradorean habitat and wildlife, specifically the eider duck. A second purpose was to attend the week-long Matamek Conference on Biological Cycles at which Gross was a scheduled speaker.

Although Burgess' journals and autobiographical writing on the conference are regrettably sparse, he provides a lavish account of the field research that preceded it. The sheer quantity of detail in his description of the Labrador expedition causes it to stand out in thirty years of journaling. Regardless of regular downpours and spray-drenched boat rides, his enthusiasm for the barren wilderness, so foreign to the New England landscape he evoked in his children's writings, is unmistakable. He clearly savored eating camp meals outdoors and sleeping on a bed of moss, and seldom complained about maneuvering in cold, cramped bird blinds with cumbersome camera equipment. Burgess' journal entries depict nature from the same perspective his books and stories did, as the rightful domain of wildlife, not people, not even scientists. The following excerpts provide a glimpse of the first days of Burgess' expedition with Alfred Gross:[15]

6/10: Fair with stiff wind. Sailed at 10 o'clock on small steamer. Springyarn [a guide] with me. Met Mr. Amory [Copley Amory, Boston businessman and sponsor of the Matamek Conference]. Made ___ of Quebec from boat on filmo [a single lens Bell & Howell motion picture camera] and #1 on graflex [a still picture camera]. ... No stops...acquaintance with a Cook named Fred. A north shore merchant of St. Johns named Foley and an Indian guide and cook named Peter and had a beer with them in Foley's room and got the best bear and moose story I ever heard.

6/11: Day dawned with rain which did not last long...Met several interesting people including Mr. Endicott of Boston en route to Moisie River Club [exclusive sport fishing club] for salmon. Saw school of white [beluga] whales in distance, brandt scoters; black back and herring gulls. Have lost time all day...Ran into bank but got off ok. ... Saw Bay whale.

6/12: A wonderful day overhead and on sea. Saw Bay and 2 Blue whales. Pair of Eider ducks, loons and gulls nesting. Parted with Mr. Amory at Matamek at noon. Several interesting landings. On deck all day with much interesting coast. No one ill. Saw Aut ___ island in distance.

6/13: Up at 5 a.m. as we approached Magpie. Another good day…Reached Havre St. Pierre, largest town on North Shore, about 200 families, at 11:20 for 2 hour stop. Went around town, had lunch and ashore again to inspect church…Blais [trading agent] took me to call on the Bishop of the whole north coast. He and his curate could speak no English, but were most cordial and delightful…Blais acting as translator. Off at about 2 P.M. Passed a school of Blue Whales and saw them clearly in the distance. One startled me by blowing alongside. Fog in evening and cold.

6/14: Last night was one of the most wonderful sunset I have ever seen, like an extended forest fire. A beautiful day with brisk wind that kicked up a sea late in afternoon. Topped off at St. Mary's [now a bird sanctuary] to land young Osborne and a Ford car which was taken off in a small boat, very exciting. Then to Harrington for some two hours, a black place with snow in the rocky hills and not a single tree in sight…At sunset to Mutton Bay where was the most picturesque place of all. Fifteen boats were alongside at one time and seven dogs taken aboard.

6/15: To bed last night at 12:05. Up at 2:50 to see unusual scenery shortly after sailing at 2:30. A wonderful passage among islands. Sighted first iceberg at 3:30 and made photo at 3:40. Dr. [Gross] went back to bed and a little later we entered islands, the prettiest part so far. Had to try three times to get him [Gross] out. Ran in to St. Augustine where we lay to for a couple hours…Finally pulled out for hour run… then in to a small place where we lay with heavy seas and fog outside, which finally got Alfred and he returned to the sea the lobster he had eaten at noon.

6/17: Up early to come through the inside passage on way to Mutton Bay…very beautiful. Saw dwarf trees on islands. Passed through tickles as narrow as they could just get through…Reached Harrington…and were met by Eli Anderson and taken to his home on island…On top of the island he had found a Horned Larks' nest with four eggs and before the steamer set sail we had blind up. Steamer saw us on the rocks as they went out and gave us a salute…was shown nest of White Crowned Sparrow.

6/18: Up at 6 o'clock to find dawn of a perfect day. Photo of robin on nest in dwarf balsam. Went by boat some ten or 12 miles to Shag rock to visit colony of cormorants. Two or three eggs in each nest. A Black-back gull's nest in same rock with three eggs. Many Herring gulls nests on neighboring island, but none with more than one egg and most of them empty — robbed. Set blind on neighboring rock from where Shags were and waited two hours but they refused to return. Took a boat to a neighboring island and found many nests of Eider ducks under thick low balsams, one with five eggs. Made photos. On cliffs found three nest of guillemots and got photos of climbing to nests, and of eggs. A rough joyous passage home to find blind blown over, but lark on her nest. After supper rest blind and anchored it with rocks. A perfect day.

6/19: A beautiful day. Over to Harrington to find we could do no work on Horned Lark. Were shown two nests of White Crowned Sparrow, one of Savannah Sparrow and Am. Pippet. Set up pup tent at nest of White Crow and Alfred and I remained and ate can of pears and crackers, peanuts and orangeade at store. Spent afternoon in blind, and got about 5 ft of bird in tussock, but she was nervous and would not go on nest. Rowed back for dinner at 6. Planned to stay over another day. At Harrington visited Grenfell Mission. Miss Purdy in charge. Helped her find dogs and were shown all over hospital. Miss Purdy's greeting was "Hello, Peter Rabbit." Both Dr. and self look like tramps.

Sir Wilfred Thomason Grenfell, M.D.

Burgess was taken aback by the discovery that in this remote area two little boys, as well as a nurse, were familiar with his stories. Later, he met the English physician and missionary, Dr. Wilfred Thomason Grenfell, who operated the hospital they visited. Grenfell was known and revered for his medical facilities in Labrador and Newfoundland and for his support of local people in the isolated area.[16] One day in July Gross and Burgess were returning from their study of eider ducks when they learned that Dr. Grenfell's yacht, *Strathcona II*, was in the harbor they were approaching. It was their good fortune to be invited aboard during the four days the vessel remained fogbound there. Burgess recalled his first impression of Grenfell in *Now I Remember*:[17]

"A tall, commanding figure of a man, clad in rough clothing befitting place and season, his kindly weathered face alight with the warmth of the smiling greetings he extended to us…here immediately before us was the man who through many years had successfully fought the combined threat and strength of that pitiless coast and the mighty storm-lashed seas of the North Atlantic. Those clear, kindly, almost gentle eyes smiling into mine reflected the force of indomitable will and complete fearlessness that lay behind them."

Roughing It

In their weeks of field work, both Gross and Burgess took thousands of feet of still and movie film from a blind, often using a telephoto lens. Burgess wrote of making their way from location to location through breaking dawns, pending darkness, and pouring rain: "We got thoroughly wet but changed clothes and no harm done." They found birds everywhere on nests, near nests, in water, on rocks, on eggs. Even the air was "full of birds." Despite adverse weather and occasional disappointments, the time was exciting, productive, and deeply satisfying. Once, while they were observing wildlife on an island with a small pond, they discovered that wildlife was observing them:

6/24: Went over rocks on east side and saw an unbelievable sight of Murres. Eggs everywhere among rocks. Mr. O. [Fred Osborne, a lighthouse keeper] pulled lobster trap before leaving and gave us the two that were in it. We roasted them for lunch. Pitched pup tent for Murres and remained two hours in rain. Explored east end of island but found only one gull's nest with two eggs. Many empty nests. Mr. O brought supplies and tent about 8 o'clock. Pitched tent and then had supper. Just as we finished discovered we were being watched by King of the island, an Arctic fox whose burrow Dr. had found in the morning. Watched us for full half an hour. Had come over ice in winter.

6/25: A perfect night's rest in sleeping bags on moss beds, and in blind at 5:30 for male eiders...Mr. O says Lewis says Puffins shed bill every years. Can carry half a dozen small fish at once to feed young, Auk will carry 2 capen at once. Harp [seals?] will not pass over not 42 feet below surface.

Mishaps were inevitable. Burgess noted one rewarding day of photographing the nests of eider ducks, puffins and auks, and tersely concluded the journal entry without elaboration: "Lost film out of camera." He broke his glasses, ran out of film at critical times, and several times got lost in an open boat among small islands on the rocky coast. He rarely commented on physical discomfort during the expedition, and only after two weeks in the wilderness noted in his journal that he was "real tired from carrying cameras up and down hill and squatting in cramped positions in blind."

They had come to observe birds, and their patience and fortitude were generally rewarded. On July 2, Burgess triumphantly reported: "A weary tramp home, dead tired, but we have our eider stuff. Now for the Guillemots, Loons, and gulls." His list of the species and nests they photographed included "Robin, Lark, Pippet, White Crowned Sparrow, Savannah Sparrow, Shag, Eider, Guillemot, Puffin, Loon, Auk, Bib Gull, Herring Gull, Plover, and Murre."

Nowhere in his journals does Burgess appear as genuinely happy, carefree, and in his element as he does in his account of the Labrador expedition with Dr. Alfred Gross, two middle-aged wildlife paparazzi stalking native birds, clambering over a rough, desolate landscape with heavy camera equipment, jubilant at their successes, stoic and newly resolved in their failures. His journal entries show Burgess' deep pleasure at being in the outdoors, his tolerance for physical discomfort, ease in unfamiliar circumstances, and his keen enjoyment of knowledgeable conversation and diverse company.

1931 Matamek Conference on Biological Cycles[18]

It was past midnight when Gross and Burgess departed by boat for Matamek, their final destination. The conference was about three hundred miles from Quebec near the mouth of the Matamek River at a wilderness camp owned by Copley Amory. The influential Boston businessman had invited thirty environmental experts and

Participants of the 1931 Matamek Conference on Biological Cycles held in Labrador, Canada included Charles Elton, William Rowan, Harry Kyle, Ellsworth Huntington, Copley Amory, and Aldo Leopold. Thornton Burgess and Alfred Gross are respectively sixth and seventh from the left. *Courtesy of Bowdoin College Library Special Collections and Archives.*

guests to meet there to discuss cyclical population and disease patterns in certain birds and animals.

"[The Matamek Conference] was unique in that it brought together for a full week in that remote place on the edge of the Labrador scientists from Scotland, England, Germany, Canada, and the United States, leaders in several fields of science that might contribute directly or indirectly to the solution of the problem to be considered," Burgess wrote. "Could a scientific study of these life cycles determine the cause or causes and so make possible accurate forecasts of years of maximum and minimum numbers of a given species?"[19]

The following journal entries describe his travel to Matamek and the first days of the conference:[20]

> 7/16: Routed out at 12:30 [a.m.] by arrival of *Sable* [vessel]. A scramble to get all our stuff together in the dark. Very rough but we finally got aboard and immediately set sail at 1:30. Were warmly greeted. Had cabins off dining room. Met Mr. Parker, gov't man in charge of Indian reservations and found him most interesting. Told much of Indian life. Speaks 3 Indian languages. Has lived much in far north. Also met Mr. Chas. Lamb of Racquette Club, St. Louis, world traveler and sportsman. … Indian bride and groom got on at Ratisqua.

7/17: Up in good season to find it raining. Sat last evening with Engineer until we reached Muigan (?) at 12:45 where Indians got off. Rain let up about the time we were to disembark towards noon. All our friends lined up to see us off. Greeted on beach by Dr. [Charles] Elton of England [ecologist] Mr. Carrier of Montreal and Dr. [William] Rowan of Edmonton [zoologist, pioneer in bird banding and migration] as well as Mr. [Copeland] Amory. [Depending on tides and boat size, an arrival at Matamek offered momentary entertainment for those on land, since shallow water often required disembarking passengers to either wade or be carried piggyback to shore.][21] After dinner went up to falls to watch salmon jump. Black flies rather bad. Like the men I have met, Dr. [Harry] Kyle fish expert of Europe, most pleasant and interesting.

7/18: A beautiful day. After breakfast all hands including Drs Gross, Kyle, Elton, Mr. Amory, Mr. Carrier, Mrs. Stiles, Springarn [guide] and Bill [Alfred Gross' son] went to Tern Island by motor boat. Found nearly all young terns dead. Gross thinks due to fog. Had dinner on a northern island. I cooked potatoes while Rowan cooked fish. Took walk with Elton and enjoyed him much.

7/19: A beautiful day. Sat around all day reading Rowan's book on Migration to be published in Sept and chatting with Dr. Kyle. Learned much from latter including fact that ell [sic] has heart in tail and climbs out of containers tail first. A delicious dinner of pork and roast beef and equally fine supper of cold dishes. Dr. Kyle and Dr. Rowan delightfully interesting. A meeting in morning to arrange programs for conference.

On Sunday conference attendees began to arrive. "Gross amazed at size [of turnout]," Burgess noted, making the sly observation that the ornithologist had been so sure participation would be negligible at this isolated site, he had barely begun to prepare his presentation on the ruffed grouse. As Burgess became acquainted with the distinguished company he would keep for a week, he made a discovery that touched him:

Some of the guests I knew by name and reputation, especially several naturalists of note. Two or three of these I had met previously. There were others whom I didn't even know by name, my work and studies having never touched their field of activity. I felt like a small boy in knee pants shaking hands with a group of grown-ups. It was then I made an astounding discovery. While most of these men were strangers to me, to most of them, excepting the European delegates, I was not a stranger at all. They greeted me as an old friend. They were familiar with my stories and approved of them. They understood and appreciated the dual purpose of what I was trying to do for children and for wild life through my little nature tales.[22]

Although his journal does not relate much about the scientific discourse at Matamek, Burgess' autobiography describes two interesting incidents. Every night at

9 p.m. a bell would conclude the day's discussions with a summons to refreshment and an animated social hour. On the first day of the conference, Copley Amory called Burgess aside. He handed him the key to his wine closet with instructions to "see that my guests have at all times what they may desire insofar as it can be supplied. I am leaving the matter in your hands entirely." (Amory did request that Burgess protect, if possible, two or three bottles of a certain rare liqueur.) Prohibition was in force in the U.S., and Burgess, only a light drinker, found he had been handed "the key to good fellowship, and for myself to a very real if temporary personal popularity."[23]

One evening, however, the children's author found himself uncomfortably in the spotlight:

> There was much swapping of experiences in remote places all over the world; telling of anecdotes and adventure. As unobtrusively as possible I listened...Finally one evening the blow fell. I was drawn forth from a quiet corner and a bedtime story was demanded. It was useless to protest. I was keenly aware that so far I had contributed nothing whatever to the splendid cause that had brought about this communion of keen minds...I had faced many audiences of children, sometimes several thousand at a time, but never with such embarrassment, such an all-gone feeling, as I now experienced as I looked over that small group. To refuse to do what was asked would be to lose face completely. Yet to tell a story designed for children of a tender age to a group of men of the highest academic range seemed impossible. The very idea seemed absurd.

Evoking humor, and no doubt eliciting laughter, Burgess requested that the group before him all imagine themselves no more than ten years old, and he would do the same. "Buster Bear's Sugar Party" was apparently well received by the learned audience. Later that year Dr. Ellsworth Huntington of Yale [whose article on the Matamek Conference appeared in *Science* that year] brought his family and some young friends to visit Burgess in Hampden. Before leaving, he asked Burgess to tell the story again. When Burgess concluded, Huntington admitted he had been curious to see if Burgess would tell it exactly the same way he had at Matamek. "Did I?" Burgess asked. "You did," Huntington replied.[24]

A Rare Invitation

In the spring of 1934, Dr. Gross invited Burgess to join a major expedition to Labrador and the Arctic with renowned explorer Admiral Donald MacMillan and Bowdoin College faculty and students on MacMillian's research vessel, the schooner *Bowdoin*. Declining the offer was apparently a financial and work-related necessity for Burgess, and in decades of journaling, it was a rare instance of bitter regret:

> "Heard over the radio that [Admiral Donald] MacMillan is to make his trip north sailing on June 9 and Gross goes with him. How I wish I could go. Got to stoke the fires that keep the boiler going for all hands — instead. Life is like that."

> "Alfred sailed today on MacMillan arctic expedition. What I wouldn't give to be with them and I had the chance. Couldn't go because of work and expense."[25]

"Work and expense" seem an insufficient explanation for turning down such a superb offer. Burgess doesn't specifically mention lack of work or pressing deadlines. At the time he was earning a substantial income with book publishing, his syndicated column, professional lectures, recordings, and undoubtedly character-related toys and merchandise. The *New York Times* reported that Burgess was one of the largest taxpayers in Massachusetts in 1925, and articles on the writer occasionally referred to him as a millionaire. Although he had suffered severe losses in the 1929 stock market crash, he and his wife Fannie lived frugally. The greatest consistent drain on his considerable income was not reckless spending, but financial assistance to family members. (On January 2, 1936, he wrote in his journal: "Why is the present generation so unable to go alone. Have worked hard all my life chiefly to support others and still must keep it up.")

One wonders if there was a greater loss in that missed opportunity to join the prestigious Arctic expedition. By substantiating his role as a serious nature writer and environmental science authority, it would unquestionably have helped reconfigure his reputation as "Peter Rabbit's godfather" and "Burgess of the Bedtime Stories." If this thought troubled him, however, there is no evidence of it in his journals. Burgess was never one to stew over old regrets. Nearly twenty years later, in 1950, he attended a lecture by Admiral MacMillan and spoke with him afterwards. In his journal, Burgess recorded a teasing remark made that evening at the expense of — and no doubt merrily shared with — his dear friend Alfred Gross: "One of the best evenings have had for a long time. Had a nice chat with [Admiral MacMillan]. Says Gross is one of the best sports and worst sailor he ever had."[26]

THE HEATH HEN

In 1923, Dr. Alfred Gross began what he considered one of the most important and challenging projects of his career, an annual census of the nearly decimated heath hen (*Tympanuchus cupido cupido*) population, a sub-species of the prairie chicken (*Tympanuchus cupido pinnatus*), the two being somewhat different in size, coloring, feathering, eggs, and nesting habits.[27] When Burgess expressed interest in the project, Gross invited him to participate in the spring population survey on Martha's Vineyard. Once a popular game bird with a wide distribution in New England and Mid-Atlantic states, the heath hen had vanished from most of Massachusetts except for the island of Martha's Vineyard, some five miles off the coast of Cape Cod.

Matt Pelikan of Oak Bluffs, Martha's Vineyard, a restoration ecologist with The Nature Conservancy, is familiar with the heath hen and its history on the island. "They're quite distinctive," he says. "They're chicken-size and chicken-like, a brown bird with barred plumage. The males have inflatable sacs of skin at their necks. I don't think in the field you could determine one from a prairie chicken, but that nearest population is in Wisconsin." By 1880, it was generally accepted that the Vineyard had the only heath hen population in the country. In 1907, the Commonwealth of Massachusetts purchased six hundred acres of land there and leased another 1,000 to secure habitat for the birds, which preferred rough, scrubby ground cover.

Over-hunting was only one factor that impacted the species. "There is a very long history of fires on the Vineyard, and in May 1916 there was a fire that burned almost one-third of the dry land area on the island," Pelikan says. "It hit at the time the heath hens were sitting on eggs. Like a lot of other birds, the females have a strong instinct not to abandon the nest, and they were immolated. In 1921, four hundred birds were reported on the island, but the next year only one hundred and seventeen were counted." Prior to the 1916 fire, there had been an estimated 2,000 birds on the island, but that devastating event was followed by a harsh winter with migration to the island of an unusual number of goshawks, which are effective predators.

"So the [heath hen] population gets small, genetic diversity is reduced, population density gets low, and males and female can't find each other during mating season," says Pelikan. "Then you get problems with inbreeding, harmful recessive genes with physical flaws or weakened immune systems. There was an inevitableness to the loss of the heath hen. The population fluctuated, but it was relentlessly downward."

In 1926, Dr. Alfred Gross had made his annual survey and in a letter to Burgess, who was unable to accompany him that year, he reported faint optimism for the heath hen:[28]

> I have estimated that there are now about 35 birds on the island. It is difficult to make a comparison with the number present last year but I am certain the birds have maintained their numbers and probably have increased. It is true that I saw only three birds when I visited the reservation last year but as I stated at the time that did not mean that there were only three birds in existance [sic].I estimated twenty five at that time but there may have been more. We use a great deal of care in making estimates checking up on all those seen by the wardens and reported by the others but at best our estimate must be more or less of a guess. I feel hopeful...I am sorry you have had sickness in your family and regret that you were not able to go to the island with me. I do wish to have you see these interesting birds. I hope the tide has turned and that the birds will begin a steady increase through the efforts now being expended by the Federation and the State Department.

Heath Hen Survey

Burgess described the experience of tracking the heath hen into its final days in his autobiography: "In the spring of 1928: I was invited by Dr. Gross to join him in the task of taking the annual census of the heath hen. This task has been in his charge since the reservation began. Making an accurate count of the birds on such a large area as the Vineyard with much of the terrain covered with scrub oak, might seem a herculean, not to say impossible, task. This was not the case."[29]

Burgess explained that the heath hens' courting ritual took place in a common area surrounded by brush and woodland. Because the birds congregated at a large open field where the males competed for a mate, it was possible to make a relatively accurate count of the birds from the seclusion of a blind: "We were in the blind before daylight, at break of day the birds would appear and begin to gather to dance, parade, fight, call and display all their peculiar charms. The blind was, in effect, a huge wooden box roofed over to keep the interior dark so that no suspicious eye could chance to catch through one of the small observation holes some movement within. There were two or three of these small openings on each side; the largest just big enough for a camera lens to get an unobstructed view."[30]

That year only four birds appeared, all male, "but those four birds went through all the courting ritual as ardently as if the bright admiring eyes of love were in truth watching every move," Burgess recalled. The next year, he wrote to Austin Clark about the 1929 heath hen census:

> There seems to be no doubt at all that there is but one left. I secured excellent photographs of this one and also motion pictures. It means that the end of a species is at hand and that thought was with me constantly as I watched the bird. It seems to me a tragedy of tragedies when a species passes out of existence. The one bird is a male. Last year at this time there were three, all males, so it was easy to foresee the end. There have been many and persistent reports of other Heath Hen on the Island, but we have run all these down and the result is just one bird.[31]

In 1930, Burgess and Gross came to the Vineyard again, and awaited the return of the lone heath hen to the field on Jimmy Green's farm.

> From the blind or hide, as some would call it, we watched the last thin stars slowly fade and the first bright shafts of the rising sun touch the distant treetops. The trees were still bare but somehow no longer with the bitter nakedness of winter. The light quickened and warmed the brown carpet of dead grass of the field which here and there was beginning to show small touches of light green. The cawing of a crow broke harshly the peace and stillness of the dawn, yet its very harshness seemed to amplify this...then in the strengthening light we saw the heath hen emerge from the thick cover of the scrub oak at the upper edge of the field. In this safe shelter he had spent the night. He did not fly. He walked, ran a few steps, walked again, then stood looking and listening, the picture of alertness. Manifestly he was well aware of the increased danger in these open surroundings. In this manner he continued to advance, watchful but without real hesitation.
>
> "In front of the blind and only a few feet from us he picked up a few grains of corn. Standing still, he stretched full height, bright eyes searching on all sides. Then spreading his tail fanwise in the same manner as his cousin the ruffed grouse, he dropped his wings until the tips all but or quite touched the ground, erected the long pinnate feathers of the sides of his neck so they stood straight above his head like the ears of a rabbit, swelled out the two bright yellow sacks like miniature oranges on the sides of his neck, took a few curious hopping steps, a sort of ritual dance, and followed this in a peculiar tooting love call. Then he stood at attention,

> looking and listening for some sign of recognition that we watching him knew could never be. The display, dance and call were repeated many times, the bird occasionally stopping to pick up a few grains of corn.
>
> It was sheer, stark tragedy. Watching that lone bird displaying all his charms, calling for a mate after the manner of his race down through thousands of years, and while I knew that nowhere in all the world was there a mate or even a companion for him, that I was watching the very end of one of Nature's creative experiments down through the ages, bathed with infinite pathos a scene that should have been fascinating and delightful.[32]

When Gross and Burgess next traveled to the Vineyard in the spring of 1931, their purpose was no longer to conduct a census, but to band and photograph the last heath hen. Burgess' autobiography reports the following account:[33]

> We knew that the end of the species was near. We wanted that end to come in complete freedom under natural conditions as Nature intended. At the same time it was extremely desirable that there should be a record of the final chapter in the life history of this bird if possible. So it was decided to trap the bird, band him, release him, and hope that the leg bones, or one of them, might be found still banded. Then the band could be returned to the bird-banding division of the Biological Survey in Washington [succeeded by the Fish and Wildlife Service], where the numbers on the band would be registered.
>
> So on March 31, 1931, at daybreak Dr. Gross and I set a net trap baited with corn. Then we retreated into the blind with hope and a long cord with which to spring the trap. It was a beautiful morning. The bird appeared on time. He did all his stunts, fed close to the blind and all around the trap, but failed to so much as look inside it.
>
> The following morning April 1, All Fools' Day, we were on our way to the Green farm while it was still dark. The weather had changed. There was a raw damp wind and heavy mist with a threat of rain. By the time we reached the farm rain was falling. We parked the car in Jimmy Green's dooryard and sat for a few minutes deciding what to do.

Gross was doubtful the bird would come out of the shelter of the brush in such bad weather, and the visibility for any photographic opportunity was poor, but they decided to take their camera equipment to the blind and hoped for the best:

> We had been in the blind but a short time when without warning and close to the trap an unfamiliar form materialized in the mist. It looked as big as a barnyard fowl. All the feathers were fluffed out, making it a forlorn looking ball of a bird. It was the heath hen. Deliberately, with no sign of suspicion, no hesitancy, he walked beneath the raised hoop of the trap. Then he began to pick up corn. … With the pull-string in my hand, I hesitated. I looked questioningly at my companion. We wanted pictures of the banding and this was anything but photographic weather.

However, the real and important purpose of that morning's trip was to band the bird. Dr. Gross nodded. I pulled the string. The trap fell.

Hastily Dr. Gross crawled out through the low doorway at the rear of the blind, scrambled to his feet and rushed headlong around the corner of the blind to secure the bird before it might injure itself in an attempt to get out of the trap. Meanwhile my movie camera was whirring away. Despite the unfavorable conditions, the results turned out fairly well.

Then, while I held the bird, Dr. Gross adjusted a band on each leg, an aluminum band on one and a copper band on the other. The numbers on the bands were afterward sent to the Biological Survey and a reward was advertised for the return to the survey of either band, should one be found. The reward never has been claimed.

A Critical Decision

When Gross and Burgess trapped the last heath hen in 1931, they placed themselves in an extraordinary position: Should they put the captive bird in a zoo or sanctuary? (The last passenger pigeon had lived at the Cincinnati Zoo until the age of twenty-one.) Or should they release it back into the wild? No regulatory agency or official was required to intercede. Circumstance dictated that the decision was theirs to make. They had discussed the options with reservation warden Allan Keniston the night before and released the bird. The next year Burgess was unable to participate in the survey and wrote Gross: "In thought at least I will be with you. It is a keen disappointment that I am not to be there in person…remember me to Allan (Keniston) and Mrs. K and to Giffie [their son]. And give my best to my old friend the Heath Hen."[34]

In February 1932, the bird reappeared at the mating ground and was seen regularly over four weeks. It did not reappear in 1933. Vineyard historian Henry Hough reported that the last authenticated date of sighting of the bird was March 11, 1932, at the James Green farm in West Tisbury. "The bird was the sole survivor of its race since December 1928, and was approximately 10 years old," Hough wrote. "It was seen at its traditional booming field at regular intervals between February 9 and March 11 of last year, and then disappeared."[35]

Dr. Alfred Gross concluded his final report that year with the solemn words: "The last heath hen is apparently dead, and the race *Typannuchus cupido* extinct." *The Heath Hen's Journey to Extinction, 1792–1933*, a pamphlet compiled by Hough, was published by the Dukes County Historical Society with photographs by Dr. Alfred Gross. It included one made in April 1931 of the last heath hen held in the hands of Thornton Burgess.

Video Record of the Heath Hen

Several years ago U.S. Fish and Wildlife Service Chief Historian Mark Madison learned of the existence of the video film of the last heath hen made by Burgess. "The Wildlife Service is in charge of overseeing the Endangered Species Act, so since 1885 we've been trying to track endangered species," says Madison. "We were really excited to find there was film footage of the heath hen, and doubly excited to find it was shot by a famous author. Watching it was amazing. We expected to see just the heath hen wandering around the forest, but what we got was Thornton Burgess hiding in a blind, popping out, and being actively engaged with this project. It opened up a whole new understanding of him and what people were doing in conservation in the 1930s."

"I don't think we have anything like it," remarked Madison. "We have nothing that has gone extinct subsequently, and we're almost certain the heath hen is gone. It's a great legacy." Madison obtained the film footage from the Massachusetts Division of Fish and Wildlife. "It was a fragile 16 MM film that we converted to beta tape and then DVDs," recalls Madison. "We took it back to Cape Cod to watch it with Bob Dwyer, head of the Cape Cod Museum of Natural History. He was blown away, and asked if he could show it that night to his board."

Madison, who grew up with Burgess' books, says, "I was glad to know that [Burgess] who had done so much to teach children about nature also had a role educating adults," he said. "Nobody paid him to make the film. He did it out of passion. It is the best type of conservation. He was really ahead of his time. It is pretty clear he was aware this was the last chance to see a heath hen, although he hoped it wouldn't go out. There were other species that went extinct as late as the 1950s, like the dusky seaside sparrow on the East Coast, and we don't have a film record of them. People always assumed they were going to save it at the last minute. Burgess and Dr. Gross prepared for the fact that we might not save the heath hen."

Fate of the Last Heath Hen

Burgess speculated in his autobiography that the last heath hen on Martha's Vineyard "might well have fallen victim to a hunting cat, a hawk, an owl, or other predator. He might even have died from natural causes, for the bird was old, presumably past his prime."[36] According to Margie Mitchell Wheeler, a realtor in Littleton, Massachusetts, the writer was wrong on all counts.

Wheeler's grandparents Harry and Ada Sillcocks had bought a summer home on Martha's Vineyard in 1930. They first came to the island to visit friends and ended up renting, and then purchasing, a large furnished house in Edgartown. Several years later Sillcocks was driving with his family in their Model A Ford near the airport, Wheeler said in a 2010 telephone interview: "I believe it was a day trip, an up-island excursion. If they were up by the airport, he wasn't going for errands. My grandparents were in the car with the four children, including my mother Peggy, who was about fourteen years old."

"The story in our family is that my grandfather ran over the last heath hen on Martha's Vineyard in the early 1930s," says Wheeler. "It happened in the summer, probably sometime in June. The bird ran across the road and my grandfather couldn't stop the car. He said he ran over this bird and killed it. They must have gotten out of the car. They were so heartbroken and shocked and horrified. They didn't tell anybody, and my mother told me not to tell anyone."

"My grandfather must have known about the bird being the last one because of publicity," says Wheeler. "I think it was hot news on the Vineyard. He was a New York lawyer and they were newcomers on the Vineyard. They wouldn't make up a story like that. There has never been any question in my mind it was the heath hen." Without evidence, it is of course impossible for experts to draw a conclusion about the anecdotal account. "I have no reason to doubt it or take it as truth," Pelikan says. Tom Chase, director of conservation strategies for the Nature Conservancy, adds: "I have heard competing stories of who saw or shot the last heath hen, but we've never seen the evidence. It could have been a domestic fowl." If true, however, the incident is ironic as well as unfortunate, for Wheeler's father Philip Street and grandfather Fletcher Street, the author and illustrator of Brief Bird Biographies, were both dedicated ornithologists.

Wildlife Photographers

In addition to providing written accounts of their field research and other work, Dr. Alfred Gross and Thornton Burgess recorded their observations of wildlife with still and motion picture photography. As the following letters indicate, they often exchanged information about their techniques, results, and camera equipment:

(Gross) Barro Colorado trip, November 1927

One of the most exciting things is a young howler monkey which Donato succeeded in getting. I have taken a whole series of photographs of him and have more than wished you were here to shoot him with the movies. … I am enclosing some prints which I know will be of interest to you…I like the picture of "Three Naturalists in the Rain Forest," but the one of you and me did not come out good. … I am taking pictures of everything that comes along when I go to the island in the hopes that it may be of use to you and to myself in connection with general articles.[37]

(Burgess) Barro Colorado trip, November 11, 1931

I have been over the [Barro Colorado] films pretty thoroughly and we have a lot of good stuff…To the seventeen subjects that we made there on the Island, I added a small honey bear, an agouti and a macaw out at San Blas. All these came out well. … I have forgotten if I told you in my last letter that six species of birds landed on the boat coming up. These included a kingfisher, a dove from Haiti, a junco off the Carolina coast (and this surprised me greatly), a warbler which I could not identify, a nighthawk and a swallow. I had a little film left in the camera and got the warbler…the exposure was all right. I have nice film of the laboratory from the water. The telephoto of the monkey limb was, as I expected, a failure, but the other lens worked all right…the little possum and his mother are bully.[38]

(Gross) Barro Colorado trip, November 15, 1927

Now I have the task before me of arranging the stuff and of getting titles. It is no small job. I have a little lantern which will take a motion picture film and with this I am enabled to test out some of the negative before having it printed...Today for first time I saw my films made during summer, the ones including the partridge, white bluebirds, etc. They are great and I have great hopes for the Panama films.[39]

(Burgess) Martha's Vineyard, February 26, 1930

Now about the camera. I don't know that there is any particular advantage for field work in having that three lens turret head. Personally, I don't see where you have use for three lenses. My experience is that two lenses are bad enough. If you should have the regular lens and the telephoto, I should think it would be sufficient. The chief advantage in three speeds would be that you could get slow-motion pictures, which you might like to take sometimes, and of course you could get a little faster picture cutting down motion. My camera has two speeds — 8 and 16. I have never used the 8. Of course that one you checked at $350 is the latest thing. With the turret head, of course, you do not have to change lenses and there are times what that is an advantage. It enables you to take a picture a long distance away and then without change get the subject when it draws in at closer range.[40]

(Burgess) Following Labrador trip, December 20, 1931

What is the make of your tripod? Fannie is giving me one for Christmas. She also gave me a range finder which I like better than the one Blais loaned us. You simply look through it and focus on the object and it gives the distance reading from 15 inches up. Now I am all set.[41]

Chapter 13

Nature and Education

The educational potential of his work was not immediately obvious to Thornton Burgess. As a professional journalist, he may have appreciated the informative quality of his work, but it had the practical purpose of earning money to support his family. The bedtime stories that launched his literary career had the original objective of sustaining a parent-child relationship disrupted by a lengthy separation. But as his authority as a children's author, lecturer and early radio host grew, Burgess used the imaginative appeal of his nature-based stories to educate by infusing them with natural science, life lessons, and humane values that resonate today.

"I was brought up on Thornton W. Burgess and his wonderful nature books, and I only wish to God that all children today were still brought up on them. No author in his lifetime ever did more to promote kindness to animals."[1]

Cleveland Amory, President
The Fund for Animals, 1982

"It would be difficult if not impossible to overstate the value of your work in nature education and in conservation. You have made a great contribution."[2]

Dr. Clyde Fisher,
astronomer, assistant curator,
American Museum of Natural History

"Burgess allowed children to envision the animal he was writing about in their imagination, to connect with that animal on an emotional level. Their love for Buster Bear wasn't the same love as for Pooh Bear. They saw Buster as a real creature with survival needs and a unique life of his own. He had a family. He interacted with the Green Forest folk on a day-to-day basis in real life, not in fantasy."

Mary Beers, head naturalist, educator
Thornton W. Burgess Society, 2010

"There weren't any woods where I grew up, and there weren't many animals. Maybe I'd see a squirrel and one time I saw a snake. So the Burgess books were where I encountered them. When I was just learning to read, Thornton Burgess opened up the woods and friendship. His books were a place I escaped to."

Frederick Lewis, financial advisor
St. Louis, Missouri, 2011

New Discovery of an Old Book

One summer evening in 2009, Judy Saunders, a veteran second grade teacher at Chatham Park Elementary School in Havertown, Pennsylvania, was visiting her friend Penny Moldovsky, a reading/literacy specialist and principal of Woodlynde, a private school in Wayne, Pennsylvania. As she idly perused Moldovsky's extensive book collection, Saunders spotted an unfamiliar title and pulled out *The Adventures of Chatterer the Red Squirrel* by Thornton W. Burgess. After scanning a few chapters, Saunders decided her students might enjoy hearing the animal stories and asked to borrow it. Moldovsky told her it was one of many Burgess books her mother Rose Baum had read and given as gifts to her children and grandchildren; she had even taken them to the nature center at the author's home in Hampden, Massachusetts.

In September, Saunders started reading *Chatterer* to her class. "I quickly knew I had found something worth its weight in gold," she says. "A few of the children went to the library to get out more Burgess books, and some bought them on Amazon. By the end of that school year, I had read six of his books to the class. This was student-driven. When I am ready to read a new book, the class votes and the majority rules. The first choice that year was always Burgess. In my eighteen years of teaching this had never happened, but I thought, 'I'm not going to fight a good thing.' It tells you everything you need to know when children go home and talk about something they did in school. I had one mother come to me and say, 'I'm confused. Who *is* this Mr. Burgess?' She was thrilled because her son had become interested in reading. For a teacher there is nothing more exciting [than to] get children to read with pure delight."

In addition to seeing the Burgess stories cultivate interest in reading and writing, Saunders discovered her second graders were developing a new attitude toward wildlife. "Burgess teaches appreciation of nature in our world," she says. "Now the children were thinking about the animals that live among us. They looked at animals in a whole different way." One day a girl sitting in a small reading group near a classroom window said, "What's that?" and pointed to a large bird, bigger than a crow, perched in one of the trees outside.

"It was a red-tailed hawk," said Saunders. "I slowly got up and called the whole class over. It was after two squirrels. It kept circling the tree, but the squirrels knew what it was doing. The children watched the talons…they could see if the squirrels got down out of the tree, the hawk would get them. After about twenty minutes, the hawk flew away. The children were entranced; it was like watching a movie. When they left that day, you could hear them saying, 'It's like the most exciting day I have had.'"

World War I-Era Students Read Burgess

Nearly one hundred years earlier another second grade teacher, Miss Edith Stocking at the State Normal School in Wayne, Nebraska, had similar pedagogical success using Burgess' syndicated newspaper stories to awaken her students' interest in reading, writing, and nature study. When she saw how class discussion was stimulated by newspaper photographs one child brought in of war-torn France "all shotted up," Stocking encouraged her students to share other pictures and stories. Their enthusiasm generated so much material that Stocking created a "post office" box with slots to store articles for any student to read: "They poured over the pictures, read phrases in the magazines, hastened to school at unheard of hours with the most unseemly reading material," including patent medicine advertisements, postcards to themselves, and letters procured from unsuspecting family members. Stocking realized her wildly successful project needed a more selective focus.

One day the teacher brought in Burgess' "Little Stories for Bed-time" column from the *Omaha World-Herald* and read it to the class. She reported the class reaction in her article "Incidental Reading Carried Along Experimental Lines" in the January 1917 issue of *Primary Education*: "And lo! The problem solved itself; for at once the tide turned in favor of 'Farmer Brown's boy with the queer shining things on his feet,' 'Peter and Mrs. Peter,' and all the little people of the old Brier Patch. Little children are eye-minded to large degree, and I seized this opportunity to work for impression, feeling convinced the wish for expression would follow."[3]

Apparently it did. Class discussions began to focus on the beauty and wonders of the natural world outside. The children asked to take the newspapers home to re-read them to parents astonished by their new-found confidence and ability to decipher advertisements as well as articles. "I had succeeded as never before in forming a tie between home, child and school," said Stocking, adding:

> We began the work in early January when the ground was clothed in a beautiful sparkling crust of snow which squeaked as we crunched our way to school. The frosty air powdered our eye-lashes, burnt our throats, nipped our cheeks, and rimed our mufflers. The window-panes were etched with wonderful frost pictures; evergreens were white wigwams under which Peter and Mrs. Peter were doubtless snuggled away safely and around which they left their tracks in plain view for our inspection…At night the hills which rimmed our horizon were outlined with faint pencil markings of darkness as they imperceptibly merged into the wintry sky as we trudged home. We looked up into the sky just before we cuddled into snuggly beds and said good-bye to the "Great, wide, wonderful, beautiful world."[4] One little girl took occasion one frosty morning to show me just how the stars had winked at her the previous night, and her little face screwed up in its odd grimace touched me more deeply than I cared to admit.
>
> The wish to be able to read aloud was the first symptom I noticed, and soon children hovered at my desk from eight o'clock on, reading paragraphs — of their own selection — from favorite chapters of the stories. The choice made was the surprising feature of the experiment to me; for usually…there was a most extensive digging and burrowing through the pigeon-holes of the post office for the exact paper desired…and almost always contained a description of the escape from danger of some of the outdoor creatures. Soon papers were being taken home to exploit the reader's ability to rustle, turn, and read them as "my daddy" did.
>
> I do not intend to convey the impression that all other incidental reading material was entirely crowded out of our room. It was not, but the bulk of the oral reading work of this type centered around the "Little Stories for Bed-time."

Edith Stocking was trained to use academic text books, but when she discovered children were smuggling Thornton Burgess columns out of the classroom under their coats, she became convinced of two things: "that children often have an insatiate desire for information" and "it is immaterial by what means they are incited with the desire to learn to read."

In his undated copy of an article/lecture titled "Can Your Child Read?", Burgess mentions a letter he received from a contemporary of Miss Stocking who taught at a small country school "in a mining section of a state in the far West." She also described her success in using one of his magazine stories to stimulate academic interest. "The youngsters were from widely scattered homes in rough wild country, and their immediate surroundings were all with which they were familiar," said

Burgess. "These constituted their entire world. The fact that even *Mother Goose* failed utterly to amuse or in any way interest those little folk did not indicate they were either dull or stupid.

"Then by chance the teacher read to them the Johnny Chuck story [which had recently appeared in a national magazine.] The next morning when she approached the school the little folk were playing Johnny Chuck. Here was a subject, a character, they knew and understood. It was one that had a place in their everyday world. Now the teacher had the key. Carefully she selected stories about other familiar friends in fur and feathers...The interest of the children was stimulated. They looked forward to the story period. They asked questions. Imagination was awakened. This led to a liking of other kinds of stories."[5]

High School Students Meet Farmer Brown's Boy

Veteran environmental studies teacher Alan Chaney, now retired, grew up reading Burgess' books and routinely assigned the stories to his senior classes at Newton South High School in Massachusetts.

"I had the kids read the story about Farmer Brown's boy looking for the redwing blackbird nest in *Old Mother West Wind*," says Chaney. "I told them when you're done, go back to find the natural history facts in it. And they read from *Blacky the Crow* which is so different from a children's book like *Frog and Toad* where the animals are riding bicycles. These Burgess stories are loaded with natural history information. You get the complete picture with them."

The teacher presented Burgess' stories in the context of both history and environmental science. "He seemed to be on the front edge of the curve," Chaney stated in a 2012 interview. "We may think of the 1960s and '70s as the time of the environment, but Thornton Burgess and Theodore Roosevelt and others who were working decades earlier for environmental conservation and preservation set the stage for it, and for today. I used Burgess to teach the difference one person can make in conservation. My students could see he knew how important it was to get kids interested. It's kids that grow up to be naturalists."

Chaney pointed out that Burgess' children's stories depicted the migration of wildlife species from one region to another. "When I was growing up I would have been flabbergasted to see a mockingbird or coyote or a turkey vulture or an opossum in my neighborhood. But Burgess published these books before the 1920s — how did he know these animals were moving into New England? Who was he talking to back then?" Chaney also had his students read Burgess' autobiographical account of banding and filming the last known heath hen.

Nature Is the Universal Teacher

Thornton Burgess would have been elated by such diverse classroom uses of his children's stories, for they substantiate his assertion that the combined power of story, imagination, and nature makes a perfect learning tool. He described his belief in the intrinsic value of nature stories and nature education in articles in *Natural History* (1922) and *Nature* (1924), as well as in various essays and lectures. "As the success of the stories grew, my own education began," he related in his autobiography. "Gradually I awoke to the understanding that entertainment was in truth incidental, merely the means of an important end, that I was in possession of the master key to education along many and diverse lines; that Nature is the universal teacher."[6]

The explanation, Burgess felt, was that human survival and progress have historically been based on observation of nature, that the special attraction of children and adults to animals is a trait that goes back to the "dawn of man" when large animals were a source of danger and small animals a source of food. "I question if there is another subject which can even approach animal life in the universal appeal to young and old," he said.[7] He recommended that nature study be taught from kindergarten through high school as a primary subject: "It is not a fad, it is a fundamental. It is the golden key to a vast storehouse of knowledge."[8]

Through his experience as a children's writer, Burgess discovered that nature stories could be uniquely instructive. As proof, he cited the success of his *Happy Jack Squirrel* stories and rhymes in promoting something as unrelated as World War I savings stamp sales. Although the subject of thrift was uninteresting to children, the animal characters were appealing, Burgess said, so the message acquired the appeal of the story. The immediate and enthusiastic response to his 1920s children's radio nature program also told Burgess that he controlled an educational tool with "undreamed of potentialities."[9]

Naturalist Stu Parsons had similar insight into the effectiveness of nature in education when he began working with live animals. After completing a graduate school internship at Manomet Bird Observatory with Massachusetts Audubon naturalists Betty Anderson and Wayne Petersen, Parsons taught nature study classes for the Thornton W. Burgess Society and found that using a live animal with children was "almost like using a puppet": "I could speak through the animal and make a connection between people and science. I would go into a classroom of kids, and stand there with my stone face. The kids were giving me their stone faces. And then I would take out a frog. Their faces would light up, and there would be that low rumble of interest, but I hadn't said a word. Until I brought out that frog, the kids' minds were all over the room. Then I had them completely focused, energized, and curious."

Drawing the attention of children to a tail or a foot easily opens up a discussion of where and how the animal lives, what it needs to survive, and its adaptation and evolution, says Parsons. He increasingly appreciated Burgess' awareness of nature's ability to reach and teach children, as well as the scientific depth of his stories. "People loved the stories and they didn't even realize what they were learning," he said. "It was subtle; it wasn't right in their faces." One of Parson's favorite stories involved Jimmy Skunk:

> It's a really simple idea, he was just looking for beetles, but a lot of people don't even know that skunks eat beetles. Jimmy wanders up the trail and he keeps disturbing other animals in their homes, a chipmunk, a toad, but he had to be fooled by Peter Rabbit to realize what he was doing. It's a fun story, but what a great

picture of animal life you get reading it. As a naturalist, I worked to engage kids in nature and then turned them over to books. Thornton Burgess engaged kids in books, then turned them over to nature education.

"I use Burgess' stories as a launch pad because they're so good for teaching natural history," agrees Mary Beers, Thornton W. Burgess Society education director. "The whimsy brings out children's imagination, and from that point, you've got them. You can bring them over to the natural history facts." Beers initiated a nature discussion with a circle of four-year-old children by personally introducing them to "Grandfather Frog." Standing before the seated children one by one, she held a very large frog at eye level, encouraging them to admire its big eyes, smooth skin, and muscular legs.

"The appeal of Thornton Burgess is nature," says author and artist Clare Walker Leslie, who teaches nature journaling and drawing. "The thing that dumbfounds me is the teacher who doesn't want to take part [in an outdoor nature exercise], and then says afterward she has never seen her class so focused, so involved, so curious, and so happy. Watch the body language of a kid holding a toad or a guinea pig. There is that hunger for the experience."

ENVIRONMENTAL EDUCATION

Nothing engaged Burgess' passion and advocacy more than environmental education.[10] In the following excerpt of his 1924 article in *Nature Magazine*, he explained why:

> The failure to give nature study its proper place in education in the past is largely responsible for the vanishing wild life and forests of today. The birthright of the nation has been wantonly wasted and is still being so wasted with result, which…is nothing less than appalling. We are told the age of larger mammals of the world is drawing to a close. A generation or two hence there will be no large wild animals left unless very radical measures are taken at once to save the species remaining… like conditions prevail in regard to many of the smaller animals. Several species of birds have become extinct within the memory of men now living. Many species of wild flowers are facing the same fate.
>
> What are we going to do about it? There is but one thing that can be done. See to it that the next generation and succeeding generations are nature lovers. The true nature lover is never destructive. Love for the living thing, the bird, the animal, the tree, the flower, prevents even the impetus to destroy. Country boys have written me that they have given up trapping. No one asked them to do it. Through reading…they learned to appreciate the fact that these little animals live lives closely parallel to their own…The boys recognized the difficulties which beset these little wild people daily in their efforts to survive. They no longer desired to add to these difficulties. They had become protectors instead of destroyers.[11]

Foundation of Beliefs

The strength of Thornton Burgess' commitment to environmental education rested upon a foundation of beliefs, some based on nineteenth century Transcendental philosophy, some on twentieth century science, some on his association with wildlife activists like William Hornaday and William Finley, some on childhood experiences, and some on his appreciation for and understanding of children. First, and above all, Burgess believed in the common ground among living creatures that offered humankind potential for connection with nature, even friendship. People undermined this potential, he said, by hurtful, abusive actions and realized it by kind, respectful actions. Second, he believed in the timeless, universal appeal of nature, and, because of it, the usefulness of nature as an educational tool for both children and adults. Third, unlike many of his generation, he believed in the destructibility of nature through human indifference and ignorance, and saw environmental education as the only means of preventing it.

Burgess's concept of an authentic relationship with nature and wildlife was formed early in Sandwich's woods, shores, and fields, reinforced by the practices of Arabella Burgess and Alice Cooke who shared her ninetieth birthday cake with a woodchuck as well as with Burgess and other human friends. Burgess sought to impress young audiences with the similarity in human and animal experiences, as in the following excerpt from an undated presentation [phrases like "little people" and "little folks" were commonly used interchangeably for children and wildlife in his day]:

> As I told you before, these little friends of ours of the Green Forest, the Green Meadows, the Old Pasture, the Old Orchard, and the Smiling Pool are real little people. Please always think of them in that way. All you little folks love good times. So do these other little folks. Their lives are just like yours. They have good times, they have bad times; they have exciting times and they never know what will happen next...If you will be friendly, they will be friendly and you will begin to know them...Such interesting little folks they are. There isn't one that isn't interesting.[12]

The theme of seeking relationship with nature rather than its destruction evolved gradually in Burgess' books and stories. It was most clearly seen through his human protagonist Farmer Brown's Boy, also called Tommy Brown. Initially no friend to wildlife, Tommy was introduced on the opening pages of *Old Mother West Wind* as he and his father were hunting down a fearful Peter Rabbit. In subsequent stories, he shot Reddy Fox, trapped Peter Rabbit, humiliated Granny Fox, and captured Grandfather Frog and then dangled him by the leg from a string.

A Model of Stewardship

The maturation of Farmer Brown's boy into a friend of wildlife was explained in Burgess' *Tommy and the Wishing Stone* series, first published in *St. Nicholas* magazine in 1914 and 1915 and later as three books published by Little, Brown and Company.[13] The fanciful storyline involved a magical stone that transformed the boy into a wild creature. This experience enabled Tommy to feel the joys and fears of a meadow mouse, a mink, a bear, or a goose, thereby learning empathy for wildlife firsthand. Burgess dedicated the books to "the cause of love, mercy, and protection for our little friends of the air and the wild-wood and to a better understanding of them."

In the "Wishing Stone" stories, Tommy's physical transformation, real or imagined, was temporary, but his moral transformation was permanent. Once indifferent to the lives of animals, the careless young hunter became Burgess' model of stewardship, exemplifying the contrast between abuse or exploitation and compassion for wildlife. Tommy's emergence as a nature lover is dramatized in *The Adventures of Bobby Coon* (1919), in which a raccoon's tree home is accidentally chopped down by Farmer Brown and his son. Burgess depicts the event as it is experienced by the animal:

> For a while he peeped out of his doorway, watching the keen axes and the flying yellow chips. Then he crept miserably back to bed to wait for the worst. He just didn't know what else to do. By and by there was a dreadful crack, and another and another. Farmer Brown shouted. So did Farmer Brown's boy. Bowser the Hound barked excitedly. Slowly the big tree began to lean over. Then it moved fast and faster, and Bobby felt giddy and sick. Then, with a frightful crash, the tree struck the ground, and for a few minutes Bobby didn't know anything at all. … You see, when the tree hit the ground, Bobby was thrown against the side of his house so hard that all the wind was knocked out of his body…though no one knew it but himself, Bobby had been badly hurt when that tree fell.
>
> Slowly and painfully Bobby climbed out. That broken leg hurt dreadfully. It was one of his front legs, and of course he had to hold that paw up. That meant he had to walk on three legs, but when he started to climb a tree, he couldn't. With a broken leg, there would be no more climbing for Bobby Coon. It was useless for him to look for another hollow tree. All he could do was look for a hollow log into which he could crawl. What should he do? For the first time his splendid courage deserted him…So he just crouched right down there at the foot of the tree he had started to climb, and whimpered. He was frightened and very, very miserable, was Bobby Coon, and he was in great pain.
>
> Farmer Brown and Farmer Brown's boy and Bowser the Hound had watched Bobby crawl out of his ruined house and start off to seek a new house. Of course, they had seen right away that something was wrong with Bobby, for he walked on three legs and held the fourth one up.
>
> The poor little chap," murmured Farmer Brown's boy pityingly. "That leg must have been hurt when the tree fell. I hope it isn't badly hurt…we can't let that little fellow go off to suffer and perhaps die," said Farmer Brown's boy, and ran forward while Farmer Brown held Bowser. Bobby heard him coming and promptly faced about ready to fight bravely. When he got near enough, Farmer Brown's boy threw his coat over Bobby and then, in spite of Bobby's frantic struggles, gathered him up and wrapped the coat about him so that he could neither bite nor scratch. Bobby was quite helpless. "I'm going to take him home and when I've made him quite comfortable, I'll come back," cried Farmer Brown's boy.[14]

Testimony to the power of this example of compassion comes from Sierra Club founder David Brower, an acclaimed twentieth century environmental activist. In his 1990 autobiography *For Earth's Sake*, Brower says his mother read most of Burgess' books to him and eventually encouraged him to read them on his own. Years later he was "blown away" when he re-read an old copy of *The Adventures of Bobby Coon*. "I discovered, after all these years, that I am Farmer Brown's Boy," Brower wrote, adding:

> Farmer Brown cut down the old dead hollow chestnut tree that was Bobby's home, and Bobby's foreleg was broken in the fall. Farmer Brown's Boy saw his predicament, gently threw his coat over Bobby, carried him home, splinted his leg, helped Old Mother Nature nurse him back to health, loved him and was loved back, then read in Bobby's eyes that he wanted to go back home to the Green Forest. Farmer Brown's Boy was forever talking gently to Bobby, feeding him goodies, petting him, as fond of him as he could be. Finally, warning Bobby about hunters, he took him back to the forest and set him free. That's all I ever wanted to do ever since.[15]

An Influence Today

Burgess' approach to environmental education continues to be credited with fostering interest and commitment to nature. "If his writing had not influenced me, I would not be working as I am at present to preserve just one of the creatures of the great forest — the bald eagle," says Terrence Ingram, executive director and president of the Eagle Nature Foundation in Apple River, Illinois.

Wayne Petersen, author of *Birds of Massachusetts*, director of the Important Bird Area (IBA) Program for Mass Audubon, and an international bird tour leader, also sees Burgess' inspiration in his work: "Looking back, Thornton Burgess is someone who had an influence on my life, my future, and what I do today." When childhood illnesses kept him housebound, Petersen's mother entertained him by reading books and stories. "Among the ones that I particularly loved were the Thornton Burgess stories, and I would ask her to read them over and over again," he says.

That connectedness with Thornton Burgess as a child evolved into a natural science focus for Petersen. In junior high school, he found others who shared his interests in birds. "By college, I was doing nothing but birding and building on my interests in natural history," he says. "I got a degree in biology and started teaching life science, then got a master's degree and was increasingly involved in ornithology. I have to think those [Burgess] stories were seminal in getting me started on that road, on my life's path. I can remember the characters now and being entranced by them."

Kat Walker and Travis Fickett of Los Angeles, California, have been home-schooling their daughter Zoe for several years. They found the *Burgess Bird Book for Children* to be an excellent resource that intertwines storytelling with factual information. "I really liked it when Jenny Wren was arguing because she was funny," remarks Zoe, six. "I also really liked it when Peter meets all the birds. It's really cool to learn about them." Her mother says they covered two to three birds per chapter, discussing their habits, food, coloration, physical attributes, nests, and habitat. "The words were easy for Zoe to understand," says Walker. "She rarely asks me what something means." After completing a Burgess chapter, they studied a bird identification website where they listened to calls and watched videos.

In Sandwich, Massachusetts, Dia Prantis home-schools her third-grade son Henry, who participates in the Thornton W. Burgess Society's book club and has read nearly a dozen Burgess books. She feels Burgess' narrative provides relevant information about wildlife: "I think children should be exposed to things that make sense to them while they're trying to make connections to their environment and the world they live in," she says. "If you're spending time outdoors, they are seeing crows and rabbits and foxes, and they know what a possum and a woodchuck are. With the Burgess books, children are able to learn about a crow's behavior, for example. It's subtly put into the story. It doesn't interrupt it, it's just there."

Canadian homeschooling parent Inge McLaurin and her husband have two boys, seven and eight, who regularly read from the family's collection of forty-three Thornton Burgess books. According to McLaurin, Burgess books such as *The Burgess Bird Book for Children* and *The Burgess Animal Book for Children* are popular on homeschooling websites because of their strong emphasis on nature study and "they aren't trying to push an agenda besides protection of nature."

McLaurin estimates her children have listened to more than four hundred Burgess chapters. "I like how Burgess begins some of them with poetry," she said in a 2012 email. "I often read the poem once, then I discuss what it means and read it again. Sometimes I get annoyed at the run-on sentences and can get mixed up and tongue-tied reading them." She also finds occasional inconsistency of information presented in one book and contradicted in another, such as whether or not Bowser the Hound can talk to wild animal characters.

"[The stories] may be a bit moral for some," she remarks, "but I do like the quietness and peacefulness of the books. I like how in almost all the books no animals get eaten. I don't mind that Burgess is so against hunters. It leads to interesting talks about how the author inserts his point of view into books. Since the series is so long, Burgess was able to write from many different characters' points of view. It allowed us to see how different 'people' can see things from so many different points of view."

McLaurin adds that many of their Burgess books belonged to her husband when he was a boy. "I like listening to him reading the books out loud to my boys," she says. "He sometimes gets up and walks around and gets quite animated. When I'm reading he will sometimes pop into the room and add a comment since he knows all the stories. There is something about walking through the woods at the start of spring that makes us want to reread the books. Seeing a muskrat swim through the water or a beaver's home out in a pond makes those wild animals seem like old friends we know. A blue jay in the sky is not just a bird, he is Sammy jay making mischief and flying through the air screaming 'Thief, thief, thief.'"

Chapter 14

Natural Science Perspective: Issues and Honors

With no credentials other than a high school diploma and his experience as a journalist, editor, and children's author, Thornton Burgess gained admission into the elite company of early twentieth century scientists and environmentalists. Chicago Tribune *journalist Robert Crombie referred to him as "one of the most famous of all nature writers." This chapter considers the impact on Burgess' career of the ethical issues of nature faking and humane values, his association with the Massachusetts Society for the Prevention of Cruelty to Animals, and highlights of awards he received.*

"Thus the story that humanizes the animal to the point of the impossible is bound to fail in its purpose from an educational standpoint. It is permissible for Peter Rabbit to talk because the child understands that in all probability there is some form of communication between animals. But it is not permissible for Peter Rabbit to climb trees or ride a bicycle. The child instantly senses the lack of truth and this of necessity weakens any lesson which the story may seek to convey."[1]

Thornton W. Burgess, 1922

"A great and beloved American died recently at the Mary Lyon Nursing Home in Hampden, Mass. where he had been a patient since December, 1963...Mr. Burgess was an Honorary Vice-President and Director of both our Massachusetts S.P.C.A and American Humane Education Society... He was...a member of the American Museum of Natural History, New York; and Honorary Vice-President of the Massachusetts Audubon Society, American Ornithologists Union, American Society of Mammalogists, and National Geographic Society."[2]

Animals, 1965
Massachusetts Society for the Prevention of Cruelty to Animals

"Anyone who objects to Burgess stories as being a harmful distortion simply doesn't know wildlife, or children."

Bradford Washburn, director
Boston Museum of Science

Nature Faking

In 1903, while Burgess was still working as a magazine editor for Phelps Publishing, the revered nature writer John Burroughs touched off a heated controversy with his article "Real and Sham Natural History" in the *Atlantic Monthly*. Burroughs charged that certain nature writers, particularly William J. Long, Ernest Thompson Seton, and Charles G.D. Roberts, had made false claims that their literary fiction was provable fact.[3] Giving voice to the criticism of other naturalists, Burroughs ridiculed such claims as foxes jumping onto the backs of sheep to escape dogs and birds mending their own injured legs with mud casts. "It is so much easier to invent your natural history than to discover it by actual observation," he said.[4]

Writers under fire simply ignored the accusations or defended themselves with articles, letters, even affidavits from alleged eye witnesses. For several years the debate engaged readers, writers, naturalists, scientists, and officials like William T. Hornaday and President Theodore Roosevelt; in fact it was the president who coined the term "nature faker."

According to Ralph H. Lutts, author of *The Nature Fakers* and editor of *The Wild Animal Story*, the controversy articulated "a conflict between science and sentiment as methods of understanding and appreciating the lives of the creatures of field, forest, and our own backyard."[5] "Americans were in the midst of a complex process of assimilating a new perspective on their relationship with the natural world," Lutts says. "This change was expressed in the educational system, recreational activities, and children's activities. The debate about the accuracy of wild animal stories was a literary expression of this process."[6]

The accusation of nature faking came to suggest that a literary work was flawed by "sentimentalism, philosophical bias, and an inability or unwillingness to use the tools of science as a source of information about nature and wildlife."[7] Although the term implies conscious deception, Lutts points out that the writers named by Burroughs were generally perceived as being more guilty of natural history romanticism and poor observation skills than deliberate fraud. "Perhaps the term is best applied to people whose sentiments about nature blind them to the real living animal in the wild," he says, "to people whose deeply held personal beliefs lead them to spin fanciful visions of nature."[8]

Aside from damage to William J. Long's career, the negative impact of the nature faking issue was minimal. It may have actually done some good by sensitizing the literary community to the expectations of the public and the scientific community, Lutts said in a 2012 telephone interview. "The nature faking issue professionalized nature writing in the sense of setting a standard for nature writers and publishers who started paying more attention to accuracy."

Some called the nature faking issue a "tempest in a teapot," but the label — and concern for the misrepresentation of nature to children — surfaced some sixty years later. In 1965, UCLA senior lecturer Frances Clarke Sayers denounced Walt Disney as a nature faker in an interview reprinted in *The Horn Book*.[9] In repudiating the statement of Max Rafferty, the California Superintendent of Public Instruction, that Disney was "the greatest educator of this century," Sayers declared: "He has, to be sure, distributed some splendid films on science and nature, but he has also been a shameless nature faker in his fictionalized animal stories."

Was Burgess affected?

Just as early twentieth century librarians, editors, and booksellers were setting standards for children's literature by determining what literature was appropriate and meritorious, those involved with natural science were also concerned with the caliber of what was being taught to and learned by children. Theodore Roosevelt wrote, "If the child mind is fed with stories that are false to nature, the children will go to the haunts of the animal only to meet with disappointment. The result will be disbelief, and the death of interest. The men who misinterpret nature and replace fact with fiction undo the work of those who in the love of nature interpret it aright."[10]

When the nature faking controversy erupted, Burgess had not yet begun to write children's books, and after he became published he generally steered clear of the stigmatizing charge. A *Rochester Democrat-Chronicle* book review of *Old Mother*

West Wind stated in 1911 that "Burgess is in no sense a 'nature faker,' and his stories create no false notions."[11] Nevertheless, the issue had a significant and permanent impact on him. As a children's author who mixed fiction with non-fiction and employed anthropomorphic animal characters to convey natural science, Burgess was particularly vulnerable to a perception of factual deception, misrepresentation, or inaccuracy. The charge of nature faking was his Achilles' heel, an ubiquitous threat to hard-earned credibility, which he described in his 1960 autobiography:

> Working alone, lacking acquaintance with any naturalist or scientist of note either through personal contact or through correspondence [when he first began to write], striving not to allow imagination to overstep the exacting bounds of truth and fact with the inevitable penalty of being branded a "nature faker," I received a long distance call that gave me a thrill I can still feel down through the years. [The call was from distinguished naturalist Dr. Clyde Fisher of the American (now National) Museum of Natural History, asking if he could fill in for Ernest Thompson Seton who cancelled a scheduled lecture.][12]

"Even decades after the height of the Nature Fakers controversy, there was much greater attention paid to accuracy," remarked Lutts, who teaches environmental history at Goddard College. Nearly forty years after John Burroughs first raised the issue, its taint was referenced in the *Springfield Republican's* article on Thornton Burgess' accomplishment of publishing his 10,000 article in 1944:

> Years ago when Theodore Roosevelt was President and he was periodically denouncing those with whom he disagreed, one of his famous controversies was with those whom he called "nature fakers." He protested against their romantic and inaccurate descriptions of animals which did things that animals never could do. Mr. Burgess has observed such a careful regards for the facts of natural history that, while he has attributed speech to his animal friends, who certainly know ways to communicate much to each other, he has escaped bitter controversies of that sort. Not the least testimony to his care in this respect and to the accuracy of his observations is the fact that with the passing of years a large part of his audience — not less than half of it he reports — has come to be composed of adults.[13]

Throughout his career, Burgess proclaimed the accuracy of his work, almost defensively at times. In February 1961, when he was eighty-seven years old, he was notified by New World Productions that a television network was interested in developing a pilot film based on his animal characters. Burgess questioned the terms, however, and responded, "the underlying value in these stories is that they are Burgess stories...the value in that name is the universally accepted reputation of the author for integrity in always holding to truth and fact in entertaining stories of Mother Nature's children and their ways, entertaining education without misleading fantasy."[14]

Given the importance he placed on credibility, Burgess must have particularly valued his friendships with renowned conservationists and scientists, not for superficial prestige, but because they enriched his life and helped safeguard his professional reputation. Author Marcel LaFollette commented that the nature faker controversy "may have been one reason that [Smithsonian curator Austin] Clark and Burgess were so concerned with promoting the idea of scientific research via radio."

The Value of Animals

The cultural attitude of Americans toward animals was an integral part of the nature faking issue. Were they living work machines? Were they romanticized furry little people? Popular books like *Black Beauty* and *Call of the Wild* portrayed, as Burgess's books did, the interior life of an individual animal. Burgess was a hunter as a young man, but he became a staunch and vocal advocate for ethical and humane practices toward animals. He often cited letters he received from boys who gave up trapping animals after learning from his books that wildlife creatures were individuals with their own lives. "What I remember of his books is the gentleness of his characters," says Mike Gradone, superintendent of Chatham (Massachusetts) Public Schools, an avid Burgess fan. "Even Reddy Fox and Old Man Coyote did what they did out of necessity. It wasn't so much about winning and losing as about everyone surviving and nature carrying on."

Massachusetts Society for the Prevention of Cruelty to Animals

A long association between Thornton Burgess and the Massachusetts Society for the Prevention of Cruelty to Animals developed from their shared objective in using children's books to promote humane attitudes and practices.[15] Burgess served on the MSPCA board of directors for decades. His 1965 obituary named the organization as sole recipient of memorial contributions. Burgess once told a reporter that as an editor for Phelps Publishing he had interviewed the elderly MSPCA founder George Thorndike Angell in 1909. If the two discussed Angell's advocacy for humane treatment of animals through children's literature, that interview may have contributed to Burgess' motivation for writing *Old Mother West Wind* the following year.

"George Angell believed that through stories we can teach kindness and respect and compassion and justice," says MSPCA president Carter Luke. "Thornton Burgess continued that tradition and was recognized by the MSPCA as an important teacher and writer, which is obviously why he was selected to be on our Board of Directors. Our philosophical belief in the rights of animals and the responsibility of people to be kind to and respect them was fundamental to Burgess."

Burgess and Angell shared similar backgrounds as well as a humane philosophy. Both had fathers who died young, leaving their families penniless. Both became successful through hard work, not largess, and both worked actively through children's literature to influence public attitudes toward animals. In 1868, two horses died of exhaustion after being forced to carry two riders in a race over forty miles of rough roads. Outraged by the abuse, Angell resolved to use his resources as a prominent Boston lawyer and philanthropist to improve animal welfare. Within one month, he had incorporated the Massachusetts Society for the Prevention of Cruelty to Animals. Within four months, he inspired passage of Massachusetts' first animal anti-cruelty laws, and within five months he produced 200,000 copies of *Our Dumb Animals*, the first MSPCA magazine. Angell personally paid to publish and distribute two million free copies of *Black Beauty*, the beloved horse story by English author Anna Sewell, which he felt clearly illustrated humane and inhumane treatment of animals.

Both the philanthropist and the writer believed that attitudes, not human nature, were responsible for cruelty and brutality toward animals — and attitudes could be changed through education. According to Luke, Angell was one of the first to recognize the correlation between cruelty to animals and criminal behavior toward people: "When he was questioned about devoting time to animals when there was so much human suffering, he replied that he was 'working at the roots.'" Luke observed that Angell and Burgess both considered animal stories effective teaching tools because they utilized the fundamental connection between humankind and animals:

> We have this incredible attraction to animals. They link us to the natural world and I think this link is part of our genes. We're attracted by the deer crossing the road or birds at a feeder. We want to see whales in the ocean. We want to live with certain kinds of animals. Animals help us understand not only the natural world but ourselves...They are part of our family. Animals are never evil, they are who they are. They are our support. I think learning more about wildlife enables us to protect the world.
>
> This natural attraction wakes us up to the fact that it is not about human beings alone because animals have feelings too. They experience pain, they can suffer and be scared. Just starting to recognize those issues in animals can turn little kids into empathetic adults. In fact, I think our humaneness may be the key to our species' survival, because if we can't learn this, we will not survive. I think the stories about animals that kids so love help us learn humaneness.

Few stories validate Luke's assertions as vividly as the plight of an Allen's hummingbird that made national news in the winter of 2010. In October, a Cape Cod woman spotted the little bird at her feeder and fed it in hopes of providing sufficient nourishment for it to leave before winter set in, but the hummingbird never left. In January, it was still feeding desperately as temperatures plummeted. "It was tiny, the whole thing was maybe three inches long, and the body was only two inches," says *Cape Cod Times* senior staff photographer Steve Heaslip, who covered the story. "To get the photos took more patience than stealth. I was there for an hour, and it was at the feeder for probably forty minutes." When sugar water from the feeder got onto its wings and froze, the hummingbird fell to the ground. Wild Care, a local rescue and rehabilitation organization, rushed to retrieve it, but was unable to keep the bird alive for more than a few days.

"The response was unbelievable," recalled manager Lela Learned. "People contacted us from as far away as Alaska and the Florida Keys. We were getting calls hourly. People came by with donations of sugar. Someone who had a greenhouse offered it, and the Wildlife Center of Silicon Valley in San Jose, California, offered to arrange a Red-eye flight to take the bird directly to them. A Pulitzer nominee even wrote a poem about him." Asked to explain the intensity of this response to one tiny creature, Learned reflected, "I think he was like a bridge. He offered a portal for nature."

The MSPCA sponsored numerous Burgess lectures at the Boston Public Library for "Be Kind to Animals Week." The women's auxiliary of the Springfield branch briefly sponsored Burgess' final 1939 radio programs, during which he offered general information about both domestic and wild animals. [On that last radio series Burgess advocated for Congressional passage of protective legislation for the bald eagle.]

Aida Flemming and International Kindness Clubs

Kindness towards animals was a value Burgess espoused early in his literary career. It was a membership requirement for his Green Meadow Club in 1914 and Radio Nature League in 1925. In the 1950s, New Brunswick newspaper editor Stuart Trueman introduced him to Aida Flemming, a well-known Canadian animal welfare advocate who was organizing Kindness Clubs in Canada. Flemming, the wife of New Brunswick Prime Minister Hugh John Flemming, corresponded with Burgess for a number of years about her work and his educational writing. [With Albert Schweitzer as honorary president, Kindness Clubs spread throughout North America, Europe, Asia, and Africa; in 1969, the U.S. Humane Society took over administration of American Kindness Clubs.]

Archival correspondence at the University of New Brunswick indicates that Flemming asked Burgess about referencing or using his books and stories for nature education in schools. In 1958, he responded: "About the books. Some of my earlier books, the Old Mother West Wind series, were put out in school editions. But that was years ago. I do not know if they are still in print. I am writing my publisher to find out. One of the series was once published in China for the very purpose you have in mind, to teach children to be kind to lesser forms of life."[16]

In that same letter to Flemming, Burgess documented his vitality in old age, as well as his enduring involvement in work: "I am feeling fine, thank you. A bit weak in the knees. In other words from the hips down I am my full age, 84, but from the hips up, age is indeterminate. My very warm regards to you and to Mr. Flemming. Should be visiting New Brunswick for a bit of fishing this coming summer, we will make an effort to pay our respects."

In another letter, Burgess provided Flemming with an example of tangible rewards of humane education and offered marketing advice on the use of radio:

> It was good to hear from you and get at first hand more about your Kindness Club. I have read through with much interest the brief you prepared. I can appreciate the amount of work you put into it.
>
> You ask if I have any of my Radio Nature League programs on tape. I am sorry to say I haven't. In those early days there was no such thing as taped programs. I have a number of my programs on file and I am going to look these up and mail you a copy of one so you may see just how I handled the radio work. If you can

by any means interest the CBC [Canadian Broadcasting Company] in a program you will have the most effective means in spreading your club work. Always the cost enters into such a program. Sometimes something can be done in the way of a sustaining program. This is what my program was for ten years. However it was confined to one station, WBZ.

I have in mind an Italian boy in one of the lower grades of the Springfield Public Schools who was what you might call "a bad egg." In school the teachers had all kinds of trouble with him and outside school he was in difficulties most of the time. Then one day he found an injured pigeon in the street. He took it home and cared for it. He took it out to a little bird hospital that my Radio Nature League was supporting. It was quite a trip out to it but he managed to make it every day or two. To make a long story short, that pigeon changed the life of that boy. He became a model of deportment in school. It was all the direct result of his response to the impulse of kindness to the injured bird. The incident gave me splendid material for my program. Permit me to suggest that you give special effort to getting a radio program…I firmly believe that more can be done through radio and TV than in any other method of reaching the public. Happily it reaches both adults and children.

Please pass my greeting to Mr. Flemming and my wishes for a successful political campaign.[17]

Burgess Honored for his Work

Of the awards Thornton Burgess received in his lifetime, the one of greatest scientific significance was the gold medal award of merit bestowed by the New York Zoological Society's Permanent Wildlife Protection Fund for his contributions to conservation and environmental education.

On January 14, 1919, Burgess and his wife Fannie took the train from Springfield, Massachusetts, to New York to attend a presentation ceremony at the annual meeting of the New York Zoological Society. It was held coincidentally on the writer's forty-fifth birthday. In his later years Burgess remembered the event as a complete surprise, but, in fact, he was well prepared. Hornaday, ever the master of orchestrated performance, had mailed Burgess scripted instructions for preferred attire, conduct, and procedures. Considering their friendship and the letter's teasing tone, Hornaday's minute directions were not intended to intimidate or impress Burgess, but simply to put him at ease, as well as to ensure the formal ceremony went smoothly:

Of course you will need to wear your glad togs. When I am halfway through my speech I will invite you to arise and come forward and confront me at the edge of the stage, virtually at arm's length. I will then finish what I have to say directly to you and pin the medal upon your manly breast. I will then step backward one or two paces and you can make your responses at first to me and then to the audience.

> The best idea will be to talk about the importance of protecting wild life and the pleasure there is in doing it. Do not compliment me about anything; but if you wish to express your satisfaction with the cooperation of the Permanent Wildlife Protection Fund in the great sanctuary-making contest and speak of the encouragement that it has been, provided it has been any, that will be alright.
>
> We must both beware of talking too long, but my speech will need to be about twice as long as yours. Of course I shall mention prominently, first your influence on wildlife protection through your stories and your audience of 6,000,000 young people, and, secondly, the importance and success of the sanctuary-making contest, which, as I understand it, owes its initiative wholly to you.[18]

As printed in Hornaday's third report to the Permanent Wildlife Protection Fund, the citation that accompanied the gold medal referenced Burgess' "distinguished services" to American children and wildlife and the fact that in less than ten years since he started writing for children, he had written 2,500 syndicated stories and twenty-seven books. The words that must have pleased Burgess as none others, however, observed his inspiring love for wildlife, his sane and logical treatment of the sport question, and most importantly, his "conscientious and correct presentations." There, before hundreds of elite, highly educated scientists, and other members of the New York Zoological Society, a high school graduate who became famous for his children's animal stories was accredited, acclaimed, and applauded.

Northeastern University Honorary Degree

In 1938, when he was 64, Burgess reluctantly took a phone call from Northeastern University vice president Carl Ell, anticipating a request for a donation. Instead, he was amazed to learn he had been selected to receive an honorary Doctor of Literature degree. He noted in his journal on May 3, 1938: "A day that brought a dream to unexpected reality. Dr. Speare came to say that it had been voted…to confer on me a doctor's degree (Honorary) at the Commencement exercises at Boston Arena on June 20. So I shall wear a cap and gown after all. It developed that he once lived in Sandwich."

Before Burgess accepted his diploma, President Frank Palmer Speare stated, "Because of your notable achievements as an editor and as a writer, because of high standing as a naturalist, and because of the knowledge and the joy in nature and wildlife which you have engendered in countless thousands through your books, syndicated articles, lectures, and radio talks, the trustees have authorized me to confer upon you the degree of Doctor of Literature." A fellow recipient of an honorary degree in law that day at Northeastern was Henry Cabot Lodge, Jr.

On June 20, 1938, Burgess wrote in his journal: "Memorable day. Off for Boston at 9 o'clock. A perfect day. Registered at Statler. To lunch at Chamber of Commerce with other candidates for degrees and members of corporation of Northeastern University. Spoke after Senator (Henry) Bridges. Dropped in to see Dr. Wigglesworth. To dinner at home of Pres. Speare. To Boston Arena where I donned cap and gown for first time…The impossible has happened. I am a Dr."

New York World's Fair Award

On April 15, 1939, Burgess received a letter from Mrs. Bernice Marshall, president of the National Life Conservation Society, notifying him of the organization's intention to honor him at the New York World's Fair the following month. "I can think of no one with the possible exception of my best friend, the late Dr. William T. Hornaday, who has done so much to create a feeling of interest and duty toward the preservation of our wildlife as you have by your very appealing stories," Marshall wrote. Dr. Ira Gabrielson, first director of the Biological Survey, and a representative of the National Park Service would be speakers for the occasion. Marshall further noted that although "conservation is not a subject that lends itself to anything in the nature of a show," the program of speeches, slides, music, and awards had generated considerable interest.

Burgess' thoughts on the day of the presentation strayed as they usually did on this date, May 18th, to the birthday of his son Thornton: "Boy 33 today. 6:30 train to N.Y. Over to World's Fair about 11. Lunch at 12 with quite a party. Sat with Bill Adams, Dr. Gabrielsen and daughter, and a Mrs. Palmer. Was largely the show at Conservation Society meeting when I was presented with medal by Mrs. Marshall... poem to me read by Mrs. Phelps." After the ceremony, Burgess attended a tea and went sightseeing before catching an 11:50 sleeper train home.

Boston Museum of Science Award

On June 1, 1936, Thornton Burgess was invited to join the board of trustees of the Boston Society of Natural History, later the Boston Museum of Science.[19] He wrote in his journal: "Drs. [Edward] Wigglesworth and [Thomas] Barbour [Harvard Museum of Comparative Zoology] arrived about 1 o'clock and assured me they were not after money but advice. Asked if I would serve as trustee of Boston Society of Natural History and discussed plans for a complete reorganization. Feel I have been honored indeed. It is recognition of the kind I most appreciate."

The next day, he noted, "Got out letters to Drs. Barbour, Wigglesworth, [Dr. Clyde] Fisher, and Sherwood." On June 6, he received confirmation of his appointment. His journals note frequent trips into Boston to attend meetings, including the May 1, 1939 meeting when he "met Dr. Babcock for first time after years of correspondence. Also met new director, Mr. Washburn...Discussed future plans. Got the midnight train for home. Glad I went down."

Bradford Washburn, the museum's new director, was a noted explorer, mountaineer, cartographer, filmmaker, pilot, and author of ten books. He had climbed Mt. Washington at the age of eleven and created the first large-scale map of Mt. Everest. Although he and Burgess initially met at Washburn's first board meeting in Boston, the director had long known of Burgess through reading his books and articles. The two kept in touch until Burgess' last years, and Washburn's wife Barbara, the first woman to climb Mt. McKinley, remembers having tea together at Burgess' home in Hampden. In 1964, Washburn would hand Burgess a gold medal award from the Boston Museum of Science.

The award was created after an anonymous donor had proposed to acknowledge the director's twenty-five years of distinguished leadership by establishing the H. Bradford Washburn, Jr. Award to recognize individual contributions to science and science literacy. The first selection committee included Richard Borden, Massachusetts Audubon Society president; Erwin Canham, *Christian Science Monitor* editor-in-chief; and Washburn. "When we decided on the objective of this prize, we listed a number of people who might have received it in the past, in order to give our committee more than a verbal feel of the award," Washburn explained in a letter to Burgess, adding:

> Then all of a sudden I realized that I owed three of these might-be recipients a great debt of gratitude for what they had done for me. So I decided to be very selfish and personal, and discussed a little idea with the donor: this year only to give the medal alone [the proposed award included a cash prize] to the three individuals whose advice, counsel, and inspiration in the exact spirit of this award have meant so much to me in my life of interest in public science education...Thornton Burgess was the first person who did more than anyone else to give me an early love of nature.

In a letter dated October 20, 1964, Washburn wrote the aged author:

> Barbara and I have just returned from Tokyo where we had a wonderful trip to see the Olympic Games...If I had not been away for nearly a month, I would have written to you much sooner. Shortly after my 25th Anniversary celebration last spring, one of our Trustees made a very large contribution to the Museum in honor of my service here—the result being a prize called the Washburn Prize.
>
> The first Washburn Prize is to be given at our Annual Meeting on November 16th. At that time, we are also going to give three additional special medals to the three individuals who had more influence than anyone else in bringing about my enthusiasm for nature and science. These three people are: You, for, as you already know, your wonderful books had a tremendous effect on my love of nature as a youngster. My mother and father read them to me from the time I could understand anything until the time I could read — and I read them avidly myself as virtually the first English prose I ever tackled alone. There is also not the slightest doubt in any of our minds here at the Museum that these same books had the same effect on literally millions of Americans throughout two full generations.
>
> I don't need to tell you once more what a tremendous debt of gratitude I owe you for all that you have done for me and millions of other youngsters.
>
> Ever affectionately,
> Brad

Kirtley Mather, Harvard teacher and author, and Dr. Gilbert Grosvenor, "master builder of the National Geographic Society," were also honored for their influence on Washburn. Dr. Grosvenor's son, Dr. Melville Bell Grosvenor, grandson of Alexander Graham Bell, was the recipient of the first Bradford Washburn prize. Although Washburn knew Burgess had suffered a debilitating stroke earlier, he urged him to attend the award presentation at the 1964 Boston Museum of Science annual dinner meeting, assuring him that he would hand-deliver the honorary medal if that was not possible. In a November 18, 1964 letter to Burgess, Washburn wrote:

> Dear Mr. Burgess,
>
> Many, many thanks for your wonderful letters. We certainly missed you on Monday night. It was a heartwarming occasion with many, many old friends present. As soon as Barbara and I can dig ourselves out from under the mountain of work I've inherited because of our recent vacation, we'll be out to see you, and bring your award to you in person. In the meantime, I am enclosing a copy of your citation so that you'll know what was said about you!
>
> Ever sincerely,
>
> Brad[20]

As promised, Washburn delivered the gold medal to Burgess at the Mary Lyon Nursing Home. It was a unique moment that manager Louis Levine recalled in his article, "Unforgettable Thornton Burgess," published in the October 1967 issue of *Reader's Digest.* "This is the highlight of my career," Burgess had whispered to Levine. "Then he wept," Levine remembered. "I had never seen him break down before."[21]

The Naturalist: Photos

Thornton Burgess canoeing with friend, location and date unknown.

Burgess on camping trip traveling by auto carrying canoes.

Burgess, with fishing guide, displays an impressive catch, probably in Nova Scotia or New Brunswick. Circa 1930s.

Burgess on bow of boat.

Burgess worked as a photo-journalist for Phelps Publishing in Springfield when he was in his 20s. This was one of his well-publicized photos.

Thornton Burgess made thousands of nature photographs like these on trips with ornithologist Dr. Alfred Gross to Panama, Labrador, Maine, Martha's Vineyard, and on photo shoots at home and in the area.

Dr. William T. Hornaday, director of the New York Zoological Society, was an ardent conservationist who is often credited with saving the bison. Left: *Courtesy of Mark Madison, U.S. Fish and Wildlife Service.* Right: *Courtesy of Greg Dehler.*

An example of women's millinery fashions that impacted bird species hunted for their plumage. *Courtesy of Mark Madison, U.S. Fish and Wildlife Service.*

A typical scene of slaughtered birds and animals that supplied public markets, date unknown. *Courtesy of Mark Madison, U.S. Fish and Wildlife Service.*

Smithsonian curator Clyde Fisher.

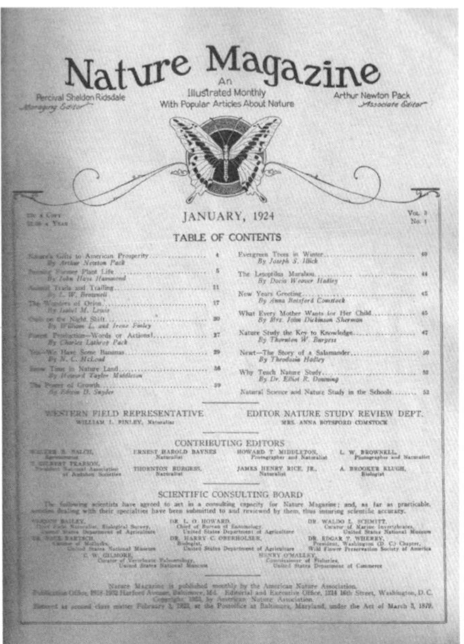

Nature Magazine

Percival Sheldon Ridsdale, Managing Editor — An Illustrated Monthly With Popular Articles About Nature — Arthur Newton Pack, Associate Editor

JANUARY, 1924 — Vol. 3, No. 1

TABLE OF CONTENTS

Nature's Gifts to American Prosperity, By Arthur Newton Pack ... 4	Evergreen Trees in Winter, By Joseph S. Illick ... 40
Farming Plant Life, By John Hays Hammond ... 5	The Leptoptilus Marabou, By Doris Weaver Hadley ... 44
Animal Trails and Trailing, By L. W. Brownell ... 11	New Years Greeting, By Anna Botsford Comstock ... 45
The Wonders of Orion, By Isabel M. Lewis ... 17	What Every Mother Wants for Her Child, By Mrs. John Dickinson Sherman ... 45
Owls on the Night Shift, By William L. and Irene Finley ... 20	Nature Study the Key to Knowledge, By Thornton W. Burgess ... 47
Forest Protection—Words or Actions!, By Charles Lathrop Pack ... 27	Newt—The Story of a Salamander, By Theodosia Hadley ... 50
Yes—We Have Some Bananas, By N. C. McLoud ... 29	Why Teach Nature Study, By Dr. Elliot R. Downing ... 52
Snow Time in Nature Land, By Howard Taylor Middleton ... 38	Natural Science and Nature Study in the Schools ... 53
The Power of Growth, By Edwin D. Snyder ... 39	

WESTERN FIELD REPRESENTATIVE: WILLIAM L. FINLEY, Naturalist

EDITOR NATURE STUDY REVIEW DEPT.: MRS. ANNA BOTSFORD COMSTOCK

CONTRIBUTING EDITORS

T. GILBERT PEARSON, President National Association of Audubon Societies; ERNEST HAROLD BAYNES, Naturalist; THORNTON BURGESS, Naturalist; HOWARD T. MIDDLETON, Photographer and Naturalist; JAMES HENRY RICE, JR., Naturalist; L. W. BROWNELL, Photographer and Naturalist; A. BROOKER KLUGH, Biologist

SCIENTIFIC CONSULTING BOARD

The following scientists have agreed to act in a consulting capacity for Nature Magazine; and, as far as practicable, articles dealing with their specialties have been submitted to and reviewed by them, thus insuring scientific accuracy.

VERNON BAILEY, Chief Field Naturalist, Biological Survey, United States Department of Agriculture; DR. L. O. HOWARD, Chief of Bureau of Entomology, United States Department of Agriculture; DR. WALDO L. SCHMITT, Curator of Marine Invertebrates, United States National Museum; DR. PAUL BARTSCH, Curator of Mollusks, United States National Museum; DR. HARRY C. OBERHOLSER, Biologist, United States Department of Agriculture; DR. EDGAR T. WHERRY, President, Washington (D. C.) Chapter, Wild Flower Preservation Society of America; C. W. GILMORE, Curator of Vertebrate Paleontology, United States National Museum; HENRY O'MALLEY, Commissioner of Fisheries, United States Department of Commerce

Nature Magazine is published monthly by the American Nature Association. Publication Office, 1918-1932 Harford Avenue, Baltimore, Md. Editorial and Executive Office, 1214 16th Street, Washington, D.C. Copyright, 1923, by American Nature Association. Entered as second class matter February 1, 1923, at the Postoffice at Baltimore, Maryland, under the Act of March 3, 1879.

Masthead of 1924 Nature Magazine featuring Burgess' article "Nature as the Universal Teacher."

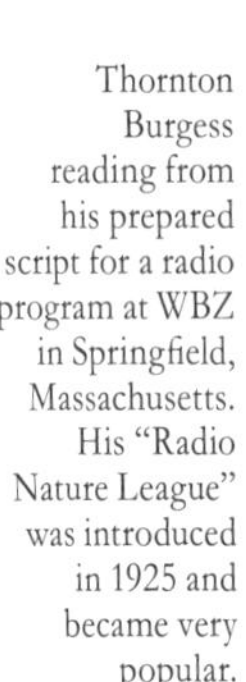

Thornton Burgess reading from his prepared script for a radio program at WBZ in Springfield, Massachusetts. His "Radio Nature League" was introduced in 1925 and became very popular.

Fannie Burgess, Alfred Gross, and Thornton Burgess (Melinna Gross undoubtedly was the photographer) enjoying a lobster picnic.

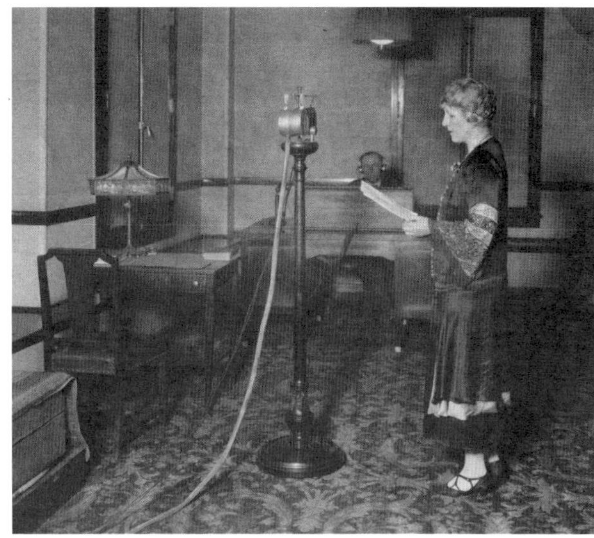

Fannie Burgess speaking during a radio program.

VINEYARD GAZETTE, MARTHA'S VINEYARD, MASS.

s in the Bird's Journe

Most Intimate Picture of the World's Last Heath Hen

In April, 1931, the lone bird was trapped and banded. Here it is, in Thornton W. Burgess's hands.

the thought of young buds, and I heard the fairy chorus of the pinkletinks ringing from reedy pools in the hollows.

Singularly fairy-like is this chorus wherever heard,

from 7 a. m. until nightfall, handicapped by a heavy wind, at times

Black Magic and the Minuet

BUSINE

Newspaper reproduction from an April 21, 1933 article about the Heath Hen. Copyright by the *Vineyard Gazette*, a weekly newspaper published on Martha's Vineyard. All rights reserved. *Courtesy of the Vineyard Gazette.*

Taken on Martha's Vineyard, this field photograph shows the now extinct Heath Hen. *Courtesy of Mark Madison, U.S. Fish and Wildlife Service.*

A stock photograph of Burgess posing with children. Circa 1950s.

Burgess autographing copies of the *Burgess Bird Book for Children.*

Stu Parson, former naturalist with Thornton W. Burgess Society, using live animals to enhance nature education.

Burgess visits children at Sandwich Henry T. Wing Elementary School, 1954.

Director Brad Washburn, with his wife Barbara, personally delivers an award from the Boston Museum of Science to Thornton Burgess at the Mary Lyon Nursing Home in 1963. *Courtesy of David Cesan.*

PART IV: THE LEGACY

Burgess by the Laughing Brook.

Chapter 15

The Legacy of Place

Laughing Brook is the name Thornton Burgess gave his beloved country home in Hampden, Massachusetts. A few years after his wife Fannie died in 1950, Burgess moved there permanently from Springfield and continued to write, adding to his thousands of children's stories, completing his autobiography and other books. Rural Sandwich had inspired his earliest children's stories with the Briar Patch, Green Meadow, and Smiling Pool, but he drew the Laughing Brook, Purple Hills, and other literary environments from the beautiful landscape of western Massachusetts and the Connecticut River Valley. In 1966, the Massachusetts Audubon Society purchased Burgess' property, now Laughing Brook Wildlife Sanctuary, where it offers outdoor education programs and manages walking trails. At present Burgess' home, writing studio, and barn are closed to the public.

"When I first bought my property in Hampden, I had from the very start the feeling that the setting was almost perfect for my work, and as time went on this feeling grew. [It] was nearly complete with the green forest, green meadows, Laughing Brook, the purple mountains and at that particular time the old orchard. All were featured in my stories."[1]

Thornton W. Burgess, c. 1960s
"An Old Man's Dream"

"There is merit in preserving his legacy because he was a pioneering conservationist, now more than ever a worthy cause."

Robert McMaster, biology professor
Holyoke Community College, 2010

"It is clear from the minutes of the [Allen Bird Club] meetings that Burgess had an influence on forming the environmental consciousness of the club, along with founder Fannie Stebbins, in urging the bird sanctuary movement. ... The Allen Bird Club's more important contributions, once the loss of habitat to development became a bigger threat than bird hunting, were to contribute money in 1930 towards land purchase for the Annie Brown Wildlife Refuge at the Parker River National Wildlife Refuge and to establish its own wildlife sanctuary, named after Fannie Stebbins, in Longmeadow in 1951. Both efforts were inspired by the early advocacy of Burgess."

George C. Kingston, historian, 2012

An Historic Country Home

In the spring of 1924, when Thornton Burgess and his wife Fannie had been living for thirteen years in Springfield, Massachusetts, he bought a second home in the country with eighteen acres of land in nearby Hampden, a small, rural town in the Connecticut River Valley. Behind the house was a wooded hill and before it lay an open field with purple hills rising in the distance. Typical of his penchant for naming places and animals, Burgess called his pre-Revolutionary home and the adjacent stream "Laughing Brook." Built in 1742, Laughing Brook is the only house in Hampden on the National Register of Historic Places. The rustic charm and setting of the ancient dwelling that snuggled into the bend of a small tributary of the Scantic River was indeed perfect for a writer who "never got over liking to be in the country," as his granddaughter Frances Meigs said. A 1916 newspaper article about the eighteenth century home described it in very Burgessian detail:

> It nestles there in the ground swells, warm and gray against the pale fields and the sky, half cloud, half blue. It must be beautiful in summer, with all its little doors and windows wide open, and the checker of shade on its lazy roof slope...Just off the kitchen at the front of the house is the old dining room. A great wood fire burns here, day in and day out practically from early October...The ancient fireplace is crammed with 18th century cooking implements, a frying pan a foot and a half in diameter with a handle at least four feet long...the three legged stewing pots, crane spits...The walls are the same as they were 170 years ago. The bare rough boards of oak a foot and a half wide, probably hand sawn, are their own adornment. The old oaken bars are on the doors, the old hinges, painted now and polished to a gloss.[2]

A Writer's Retreat

Burgess maintained that he could write anywhere, but Laughing Brook became his favorite workplace. Steps led up to a one-room bungalow on the steeply pitched small hill, a glacial esker, behind the house. Later, when arthritis prevented him from climbing the slope, he moved his workplace to the barn. As a devout fisherman, he must have been delighted to discover it was possible to fish in the burbling stream just below his new studio's window. The antique country house was ideal for hosting friends, family, and professional colleagues, including illustrators Lemuel Palmer, Phoebe Erickson, and Harrison Cady and their spouses. Awed children and total strangers stopped to chat, collect his autograph, or deliver injured animals into his care. When he sat outdoors in the summer, he would wave back at people who recognized him because, as he joked to his neighbor Polly Philpot, "I have to — they buy my books."

The presence of Burgess' immediate family, including ten grandchildren, fill the pages of his journals, as they were a vital, enriching part of his life in Springfield and Hampden. He had one son, Thornton W. Burgess III, who married Mildred Peterson and had three children: Nancy, Thornton Burgess IV, called "Brother," and David. Burgess' second wife Fannie Johnson had two children from a previous marriage, Chester Johnson and Helen Johnson Kohloss Bradford. Chester and his wife Ruth Spaulding had two children, Bobby and Willis, while Helen married twice and had five children: Robert, Jean, Frances, Rosemary, and William. Fannie's grandchildren were technically Burgess' step-grandchildren, but he considered them his own.

"I have great memories of their house," says grandson William Bradford of Newport, Rhode Island. "I remember the meals that came out of that little kitchen and the blue and white plates Nanna had all around. We'd have the greatest scrambled eggs, Grampa's specialty. There was a little putting green golf course right outside the back door. In the summer we'd all be outside, and the water would be boiling on the outside grill, and Grampa would say, 'Alright, William, time to go across the street and get the corn.' As a little kid, it was like a paradise, with snakes and the skunks Mike and Ike. They were cute as heck."

Bradford recalls being the one to gently tell his elderly grandfather it was time to relinquish his driver's license: "I wrote him a letter and told him how much he loved everybody in Hampden, and if he ever injured anyone he would never forgive himself." Burgess replied that he had gotten behind the wheel of a car for the last time, Bradford says. "He said how hard it must have been for me to write that letter, and how much he appreciated it. There were tears running down my face when I read it."

"We used to go visit him in Hampden every summer," remembers granddaughter Nancy Hughes, who grew up with her mother and brothers in Cambridge, Massachusetts. Her father joined the Army to serve in Germany during World War II and then worked in Saudi Arabia for the Arabian-American Oil Company, formerly California-Arabian Standard Oil Company, now Chevron. "We had great times with Grampa at Laughing Brook," says Hughes. "He was always busy writing, but of course he would never say, 'Oh I'm too busy to visit with you.' He was a very sweet, gentle person. I don't think he ever said a mean word about anybody." Affection between Burgess and his grandchildren was mutual. He wrote in his 1947 journal of lecturing for the fifth consecutive year at the Boston Public Library: "Hall nearly filled despite heat. Mildred and children there and we took them out to their home where we had supper. The children are dear, all three of them."[3]

Frances Meigs describes a deeply loving relationship with her grandparents, Thornton and Fannie, in her memoir *My Grandfather Thornton W. Burgess*, crediting them with providing her and her siblings with essential nurturing and stability. "My mother and father weren't there that much, so we loved coming to our grandfather's house," she said. "I was always on Grampa's lap. We children just absorbed him."

Dedicated Gardener

Burgess was an avid gardener at Laughing Brook. "He kept extensive flower beds to the right of the house, and he cultivated a thirty- by forty-foot vegetable garden across the street until the 1955 flood took out a bridge and silted it over," recalls David Cesan, the son of Ernestine Johnson, Burgess' secretary in Hampden. The writer's journals recorded many years of bountiful harvests of peas, beans, beets, broccoli, kohlrabi, carrots, onions, tomatoes, corn, and numerous other crops he started as seeds or seedlings in the spring and carefully tended through the summer. "He loved that vegetable garden," says Cesan. The pleasure Burgess derived working at Laughing Brook is confirmed in his journals, as is his physical hardiness. He was in his seventies when he wrote the following:

> Cleaned barn, or helped to do it. Did some work on hill. Watched female hummingbird apparently starting a nest in oak tree in plain view of window beside which I work. First noticed birds apparently picking the lichens from trunks of trees and flying to same spot on limb of oak. Could see nothing on it for a long time, but late in afternoon could see what looked like possible foundation...Hummer busy all day and nest shaping up rapidly. Sits in it while she adds material and shapes it around her.

> Another very lovely day. It couldn't have been better...Did two stories and some work about the place...Humming bird among oaks near last year's nesting place. Young Rabbit kicking up his heels in play and feeding between garden and the

long bed. Out there for over half an hour about sunset. More corn ready. Probably continuous supply from now on. Glad I put in early variety.

A bright day with a cold, tiresome wind...worked until 4:30 p.m., planting three double rows of sweet and garden peas, full rows of carrots and beets, and short rows of lettuce, kohlrabi and cabbage...Hen pheasant in clover near garden. Radishes breaking ground.

To Hampden by 8:30...Got east side mowed, planted 1 row of string beans, 5 hills of cukes, putting plenty of well-rotten manure in earth, and 2 rows of popcorn. Got 10 hills nearly prepared for melons when rain forced me to quit...Home by 5 o'clock, wet and tired.[4]

The Writing Studio

Burgess was a light drinker whose gambling was generally limited to penny ante poker and church-sponsored raffles. His use of the one-room building at Laughing Brook as a solitary, peaceful writing studio was a sharp contrast to the merry partying for which it was originally intended. A 1952 article describes the property's purchase in the early 1920s for use as a sportsmen's clubhouse:

The old Stebbins place [later Laughing Brook] was acquired by a group of Springfield business men for the Massasoit Fish and Game Club. Edward Coates [a Springfield liquor store owner] was among the sponsors. Each Saturday evening during the summer months, the members of the club gathered in the old dining room for a supper that included such delicacies as brook trout, squab and chicken...Part of the time, Damon N. Coates [identified in his obituary as a diamond merchant], brother of Edward Coates, lived in the house...During the time the house was controlled by the Massasoit Club, the little house on the hill was built.[5]

A 1922 public notice stated that "a new building on the knoll in the rear of its present clubhouse," was to be erected by the Massasoit Fish and Game Club.[6] Its purpose is made clear in a 1983 oral history collected by Josh Lane from Hampden resident Gertrude Lyons who personally knew the Coateses:[7]

"Mary [Damon Coates' wife] didn't like all this gambling and drinking, and so they built that little house up on the hill. That's where they used to do their gambling. They didn't come into the house except to eat. The Saturday night I was there (to help prepare and serve the meal) they had a pheasant supper, and Mary had somebody come up from Springfield to help her put on the dinner. It was very interesting. These fellows would come out and go hunting and fishing and then they'd come back, and...they'd have to go up on the hill to do their carousing."

For Burgess, however, the rustle of leaves and peaceful gurgle of the stream rounding the bend beneath his writing studio were sufficient entertainment. He kept the large, single-room bungalow sparsely furnished with a few tables, a rush-seated chair, a metal framed bed, scattered rugs, file cabinets, a book case, and a mahogany writing desk, which faced the only doorway and the house visible below. On the desk he typically kept his black Remington manual typewriter, a dictionary, pencils, erasers, paper, and notes. A calendar and a few of Harrison Cady's paintings adorned the walls. Overhead were exposed wooden beams, deer antlers, and a pair of snowshoes. "And there were papers everywhere," says Meigs. When Burgess' mobility decreased, he moved his work space to the barn, creating a knotty pine sitting area and shelf-lined study with five tall file cabinets.

Burgess spent good and happy years at Laughing Brook, living there permanently after 1955. His journals noted that problems there generally related to the water heater, flooding and/or drought, and regular vandalism to the property, a tempting target near the roadway. In 1945, he recorded: "Shutters torn off, window forced open in main room, transom windows broken, back door left open, window broken in studio but nothing taken, and window in tool house broken, but was nailed down so nothing taken...Think it was boys."[8] On the Fourth of July, he usually stayed up through the night to ward off destructive visitors. His wife's poor health caused Burgess to contemplate giving up the Hampden property, but it was a fleeting consideration.

Strokes and Sadness

In 1963, Burgess, then 89, was strickened by a cerebral hemorrhage and moved permanently to the Mary Lyon Nursing Home in Hampden from Laughing Brook. Someone later found on his desk the last couplet he composed there: "Some folks are seldom thought of 'till / They leave a gap that none can fill."[9] He had experienced a mild stroke in 1950 after shoveling snow from the long driveway at 61 Washington Road in Springfield, but soon recovered. Within weeks, however, his wife Fannie also had a stroke. She died later that year on August 16, 1950.

"My Lady, my beloved, passed at 9:15 and my heart is broken," Burgess wrote in his journal. "I am utterly desolate. Fances [*sic*] came, bless her. Robert arrived in p.m. Wm. left for home."[10] In the days that followed, an anguished Burgess wrote repeatedly of the effort to "hold my self together." Nothing illustrated the depth of his grief more than his journal's repeated refrain: "'I'm glad I belong to you' — My Lady." For more than a year, he began each day's entry with these words of tenderness that his wife, who he nicknamed "Lady," had apparently once written or spoken to him. As always he coped with hardship by immersing himself in work and in nature:[11]

> A hard day. Work my one relief. Frances, God bless her, helped me do 7 stories... Up at six and drove 30 miles among the hills.
>
> A wet day as if the very skies wept with me. Again Frances proved a sustaining support. We did 6 stories and I mailed two sets to Cady. Now 5 weeks ahead... Cannot get control of my self. My home and my heart are empty.

Immediately after Fannie's death, Burgess sought refuge on the Cape among old friends and familiar places. Protectively accompanied by several grandchildren, he spent a week there, staying at the Coonamesset Inn in Falmouth near one of his grandchildren and visiting his hometown:

> To Sandwich. Saw Aunt S. [Alice Cooke] for few minutes. Also Eliz. Clark. Found graves of Thomas and Dorothy Burgess from whom I am 9th generation.
>
> A lovely day…Stopped at cemetary [sic]. Burgess lot not too well kept. Drive to Canal, town neck and walked to beach. Visited two fish hatcheries…Spent evening talking over old days with Geo Dennis. Took my mind off my loss.
>
> Drove around [Shawme] pond in early morning. To see Aunt Sally about 9. To [First Church of Christ] church at 11. First time to service there since I left town 58 years ago. Sat at back and slipped out before others so as not to meet a lot of folks. Flora Spurr's daughter recognized me going in. Walter Fish spoke when I came out…[in evening] After dinner…talking with Richard Bourne and others until 12.
>
> Best day so far. Showed Paul [husband of granddaughter Jean Montville] places of interest. To Sandwich Fish Hatchery where brook trout are raised, Bob MacComber in charge. Young Raymond assisting…at Game Farm where we saw Bob White and pheasants, also fawn. Lunch at Cahoon's lunchroom of which Aunt Sally told us. To beach…we all had dinner at the Yankee Clipper.[12]

As his wife's co-executor, he was shocked to learn that she had accumulated a considerable fortune — "probably double the maximum of what I would have guessed" — which she left primarily to her daughter and grandchildren. Burgess' own income was substantial, so he was not hurt or disturbed at being excluded as a beneficiary and noted simply: "I am disinterested…She knew I didn't need it."[13]

Widowed for the second time, Burgess continued to write, travel, and garden. In 1958, he sold the Springfield house he had bought in 1905. That transaction was complicated by the fact that Fannie Burgess, who handled most of the couple's finances, had years earlier inexplicably put the Washington Road property in her own name, willed it to her daughter Helen, and given Burgess life tenancy.

In the process of putting his own affairs in order, Burgess contemplated the fate of the Hampden home he cherished and wrote a two-page essay titled "An Old Man's Dream." It expressed his heartfelt desire to preserve specifically for children the place where he had written thousands of his stories:

> Now in my old age, I face the problem of what is to become of "Laughing Brook" as I named the place, when I pass on. The more I think of it, the more it hurts. It is very difficult to think of "Laughing Brook" placed in the hand of no-one-knows-who and the place forgotten. It is not a showplace but I submit it is attractive! It has drawn visitors from all over the United States and Canada through

> the years. I admit to a great degree of egotism to think that it would be preserved as a sort of mecca for the children of the future! ... The suggestion was made that it might be bought and given to the town! To preserve just as the author's home and where he spent his last days which was the birthplace of so many, many stories known by children all over America. This has started another dream; the possibility of some organization taking over the property and maintaining it.[14]

"An Old Man's Dream"

After Burgess' death in June 1965, the Hampden Lions Club obtained an option on the property in the fall. Their purpose was specifically to keep it from auction or private sale until they could find a buyer that would fulfill the hopes Burgess expressed in "An Old Man's Dream." Headed by Lions Club president Louis Levine, director of the Mary Lyon Nursing Home, a search committee actively sought a buyer for more than a year. Among those Levine contacted was Charles "Chuck" Roth, then education director of the Massachusetts Audubon Society.

It was a promising lead, for Burgess had long-standing ties to the conservation organization. Although his papers generally fail to distinguish between the National Audubon Society and the Massachusetts Audubon Society, Burgess' relationship was primarily with the state organization, which enrolled him as a sustaining member in 1919 and named him an Honorary Vice-president in 1940. Mass Audubon provided an important forum for the conservation issues he supported, and its Tremont Street lectures featured prominent individuals Burgess knew as colleagues and friends, including Dr. William Hornaday, William and Irene Finley, Dr. Clyde Akeley, Edward Avis, Harry Oberholser, Dr. John C. Phillips, and Louis Agassiz Fuertes. Burgess' obituary in the *Springfield Republican* stated that he himself gave "hundreds of lectures for Audubon and school groups."[15] He described one Audubon lecture at the Statler Hotel ballroom in Boston: "Nearly 1200 present, double any previous attendance in series. Large sale of books which I autographed. Great demand for autographs for hour after lecture."[16] He was about to launch a new lecture series for Mass Audubon when his first stroke occurred. He wrote in his journal on February 24, 1950:

> Wired cancellation of six Audubon lectures. Dr. forbidding all thought of trying to fill engagements although they are two weeks away and more. [Russell] Mason of Audubon Society [Mason was then executive vice-president of the Massachusetts Audubon Society] called and would like use of film, which I granted.

Two weeks later the replacement lecturer came "to get film and for me to prime him on the pictures." Richard Walton's co-authored *Massachusetts Audubon Society: The First Sixty Years* mentions Burgess' participation in an Audubon nature lecture series: "During the 1950s, under the aegis of the National Audubon Society, the [Massachusetts Audubon Society] program maintained its popularity with such speakers as Roger Tory Peterson, Thornton W. Burgess, and Richard Borden [Mass Audubon president]."[17]

Mass Audubon Purchases Burgess Home

When Lou Levine inquired about Mass Audubon's interest in taking Laughing Brook on in the spirit of "An Old Man's Dream," Chuck Roth was pleased.[18] He personally knew and admired Burgess, but advised Levine that the organization had a restrictive policy. "We wouldn't take property unless there was endowment to maintain it," he says. As a result, [Emily] Paddy Wade, a longtime member of the Massachusetts Audubon Society's board of directors, managed a successful fund-raising drive for the necessary endowment monies for Laughing Brook. "I felt very strongly that it should be kept as Burgess' place," Wade says. "I thought his writing was important and his legacy should be preserved. Children would be able to go there and tie it all together. And I thought Laughing Brook was an asset for Mass Audubon. It was located in an area we didn't have anything, and this was near Springfield, so it was an advantage for the inner city kids and school kids and families."

With the November 1, 1966, purchase of the buildings and 17.8 acres of land at Laughing Brook for the price of $28,144[19], Mass Audubon acquired the contents of Burgess' office and library, including first edition books by Anna Botsford Comstock and Dr. William Temple Hornaday. "As I went through his things, I was dumbstruck," says Roth. "There was so much more there I didn't even know about." Mass Audubon later conveyed to or shared archival materials at Laughing Brook with the Thornton W. Burgess Society in Sandwich and the Massachusetts Historical Society.

Soon after the Massachusetts Audubon Society bought Laughing Brook, it announced plans for a multi-million dollar nature center with an emphasis on wildlife and rural settings.[20] In 1967, the first caged animals arrived at Laughing Brook Wildlife Sanctuary. Three deer and an enclosure were provided by Louis Levine and the Lions Club, which later also contributed a raptors' cage. Chuck Roth recruited Miriam Dickey at Boston Children's Museum as an educational assistant and David Bonney at the Museum of Science as Laughing Brook's first director.

More cages and animals were added, including a coyote, skunks, rabbits, woodchucks, and a hawk. Mass Audubon created hiking trails with signage and printed guides, gave tours of the property, and opened a gift shop that sold Burgess' books and the penny candy he had nostalgically specified in "An Old Man's Dream." Burgess' one-room writing studio was used for evening lectures and slide shows. By 1970, Laughing Brook Wildlife Sanctuary had three paid staff members and seventy-five volunteers. Edith Huck of Longmeadow and Sandwich belonged to the large, close-knit group of Laughing Brook volunteers. "It was a very busy place," she remembers. "We had school field trip groups all the time."

Happy Memories

"We ran tours of the house as an historic site, and tried to keep it and the furnishings as they had been before," Roth says. "We held Burgess story hour in the borning room off the kitchen. The live animals were a big attraction." Among the hundreds of weekly visitors was historian Julie Arrison, author of *Franklin Park*, who grew up in nearby Chicopee. Her parents passed on their love of Burgess stories and often took their daughters to visit the Laughing Brook Wildlife Sanctuary. "It was a place with walking trails and animals, a place to learn about nature and Thornton Burgess," says Arrison. "Even in the early 1980s, Burgess had a lasting impact on my sister and me as someone who taught children about nature. As an adult I realized how peaceful and serene the wildlife sanctuary was. I have a good family memory of Laughing Brook, of the animals, nature, and a nice Sunday afternoon with my parents. For me, there is a happiness there."

An important part of that happiness was Polly Philpott, the unforgettable Laughing Brook volunteer who portrayed "Old Mother West Wind" for more than twenty years. During a 2010 interview in her home, Philpott, then ninety-three, sat in a wheelchair, white hair pulled back into a youthful ponytail. Rabbit figurines dotted her coffee table, and awards and framed photos of her in costume as Old Mother West Wind covered the living room walls. In 1955, she and husband Dalton had moved across the street from Thornton Burgess, then a widower, and became friends. Dalton and Burgess regularly fished for trout in the stream that ran along their properties. Polly will never forget the time her nine-year-old daughter Darlene's horse Honey bolted. Burgess, in his 80s, planted himself in the middle of the road and waved his arms to try to head it off.

Philpott enthusiastically described the early days of Laughing Brook Wildlife Sanctuary when she represented in costume Old Mother West Wind, the all-knowing, ever-firm, just, and caring maternal character who oversaw Burgess' fictitious world. "In the beginning I had wings and wore a hooped skirt," she says, laughing. Philpott entertained and enlightened tourists and visitors at the sanctuary, and also traveled to out-of-state schools and hospitals. "She was incredibly good with children," says former Laughing Brook program coordinator Tom Tyning, now an environmental studies professor at Berkshire Community College. "The first time I met her I was cleaning animal poop out of cages. I looked up and here was this giant creature in a hoop skirt who just started talking to me." As a volunteer Philpott enjoyed pointing out Burgess' personal possessions, including an antique hooded cradle, his Salem rocker, and a hummingbird's nest, but says that her favorite job at the wildlife sanctuary was giving wild animal presentations.

Funds for a Nature Center

In 1970, a Friends of Laughing Brook committee launched fund-raising plans for an education/nature center.[21] Although it fell short of its $90,800 goal, it contributed significantly to facility improvements. Over the next three years Laughing Brook supporters implemented a course of action for a major funding-raising drive co-chaired by David Starr, a Springfield newspaper publisher, and David Anderson, a Springfield attorney. In order to obtain approval from the Greater Springfield Capital Funds Advisory Committee, Friends of Laughing Brook signed a Memorandum of Understanding with Mass Audubon in 1978. With the state organization's contribution of $92,000, the Friends exceeded their fund-raising goal of $460,000. Construction for the new nature center began in October 1979 and opened within a year. A decade later Mass Audubon undertook a $1.2 million renovation at Laughing Brook in order to deal with heavy visitor traffic, flood damage, and changes to the regulation of captive wildlife facilities. The work was completed in 1990.

"It was a remarkable place," says Tyning. "It was exhausting and totally fun. There was nothing like Laughing Brook at its height. The staff was working hard, people were getting the message, donations were pouring in, and even with the fancy new building nobody ever lost the connection to Burgess." In the early days the staff did everything from cleaning bathrooms to cage cleaning, Tyning recalls, and volunteers helped run all aspects of the operation and put on special events. "There were at least thirty to forty thousand visitors coming through for walks, talks, and demonstrations, even more if you include special programs," he said. "We also co-sponsored events with the local Allen Bird Club."[22]

Laughing Brook staff member Helen Bates was "the soul of Laughing Brook," says Tyning. "She made sure the volunteers used accurate information and were polite to visitors." Bates worked in the same knotty pine office that Thornton Burgess had occupied fifteen years earlier, amid the writer's file cabinets filled with original hand-typed syndicated bedtime stories files. "He actually had his typewritten story and the newspaper clipping of it stapled together in order by dates," says Tyning. "One day I went into a closet and found a shoebox full of black-and-white pictures with their negatives. I started thumbing through them and saw one I couldn't believe. It was a photograph of the last heath hen. And in Helen Bates' office I found an essay [Burgess] wrote when he went out with an ornithologist [Dr. Alfred Gross]. It was one of the most remarkable pieces of writing I'd ever seen. Here was the Burgess most people connected with Peter Rabbit writing one of the most poignant pieces of commentary on extinctions I'd ever read. It was very inspiring to me as a young naturalist coming into the field.

"Helen was fond of saying, 'Try to find out something that is not accurate about what Thornton Burgess' animals are doing,'" Tyning recalls. "He was a really good naturalist, and it made his characters believable to kids. He had a solid background in biology and he was out in the field communicating with the best men and women of science." He points out that in addition to the value of Laughing Brook's historic connection to an influential early twentieth century naturalist and nature writer, the wildlife sanctuary attracted and helped prepare young people for careers in conservation. "We had a big group of teenagers coming in to work, and some became major players in conservation and natural science throughout the country."

Wildlife Program Ended

To a considerable degree, the commitment of local residents made it possible for the sanctuary to meet demands for programming, space, and services. The corporate connections of Helen's husband Moreton Bates with Mass Mutual and Dalton Philpott with the Montsanto Corporation, for example, secured important financial backing for the sanctuary. "There were enormous numbers of people who were not involved with Mass Audubon, but they knew the sanctuary and were eager to support it," says Tyning. "They would get food and bedding for the animals. It was a place everybody knew, not only kids but adults."

Despite its overflow crowds, however, Laughing Brook began to experience debilitating loss of attendance, volunteers, and financial support in the 1990s.

Economic recession in the late 1980s had impacted school budgets, causing field trips and visitation to decline. "Several things were going on at the same time," says Tyning. "There was a huge economic drop, a mini-depression that affected us at Laughing Brook, and in the '80s there was a trend of getting away from static exhibits at zoos and museums, a trend in nature education that said people should be learning about what is right around them. There was a sense that a place like Laughing Brook could get along without relying on animals in cages, but it also seemed clear that having the animals would bring people out." Although there was a corporate sense that a facility like Laughing Brook didn't need to rely on the attraction of caged wildlife, it was evident that live animals were an important draw.

In 1992, Mass Audubon announced that the live animal facilities, though very popular, were too expensive to operate and would be phased out. Only two years after its major renovation/expansion project, Mass Audubon president Jeremy Bertrand sold and relocated the animals, removed the new exhibit, and laid off staff, leaving the sanctuary open primarily for bird watchers and hikers. Bertrand explained the action was due to Laughing Brook's exorbitant expenses, which depleted resources for other Mass Audubon sanctuaries. Hampden residents Polly Philpott and David Cesan blame the sanctuary's problems on elimination of the wild animal program.

The action greatly upset volunteers and local supporters, many of whom had financially contributed to and were highly invested in the Laughing Brook Wildlife Sanctuary programs and property. Some who had expected to will land to Mass Audubon withdrew their offers and resigned from the organization. Burgess family members Frances Meigs, Nancy Hughes, and Thornton W. Burgess IV became concerned about the apparent abandonment of Burgess' house and barn and the degraded condition of his writing studio, which was eventually cordoned off with "no trespassing" tape. Frances Meigs said the poor state of Laughing Brook had prompted her to write her memoir, *My Grandfather, Thornton W. Burgess*: "I saw the condition of the house and became afraid my grandfather was being forgotten."[23]

Spring flooding in 1997 caused further deterioration at Laughing Brook. As local commitment evaporated, attendance dropped to 2,000 in 2003. The situation worsened when the education center, for which both Mass Audubon and Friends of Laughing Brook had invested hundreds of thousands of dollars for initial construction, upkeep, and renovation, was torched by a local arsonist on September 1, 2004. The vacant, uninsured building was subsequently demolished by the town as a safety hazard. To make matters at the sanctuary worse, flooding in 2005 caused more damage to three bridges.

Among those disturbed by conditions at the historic property at Laughing Brook was Michael Dobbs, managing editor of *Reminder Publications*, who has fond memories of reading Burgess' stories and visiting Laughing Brook Wildlife Sanctuary as a boy. "If they're (Mass Audubon) not into preservation of historic resources, they should say so and partner with someone who is," he says. Springfield blogger Bob Shaunessy, who has documented the physical state of Laughing Brook since 2008, comments, "Laughing Brook was once the epicenter for nature education in Western

Massachusetts. What happened to this former jewel of a Massachusetts Audubon Society reservation?" A longtime supporter of Laughing Brook and the Thornton W. Burgess Society, Nancy Hladik of Penfield, New York, submitted a letter to the *Wilbraham-Hampden Times* that described her "continued frustration" over Mass Audubon's "lack of interest" in the buildings associated with children's author and naturalist Thornton Burgess.

According to Mary Shanley-Koeber, director of Mass Audubon's Connecticut River Valley Wildlife Sanctuaries, the steep slope, severe erosion, and storm damage at the site of Burgess' writing studio made structural restoration there extremely difficult at best. She had noted that contractors asked to assess the site in recent years all recommended demolition, "which was not an acceptable solution."[24]

In the fall of 2010, Mass Audubon hired Traditional Housewrights [in Sandwich, Massachusetts, now Old Colony Housewrights] to provide emergency stabilization for Burgess' writing studio. The roof, walls, and porch were in critical condition when contractors Joseph Roy and Justin McCarthy began work at Laughing Brook. "It had to do with the initial construction," says Roy. "There were wood timbers [resting] on the ground. It was built like a clubhouse for guys." The builders braced the porch and interior walls, essentially tying one end of the building to the other, replaced half the roof, and braced the chimney, which was in imminent danger of collapsing. "It was never built for longevity," says McCarthy. "It was stick framing with two by fours and nails."

In January 2012, the contractors returned to the site to pour sixteen new concrete footings to support the structure and porch. They saved about one-third of the existing sills and replaced the rest. "We were repairing a structure, not ripping it down," says McCarthy. "We used modern materials and methods and made improvements when we could. Whenever we had to add material, we did it to today's standards." A full restoration of the writing studio was ultimately completed in May 2012. Mass Audubon's plans for the renovated building have not been determined at present.

In 1996, former Hampden State Representative Mary Rogeness wrote in the *Beacon Hill Byline*, "How did this battle between the partners in operation come about? The [Massachusetts] Audubon Society and Laughing Brook [Wildlife Sanctuary] are both synonymous with environmentalism."[25] Ardently engaged in critical environmental issues of his day, Thornton Burgess would surely have been intrigued to find his cherished Hampden home and writing studio a focus of debate on whether to advance conservation through land acquisition/management or historic preservation/maintenance. However, for some area residents, Burgess family members, and devotees of the children's nature writer and naturalist, the heart of the matter continues to be default on a promise to fulfill "An Old Man's Dream."

A STORY: AFIELD ON THE GRAVES FARM

"I was afield in woods or on the marshes at every opportunity, usually alone. Studying the wild things and their ways."[1]

Thornton Burgess often commented that he learned about nature from books and authorities, and by studying nature when he was "afield," whether exploring Cape Cod's pine woods and salt marshes or Labrador's barren wilderness. When he moved to western Massachusetts, Burgess found different landscapes to investigate with a pair of binoculars and undoubtedly a notebook in his pocket. A reporter once asked him, "What is a Cape Codder like you doing so far inland?" He had replied: "I like the hills." Although he must have had many favorite places to go wandering and birding in the local countryside, the Graves Farm is known with certainty to be one because of a strange discovery by the Williamsburg (Massachusetts) Historical Society.

A westward-looking panorama of the Graves Farm taken in the late 1920s. *Courtesy of the Williamsburg Historical Society Graves Farm Collection.*

Less than thirty miles away from Burgess' home in Springfield, the Graves family's dairy farm had hundreds of acres of open land, the kind that inspired his children's stories, satisfied his desire to be outdoors with wildlife, and brought him peace of mind. Eric Weber and Ralmon Jon Black are intimately familiar with the farm; Eric as Graves Farm historian for the Williamsburg Historical Society and Ralmon as the town's historian and archivist who lives on nearby land that has been in his family for eight generations. Eric can easily explain the farm's appeal to a naturalist like Burgess:

> In his day, the farm was a patchwork of mowings, pastures, orchards, barnyard, flower beds, vegetable gardens, small tilled areas producing a variety of row crops, and extensive woodlands both wet and dry, on rich soils and poor rocky ones, all threaded by little farm roads and by Joe Wright Brook and Benoni Day Brook. Along Joe Wright Brook in the northern part of the farm's roughly 500 acres was (and still is) a deep talus-strewn gorge far too rugged even to harvest trees from, bordered on its east side by overhanging cliffs.

> A birder on foot could easily wander in one hour through eight or ten distinctly dissimilar habitats on the farm and reasonably expect to see the bird species endemic to each one of them, without having to drive all over western Massachusetts or even go very far from Burgess's home to do it. It was the enormous variety of ecological niches afforded to wildlife by the farm that made it extraordinary. And [brothers Dwight and John Graves'] faithful and enthusiastic devotion to recording whatever they saw, enabling a visitor to know what s/he might hope to see and where, was an added attraction.

Farm records showed that well-known area naturalist Samuel Eliot, co-author of *Birds of the Connecticut River Valley*[2], went birding at the Graves farm, but there is no written evidence of Burgess being there. "I vaguely remember my grandmother saying that Thornton Burgess had come and visited it," says Ralmon. Eric, too, knows of "scraps of stories, second- or third-hand from birders or local people" about Burgess being at the farm. And he has a wintertime photograph of two men standing with a smiling young John Graves, who, with his brother Dwight, owned the farm. The oldest of the three is a solid-framed older man wearing a good overcoat with binoculars around his neck. He is holding his eyeglasses and as a result is squinting in the sunlight. Based on comparison with other photographs, there is little question that the man is Thornton Burgess.

Dwight and John were the last family members to work on the Graves dairy farm, two life-long bachelors who were "reclusive hermits, unmarried old geezers with the same intellectual curiosity as Burgess," says Ralmon. "They were observers out on the land, and they kept lists of bird sightings, especially first sightings in the spring or an unusual sighting in the winter, like an albino. They'd report regularly to birders like Burgess and Eliot and send them a postcard or a letter describing what they saw."

According to the historian, Burgess appears to have influenced the brothers in two ways. Although the writer's "Old Man's Dream" proposal for sale and development of his own home in Hampden never specifically mentioned the Massachusetts Audubon Society, there are numerous anecdotes about Burgess' advice to the Graves brothers to give or sell their farm to the state organization. "What he said may have inspired them to leave their farm to Mass Audubon," says Ralmon.

In 1990, it was arranged that Mass Audubon would buy the 450-acre Graves farm from John and Dwight with life tenancy. When the surviving brother Dwight died in 1994, Mass Audubon took possession of the farm, now a wildlife sanctuary. The brothers had bequeathed their tangible, personal property to the Williamsburg Historical Society. "We had a window of time to remove everything of historical interest from the farm," says Ralmon, then chairman of the Collections Committee.

"In two centuries, the Graves family had never thrown anything away. The farm was a time capsule. You could go into their parlor and read about the 1938 hurricane. The house had been kept heated so the papers weren't in bad condition at all. There were periodicals going back to 1840. Over in the corner behind the bed in the guest room was a 1740 musket with bayonet, probably a battlefield pickup from the French and Indian Wars. There was a broadside issued by John Hancock on Evacuation

Day in Boston calling the people to fast and meditate for the good of the Cause of Liberty. We found an 18th century straw splitter and yarn winder, thousands of bread wrappers, one hundred and fifty expended ballpoint pens, diaries of their mother and grandmother, farm records, and many notebooks recording their bird sightings which were turned over to the Massachusetts Audubon Society."

There, among those historical treasures, members of the Collections Committee made the remarkable discovery of boxes containing hundreds, possibly thousands, of empty envelopes addressed to Thornton Burgess. "There were bushels of envelopes from all over the U.S. and the world. Even one from Walt Disney," says Ralmon. His explanation? The writer maintained active correspondence with people around the globe and the Graves brothers collected stamps. "I suppose Burgess saved his envelopes with the stamps to pass on to them," says Ralmon. "That was his thank you."

His theory would account for an April 1945 entry in Thornton Burgess' journal: "Dwight Graves, Johnnie and Mrs. Graves stopped by for brief call. Had two boxes of envelopes for Dwight. Gave him a copy of last book."[3]

Note: Williamsburg historians Ralmon Jon Black, Eric Weber, and Geoffrey LeBaron, coordinator of the Audubon Society International Christmas Bird Count, provided this information. The photograph below shows, from left to right, Thornton W. Burgess, John Graves, and unidentified man at the Graves Farm, circa 1940s. *Courtesy of the Williamsburg (Massachusetts) Historical Society Graves Farm Collection.*

Chapter 16

THE LEGACY OF INSPIRATION

Although Burgess grew up in Sandwich village, or "uptown" as some older residents still say, daily life, employment, and boyhood wanderings often took him into East Sandwich a few miles away. In both areas, the Thornton W. Burgess Society manages sites that inspired the settings for his stories and his love of nature. For many years the Thornton W. Burgess Society has operated the Green Briar Nature Center and Jam Kitchen and the Thornton W. Burgess Museum, and offered year-round environmental education programs for adults, children, families, and schools. At present, the museum is closed.

"What has sustained this organization is the environmental mission — and children themselves."

NANCY TITCOMB, FOUNDING MEMBER
THORNTON W. BURGESS SOCIETY, 2009

"I've always admired Thornton Burgess because he did such a wonderful job popularizing children's literature. To me Burgess' legacy is the accessibility of his children's stories."

PAT ROGERS, ARTIST/CURATOR
THORNTON W. BURGESS SOCIETY, 2009

"Green Briar is a place where you can still see Thornton Burgess' Smiling Pool and Peter Rabbit's Briar Patch. You can picture Ida Putnam in her white tie-up shoes and starched, white uniform standing in front of the burners and the big kettles at Green Briar like she did 100 years ago. This is history you can touch."

JOHN AKELEY, VOLUNTEER
THORNTON W. BURGESS SOCIETY, 2010

"So often people focus on one plant or animal because they see the beauty in that particular one, but Burgess saw the beauty and value of many animals and plants. He told children about interaction within the entire environment, about what an important place it is that provides food, water, and space. We're all competing for food, water and space, but animals have to be especially aware of the other animals around them. What a great lesson his stories are for us."

MARY BEERS, EDUCATION DIRECTOR,
THORNTON W. BURGESS SOCIETY, 2010

BIRTHDAY CELEBRATION IN SANDWICH

As a man who genuinely enjoyed celebrating his birthdays with friends and family, Burgess would have loved the one-hundredth birthday party his hometown held for him in 1974, a three-day gala that included a parade, pet show, and an original musical. Organizers collected and displayed memorabilia in his aunt Arabella Burgess' house in the village. Congratulations and tributes included telegrams from Bradford Washburn, director of the Boston Museum of Science, and Arthur Thornhill, Jr., president of Little, Brown and Company, as well as a floral display from New Brunswick premier Hugh John Flemming, and his wife Aida, who knew Burgess from his many trips to New Brunswick and a common interest in animal welfare.

The celebration coalesced interest in the Burgess legacy among a core of residents, but the growth and development of the Thornton W. Burgess Society is universally credited to the vision, energy, and irresistible talent for persuasion of East Sandwich bookseller Nancy Titcomb. After she and husband Ralph established Titcomb's Bookstore in the late 1960s, she became intrigued by the strong interest customers showed in the author of *Old Mother West Wind.* "People were looking for different editions of his books, anything related to Thornton Burgess, and they expected us to have something in stock because he was born in Sandwich," she says.

When Titcomb discovered the centennial anniversary of Burgess' birthday was approaching, she and others met with the Board of Selectmen to discuss holding a special celebration of the town's most famous citizen. "Our thought was to celebrate this man who had contributed so much, who opened up the natural world for millions of children," she says. "It would have been a milestone for any author to have their work so well received and at that time to have their books translated into other languages, but he was also on the radio and in the newspapers." At the time, the Sandwich Women's Club was undertaking badly needed restoration of a town-owned historic property, the Deacon Eldred house, where Burgess had fished, played, and watched his aunt summon turtles and eels to the dock behind her house.

With its central village location and tie to the writer, the house was an advantageous site to display Burgess books and memorabilia. After the Thornton W. Burgess Society incorporated in 1976, it established a museum there for permanent exhibits, a gift shop, archives, and special activities and events. Within ten years, more than 65,000 people a year were visiting the museum, and Nancy Titcomb and other volunteers accumulated countless stories from visitors who knew Thornton Burgess' books and stories. "One day I'll always remember, a couple of burly guys drove up to the museum on big Harley-Davidson-type motorcycles," recalls former museum manager Karel Huber. "We wondered what we were in for. It turned out that one of them had loved Thornton Burgess stories as a kid and wanted to stop and see the museum. He had the best time and ended up buying a number of books."

On another occasion, Gene Schott, executive director of the Thornton W. Burgess Society, was giving a tour at the museum. As he related Rose Kennedy's statement in her autobiography *Times to Remember* that Burgess' *The Adventures of Reddy Fox* was a favorite boyhood book of her son John F. Kennedy, a woman from Springfield, Massachusetts, interrupted him. Her father had been a personal friend of JFK's, she said. Knowing his love of Burgess' books, he contacted the elderly author in Hampden to obtain an autographed copy for the President. "She told us that when her father handed the book to Kennedy at the White House, he sat right down in his rocking chair and began to read it," says Schott.

An Extraordinary Burgess Story

In 1999, a visit to the museum by a military veteran from Missouri and his wife brought to light an extraordinary story that spans the twentieth century, connecting his family to a World War II letter to Thornton Burgess, as well as the famous

1903 expedition to Yellowstone of President Teddy Roosevelt and naturalist John Burroughs. In 1944, the publication of Burgess' 10,000th syndicated story generated considerable publicity, including a major article in *Life*. As a result, he received many personal letters of congratulations, including the following special request from Captain Dorsey Hurd Cullen writing from "Somewhere in Eastern France":

> My Dear Mr. Burgess:
>
> A copy of *Life* for August 28 has reached this Front and in reading the article about you many happy memories were brought back to me. One of my earliest recollections is of my mother reading to me about Peter Rabbit, Jimmy Skunk, Bobby Coon and the rest of their many friends. It helped a great deal in developing in me a love of Nature and its animals. I kept, through the years, a complete set of your many books, and until the war sent me overseas I would read those stories almost every night to my own children. That has been almost two years ago when embarkation took me to England, and later to the beaches of Normandy in June.
>
> My children know and love your stories well, and in that connection, I would like to ask a favor. It would prove a wonderful Christmas gift to them if you could see fit to write just a short story about Peter Rabbit and his friends for my children and send it directly to them. I am sure their happiness would be complete. With your wealth of understanding of children I'm sure you know just what I mean. For your information their names and ages are as follows:
>
> Isabel Kathleen – 9 years
> Dorsey H, Jr. – 6 years
> Philip K. – 5 years
> Peter – 2½ years
> Raymond – 1 year
>
> I will feel most grateful if you can see fit to do this for me. May you and yours have a very Merry Christmas in those wonderful States of ours.[1]

Burgess sent the children the requested story, adding a special letter from Peter Rabbit and a note to their mother explaining why he was writing. He also wrote Cullen, saying it had made him very happy to comply with his request, but he never heard from either the Army officer or "that precious family in Virginia" and concluded that "something somewhere was amiss," accepting that he would probably never know more.

More than fifty years later, in September 1999, Colonel Peter Cullen of Kansas City, Missouri, a decorated Army veteran of the Vietnam War and Operation Desert Storm, made a trip with his wife Leslie to the East Coast after retiring. Having been recently diagnosed with a serious illness, he had decided to do some traveling. "We stopped by the Thornton W. Burgess Society Museum because he remembered his father had such a fondness for the books," said Leslie Cullen in a 2012 telephone interview. During their visit, the museum staff obtained enough information to realize that Col. Cullen was one of the children mentioned in the World War II letter from "Somewhere in France" that Burgess mentioned in his autobiography. "My husband was stunned when the ladies at the museum knew who he was," says Leslie Cullen. "They said, 'You're the Peter from the story!' They were so tickled to meet him. He was overwhelmed."

"It was pure chance that we were there," says Cullen. "There was no specific reason we were in Sandwich, we just happened upon it, and he remembered his father had loved the Burgess stories. We went out and looked at the little pond behind the museum. The ladies said this is where Thornton Burgess learned about nature. It was such a peaceful little scene.

"My husband bought the autobiography," she said. "We looked up the story about our family and later sent it to his brother Dorsey in California. The ladies at the museum told us how unhappy it made Thornton Burgess that he never heard what had happened. We were embarrassed because he had been so gracious about writing the letter." Peter's sister Mary, who was born after their father sent his 1944 letter to Thornton Burgess, continues the story: "I remember hearing about this, but not seeing the letter," she says. "What horrified me was that my parents never acknowledged the children's story. They obviously received it. [The Cullen family still has the story.] None of us can understand why Mother didn't write the letter, but I can imagine my father saying to my mother after they received this wonderful letter, 'I'll take care of it.'"

Given wartime mail delivery and the volume of Burgess' mail, especially following the *Life* article, there is little question that the Cullens' letter simply failed to reach its Springfield, Massachusetts, destination. Thornton Burgess scrupulously responded to all who contacted him, whether grade school children or renowned naturalists. His wartime journals made clear his longing to contribute to the war effort, so acknowledging a letter from a battlefront veteran or his family would have been a top priority. If he received the family's letter, he would have unquestionably written back to express his pleasure in fulfilling the fatherly request of a U.S. Army captain serving in Europe and in learning he was safe.

The Cullen family has another fascinating connection, more indirect, to Thornton Burgess. The grandfather of Isabel, Dorsey, Peter, Philip, Raymond, Mary, and three other siblings was also named Colonel Dorsey Hurd Cullen. It was his wife who read Burgess' stories to the children's father, the writer of the World War II letter. Born in 1869, five years older than Burgess, this earlier Dorsey Hurd Cullen was an Army veteran of the Spanish American War. In 1903, he served as a special wilderness guide to Yellowstone National Park for two famous men who knew and were known by Thornton Burgess: President Theodore Roosevelt, whom Burgess admired and from whom he sought an endorsement of his Green Meadow Club, and naturalist/author John Burroughs, who supported Burgess' Green Meadow bird sanctuaries. On that well-documented trip, Burroughs and Roosevelt would have unquestionably discussed the Nature Faker controversy, a subject that would later touch but not tarnish Burgess's reputation as a careful nature writer for children. Speculation that Col. Dorsey Cullen took part in such discussions is irresistible.

Growth and Development

The Town of Sandwich's 1974 centennial celebration of Burgess' birthday was highlighted by purchase of a 52-acre parcel on Robert and Sarah Swain's dairy farm that encompassed the original "Briar Patch" Thornton Burgess frequented as a boy. Sandwich native Barbara Bassett grew up in that East Sandwich area; as a girl, she had lived across the street from Burgess' childhood friend Lil Tangney and on the opposite side of Gully Lane from his old friend Alice Cooke. ("Gully Lane was definitely a gully when there was rain," she says.) Bassett was familiar with the "gobs of bull briars" on the dirt road behind the small spring-fed pond Burgess named "Smiling Pool."

Like Burgess, Bassett picked blueberries, wild grapes, and currants there with her grandmother. Halfway up Discovery Hill Road, above Green Briar Jam Kitchen and the pond, she remembers gathering the mayflowers Burgess loved. "They were on a creeping, low-growing vine that grew in pine forests," she says. "It didn't grow very high, maybe three or four inches. You cut them with scissors because if you did it by hand, you'd pull up the roots."

The new Briar Patch Conservation Area of woodlands and wetlands was developed with two miles of walking trails and signage. An entrance on Gully Lane is identified with a plaque and the words: "[Thornton Burgess'] love of nature and the foundation for his animal stories originated in this woodland." According to naturalist Mary Beers: "When you point children to the Briar Patch, they can't believe they're going to set foot in it. They've just imagined it from the stories, and now they can see it."

When the Thornton W. Burgess Society purchased Green Briar Jam Kitchen in 1979 for $82,500, it created a physical link between the Briar Patch conservation land and what would become the organization's operational headquarters and nature center. The three-acre property included an historic house with a broad country porch and an attached production kitchen equipped with two long rows of black, gas-fired burners. Set back from a busy roadway, the house and kitchen were situated at the edge of a small, spring-fed pond that abutted woodlands and a working cranberry bog as well as the Briar Patch, an ideal location for outdoor education and nature classes.

Within ten years of its inception, the Thornton W. Burgess Society had 2,500 members and one hundred volunteers. It operated a museum, nature center with educational programs, an historic jam kitchen, and two gift shops. An outreach program donated free twenty-volume sets of the Burgess Adventure series to schools and libraries throughout North America, from Salmon Falls, Maine to Cupertino, California. By 1995, the organization had contributed materials to 350 schools. "The thing that always impressed me about the Thornton W. Burgess Society was the hard work and dedication," remarked former head naturalist Stu Parsons. "Where were the 'sugar daddies' — they didn't exist." Prominent local artists like sculptor Alvin White and jeweler Nina Sutton helped finance operations by creating original designs for glass cup plates. These colorful pieces that depicted Burgess' characters and habitats became lucrative collectibles. Sutton recalled that years before the Thornton W. Burgess Society was formed, she and husband George knew Burgess as a welcome visitor to their home:

> I first met him when he gave me permission to sell ceramic figures I had made of his animal characters. It was always a happy day when he came to Sandwich and stopped to visit us. The car would drive up, [Frank and Kathy Jones] would drop him off, and he'd suddenly appear. My mother Nina Baer collected Sandwich glass and they'd talk for hours about the old Boston & Sandwich Glass Company. He'd tell stories and brought our kids his records. I would have loved for him to know about the Burgess Society and the museum.

Burgess never lived at the museum site in the village or the Green Briar property in East Sandwich, but both places were relevant to his boyhood in Sandwich. He fished from his aunt's dock on Shawme Pond in the village, a few minutes walk from his various homes there. The jam kitchen's original owner/operator Ida Putnam and her brother John were good friends of his. Volunteers who cleaned out the house in the 1970s were delighted to discover a book Burgess had playfully inscribed with the words, "To Ida, It's a wonderful thing to sweeten the World which is in a Jam and Needs Preserving."

Since the property abutted the former home of William Chipman, the commercial pond lily grower for whom Burgess worked as a young boy, Green Briar was part of the familiar route he took collecting and delivering Chipman's mail, telegrams, and packages at the Sandwich post office. The walk through woods and pastureland was about three miles round-trip or six if he started from his home in the village. Thornton Burgess always credited those solitary hours with first instilling his love of nature and wildlife.

Green Briar Jam Kitchen

In 1903, Ida Putman began selling jam and jelly from her mother's kitchen at Green Briar to a ready market of summer people and visitors. Burgess and his mother had left Sandwich about ten years earlier, but throughout his life he kept in touch with Putnam. During his visits to Sandwich, he usually stopped at the jam kitchen to catch up on local gossip and pick up a few jars of her delicious wares. Beach plum jelly was reportedly Burgess' favorite. Putnam modernized and expanded the facility in 1916. Three years later Martha Blake, then a teenager, joined the staff and eventually became her assistant. Blake bought the operation and property from Putnam in 1951. The year before she sold it to the Burgess Society, Martha Blake single-handedly put up 11,000 jars of jam, jelly, and conserves. All Green Briar's fresh fruits used to be picked locally; today cranberries and beach plums still are.

The Thornton W. Burgess Society originally had no intention of commercially operating the jam kitchen, but Blake enticingly left behind her equipment and — most valuable of all — her recipe box. Some of the century-old Green Briar recipes are original to culinary expert Fannie Farmer, author of the famous *Boston Cooking-School Cook Book*, published by Little, Brown, Thornton Burgess' publisher. Farmer worked as a cook for Ida Putnam's uncle William Foster in Newton, Massachusetts, so the two women may have met there or in Sandwich when the Fosters moved into their East Sandwich summer home near Green Briar.

According to Barbara Bassett, in 1939 Thornton Burgess and Ida Putnam invited the Spring Hill Ladies Club, a neighborhood social group in East Sandwich, to Green Briar for a slide show. "It was all old ladies and myself," remembers Bassett, then seven, who speculates that she was included for lack of a baby-sitter. Among the guests she names her grandmother Catharine Bassett, Lil Tangney, Martha Blake, Ida Rouse, who also worked at the kitchen, and "two sisters from uptown, Nellie Pope and Nanny Jones." The group gathered in Ida Putnam's stock room where shelves along the walls were filled with jars of cooked jam and jelly. "The only remembrance I have of his talk is Thornton Burgess standing beside the screen and chairs all around," says Bassett. "He showed slides of where he had been in the Caribbean [likely his 1927 trip to Barro Colorado with Dr. Alfred Gross]."

Nature Education

With a successful capital campaign and a benefactor's generous donation, the Thornton W. Burgess Society completed construction in 2007 of a two-story education center that provided for expansion of education programs, office space, and live animal exhibits. Through a license agreement with the Massachusetts Division of Fish and Wildlife, the Burgess Society also operates nature programs along the tidal waters of Scorton Creek in East Sandwich. A former game farm for stocking pheasant and quail, the 93-acre site's diverse environments include a salt marsh, freshwater pond, and forest and meadow lands. Green Briar education staff utilizes it for grade school field programs and nature education classes that include bird watching and night-sky observation. "To me, it is all like a big puzzle fitting together," former Burgess Society president Nancy Titcomb remarked.

Whether providing library presentations that focus on Burgess' stories or school programs that concentrate on natural science, the basic goal of all Burgess Society education programs is to engage children in nature. Jennifer Lukas Hemr, a science teacher at Riverview School in East Sandwich, worked at the Burgess Society's nature center in the mid-1990s. "It was the best job I ever had," she says. "Green Briar started me on my path as a science teacher, and definitely helped form my philosophy of teaching and learning. We would take kids to the salt marsh or ponds to study wetland species. It was great hands-on learning. The kids were always laughing and having a great time. I never dealt with any behavior problems because everybody was involved with learning."

When her three children were young, writer Stephanie Boosadha of Yarmouth, Massachusetts, took them to the Thornton W. Burgess Museum and Nature Center every Saturday. "The programs were down-to-earth, they kept true to nature and to the Burgess stories we read," she says. "The kids would go to bed listening to a cassette tape of his stories, and my son wouldn't go to sleep until it was over. He loves animals, and I swear it's the Burgess books."

The Burgess Society education staff includes both field naturalists who conduct outdoor programs and teaching naturalists who work with over forty-five schools annually. For children today Burgess' environmental message is especially critical, observes former Burgess Society executive director Jeannie Johnson.

Nature Programs for Families

Among the families that take part in Thornton W. Burgess Society programs are Marianne Millette-Kelley, a K-5 librarian, and her daughter Abby, nine, who regularly visit Green Briar to walk the trails, read books, and take jam classes. "Green Briar is one of the most serene places I know," says Millette-Kelley. "Within fifteen minutes of getting there, you feel wonderful. I think it has to do with the light and the color." Abby added, "You go there and get relaxed. And it's full of butterflies." Millette-Kelley remembers the summer her daughter took eighteen workshops and seven jam classes: "It was the most wonderful summer I can remember. She'd take the science classes and come home feeling smart and respected. I loved watching her self-confidence grow."

Former first grade teacher Tricia Spillane's family has belonged to the nature center for six years. Attending the Burgess Book Club monthly meetings and listening to Burgess' stories, Spillane says, has helped her three children develop their imagination: "We're not a big TV family, and the Burgess books fit nicely into that lifestyle. Nature is a big part of our lives. The children enjoy listening to the stories. For me, one of the benefits is that [the stories] have clean language and the animals are nice to each other. For that time frame, books like *Old Mistah Buzzard* give us an opportunity to talk about social changes that we can relate to Martin Luther King and Ruby Bridges."

When Jennie Gilkie grew up in Sandwich, she loved coming to the Burgess Society's facilities and events with her mother Judy. Although she now lives in Brooklyn, Gilkie gets special pleasure in returning to Green Briar Nature Center with her husband Derek and their daughter Anna Grace Lucci, seven. "Classes at the nature center have been outstanding for teaching Anna Grace to appreciate nature," says Gilkie.

Staff members take Burgess Book Club members outdoors to look at the animals and habitat Burgess wrote about. The group currently has seventeen members ranging in age from six to twelve. "I'll bring in the skull and fur of an animal in the book we're reading, so they've got a direct link to Burgess' writing," says Beers. "They read the stories, and then they see the real thing." Susan Cummings' daughter Grace Ripley, age seven, comes regularly to the book club. "At first I thought, is Grace really going to get into it," says Cummings, "but Mary brings in pelts of a beaver or fox, whichever animal she is reading about, so the discussion is mostly on the animal itself." Grace says, "I can remember a part of the Jimmy Skunk story when Reddy Fox was chasing Peter Rabbit, and then he hid, and Jimmy Skunk sprayed Reddy instead." She likes the fact that the animals talk and explain their feelings. "Say someone hurt my feelings and makes me mad," Grace says. "I could tell my parents. And they [animals in the stories] can tell their feelings too."

"The Burgess stories teach about getting along and appreciating where you live," observes writer Stephanie Boosadha. "He talks about taking care of the land, and then you realize this was written one hundred years ago." When her oldest daughter started hearing the stories a second time as they were being read to a younger sibling, she thought they were different stories, says Boosadha. "She began to see that they were really about people and relationships. Sometimes the characters argue and don't make up because they're stubborn. This resonates with kids, maybe with something that happened in school that day."

Nature Study Teachers and Learners

Project L.I.F.E. (Lessons in Field Ecology) is an award-winning educational program developed in 1982 by the Burgess Society staff to teach elementary students about their native environment. A key component of Project L.I.F.E. is training high school seniors to be able to present an environmental study curriculum to fourth graders. The program's effectiveness lies in the fact that it engages two different age groups that interact as teachers and learners. "This is a magnificent tool for environmental education," says Gil Newton, a Sandwich High School botany and environmental technology teacher who has been involved with the program for more than a decade.

After his students receive instruction from Burgess Society naturalists, they go into Sandwich fourth grade classrooms, which comprise about three hundred students. "The seniors will teach three classroom lessons and one field lesson in forest ecology," says Newton. "When they start off, they're apprehensive because only a few have had any experience in teaching. They learn very quickly that they have to study the material to be able to present it clearly to younger students. They also discover they're really enjoying themselves."

"It's not just dispensing information," observes Beers. "The high school students are being exposed to what it is to be a teacher. One of the most rewarding aspects of Project L.I.F.E. is having the high school students consider teaching as a career because of this experience." Beers notes that teaching environmental education through every means possible has become increasingly important. "Children can quote statistics about a tropical rainforest, but they know very little about the forests on Cape Cod. Many of them read about bears and rattlesnakes living in the woods and believe they live in the woods here."

A Wildflower Garden

A mulched dirt path winds through the lavishly colorful wildflower garden that botanist Dr. Shirley Cross designed at Green Briar Nature Center. In 1979, she convinced fellow board members to relinquish an area intended for lawn and parking space to develop an educational garden.

The Shirley Cross Wildflower Garden specimens range from mosses and grasses to various iris, poppies, mallows, and roses. Plantings are grouped for shade, marsh, and sun environments. Some varieties that flourish there include pitcher plants, cardinal flower, marsh mallow, trailing arbutus, and a rare *Franklinia alatamaha*. With more than three hundred native and exotic species, the garden inspires staff as well as visitors. Former director Jeanne Johnson says: "When you were having a crisis in the non-profit world, you could look out the window and see kindergarteners looking at butterflies with a naturalist in the wildflower garden. That always kept me fulfilled."

Wildflower garden at the Green Briar Nature Center.

Chapter 17

The Legacy of Memories

As a writer, conservationist, naturalist, lecturer, and radio host, Thornton Burgess was a well-known public figure in the first half of the twentieth century. But what of the personal life of the man who was "Grampa" to his grandchildren and "Spiffy" to Tobago friends in the 1950s who teased him for wearing a bow tie on a Caribbean island? This chapter considers the legacy of memories preserved by those who knew him best and by Burgess' personal papers. [Thornton Burgess is usually referred to here as "Burgess" and his son as "Thornton."]

"He lived his work."

Frances B. Meigs, granddaughter

"His love of nature was a true love; it wasn't just something for him to get money from."

Joyce Libby, former physical therapist
Mary Lyon Nursing Home

"He was a great humanitarian, and had tremendous regard for all living things, human or animal. He was quite a man."

Thornton W. Burgess IV, grandson

"He'd take us to the grist mill on Shawme Pond, and tell us how he fished behind his Aunt Arabella's house. I can remember vividly looking at the town beach, and thinking 'this is where the whale came up, the one he remembered seeing as a little boy of five.' He remembered it as a sad story, and as a child hearing it, I felt like I wanted to comfort him. Those mixed emotions stayed with him."

Frances B. Meigs, granddaughter

"I can think of nothing more disheartening as to go through life adding nothing to the sum of human knowledge, progress, and happiness."[1]

Thornton W. Burgess, 1929

Habits, Traits, and Appearance

Born and raised an independent, self-reliant Cape Codder, Thornton Burgess was in some ways an uncomplicated man who lived a complicated life. He outlived two wives: Nina, who died in 1906 within twenty-four hours of childbirth, and Fannie, who died in 1950 of multiple chronic conditions. He grieved the loss of both women deeply and long. With Nina, he had one son, and with Fannie two step-children. In all, he had ten grandchildren. Although Burgess was a family-centered homebody, he was comfortable traveling to distant cities and foreign countries and thought nothing of putting hundreds of miles on his Packard to visit friends and family around the Northeast. He wrote simple animal tales for children and filled them with scientifically authoritative facts and information. Although he was internationally known as a writer, he considered naturalists and biologists "my own kind."

In early photographs, Burgess appears to be a tall, thin, somewhat homely figure, a serious, scholarly young man, but as he aged, his frame became more substantial and newspaper articles often mentioned his "twinkling eyes." *Life* staff writer Paul O'Neil described him as "a big (6 feet, 180 pounds), rugged looking, white-haired old man who has weathered the emotional and physical vicissitudes of life with remarkable élan."[2] Thornton W. Burgess Society president Wendy Maggio remembers shyly asking Burgess to autograph books when he stopped in Clarence Cahoon's snack shop in Sandwich in the 1950s. "He had a lovely face, a lovely expression, and a gentle presence about him," she says.

Although not athletic, Burgess was a remarkably strong and hardy man. At seventy-one, he wrote in his journal: "30 degrees this morning. Started work at Hampden at 7:30 and quit in heavy shower at 4, with half an hour for lunch. Mowed and raked thoroughly. Spaded, raked, and fertilized second front bed and set pansies." More than ten years later, he wrote friends that he was swimming daily laps in the warm waters off Tobago where he wintered in later years.

A Modest Man

By most personal accounts, Burgess remained genuinely modest and unpretentious despite decades of celebrity, and he never lost an intrinsic naiveté, which worried some family members who believed he was vulnerable to opportunists. *New York Times* book reviewer Hal Borland observed, "Mr. Burgess never became sophisticated, which is perhaps the key to his stories. He is still in awe of what happened to him, boyish in appreciation of praise and approbation."[3] In organizing his papers, archivist Bethany Rutledge noticed that Burgess seldom elaborated on professional accolades or reflected on his writing. "If you didn't know he was this hugely successful author, you might not suspect it," Rutledge remarked. "A sentence here and there references his career, but they could have been diaries kept by any man who liked to keep a garden or go on road trips."

While fame undoubtedly pleased Burgess, it also seemed to amuse or surprise him as an unexpected consequence of his efforts. When Northeastern University staff asked him to provide biographical information for the graduation ceremony at which he would receive an honorary doctoral degree, he told them, "It is the most uninteresting subject I know of…would rather write a Bedtime Story." He resisted the urgings of Little, Brown president Arthur Thornhill and editor-in-chief Alfred McIntyre to write his autobiography. "I still can't see it," he said in 1945. It was another three years before he finally signed the contract for *Now I Remember*, and ten more before he submitted the manuscript. His disinclination to claim attention was reflected in the first paragraph of his autobiography, which concludes with the disclaimer: "This…is simply a record by me, of me, for me, and perhaps of no real interest to anyone but me."[4]

The record of Burgess' life and accomplishments, however, was clearly of widespread public interest. When he was eighty-six years old, he was inundated by media attention and letters of congratulations from around the world — "very flattering and at times embarrassing" — at the publication in 1960 of his 15,000th syndicated newspaper story. "I am amazed," he remarked in his journal. "And this after 50 years."

> There was a succession of newspaper men and photographers here at my home including a staff writer from *Life* who spent a couple hours a day with me for six consecutive days. By the time he was through I was in a mental vacuum. And *Life's* photographer is due any day now. The AP photographer was here all one afternoon and shot me all over the place. I was in Boston for three strenuous days, on two TV shows and one radio, lunches, interviews and autographing books. Last week I had two days of the same in New York. … Found letter from the Canadian Broadcasting Corporation saying they would like to arrange for a TV interview. … As a result both books [*Now I Remember* and *Old Mother West Wind Golden Anniversary Edition*] seem to be going very well.[5]

Temperament and Outlook

Although Burgess was generally considered to have an agreeable, optimistic disposition, he earned a reputation in later years for being a curmudgeon. His friend Polly Philpott attributed this to an increasingly serious hearing loss that many were unaware of. Deafness made the interpersonal communication and repartee that he savored difficult, if not impossible, and forced him to abandon the lecture circuit, long a source of income and stimulation. After attending a church Valentine party in 1947, he wrote: "Hearing very bad. Guess I'm in for a complete loss." Frances Meigs said physical ailments, from advanced arthritis in his knees to dizziness, contributed to her grandfather's irritability. "His legs were often killing him, and he'd be up half the night with cramps," she says. "He couldn't do the things he used to do."

Nursing aide Nancy Jones Sazma Phillips worked with Burgess at the Mary Lyon Nursing Home. "I was nervous because I'd always known him as a neighbor," she says, "but he had a wonderful sense of humor. He took everything in his stride. I learned a great deal from him. He'd say, 'when you look at leaves changing, think of the new leaf pushing off the old leaf.' He'd tell me you have to be kind and considerate to animals." Many years earlier her church's youth fellowship held a scavenger hunt in Hampden, and she remembers her group stopping at Burgess' house in search of a certain dime and a cracked saucer. "He had the dime and went out to the kitchen to look for a saucer, and all of a sudden we heard a crack," she says. "We knew what he had done."

A physical therapist at the Hampden facility, Joyce Libby remembers Burgess as an easy patient. "He was eager to get better and get outside," she said. "He loved to sit down by the Scantic River. It was getting back to the nature he loved. Once, someone from the Cape sent him some trailing arbutus. He was so pleased to have those flowers. His love of nature was a true love; it wasn't just something for him to get money from."

While reading through the extensive archival correspondence between Burgess and Smithsonian curator Austin Clark, author Marcel LaFollette observed a difference in the response of the two men to obstacles. "In the phrasing of [Burgess'] letters, he always read to me as someone who is comfortable in his own skin," she says. "He just jumps in and feels good about things, which was quite the opposite of Clark, who occasionally was quite bitter about not getting this or that. If Thornton Burgess has a disappointment, he just turns around and finds another route." She also notes that Clark was involved in the Washington social scene. "But it sounded like Thornton Burgess didn't play those games…He wasn't seeking out a social advantage."

Importance of Family

Attending community and church functions with his wife Fannie was definitely more Burgess's style during the years he lived in Springfield and summered in Hampden. They dined out two or three times a week at Stannard's or Brigham's and hosted friends and his professional contacts, but family was always their priority. Burgess' involvement in the lives of children, and his fondness for them, is unmistakable. In his journal he wrote, for example, of Thornton's youngest boy, saying: "David's 3rd birthday and he had two little girls in. He is a dear little fellow. And Brother (Thornton IV) and Nancy are equally dear." Burgess accompanied grandchildren to doctor appointments, sporting events, and school activities. He cooked them his famous scrambled eggs and quahog chowder. He was partial to babies and young children, said granddaughter Frances Meigs, explaining that when they got to be teenagers, he wasn't so sure of them. Judging from his journals, Burgess' wariness was well-founded:

> Threatening snow all day but did not materialize more than a flurry. To Hampden with gifts, taking Wm. [age 10]. Got his lunch and then took him to Museum. Saw Christmas pageant in Planetarium. Spent more than 2 hours in… station of bus line waiting for Jean [age 19]. Rosemary [age 17] with me. Got home around 11:30 to find that Jean had finally phoned that bus had broken down and someone had brought her to city and she was at Doria Smiths. Drove around for her…She wasn't ready to come home. So home and to bed in disgust.[6]

One grandson accumulated speeding fines and repeatedly used Burgess' car without permission while another ignored loan payment deadlines, incurring court fines that Burgess was obliged to cover. Having worked since childhood to avoid financial debt, Burgess struggled to understand youngsters who squandered opportunity after opportunity (which he had often arranged) for employment and an education, but misdeeds were forgiven as soon as the young offender took a step in the right direction. Burgess proudly noted family birthdays and accomplishments in his journals. When Frances Meigs had her first child, he wrote: "Little Frances, (Caroline "Candy" Keel Walton) 7 lbs 14 oz, born this afternoon at Newport News, Va. Hard to sense that our own Frances has grown to motherhood."[7]

Adult grandchildren kept in touch and returned for visits to Springfield and Hampden with spouses and their own children. William Bradford recalls driving to New Hampshire with his new wife for their honeymoon. When they reached a certain fork in the road, he said, "If we go right at this intersection, we go to Sunapee, and if we go left, we go to Hampden to see Grampa, and we both said, 'Let's go left.'"

Money Issues

While Burgess was able and practical in daily affairs, it was clear from his earliest employment as a bookkeeper in Boston that he had little taste or aptitude for business matters. He and Fannie kept separate financial accounts, but she handled most of the couple's joint affairs. "Almost everything was in her name," said Meigs, who described her grandmother as a smart, clever investor fascinated by money. "Nanna, either by shrewd intuition or good advice, had liquidated her personal stock holdings in September 1929 and had bought gold, thereby suffering no losses in the stock market crash," Meigs wrote in her memoir.[8] If Fannie indeed possessed and shared inside information with her husband, he must have chosen to ignore it, for Burgess was hard hit by the Wall Street stock market crash and lost savings as well as $10,000 he had invested two days earlier.[9] Though he eventually recovered financially — the *New York Times* and *Life* both reported that Burgess became a millionaire from book royalties, syndication contracts, and other work — the cash assets evidenced by his will were relatively modest.[10]

Given his professional earnings and temperate lifestyle, the need for money is a surprisingly common theme in Burgess' journals. There were no social excesses to speak of, for he drank seldom or in moderation and did not gamble for more than pocket change stakes. In addition to his two homes in western Massachusetts, Burgess owned Golden Grain Farm in Saskatchewan[11] and a fishing camp on Bolton Lake in New Brunswick[12], but these were country getaways, not lavish estates with swimming pools and multi-car garages.

The greatest drain on his income was unquestionably his family, as Burgess himself observed: "I seem to be working constantly only to bail others out of their financial problems." But the ethic of family caring for family was deeply ingrained, and, as he and his mother had been supported, he willingly provided financial assistance throughout his life to at least fifteen family members. He financed Thornton III's purchase of a gas station and in 1936 alone paid more than $15,000 to clear his wife's son Chester of debt. "He was very generous," said grandson Thornton IV. "He sent Mother money on a regular basis, and if there was a medical situation, he was happy to contribute or help finance it."

Burgess' wife Fannie was also very generous in supporting her family. Her daughter Helen's four children came to live with the Burgesses several times in the 1920s. After she divorced and remarried, Helen moved to England with her new husband, William Bradford, to look for housing, leaving her four children with their grandparents. According to Frances Meigs, Bradford felt that he should be responsible for only half the upkeep of the household, "and the rest — including schooling, clothes, nanny, travel, and anything else that came under the heading of financial support for Helen's children — would have to become Nanna's responsibility."[13]

Difficult Relationship with His Son

"The Bedtime Story Man" had a unique ability to relate to children, but as a father, Burgess struggled to understand his only child, Thornton III, who had inspired the stories that launched his literary career. Scattered throughout Burgess' journals are brief reflections of sharp regret and sadness:

> "An unclear day. T's 31st birthday. I wonder where he is and what he is doing. Poor boy and poor father. Thirty years worth of heartache." (1937)

> "I am 64 this day and Son is 10 years married this day. He is on my mind constantly." (1938)

> "He is out [East visiting from West Coast]. Letter bitter. Asks for aid. Of course I had planned to give this anyway...Poor boy. My heart aches for him." (1939)

> "Better tone. Addressed me as Dad this time. God grant he has set his foot on the right path." (1939)

Burgess does not appear to dwell on the fact that in infancy both he and his son lost a parent, nor does he attempt to analyze the potential role of guilt or resentment in their relationship. The year after *Old Mother West Wind* was published in 1910, Burgess married Fannie Johnson, a second marriage for both, and the blending of the two families was apparently difficult. Frances Meigs' memoir describes a contentious and strained atmosphere in Burgess' home in the early years when he was beginning to earn a living as a children's author. Loss of his job two months after remarrying intensified pressure to earn money, and a proliferation of assignments the next year heightened demands on his time.

In February 1912, Burgess began to produce six syndicated stories a week for a trial period of six months. That spring J. H. McFarland Company sent him on a one-month tour of Florida to research and photograph material for horticultural and agricultural catalogues. After he returned, he worked long days preparing the advertising copy. On June 18, 1912, his mother Caroline died, the grievous loss of a caring, stabilizing, reliable presence for him and young Thornton. That year he wrote *Mother West Wind's Animal Friends* for Little, Brown and *The Boy Scouts of Woodcraft Camp* for Penn Publishing Company.

One lesson Burgess had retained from the impoverished circumstances of his childhood was the absolute necessity of financial independence. The time he devoted to parenting in these early years was obviously minimal. His young son Thornton became increasingly "angry and rebellious," says Meigs in her memoir, noting that on one occasion local officials were called to intervene. In later years, her grandfather "blamed himself for Thornton's unhappiness and chastised himself for not having been home when Thornton was young, for being driven to his writing, for missing his son's childhood...He knew that at times he hadn't listened well or had failed in empathetic understanding or had missed an opportunity to take a strong moral stance."[15] But Burgess' priorities were work and financial security.

Burgess' transcribed journals begin on January 1, 1928, when the writer was fifty-three years old and his son was twenty-one. The very first entry of the first page offers a précis of the family's issues:

> Helen [his wife's daughter] and family to dinner. Day cloudy, slightly cooler, but far from the cold wave predicted. Home all day. ... Wrote T's [Thornton Burgess III] fiancée [Mildred] that I disapprove of the proposed marriage January 14 on the grounds that Son is not prepared financially or in his work for such a step.[16]

Gathered at the dinner table were Burgess, his wife Fannie, and her 29-year-old daughter Helen and her children, aged six, five, three, and one, whom Fannie was supporting. Burgess' own son Thornton, twenty-one, had made wedding plans that his father opposed in the belief that he was not sufficiently established financially or professionally to support a wife. The proposed wedding date of January 14 was Burgess' birthday. This choice undoubtedly added to the pique of a father who had worked steadily since boyhood and had saved money for years in preparation for marriage. However, when Burgess had been his son's age, he, too, made what appeared to be an unwise decision. Much to his grandfather Charles' great disappointment, Burgess abandoned reputable employment as a bookkeeper in Boston for an office boy's job with a publisher — a leap of faith in the hope of future happiness and prosperity. Burgess does not appear to have considered that perhaps his son Thornton at twenty-one believed marriage offered him the same hope.

There is no question that Burgess' response to Mildred offended the young couple. They replied that they would not change their plans and did not invite Burgess and Fannie to the ceremony. "It is a bit difficult that I have no part in them and that I shall not see him married," wrote Burgess, posturing calm acceptance. Although he and Fannie were in New York the day of the wedding there, having made enjoyable plans to see an automobile show and meet up with Harrison and Melinna Cady, Burgess "did not feel good" and spent most of the weekend resting.

In the years that followed, Burgess' journal records constant concern for his son and his young family. Thornton was away frequently and then permanently while his wife Mildred and their three children remained in Cambridge, Massachusetts. A well-meaning aunt told Thornton's daughter Nancy that her father had died of tuberculosis (her great-grandfather's cause of death). "But I didn't believe it," she says. "Finally when I was eighteen, I got a letter from him. I had prayed every night that I would hear from him. It was like a miracle." Her father had joined the Army and served as a mechanic during World War II. Burgess recorded in his journal on June 13, 1945: "Mildred wrote that Nancy hears from her father now in Luzon [northernmost island in the Philippines]. Was in Germany. Expects to go to China."

Thornton was stationed in Luzon until 1950. He then worked as an electrical contractor and lived for more than ten years in Saudi Arabia, eventually moving to California. "We called him 'Grandpa from Arabia,'" says Debra Hanna, Nancy Hughes' daughter. From his visits Hughes remembers her father as a very handsome, smart man with a good sense of humor who liked to cook. [Photographs of Thornton suggest a poised, austere manner and a physical elegance his father lacked.] "I always adored him," Hughes says. "When he stayed with us, he was a lot of fun, and he took me every place with him." They never discussed his childhood in Springfield. When Burgess learned of his son's wartime activities, he proudly remarked that Thornton was the only member of the family to serve in the war.

A Happy Reunion

As they grew older, father and son kept in touch periodically, but near the end of their lives there was proof of genuine healing in the relationship. In February 1960, Burgess received an itinerary of his son's trip to meet him on Tobago where he wintered in recent years. Thornton's second wife Gladys would accompany him. The couple arrived on April 25th and then left with Burgess for New York and Massachusetts. His journal recorded the family's times of closeness:

> 4/25/1960: Met them at the airport. A happy reunion. Son seems a real man of the world. A good talker. Mixes well. [I] Like Gladys.
>
> 4/26/1960: Son's pocket radio stolen while at dinner last night. Too bad...Son and Robert [Burgess' grandson?] hit it off well.
>
> 4/30/1960: David and Ruth [Thornton's youngest son and wife] here for the night. Son gave dinner party with three friends from New Jersey. All day he has taken wonderful care of the old man.
>
> 5/7/1960: Son and Gladys off with David and Ruth to see Nancy and Brother [Thornton's older two children, then living in Massachusetts].
>
> 5/15/1960: Son off from Bradley Field for Idlewild at 5 PM...from restaurant window watched son board his plane and take off...It has been a happy reunion.
>
> 5/18/1960: Fifty-four years ago today that Son was born and his Mother taken to her Heavenly home. So very glad that this rift in relations with son is happily ended. He has developed into a man of the world beyond my hopes. Had adjusted relations with his children and this makes me very happy.

During a subsequent exchange of letters with his son, Burgess noted there was "small chance of [Thornton's] return to America under a year at best," so evidently Thornton was still working abroad in some capacity. In early spring 1964, Thornton came to visit his father at the Hampden nursing home. Shortly after returning to his residence at Granada Hills, California, Thornton was found in his car, dead at fifty-seven, apparently of a heart attack. One close friend said Burgess remained inconsolable, but he wrote with odd detachment to his Canadian friend Stuart Trueman:

> Dear Stuart, how goes the history of New Brunswick [a writing project of Trueman's] and are you and Mildred going to try for Salmon this year. There is no special news here except that I have suffered the loss of my son who died at his home in California last Tuesday.[17]

Whether from grief, shock, or denial, Burgess registered more distress at the recent death of a friend's spouse than of his own son. His next letter to Stuart Trueman, June 6, 1964, was equally cool and unemotional: "I appreciate your words of sympathy in the loss of my son. It was very sudden. He was strickened in his car. They found him pulled over to the side of the road. Thus has closed one chapter of my life."[18]

But further sadness awaited him. A married couple, Kathy and Frank Jones, had stepped into Burgess' life after his wife Fannie died in 1950, helping him with daily affairs and maintenance at 61 Washington Road and Laughing Brook. They eventually moved in with him as caretakers, traveling companions, and special friends, and he had embraced them as family with characteristic generosity and affection. The Joneses remained at Laughing Brook after Burgess' stroke necessitated his moving to a nursing home. Frank died of emphysema a few months before Thornton III's 1964 visit, and it became evident to all, even Burgess who doted on her, that it was unsafe for Kathy to remain alone at Laughing Brook. She moved to East Longmeadow, Massachusetts, on May 18, 1965, and died the next day in a house fire caused by a burning cigarette.[19] Within little more than a year, Thornton Burgess had lost three people he cherished. Ernestine Johnson accepted responsibility for bringing the terrible news of these deaths to him.

Quality of Life

Despite the serious incapacities and limitations of his last few years at the Mary Lyon Nursing Home, Burgess continued to find meaning and enjoyment in his life. Naturalist Chuck Roth of the Massachusetts Audubon Society was a regular visitor. Roth first met Burgess at fifteen when the author came to artist Phoebe Erickson's Connecticut home to discuss her illustrations for one of his books. "She was my mentor, almost like my second mother, and she felt I should be included," says Roth. In the years to come, he visited Burgess at home in Springfield and Hampden, and finally at the Mary Lyon Nursing Home, where he would occasionally bring a live animal into Burgess' room. "He loved having the animals there and insisted I take them around and show them to the others," says Roth. "It was a thrill for him and for me. We talked about how his books were doing, but most of the time we talked about the animals I had brought. That was one of his great pleasures."

After Burgess' stroke, he was unable to speak, so director Lou Levine was shocked one day to hear the writer's voice coming clearly from his room. When he walked in, Levine found Burgess sitting up in bed with several children gathered around him. He was mouthing the words to one of his stories while a recording of it played. "He had promised them a story and didn't want to let them down," explained Hampden neighbor Polly Philpott. In his 1967 article in *Reader's Digest*, "My Most Unforgettable Character: Thornton W. Burgess," Levine described the writer as "a very distinctive person" who gave special names like "Little Breeze," "Sunny," and "Bartender" to his nurses, as he had to his animal characters. "He revitalized his fellow patients," noted Levine.[20]

Knowing Burgess' passion for fishing, Levine made arrangements to dam a small stream behind the nursing home, which the Massachusetts Division of Fish and Game stocked with trout. Once when Burgess was feeling poorly, Levine suggested he forgo fishing, but Burgess responded that he couldn't disappoint the men who had gone to such trouble. "And since I'm not supposed to know it, the only way I can thank them is by enjoying what they've done for me."[21] Levine was present when Boston Museum of Science director Bradford Washburn, accompanied by his wife Barbara, personally delivered the museum's honorary award to Burgess.

Throughout his life, Burgess corresponded with an incalculable number of family members, friends, scientists, publishers, artists, and readers. There was no one, however, with whom he maintained as long and steady a correspondence and friendship as with his great friend and illustrator Harrison Cady. In 1959, when Burgess was still living at Laughing Brook, Cady came to visit for a week. The purpose of the trip was ostensibly to work and celebrate his eighty-second birthday with an old friend, but it undoubtedly also helped relieve Cady's lingering heartache at losing his wife Melinna three years earlier. Burgess' wife Fannie had died in 1950. "Good to see him and think he is glad to be here," Burgess wrote. Although the weather was miserable, Cady worked in the barn on syndicated story illustrations while Burgess puttered around.

On the day of Cady's birthday, they drove to the Cape where Burgess had a planned a surprise dinner party at the Coonamesset Inn in Falmouth. "Wet trip but happy affair," he noted. When Cady departed for home, it is unclear to whom Burgess referred when he wrote: "Harrison off at 2:45. Near tears." Five years later, when Burgess was ninety, he wrote the following letter to Cady. It reflects the warmth, humor, and ease in their relationship, as well as Burgess' continued engagement with life and work:

> Dear Harrison,
>
> Hi! Boy! Spring is really here and like the birds heading north I'm on the move, the difference being that my motor is very, very slow...By the way, did I write you that I had a record of two stories released in February. A letter from my publisher said he was going to see what they could do about utilizing the record with the books. The record is really good.
>
> Arthur Thornhill, chairman of the board of Little Brown, former president, says the voice sounds exactly as it did when he went out with me on my lecture dates many years ago. It was so many years ago I can hardly recall I use[d] to go on a[lecture] platform.
>
> I presume you will go to Rockport as usual this year. Watch your step when you reach the 87 mark. Maybe by that time I shall be home and I wish we might

have another Cape Cod celebration. I feel that won't be possible. You are still young and I feel in that respect. Ninety years have passed over my head, but I refuse to admit I am an old man!

I get out every day in a wheel chair, pushed by my nurse and the only thing that keeps me from going fishing on the grounds in back of this home is the fact that I don't think she could push me back up.

"As ever yours with much affection,

Thornton W. Burgess"[21]

In early June 1965, Canadian editor Stuart Trueman was returning home from a trip to Washington, D.C. and impulsively decided to stop in Hampden to visit his friend at the Mary Lyon Nursing Home. He found Burgess frail, weak, and uncharacteristically tearful. "He spoke slowly, but his speech was difficult to comprehend," Trueman said. "He seemed to be saying what he was going to write about next."[22] Thornton Waldo Burgess died two days later, on June 5, 1965.

Chapter 18

The Legacy of Influence

A writer's legacy is ultimately the lasting impact of his or her beliefs, body of work, and vision. For children's author Thornton W. Burgess, belief, work, and vision were inseparable from love of nature. This chapter is a collection of edited interviews that reflect the thoughts and opinions of diverse individuals who have found Thornton Burgess' legacy relevant in their lives and work, and in today's world.

Kathleen "Betty" Anderson

Founder, Manomet Center for Conservation Sciences (formerly Manomet Bird Observatory)

In cooperation with East Coast efforts by Chandler "Chan" Robbins of the U.S. Fish and Wildlife Service and James Baird of the Massachusetts Audubon Society, Betty Anderson established Operation Recovery, a bird-banding station in Duxbury, Massachusetts, and subsequently founded the Manomet Bird Observatory, which, at that time, was only the third bird observatory in North America. In 1974, she was one of the first women elected to join the Nuttall Ornithological Club, and, to date, the only woman to serve as president. She has received numerous professional accolades and awards, including the 2007 Massachusetts Division of Fisheries and Wildlife's Governor Francis W. Sargent Award and the 1995 Arthur A. Allen Award from Cornell University's Laboratory of Ornithology.

When I was a small child, we got the old *Boston Post.* It had the Thornton Burgess stories, and Daddy would read them every night. We'd sit on the arms of the chair and on his lap. When I was seven or eight, I cut the stories out of the paper and kept a scrapbook of them. Eventually we were given the books. The stories gave the animals personality, they were like people. Oh, how I loved them!

We were country. I was born in Montana, but grew up in Carver, Massachusetts by a lake. The village was at the other end of the lake, and other than summer people there were no children to play with. We had each other and the critters. My father, Ernest W. Shaw, was born in 1875 and as a young man he went west as a homesteader. He joined the U.S. Forest Service when it began, and when he ended up he was a supervisor of Absaroka National Forest in Montana, at that time the largest in the United States, and he loved nature. My mother grew up in Montana, thirty miles from the nearest town. She learned to count by the nails on a wooden keg. I can still remember seeing my first bald eagle. Daddy saw it sitting on a pine tree branch, and called us out of the house. We had a great big calendar, and Mother would write on it the number of eggs she brought in, and when peas came up. All of us would bring in our nature notes. We reported the first robin and the first dandelion, the first and last frost, and seeing the first woodchuck.

So, Thornton Burgess was read to us every night, and his animals were part of our lives too. To me, as a child, he was a magic man. I've been a naturalist all my life, and those books influenced me more than anything else. Along with an appealing story, the facts behind the story were absolutely accurate in the descriptions of the habitats the critters lived in, what they needed, their behavior. Each book was written from the point of view of either the predator or the prey, depending upon the subject. So children who read them, or were read to, absorbed a huge amount of accurate information.

As I grew older and began to see these animals myself, I felt quite familiar with them. They were where I expected to find them, doing things that were to be expected. Johnny Chuck was out in our hayfield, the barn swallow was nesting in our barn, the weasel got into our hen house, which made my mother furious, and my father saw a rabbit amongst his vegetables. Of course it helped that I grew up in the country, but as a child I felt I already knew a lot about these birds and animals. Thornton Burgess was obviously a careful and astute observer himself. His animals had cute little names, but he could not have written in such a charming way if he was trying to imagine the animal from a picture book or from a scientific reference. It's why those books influenced so many children, whole generations. I'm still buying them, for my great-grand children now.

North Cairn

Nature Writer

An environmental writer for the Portland (Maine) Press Herald, North Cairn shares Burgess' inclusive passion for the natural world. For many years she lived on Cape Cod, where she wrote an eloquent, award-winning newspaper column on nature, wildlife, animal companions, and the human condition. Her book By Monomoy Light: Nature and Healing in an Island Sanctuary *(2000) describes three summers she spent on an island wildlife refuge off Chatham, Massachusetts. She has taught non-fiction writing at Mount Holyoke College, Suffolk University, and Hope College.*

I think it's been a traditional mistake to think of ourselves as apart from nature. Of course we are within nature. Of course we are. It's just the species we are that makes it possible for us to think of ourselves as separate from the earth in which we come and live out our existence. I think what's important is that we have to have places that are preserved, that communicate to us not only what wilderness is. I believe it is imperative to the human psyche or wild spirit because wilderness is the place where we discover our right size again in creation.

Someone said you go to wilderness not to find yourself, but to lose yourself. I think what is meant by that is that human history teaches us as a species we are arrogant and grandiose and self-absorbed, and the return to wilderness teaches us how small and helpless we are. For me and for many, nature is truly the most profound and liberating experience you can have.

Suddenly you discover your minute size and importance, and all the heavy concerns and the heavy responsibilities take on a much more realistic proportion when they are juxtaposed with wilderness, infinity, and something not made. We escape the artificial and made world, and in wilderness we began to participate in the great rhythms of the oceans, the land itself, and it has nothing to do with us. We're just there, being the lucky observers of the innocence and violence of nature, its beauty and grandeur. As a writer, I can say it [nature writing] reminds a community of the tremendous gift we've been given, it puts people in touch with the natural world, within and without, the nature in them and the nature that transcends them.

What does this have to do with Thornton Burgess? If you can do that for children, you're doing something very important, because if you can get them connected to the natural world in a way that feels to them essential, you have connected them to it for life. Burgess made animals into beings that we could understand. For many centuries the only role animals had was to fill a function as a means of food or labor, but Burgess, in writing for children and by giving animals true anthropological characteristics, made them our companions. I believe the human responsibility in all things, to all things, is stewardship. We're caretakers of the earth, and you don't bother to take care of something that has no connection to you. Burgess helped children see the natural world — birds, raccoons, snakes — as connected to them and somehow kin to them, and when we feel that kinship to the natural world, caretaking is instinctive.

What also strikes me in reading about Burgess is he was a child whose human relationships were interrupted; he had the loss of a father and was raised by a mother who was an orphan. These are traumatic foundational experiences, and it is quite often only through animals that wounded people are able to reconnect. Burgess' stories provide a safe environment in which a child — a vulnerable, growing human being — can find connection and hope and beauty in the world, as well as fun and light.

To be able to create that space, that world, for a child, through a story or a book, is a tremendously redemptive act for the whole species. When we talk about connecting with nature, we're talking about survival of humanity and the planet itself. The numbers of species expected to be extinct in the next forty years ought to bring us to our knees every day. It is staggering. What we are and what we make out of ourselves is the promising future or the absolute void. We need to continue to find ways to get people to realize that their understanding of the natural world is vital to their children and their children's children, for generations to come.

Thornton Burgess knew that.

Dr. Tom French

Assistant Director of Massachusetts Division of Fisheries and Wildlife

More than twenty-five years ago, Dr. Tom French was appointed head of the Massachusetts Division of Fisheries and Wildlife's Natural Heritage and Endangered Species Program that has overseen the recovery of numerous species of native plants and animals. He works in cooperation with the U.S. Fish and Wildlife Service, federal and state agencies, and private conservation organizations. He climbs trees to band bald eagle chicks and occasionally cleans huge whale skeletons in his backyard.

My first impression of Thornton Burgess is the obvious — he did an incredible job in his enormous volume of writing in generating public interest in nature and wildlife. One of the problems we have these days, and I think we had it even back then, is bridging the gap between the general, untrained, not particularly interested public and issues of wildlife and science and conservation. Trying to figure out how to engage the general public has always been a difficult challenge.

The most successful case I've been involved with has been our second peregrine falcon nest on a skyscraper in Springfield, Massachusetts, the highest building in the city. When the nest tray was first put up, a local cable station was permitted to install cameras in the small office adjacent to the window on the twenty-first floor. This was early on, when there weren't these kinds of cameras focused on bird nests. When the falcons began nesting, people started calling it the Falcon Channel. It was on twenty-four hours a day, and we had a viewing audience of 200,000 in Springfield.

In the first year, there were two chicks, and people called in, saying there is something wrong with the smaller chick. We sent somebody down there to look at it, and they confirmed that the chick was dying, right there on the camera. They let me tie a 150-foot rope to the upper railing on the twenty-third floor, and I rappelled down to the twenty-first floor to get the chick out of the nest. The parents hit me so hard they knocked the helmet and glasses off my head. I caught the helmet, got the chick, and we took it to Tufts Veterinary School in Grafton. They found it had a piece of meat stuck in its throat. We kept it eight days. It doubled its weight, and we took it back. Everybody in Springfield knew every detail. It ended up on Tom Brokaw's *NBC Nightly News*, Peter Jennings' *ABC World News Tonight*, and *CNN Evening News*.

My point is this: It was a case where people who weren't interested in wildlife were completely hooked on following all the trials and tribulations of this family of falcons because they knew them personally and individually. Burgess did the same thing with his stories. He did it very well, and he did it with a younger audience that was developing their values, which is the right age to catch.

Before the 1918 Migratory Bird Treaty Act was passed, when there was market hunting, you could kill as many ducks as you wished, any time you wished. And as for raptors — hawks and owls — there was no federal law against killing them until the 1972 amendment to our treaty with Mexico. Public attitude has completely changed now. We use words like *majestic* and *proud* to describe hawks and owls, but around 1945, there was a book on raptors of the Northeast that said the peregrine falcon "can be tolerated in small numbers," and for most of the others it was kill every damn one you can. Burgess was really that much more important because he helped give people a better feel for and an understanding of nature at a time when public attitude was largely negative for some types of animals.

Rosemary Talmadge

Director of Organizational Development at LaGuardia Community College

An internal consultant at LaGuardia Community College in Queens, New York, a school with a diverse campus of more than 20,000 credit students from 160 countries, Rosemary Talmadge helps "engage everyone on the campus in change initiatives." When the editor of a college journal asked her to contribute an essay on mindfulness and sustainability, both unfamiliar fields to her, she accepted the challenge. "As I wrote it, it was surprising to me that this link between the planet and mindfulness meant so much to me," she says. Talmadge also discovered her paper had an unexpected connection to her father and Thornton Burgess. The following is an excerpt of Talmadge's introduction to "In Transit," in The LaGuardia Journal of Teaching and Learning (spring 2011).

Practices for cultivating mindfulness or attentiveness may take many forms: meditation, for example, or writing, running, and yoga. My first teacher of mindfulness was my father, whose instruction might have some bearing on my discussion of systems thinking and mindfulness. One of eleven children, my father was a city kid who left high school at seventeen to join the Marine Corps. When I was six, we moved to a dreary, brick apartment complex in Norfolk, Virginia, near the back gate of the naval base where he was stationed, and it was there that my awareness of ecology began. One day while browsing in the PX, my father came upon and bought a set of *The Bedtime Story-Books* by conservationist and author of children's stories, Thornton W. Burgess. Our small apartment became a kind of mindfulness boot camp as each night after dinner, while my mother washed the dishes, my father read to us from these books. My younger sister and I came to love the animals of Burgess's *Mother West Wind*, worrying every time Farmer Brown's mindless son threatened the tranquility of their lives in the Great Forest.

My father had little first-hand experience with the wonders of the natural world, but he soon became a master at introducing them to us. Fastening a string of seed on the concrete sill, he drew a flock of birds to our bedroom window. Delighted with this success, he brought us a field guide to identify them and he taught my sister and me to sit quietly to observe them and learn their calls. One day, we found a nest and in it a perfect blue egg which we presented to our father. He was less happy with our gift than we had hoped. Surprised, we offered to return the egg, but he patiently explained that it was not possible to undo the damage we had done. Without training or experience, my father was teaching us the principles of thinking ecologically: to be mindful of our connection to the natural world, to know that we are a part of something larger than ourselves, and to understand the consequences of our actions on the world around us.

HONI ANN BOUDREAUX

Farmer

Honi Ann Boudreaux and her husband Glen own and operate a 107-acre Jolie Vue Farms northwest of Houston, Texas. When they bought the farm in 1989, their goal was to convert an over-grazed, sterilized environment into an oasis for native vegetation and wildlife as well as for the healthy production of grass-fed pastured beef and free-range chicken and pork. In 2010, Honi took a break from spreading manure around peach trees with a front-end loader to talk about her favorite children's author.

I never knew Thornton Burgess, but I loved his books. My grandmother started me on those books when I was a very young girl, and I still have many of them today.

I'm getting my grandchildren to read them now. I still count those books as the basis of my knowledge of the outdoors and of wildlife. In 1956 or so, my grandmother had started buying my sisters and me *The Adventures of Bobby Coon*, *Old Mother West Wind*, and other Burgess books. She bought them every birthday, every Christmas, and we read them avidly. We still enjoy them. The world was getting into the cutsie books, nothing against Dr. Seuss, but I would really *read* those Burgess books and we'd talk about them.

We were an outdoors family. My grandmother was always taking us on a bird watch. She was born in Indian Territory in Oklahoma in 1898. Her mother would draw a line in the sand and say, "Don't go past this." So she grew up in a rural area, and she kept her love of nature when she came to Houston with her father after her mother died. The great thing that broadened her horizons was she was hired as a secretary for three wealthy ladies. They would go to Idaho and other places, and this one elderly lady liked to watch wildlife, so my grandmother got to see wolves and cougars and coyotes in packs, and things southeast Texas didn't have. We would always get pictures and stories from her about the animals she saw. At the end of her life, we started a bird-watching club for her at her assisted living home.

As we grew up, we learned that everything Thornton Burgess put in those stories was light-hearted and fun, but the things he said about the animals were true. Raccoons do like to go through the hen house, and skunks do eat beetles, and jays will dive-bomb you if they think you're a threat. And you can get mockingbirds to imitate each other. I just loved that the books were about real nature, how maybe one animal starts on a journey for corn, and he gets lost or scared, and it takes three days to get home.

We had beavers in our creek here, and when I watched them I remembered in the Burgess story about how beavers took down saplings. And when we're mowing, we'll always find that the mama mouse or bunny puts the babies right against a road, because a fox wouldn't go there. The little animals know that a predator doesn't want to be seen, and so did the ones in Thornton Burgess' books.

Nikki Giovanni

Poet, Author, College Professor

Nikki Giovanni is a distinguished professor at Virginia Tech who addressed the campus with a poem composed after the horrific 2007 campus shooting. Her two dozen books for children and adults have received wide recognition, including the Coretta Scott King Award, Caldecott Honors, NAACP Image award, nominations for the National Book Award, and a Grammy nomination for her spoken word album, "The Nikki Giovanni Poetry Collection." Ms. Giovanni participated in the 2009 bicentennial celebration at the Lincoln Memorial by reading her poem, "At This Moment." She was voted "Woman of the Year" by Essence, Mademoiselle, *and* Ladies Home Journal. *Her most recent book is* The 100 Best African-American Poems* But I Cheated (2010).

I guess it was my mother who introduced me to the *Old Mother West Wind* series. I liked the Merry Little Breezes and Mother West Wind. Like any mother she had jobs to do, she leaves the Little Breezes to play in the meadow while she goes off to send ships sailing and do all the important work mothers have to do. I thought it was wonderful. I always loved that it was a series, that there was another story and another.

I was in the fourth grade when I started reading Burgess. I grew up with my grandmother in Knoxville, Tennessee; my parents lived in Cincinnati. It was a rural area, so we had a book mobile, and I remember a terrible thing happened. I used to like to make bubbles. I was reading *The Cave Twins* and knocked the bubbles over onto the book so Mommy had to buy the book. I was feeling so bad, it was probably $2.50. It taught me not to read with bubbles. Granny Fox would have done the same thing my mother did. If Reddy knocked something over, she would have said "I'm sorry, but you cannot do this," but she wouldn't have tried to humiliate him.

My great-grandmother Cornelia lived with us, she was something! We called her Mama Dear, and I remember her saying: "I smell trouble on the way /Yes, I do! Yes, I do! / Hope it ain't a'gwine to stay, / Yes, I do! Yes, I do!" Mama Dear was born the free child of slave parents, so the rhyme would have been something she heard and knew. It was something that was out there. Now we have practically no sense of smell, but we used to smell rain and fear. In fact, Thornton Burgess used this rhyme in *The Adventures of Reddy Fox* [see sidebar]. Given the time he was working in, there is every reason to think he had heard African-American Spirituals as well as Blues.

At my home I have a meadow I've taken back to natural Virginia. We pulled out everything that wasn't native, now the birds can feed all year round. My friend Alice Walker has one hundred acres and I have two acres, but it is comfortable. It is balanced now. I have a variety of wildlife — field rats, mice, skunks, possums, rabbits. You see them all winter. I never come home without looking at my lawn because they'll be sitting out there. I come very slowly. I'm sure I was influenced by Burgess, because I think of all of these creatures as being my friends. Mother Nature tries to keep a balance. When I was ten, I did see that balance in the stories, and I did see that patience in Granny, that things come when they should. The stories were incredibly important to me.

I remember being delighted with Reddy, because the things he tried I would never ever have tried to do. He was so adventuresome. None of the characters I knew ever ate each other. The foxes would eat the chickens, but they were never our friends. Reddy didn't eat "Susie Chicken." It was always that he ate "a" chicken. And that kept you from worrying.

To me we were contemporaries, me and Reddy. I wasn't thinking: This is the way you treat Nature. There was a sense of camaraderie, they [the animal characters] were not different from me, nor were they dangerous. And you delighted in all of that, even the Merry Little Breezes, somehow they all became real to me. It wasn't, oh, winds are important, but, yes, I'd like to play with the Merry Little Breezes. And I still feel that way. It is forty-eight degrees outside today, and when I went out to look at my fish, and the breezes were there, I found myself smiling. I don't know if I learned that from Burgess or I brought that to Burgess.

Human beings are not good neighbors. If more kids read more books like Thornton Burgess', they would probably have more respect. They wouldn't be afraid of differences. If youngsters were reading *Mother West Wind*, they would know that tragedies occur, the life cycle goes on, you cannot defend against everything. What I do know about Granny and Reddy and the Green Meadow is you are always watchful, you use ordinary prudence. That's the price you pay for life. There is an old Negro spiritual that says "Watch right and pray," and that's what we all [have to] do. "Watch right" means "watch correctly." Those are the two things that will get you over things that are get-overable. Some things are not. But you can't spend your life being afraid, otherwise you would need to lock yourself up somewhere.

Things happen, that's why you have to use ordinary prudence. I had a student from England who had never had grits. So I made them for him. When I got to the campus that morning, it was still dark. Because I work at a university and things happen in big places, I turned off my car and looked around. I used ordinary prudence. I'm of the Civil Rights generation. We came up knowing that today was all you had. So you have to do today's job today, because tomorrow is not promised. You may be in jail tomorrow. You may be dead tomorrow. So you maximize, and that becomes a habit. It's a good habit.

The books my children grew up with didn't teach them compassion or love or ordinary prudence. I think that Burgess deserves more, and young readers would benefit from reading him. He has not gotten his due.

EXCERPT FROM *THE ADVENTURES OF REDDY FOX*[1]

"Whenever Reddy saw Farmer Brown's boy he would say with the greatest scorn: "Who's afraid of him? Not I!"

"So as Reddy Fox thought more and more of his own smartness, he grew bolder and bolder. Almost every night he visited Farmer Brown's henyard. Farmer Brown set traps all around the yard, but Reddy always found them and kept out of them. It got so that Unc' Billy Possum and Jimmy Skunk didn't dare go to the henhouse for eggs any more, for fear that they would get into one of the traps set for Reddy Fox. Of course they missed those fresh eggs and of course they blamed Reddy Fox.

"Never mind," said Jimmy Skunk, scowling down on the Green Meadows where Reddy Fox was taking a sun bath, "Farmer Brown's boy will get him yet! I hope he does!" Jimmy said this a little spitefully and just as if he really meant it.

"Now when people think that they are very, very smart, they like to show off. You know it isn't any fun at all to feel smart unless others can see how smart you are. So Reddy Fox, just to show off, grew very bold, very bold indeed. He actually went up to Farmer Brown's henyard in broad daylight, and almost under the nose of Bowser the Hound he caught the pet chicken of Farmer Brown's boy. 'Ol Mistah Buzzard, sailing overhead high up in the blue, blue sky, saw Reddy Fox and shook his bald head.

"Ah see Trouble on the way;
Yes, Ah do! Yes, Ah do!
Hope it ain't a gwine to stay;
Yes, Ah do! Yes, Ah do!
Trouble am a spry ol' man,
Bound to find yo' if he can;
If he finds yo' bound to stick.
When Ah sees him, Ah runs quick!
Yes, Ah do! Yes, Ah do!"

"But Reddy Fox thought himself so smart that it seemed as if he really were hunting for Ol' Mr. Trouble. And when he caught the pet chicken of Farmer Brown's boy, Ol' Mr. Trouble was right at his heels."

The Legacy: Photos

Laughing Brook, Burgess' home in Hampden, Massachusetts.
Courtesy of David Cesan.

A view of Burgess' home at Laughing Brook from his writing studio behind the house. *Courtesy of David Cesan.*

Burgess and Fannie with rabbit.

Burgess and his wife Fannie before the 17th century fireplace in their home at Laughing Brook. *Courtesy of David Cesan.*

Undated photo of Burgess (with trademark bow tie) and wife Fannie in front row, with friends and/or family.

Bradford children holding owl, circa 1932.

Thornton Burgess' granddaughter Frances Bradford Meigs, who recorded memories of her beloved grandfather in a memoir published in 1998, *My Grandfather, Thornton W. Burgess.*

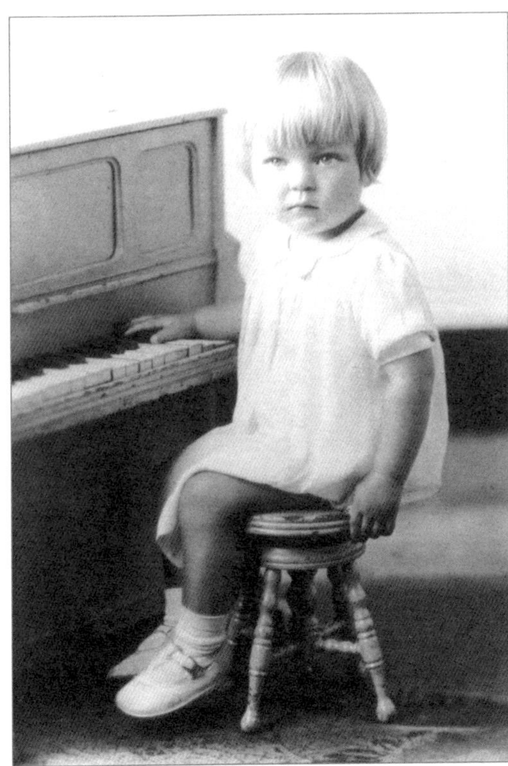

Burgess' granddaughter Nancy Burgess at a piano.

Burgess with great-granddaughter.

Students listen to their guest speaker during "Burgess Day" at the Henry T. Wing School in Sandwich, Massachusetts, circa 1954.

Thornton W. Burgess with Henry T. Wing School teacher Velma Consolini at "Burgess Day," circa 1954.

Thornton Burgess visiting the Sutton family at their home in East Sandwich.

Martha Blake, left, working with her staff at the Green Briar Jam Kitchen.

Ida Putnam's well-stocked showroom of jams and jellies, circa 1930s.

Thornton W. Burgess III while serving in the U.S. Army, possibly taken in the Philippines.

Thornton W. Burgess III in his 30's with his daughter Nancy, circa late 1930s.

Thornton W. Burgess III in Amsterdam.

From left: Thornton III, Burgess, and unidentified man, circa 1960s.

In the mid-1950s, Thornton Burgess began vacationing, then wintering, on the Caribbean island of Tobago where he continued to write books and syndicated stories.

In the late 1950s, Thornton Burgess traveled to Tucson Arizona. He visited the Sonora Desert Museum where he enjoyed learning about Southwestern wildlife, such as this bobcat, and also met Chuck Roth's son who worked there.

According to David Cesan, this photograph was taken at the Mary Lyon Nursing Home by his mother Ernestine Johnson about 1964. It was the last time Thornton Burgess and Harrison Cady saw each other. *Courtesy of David Cesan.*

Thornton Burgess and his secretarial assistant Ernestine Johnson at the Mary Lyon Nursing Home in Hampden, Massachusetts, circa 1964. *Courtesy of David Cesan.*

Thornton W. Burgess, circa 1960.

Thornton Burgess Society's Putnam Education Building at Green Briar Nature Center.

Shirley Cross in her wildflower garden at the Green Briar Nature Center.

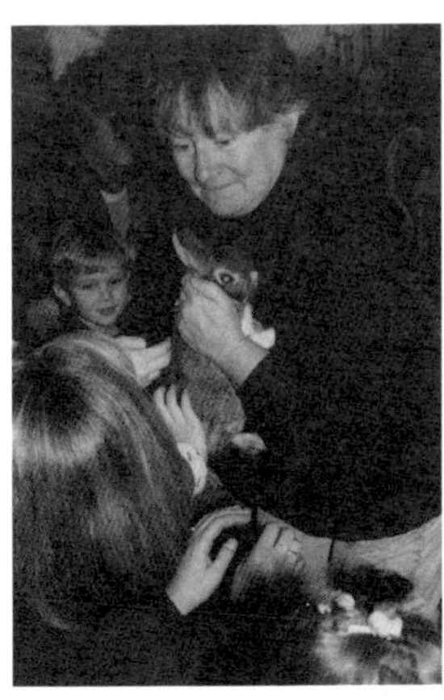

Head naturalist Mary Beers at Green Briar Nature Center.

A nature scene at Laughing Brook Wildlife Sanctuary in Hampden, Massachusetts.

The sign at the Massachusetts Audubon Society Wildlife Sanctuary. *Photos courtesy of Hellsacres blog.*

Green Briar Jam Kitchen and spring-fed pond in East Sandwich, Massachusetts.

ENDNOTES

Unless otherwise noted, the personal journals and correspondence of Thornton W. Burgess have been made available by the Thornton W. Burgess Society. All journal entries referenced here are those of Thornton W. Burgess.

Abbreviations
Note: The following abbreviations can be found in the endnotes that follow:

AHC: Austin Hobart Clark
AOG: Dr. Alfred Otto Gross
BCLA: A.O. Gross Papers, George J. Mitchell Dept. of Special Collections & Archives, Bowdoin College Library, Brunswick, Maine
HGARC: Howard Gotlieb Archival Research Center at Boston University, Boston, Massachusetts
NMNHA: National Museum of Natural History Archives, Washington, D.C.
PANB: Provincial Archives of New Brunswick, Fredericton, New Brunswick
SAHC: Sandwich Archives and Historical Center, Sandwich, Massachusetts
SIA: Smithsonian Institution Archives, Washington, D.C.
TWB: Thornton W. Burgess
TWBSA: Thornton W. Burgess Society Archives, Sandwich, Massachusetts
UNBASC: University of New Brunswick Archives and Special Collections, Harriet Irving Library, Fredericton, New Brunswick
WTH: Dr. William Temple Hornaday

Introduction

1. Catalogue of the Thornton W. Burgess Collection, an inventory of the author's personal library made by Wayne Wright for the Thornton W. Burgess Society, p. 32. *Courtesy of the Thornton W. Burgess Society.* Note: In the forward of his book, Hornaday wrote a deeply-felt belief that he and Thornton Burgess shared. "Most sincerely do I wish that the boys and girls of America, and of the world, may be induced to believe that the most interesting thing about a wild animal is its mind and its reasoning...If the feet of the young men would run more to seeing and studying the wild creatures and less to the killing of them, some of the world's most valuable creatures might escape being swept away tomorrow, or the day after.
2. *One Hundred and Fifty Years of Publishing* (Boston: Little Brown and Company, 1987), p. 67.
3. *Journal*, TWB, October 1 and 4, 1954. TWBSA.
4. David Brower, *For Earth's Sake: The Life and Times of David Brower* (Salt Lake City: Gibbs-Smith Publishing, 1990), p. 445.
5. John Goldthwaite, *The Natural History of Make-Believe* (New York: Oxford University Press, 1996), p. 337.
6. Thornton W. Burgess, *Whitefoot the Wood Mouse* (Boston: Little, Brown and Company, 1922), pp. 58-63.
7. Undated letter, Dr. Theodore Reed to TWBS. TWBA.

Chapter One

1. Thornton W. Burgess, *Now I Remember* (Boston: Little, Brown and Company, 1960), p. 4.
2. Burgess, *Remember*, p. 5.
3. TWB to Stuart Trueman, December 8, 1963. Courtesy of University of New Brunswick Archives and Special Collections (UNBA&SC).
4. Burgess, *Remember*, pp. 5-8.
5. *Sandwich Observer*, January 17, 1874. *Courtesy of Sandwich Archives and Historical Center (SAHC).*
6. Letter, Capt. Charles I. Gibbs to Louisa A. Gibbs, Nov. 11, 1961. "We hear...that our shell stove the battering ram so badly that two steamers were required to tow her up river one on each side to keep her afloat." Property of author.
7. *Seaside Press*, October 31, 1874. SAHC.
8. Obituary notice, SAHC. Note: The notice is incorrect. Thornton W. Burgess, Sr. was buried at Bay View Cemetery. Charles and Louisa Gibbs and their children are buried across the street in the Freeman Cemetery.
9. Burgess, *Remember*, p. 10.
10. Historic details of life in Sandwich in this chapter came from the *Sandwich Observer*, May 1, 1884; Burgess' autobiography; the Sandwich Archives and Historical Center; and the Thornton W. Burgess Society. Sandwich historian Barbara Gill and Jerry

Ellis of Bourne contributed helpful information.

11. *Sandwich Observer*, May 1, 1884. SAHC.
12. Burgess, *Remember*, letter of November 24, 1894, p. 64.
13. Ibid., letter of June 17, 1894, p. 61.
14. Ibid., p. 20.
15. Ibid., letter of June 10, 1894, p. 60.
16. Russell Lovell, *The Cape Cod Story of Thornton W. Burgess* (Sandwich: Thornton W. Burgess Society, 1974), p. 42.
17. Burgess, *Remember*, p. 242.
18. Ibid., p. 244.
19. Robert Conant Ellis, *The Life and Short Stories of Eleanor Conant Yeager*, pp. 79-80.
20. Thornton W. Burgess, *Happy Jack* (Boston: Little, Brown and Company, 1918), pp. 119-125.

Chapter Two

1. Thornton W. Burgess, *Now I Remember* (Boston: Little, Brown and Company, 1960), p. 20.
2. Letter, TWB to Marion Day, February 23, 1948. *Courtesy Thornton W. Burgess Society Archives* (TWBSA).
3. Burgess, *Remember*, p. 9.
4. Ibid., p. 21.
5. Ibid., pp. 22-23.
6. Ibid., p. 23.
7. Thornton W. Burgess, *At Paddy the Beaver's Pond* (Boston: Little, Brown and Company, 1950), pp. 128-129.
8. Burgess, *Remember*, pp. 22-27.
9. Information about cranberry harvesting obtained from *Sandwich Observer* (1884-1885) and Joseph Thomas' *Cranberry Harvest* (New Bedford: Spinner Publications, 1990), pp. 61-62.
10. Burgess, *Remember*, pp. 32-33.
11. Ibid., pp. 27-28.
12. Thornton W. Burgess, *The Dear Old Briar-patch* (Boston: Little, Brown and Company, 1947), pp. 3-4.
13. *Sandwich Observer*, May 8, 1884. SAHC.
14. George Haines to TWB, April 28, 1902. TWBSA.
15. William H. Woodwell, *My Way Around* (memoir), 1953. TWBSA.
16. *Journal*, January 7, 1952. TWBSA.
17. Poem and correspondence, TWB to Lillian Haines Tangney, TWBSA.
18. Text of TWB speech, 1939 Sandwich Tercentennial Celebration. Author's collection.
19. Russell Lovell, *The Cape Cod Story of Thornton W. Burgess* (Sandwich: Thornton W. Burgess Society, 1974), p. 90.

Chapter Three

1. Thornton W. Burgess, *Now I Remember* (Boston: Little, Brown and Company, 1960), p.50.
2. Ibid., p. 48.
3. TWB to George Haines, Oct. 27, 1892. TWBSA.
4. Originally submitted to *The American* as an autobiographical article titled "When the Tide Began to Make," this was presumably the article published by the magazine in May 1919 retitled "The Gold Mine I Discovered When I Was 35." TWBSA.
5. Burgess, *Remember*, pp. 50-56.
6. Note: *Forest and Stream's* editor was conservationist George Bird Grinnell who worked for the preservation of bison and American wildlands. As a founder of the New York Zoological Society, Grinnell may have attended the 1919 annual meeting and award ceremony at which Thornton Burgess was honored for distinguished service to wildlife.
7. Michael W. Dowhan, Jr. *Thornton W. Burgess, Harrison Cady: A Book, Magazine and Newspaper Bibliography* (New York: Carlton Press, Inc., 1990), p. 261. Note: Dowhan lists Burgess' various pseudonyms as: Arthur Chapouille; B.T. W.; B.W. Thornton; Frank Presbrey; T. B.; T. B. W.; T. B. Waldo; T. W. B.; Waldo, W.B.T., W. B. Thornton; W. B. Waldo; and W. T. B.
8. Burgess, *Remember*, pp. 50-51.
9. Ibid., p. 51.
10. Ibid., p. 56.
11. Ibid., pp. 72-73.
12. TWB to Caroline Burgess, November 29, 1895. TWBSA.
13. Burgess, *Remember*, pp. 74-77.
14. Note: According to *Henning Report* columnist David Travers-Adolphus, Burgess' column was preceded by "The Horseless Age," a New York subscription-based weekly first published in 1895.
15. Burgess, *Remember*, p. 94.
16. Correspondence courtesy of New York State Historical Association, Christman Family Papers, Special Collections.
17. The Thornton W. Burgess Research League web blog maintained by Peter Oehlkers was a valuable resource in writing this chapter.
18. Bethany S. Rutledge, "Nina: The First Mrs. Burgess," *Burgess Book Collectors Bulletin*, Vol. 33, No. 1, April 2002, p. 3. TWBSA.
19. Ibid., p. 4.
20. Ibid., pp. 4-5.
21. Meigs, *Grandfather*, p. 24.
22. Burgess, *Remember*, p.p.108-109.
23. Meigs, *Grandfather*, p. 26.
24. Burgess, *Remember*, p. 115.

Chapter Four

1. Thornton W. Burgess, "When the Tide Began to Make," copy submitted to *The American*, p. 2. TWBSA.
2. Unidentified 1913 advertisement quoting *Journal of Education*. TWBSA.
3. Burgess, *Remember*, p. 98. Note: In repeated references to this trip, Burgess does not identify his son's grandmother as Caroline Burgess or Mary Osborne.
4. Ibid., pp. 98-99. Note: Hebert F. Jenkins was presumably the "editorial representative" who visited Phelps Publishing and first brought Burgess' children's stories to the attention of Little, Brown. When Burgess noted Jenkins' death in his journal on January 31, 1960, he commented: "Too bad he could not have lived to see the Golden Anniversary edition of my first book [*Old Mother West Wind*] which he discovered." Jenkins joined Little, Brown in 1901

and with Alfred McIntyre was promoted to head of the editorial department in 1913.
5. Ibid., p. 111.
6. Ibid., p. 112.
7. TWB to Stuart Trueman, December 8, 1959. *Courtesy of University of New Brunswick Archives and Special Collections* (UNBA&SC).
8. Jason Rogers, *Newspaper Building* (New York: Harper & Brothers, 1918), pp. 142-143.
9. Burgess, *Remember*, p. 114.
10. Ibid., p. 318.
11. *Journals*, January 28–March 3, 1949.
12. Burgess, *Remember*, p. 100.
13. Advertisement clipping, 1915, no source or date. TWBSA.
14. *The Bulletin of the Massachusetts Audubon Society*, Vol. IV, No. 5, 1920, p. 4.
15. Thornton W. Burgess, *The Crooked Little Path*, (Boston: Little, Brown and Company, 1947), pp. 3-4.
16. Burgess, *Remember*, pp. 139-140.
17. Joseph Debraggio and Robert Kelley, "The Mighty 7th War Loan," pp. 7-9. Note: Inspired by use of the iconic image of Marines raising the U.S. flag at Iwo Jima, the government's 1945 Seventh War Loan drive became the most successful of all World War II fund-raising efforts, raising $26 billion toward a goal of $14 billion during a six-week campaign.
18. *Journals*, March 15–April 14, 1945.
19. *Boston Herald*, October 30, 1938. TWBSA.
20. *Journals*, October 26-27, 1934. Marie Peary, known as the" Snow Baby," was the daughter of Admiral Robert and Josephine Peary and the first Caucasian child born in the Arctic.
21. *Journals*, annual financial notes 1921-1939.
22. TWB to Dana, September 19, 1951. TWBSA.
23. Boy to TWB, January 30, 1927. TWBSA.
24. *Boston Globe*, April 1915, on writing his 1,000th story. TWBSA.
25. Burgess, *Remember*, pp. 266-268.

Chapter Five

1. Wayne W. Wright, *Thornton W. Burgess: A Descriptive Book Bibliography* (Sandwich: Thornton W. Burgess Society, 2000), p. 15.
2. Burgess, *Remember*, p. 301.
3. *One Hundred and Fifty Years of Publishing* (Boston: Little, Brown and Company, 1987), pp. 57-65.
4. Ibid., p. 67.
5. *Journal*, TWB, February 25, 1949.
6. TWB to Kathy and Frank Jones, March 5, 1959. Courtesy of David Cesan.
7. Information on John Eggers Company provided by Wayne Wright.
8. Trade flyer, Grosset & Dunlap, circa 1950s. TWBSA.
9. TWB, "Making Men of Them," *Good Housekeeping*, July, 1914, pp. 3-12.
10. Ibid., p. 4-6.
11. Ibid., p. 8.
12. Burgess, *Remember*, p. 257.
13. Wright, *Bibliography*, p. 147.
14. Nelson Poirier, "Thanks Mom and Mr. Toad," *Brunswick Times*, February 27, 1999.
15. *Journal*, October 23, 1960.
16. Note: The Thornton W. Burgess Society collections include the twenty-volume set published in Japanese.
17. Anime News Network has a list of "Fables of the Green Forest" productions and programs.
18. Advertisement for Bodley Head Ltd., "Publishers Circular and Booksellers' Record," October 10, 1931. TWBSA.
19. Wright, *Bibliography*, pp. 147-153.
20. Burgess, *Remember*, pp. 334-335. Note: He refers to *The Bride's Primer* (1905) and *Old Mother West* Wind (1910).
21. Wayne Wright, "Three Illustrators of Burgess Books," *Burgess Book Collectors Bulletin*, Vol. 29, April 2000, p. 1.
22. Michael W. Dowhan, Jr., *Thornton W. Burgess, Harrison Cady: A Book, Magazine and Newspaper Bibliography* (New York: Carlton Press, Inc., 1990), Introduction. Dowhan notes that Harrison Cady worked for *Life* for twenty-six years, *People's Home Journal* for twenty-one years, and *American Boy* for twenty years in addition to illustrating Burgess' books and stories.
23. John L. Cooley (interviewer), *O Rare Harrison Cady: The Life of Harrison Cady* (Sandy Bay Historical Society, 2009), pp. 73-75. *Courtesy of Sandy Bay Historical Society.*
24. Dowhan, *Burgess, Cady Bibliography*, p. 244.
25. "H. Cady Art at Sotheby's," *Burgess Book Collectors Bulletin*, Vol. 13, October, 1994, p. 2.
26. Robert McCracken Peck, *A Celebration of Birds*, (New York: Walker and Company, 1982), p. 1.
27. Peck, *Celebration*, p. 89.
28. Ibid., p. 22.
29. *Journal*, October 1 and 4, 1954.
30. *One Hundred and Fifty Years of Publishing*, p. 67.
31. Interview with editor Stuart Trueman, *Evening-Times Globe*, October 8, 1963.
32. Louis Levine, "Unforgettable Thornton W. Burgess, *Readers Digest* (reprint), October 1967, p. 3.

Chapter Six

1. *Journal*, December 31, 1947.
2. Ibid., February 19, 1948.
3. Ibid., February 21, 1936.
4. Burgess, *Remember*, p. 49.
5. Obituary, *New York Times*, June 7, 1965, p. 84.
6. Affidavit, December 27, 1940. TWBSA.
7. Harry Dow, "Burgess 'Quaddies' – Popular Collectibles," *Burgess Book Collectors Bulletin*, Vol. 16, November 1995, p. 1. TWBSA.
8. Ibid., p. 2.
9. Information on Burgess collectibles provided by Gene Schott and John Richmond.
10. Burgess, *Remember*, pp. 227-228.
11. Notice, *The Billboard*, April 18, 1953, p. 16. TWBSA.
12. Wayne Wright provided this information.
13. *Journals*, January 23-April 18, 1940.
14. Bradford Washburn to TWB, May 24, 1940. TWBSA.

15. Russell Mason to TWB, May 24, 1940. TWBSA.
16. William H. Carr to TWB, June 6, 1940. TWBSA.
17. Hazel L. Muller to TWB, June 24, 1940. TWBSA.
18. F. C. Walcott to TWB, July 10, 1940. TWBSA.
19. *Books of the Week*, July 29, 1940. TWBSA.
20. AHC to TWB, May 29, 1940. SIA.
21. *Journal*, December 12, 1948.
22. *Journal*, December 21, 1948.
23. News item, *The Press-Union*, Atlantic City, New Jersey. June 3, 1949. Courtesy of University of North Texas.
24. A paper on Gordon Knox and the Princeton Film Center (February 11, 2009) was provided by his son Toby Knox.
25. TWB to Kathy Jones, April 14, 18, 1957. Courtesy of David Cesan.
26. Article or lecture text (draft copy), Thornton W. Burgess, "Can Your Children Read?", p. 5. TWBSA.
27. Ziv International website.
28. Internet posts about the program indicate that the theme song of *Fables of the Green Forest* was also popular. The following lyrics are on Rick Ambrozic's website

"Trouble! Trouble! Trouble! Buster Bear's pursuing trout,
Reddy Fox's radar snout has sniffed out his prey!
In the Green Forest, the Green Forest,
The Laughing Brook chuckles all day.
Paddy Beaver's building a dam,
Joe the Otter tells him SCRAM!
Chatterer is on the lam.
Oh what a sight!
In the Green Forest, the Green Forest,
You may see the occasional fight.
Peter Rabbit hippity-hops,
The mean old weasel growls,
Grandpa Froggy flippity-flops,
And Sammy Blue Jay scowls.
There are martens, mink and sable there,
Toads on mushroom tables there,
Four and fifty fables there...
With friendship and strife.
In the Green Forest, the Green Forest
The stories you've read about all come to life,
Yes, the stories you've read about all come to life!"

29. *Fables of the Green Forest* (TV show), Anime News Network website.
30. *Journal*, October 30, 1947.
31. *Journal*, September 19-20, 1960.
32. TWB to Stuart Trueman, October 12, 1960. UNBA&SC.

Chapter Seven

1. Annie Carroll Moore, *Roads to Childhood* (New York: George H. Doran Company, 1920), p. 51.
2. Brian King, "Visits in Our Valley," source and page unknown, October 11, 1959. TWBSA.
3. Burgess, *Remember*, p. 229.
4. TWB to Stuart Trueman, June 26, 1963. UNB&SC.
5. Burgess, *Remember*, p. 219.
6. Ibid., p. 217.
7. Ibid., p. 230.
8. Ibid., p. 216.
9. *Journal*, Feb. 19, 1948.
10. Walter Oriskany to TWB, 1959. TWBSA
11. Thornton W. Burgess, "Nature as the Universal Teacher," *Natural History*, March-April, 1922, p. 139.
12. Burgess, *Remember*, p. 8.
13. Note: In November 2008 PBS aired "The Wolf That Changed America," a television program based on Ernest Thompson Seton's story of the capture of Lobo, a legendary wolf and his mate [see this chapter, p.14]. One parent posted the following online comment: "I would suggest very strongly that if you show it again it should have a parental advisory. I allowed my 8-1/2 year old to watch it and I am very sorry that I did. It was almost as if something in her died when Lobo died. She woke up the next morning in tears and said that she was trying to pretend that it wasn't a real story and that Lobo was really alive. I think the cruelty of what that man did to that animal really stunned her. Or perhaps it was just too graphic a presentation of the destructiveness of humans in general for her to take. We have never had a problem like this with any nature program before. It was an excellent and powerful presentation but not good for children, at least not this one."
14. Thornton W. Burgess, *The Adventures of Old Man Coyote* (New York: Grosset & Dunlap, 1916, 1944), pp. 21-25.
15. Thornton W. Burgess, *Old Mother West Wind* (Boston: Little, Brown and Company, 1910), pp. 4-5.
16. Thornton W. Burgess, *The Adventures of Buster Bear's Twins* (New York: Grosset & Dunlap, 1921, 1951) pp. 94-100.
17. Thornton W. Burgess, *The Adventures of Granny Fox* (Boston: Little, Brown and Company, 1920), pp. 78-79.
18. Thornton W. Burgess, *The Adventures of Bob White* (New York: Grosset & Dunlap, 1919), pp. 101-103.
19. Thornton W. Burgess, *The Adventures of Jerry Muskrat* (Grosset& Dunlap, 1954) pp. 187-192.
20. TWB to Aida Flemming, April 25, 1955. *Courtesy of the Provincial Archives of New Brunswick.*
21. TWB to Austin Clark, September 26, 1925. *Courtesy of Smithsonian Institution Archives.*
22. Austin Clark to TWB, September 28, 1925. Smithsonian Institution Archives.
23. John Goldthwaite, *The Natural History of Make-Believe* (New York: Oxford University Press, 1996), p. 341. Note: In Chapter Eight endnotes, Goldthwaite further discusses the connection he finds between Burgess' 1944 book and the E.B. White classic *Charlotte's Web.*
24. *Journal*, June 23, 1945.
25. John Goldthwaite, *The Natural History of Make-Believe* (New York: Oxford University Press, 1996), p. 338.
26. John Burroughs, *Squirrels and Other Fur-Bearers* (Boston and New York, Houghton Mifflin, 1875), pp. 1-2.
27. Thornton W. Burgess, *50 Favorite Burgess Stories* (New York: Grosset & Dunlap, 1944, 1946), pp. 4-44.
28. Ernest Thompson Seton, *Wild Animals I Have Known* (New York: Charles Scribner's Sons, 1898), pp. 46-47.

29. Linda Lear, *Beatrix Potter: A Life in Nature* (New York: St. Martin's Griffin, 2007), p. 131.
30. Thornton W. Burgess, *The Adventures of Ol' Mistah Buzzard* (New York: Grosset & Dunlap, 1919, 1947), pp. 36-37.

Chapter Eight

1. Draft of article, "The Gift of Gifts for a Child," submitted to *Publishers Weekly*, September 26, 1923. TWBSA.
2. Eden Ross Lipson, *New York Times Parents' Guide to Best Books for Children* (New York: Three Rivers Press, 2000), p. 635.
3. Thornton W. Burgess, *Mother West Wind "Where" Stories* (Boston, Little, Brown and Company, 1918), p. 137.
4. Thornton W. Burgess, *The Adventures of Bowser the Hound* (New York: Grosset & Dunlap, 1920, reprint by permission of Little, Brown and Company 1948), p. 22.
5. Thornton W. Burgess, *At Paddy the Beaver's Pond* (Boston, Little, Brown and Company 1950), pp. 3-4; 19-20; pp. 35-36.
6. Lucien L. Agosta, "Thornton W. Burgess," *Twentieth Century Children's Writers, 2nd Edition* (New York: St. Martin's Press, 1983), p. 140.
7. Margaret Bush, "New England Book Women: their increasing influence – Caroline Hewins, Anne Carroll Moore, Alice Jordan, and Bertha Mahony," *Library Trends*, spring 1996.
8. Bush, 'Bertha Mahony: the WEIU and the Bookshop,' "New England Book Women," *Literary Trends*.
9. Bertha E. Mahony and Elinor Whitney, *Realms of Gold* (Garden City: Doubleday, Doran & Company, 1929), pp. 107, 112, 590, 712.
10. Thornton W. Burgess, *Now I Remember* (Boston, Little, Brown and Company, 1960), p. 120.
11. Leslie Linder, *A History of the Writings of Beatrix Potter* (New York: Frederick Warne & Co Inc., 1971), p. 109.
12. Linder, *History of Writings*, p. 109.
13. Ralph H. Lutts, *The Nature Fakers* (Charlottesville: University of Virginia Press, 1990), p. 87.
14. Thornton W. Burgess, *Now I Remember* (Boston: Little, Brown and Company, 1960), p. 98.
15. Linda Lear, *Beatrix Potter: A Life in Nature* (New York: St. Martin's Griffin, 2007), p. 131.
16. Souces of information in this section were taken from the Linder and Lear biographies and Burgess' autobiography.
17. Mark I. West, "The Response of Children's Librarians to Dime Novels and Series Books," *Children's Literature Association Quarterly*, Volume 10, Number 3, Fall 198, pp. 137-139.
18. Christine Jenkins, paper, "From Fireplace to Marketplace," *The Cycle of Story*, University of Illinois, p. 85.
19. Thornton W. Burgess, *The Adventures of Little Joe Otter* (New York: Grosset & Dunlap, 1925, published by arrangement with Little, Brown and Company, 1953), pp. 57, 7, 32, 19.
20. Thornton W. Burgess, undated essay, "Books and the Child." TWBSA.
21. Annie [Anne] Carroll Moore, *Roads to Childhood*, (New York: George H. Doran Company, 1920), pp. 50-52.
22. *Journal*, October 28, 1939.
23. Orville Prescott, *The Five-Dollar Gold Piece* (New York: Random House, 1956), p. 8. Note: In his 1965 book, *A Father Reads to His Children*, Prescott comments on childhood reading: "It is much easier to learn to love reading as a child than later. When all the world is fresh and new and the ancient art of storytelling seems most magical, most boys and girls can most naturally acquire the habit of reading, which, once acquired, can never lose its power to delight and to inform."
24. Jill Lepore, "The Lion and the Mouse," *The New Yorker*, July 21, 2008.
25. Linda Lear, *Beatrix Potter: A Life in Nature* (New York: St. Martin's Griffin, 2007), pp. 312-317.
26. Jacalyn Eddy, *Creating an Empire in Children's Book Publishing, 1919-1939* (Madison: University of Wisconsin Press, 2006), p. 4.
27. Bush, "New England Book Women," *Library Trends*.
28. Elizabeth D. Schafer, "Thornton W. Burgess," *Guide to Literary Masters and Their Work*.

Chapter Nine

1. Thornton W. Burgess, "Nature as the Universal Teacher," *Natural History*, Vol. XXII, No. 2 (1922), p.137. TWBSA.
2. Burgess, *Remember*, p. 332.
3. Burgess, *Remember*, p. 129.
4. Jason Rogers, *Newspaper Building* (New York: Harper & Brothers, 1918), pp. 142-143.
5. TWB, "Bedtime Story Club," *Milwaukee Journal*, (October 3, 1915), p. 9. TWBSA.
6. Burgess, *Remember*, p. 119.
7. Ibid., pp. 121-125.
8. Ibid., p. 123.
9. Moody Gates' letter, *People's Home Journal*, Vol. 1, No. 1 (May 1, 1914). TWBSA.
10. TWB, "Mother Nature News," May 1, 1917.
11. TWB, "A Plea for Our Feathered Friends," *New England Homestead*, December 24, 1904, p. 22.
12. "A Conspicuous National Service," *People's Home Journal*, pp. 10-11. TWBSA.
13. William T. Hornaday, *Statement of the Permanent Wild Life Protection Fund, 1917-1919*, Vol. 3, (1920), p. 69.
14. "A Conspicuous National Service," *People's Home Journal*, undated, p. 9.
15. Advertisement, *People's Home Journal*. TWBSA.
16. "A Conspicuous National Service," *People's Home Journal*, undated. Endorsement statements on pages 7, 19, 21, and 28.
17. Hornaday, *Statement*, p. 32.
18. Note: In William Hornaday's *Thirty Years War for Wild Life* (New York: Charles Scribner's Sons, 1931) he praises the *People's Home Journal's* campaign, saying, "It is impossible to imagine the pursuit of a cause for public benefit at a higher plane."
19. Hornaday, *Statement*, "Two great campaigns for wild life sanctuaries," pp. 71-72

20. "A Conspicuous National Service," *People's Home Journal*, undated, pp. 24-25.
21. "A Conspicuous National Service," *People's Home Journal*, undated, pp. 22-23.
22. Hornaday, *Statement*, p. 69.
23. Ibid., p. 69.
24. "What About Your Pledge?" *People's Home Journal*, Vol. XXXIV, No. 8, August, 1919.
25. William T. Hornaday to TWB, July 25, 1917. *Courtesy of Gregory Dehler.*
26. A Splendid New Green Meadow Club Sanctuary, "Mother Nature's News," August, 1919, Vol. XXXIV, No. 8, p. 1.
27. Several sources credit the Green Meadow Club bird sanctuaries program with posting eight million acres. A 1939 article by publisher/editor Marlen E. Pew, Jr. in *Editor and Publisher* states: "Through his Green Meadow Club, which was built up through his newspaper stories, [Thornton Burgess] had established bird sanctuaries covering more than 8,000,000 acres."
28. *People's Home Journal*, "A Conspicuous National Service," undated, p. 9.

Chapter Ten

1. William T. Hornaday, *Our Vanishing Wild Life* (New York, New York, Charles Scribner's Sons, 1913), p. 7.
2. WTH to TWB, November 1, 1916. TWBSA.
3. *Journal*, February 24, 1940.
4. Burgess, *Remember*, pp. 127-128.
5. WTH to TWB, January 24, 1916. TWBSA.
6. WTH to TWB, February 2, 1916. TWBSA.
7. Burgess, *Remember*, p. 132.
8. Kurk Dorsey, *The Dawn of Conservation Diplomacy* (Seattle, Washington: University of Washington Press, 1998), p. 167.
9. Dorsey, *Dawn*, pp. 16-18.
10. WTH to TWB, January 21, 1916. TWBSA.
11. Hornaday, *Vanishing*, p. 44. He notes this information was provided by E. L. Ewbank, T. Gilbert Pearson, H.H. and C.S. Brimley.
12. William T. Hornaday, *Statement of the Permanent Wildlife Protection Fund, 1917-1919*, Vol. 3, (New York, New York: The Fund, New York Zoological Park, 1920), p. 29.
13. William T. Hornaday, "The Zero Hour for American Game," *Nature*, January 1924, p. 56. TWBSA.
14. Hornaday, *Vanishing*, p. 11.
15. WTH to TWB, Feb. 23, 1916. TWBSA. Note: According to Gregory Dehler, author of *William Temple Hornaday: An American Crusader for Wildlife*, Hornaday was fond of employing catchy expressions, and first used the phrase "gauntlet of guns" in his 1914 four-volume set *American Fireside Edition of Natural History*.
16. Thornton W. Burgess, *The Adventures of Poor Mrs. Quack* (New York: Dover Publications, 1919, 1993), pp. 8-9.
17. Burgess, *Mrs. Quack*, pp. 12-17.
18. Burgess, *Mrs. Quack*, pp. 45-46.
19. WTH to TWB, November 1, 1916. TWBSA.
20. Ray P. Holland Papers, "Enforcement of the Migratory Bird Treaty, 1872-1974," Olin Library Special Collections and Archives, Wesleyan University.
21. Note: Dr. Tom French, assistant director for the Natural Heritage and Endangered Species Program of the Massachusetts Division of Fisheries and Wildlife provided information on the history of the Migratory Bird Treaty Act.
22. Interview, Chandler Robbins, May 3, 2010.
23. Thornton W. Burgess, *The Adventures of Lightfoot the Deer* (New York: Grosset & Dunlap, 1921) pp. 94-95.
24. Burgess, *Lightfoot*, pp. 108-110.
25. Thornton W. Burgess, *The Adventures of Bob White* (New York, New York: Grosset & Dunlap, 1919), pp. 117-118.
26. Burgess, *Bob White*, p. 121.
27. Ibid., pp. 134-135.
28. Burgess, *Remember*, p. 132.
29. Ibid.
30. Ibid.
31. Hornaday, *Statement*, p. 111.
32. WTH to TWB, March 29, 1917. TWBSA.
33. WTH to TWB, Oct. 28, 1918. TWBSA.
34. Hornaday, *Statement*, p. 48.
35. Burgess, *Remember*, p. 126.

Chapter Eleven

1. *The Washington Post*, Jan 31. 1926, p. AF 10.
2. TWB to Alfred O. Gross, January 7, 1926. Bowdoin College Library Archives and Special Collections (BCLASC).
3. Austin Clark to TWB, June 20, 1925. Smithsonian Institution Archives (SIA).
4. Benjamin Beardsley to TWB, undated. Thornton W. Burgess Society Archives (TWBSA).
5. Charles Popence to TWB, June 1, 1922. TWBSA.
6. Burgess, *Remember*, p. 142.
7. Ibid., p. 142-143.
8. Radio script, Jan 21, 1925, p. 4. Howard Gotlieb Archival Research Center (HGARC).
9. Ibid., p. 6. HGARC.
10. Ibid., p. 5-6. HGARC.
11. Burgess, *Remember*, pp. 304-306.
12. Radio script, January 21, 1925, p. 5. HGARC
13. *Christian Science Monitor*, February 18, 1925, p. 9. TWBSA.
14. Radio script, January 7, 1925, p. 4. HGARC.
15. Radio script, January 14, 1925. HGARC.
16. Radio script, January, 21, 1925. HGARC.
17. Note: Burgess patented a bird house pattern which he sold for one dollar.
18. Burgess, *Remember*, p. 145.
19. Radio script, July 15, 1925. TWBSA.
20. Radio script, Aug. 19, 1925. TWBSA.
21. Radio script, May 25, 1925. TWBSA.
22. Radio script, May 13, 1925. TWBSA.
23. Note: According to bird song expert Edward Avis, the song sparrow was the most versatile singer and the bobolink's song the most difficult to replicate.
24. Burgess, *Remember*, pp.146-147.
25. Harry Chutham to TWB, June 29, 1930. TWBSA.
26. Ivan Baylry to TWB, May 20, 1925. TWBSA.
27. Marcel C. LaFollette, *Science on the Air* (Chicago, Illinois: University of Chicago Press, 2008), p. 27.

28. LaFollette, *Science*, p. 31.
29. Austin H. Clark to TWB, June 29, 1930. SIA.
30. TWB to AHC, June 10, 1925. SIA.
31. AHC to TWB, June 1, 1925. SIA.
32. *Popular Radio*, undated. TWBSA.
33. TWB to AHC, June 17, 1925. SIA.
34. TWB to AHC, June 19, 1925. SIA.
35. AHC to TWB, date unknown, 1925. SIA.
36. AHC to John C. Phillips, September 29, 1925. SIA.
37. LaFollette, *Science*, pp. 32-33.
38. Ibid., p. 28.
39. TWB to AHC, July 25, 1928. SIA.
40. AHC to TWB, July 26, 1928.SIA.
41 AHC to TWB, July 30, 1928. SIA.
42. TWB to AHC, Sept. 24, 1928. NMNHA.
43. AHC to William Maxon, May 10, 1935. NMNHA.
44. TWB to AHC, August 15, 1929. NMNHA.
45. AHC to TWB, August 19, 1929.NMNHA.
46. TWB to AHC, December 3, 1929. NMNHA.
47. AHC to TWB, December 5, 1929. NMNHA.
48. AHC to TWB, March 24, 1930. NMNHA.
49. Telephone interview, Marcel C. LaFollette, September 6, 2011.
50. Radio script, August 19, 1925. TWBSA.
51. TWB to AOG, February 25, 1926. BCLASC.
52. LaFollette, *Science*, p. 37.
53. William L. Finley to TWB, January 28, 1924. TWBSA.
54. Worth Mathewson, *William L. Finley, Pioneer Wildlife Photographer* (Corvallis, Oregon: Oregon State University, 1986), p. 12.
55. *Journal*, May 9, 1946.
56. Radio script, July 22, 1925, p. 9. TWBSA.
57. Radio script, May 20, 1925. TWBSA.
58. Burgess, *Remember*, pp. 152-156.
59. Radio script, June 3, 1925. TWBSA.
60. "Disembodied Voice Leads Multitudes," *Hartford Courant*, October 28, 1929, p. E16.
61. TWB to AHC, February 8, 1935. SIA.
62. "Disembodied voice," p. E16.
63. Ibid.

Chapter Twelve

1. Olin Pettingill, "The Legacy of Peter Rabbit," *Audubon*, Sept, 1983, Vol. 85, No. 5, p. 101.
2. Raymond Paynter, Jr. "In Memoriam: Alfred Otto Gross," *The Auk*, July 1971, pp. 521-527.
3. Pettingill, *Audubon*, p. 101.
4. Alfred O. Gross to TWB, January 13, 1914. Bowdoin College Library Archives and Special Collections (BCLASC).
5. AOG to TWB, January 2, 1925. BCLASC.
6. Pettingill, *Audubon*, p. 101.
7. AOG to TWB, November 2, 1925. BCLASC.
8. AOG to TWB, November 28, 1925. BCLASC.
9. Burgess, *Remember*, p. 148. Note: Burgess was particularly interested in learning the number of specimens the Radio Nature League provided because this information would give sportsmen and bird watchers who had supplied them concrete evidence of the value of their help and of the Radio Nature League. The duration of the study and information about raw data made tracking the source of specimens difficult, but Dr. Arthur Allen, Gross' partner in the ruffed grouse study, reported to Burgess in 1926 that they received three hundred twenty-eight total specimens that year through the Radio Nature League.
10. TWB to AOG, June 15, 1928. BCLASC.
11. Note: According to the fourth annual report on the Barro Colorado facility written by Dr. Thomas Barbour, other scientists who visited that year included Dr. Frank Chapman, curator of the American Museum of Natural History; Dr. Josselyn Van Tyne of the Museum of Zoology at the University of Michigan, and Dr. George Wislocki of John's Hopkins University.
12. Burgess, "Radio Nature League Newsletter," November 20, 1927. BCLASC.
13. Burgess, "Radio Nature League," December 18, 1927. BCLASC.
14. TWB to Austin H. Clark, October 26, 1927. *Smithsonian Institution Archives* (SIA).
15. *Journals*, June 10 to June 19, 1931.
16. Burgess, *Remember*, pp. 293-296.
17. Ibid., p. 295.
18. Note: Thornton Burgess' description of the 1931 Matamek Conference on Biological Cycles in Chapter 22 of his autobiography may be the only layman's account in existence. His observations as a professional writer provide a unique view of the conference participants and activities. In December 30, 1931 Burgess wrote Alfred Gross: "I sent the Matamek reel down to Dr. [W. Reid] Blair [director of the New York Zoological Society] and have it back again but not a word from him. Have the copy of [William] Rowan's book via you and am glad to have it. Have written him and sent his little girl one of my books. Also received a group enlargement from DeLury. It is a bit muddy, not as clear as your groups." BCLASC.
19. Burgess, *Remember*, p. 200.
20. *Journal*, July 16-19, 1931.
21. Burgess, *Remember*, p. 202.
22. Ibid., pp. 202-203.
23. Ibid., p. 203.
24. Ibid., p. 204-207.
25. Journals, April 4, 1934 and June 16, 1934. Note: Like Burgess, Macmillan was born in 1874 on Cape Cod, in Provincetown. He accompanied Admiral Robert Peary to the North Pole in 1908-1909.
26. *Journal*, February 6, 1950.
27. Interviews on the heath hen with Matt Pelikan, restoration ecologist, Tom Chase, director of conservation strategies for The Nature Conservancy, and writer Tom Dunlop contributed to this portion of the chapter. U.S. Fish and Wildlife historian Mark Madison also contributed information and photos. To obtain a copy of the agency's heath hen DVD, contact him at Mark_Madison@fws.gov.
28. AOG to TWB, April 22, 1926. BCLASC.
29. Burgess, *Remember*, pp. 178-179.
30. Ibid., p. 179.
31. TWB to AHC, April 12, 1929. National Museum of Natural History (NMNH).

32. Burgess, *Remember*, pp. 181-185.
33. Ibid., pp. 183-185.
34. TWB to AOG, March 27, 1932. BCLASC.
35. Henry Hough, "The Heath Hen's Journey to Extinction, 1792-1933" (Martha's Vineyard: Dukes County Historical Society, 1933).
36. Burgess, *Remember*, p. 182.
37. AOG to TWB, November,1927. BCLASC.
38. TWB to AOG. November 11, 1931. BCLASC.
39. AOG to TWB, November 15, 1927. BCLASC.
40. TWB to AOG, February 26, 1930. BCLASC.
41. TWB to AOG, December 20, 1931. BCLASC.

Chapter Thirteen

1. Cleveland Amory to TWBS, September 3, 1982. TWBSA.
2. Burgess, *Remember*, pp. 332-333.
3. Edith Stocking, "Incidental Reading Carried Along Experimental Lines," *Primary Education*, January 1917, pp. 8-9. TWBSA.
4. Note: This is the first line of a charming poem by William Brighty Rands, not a Burgess quote.
5. TWB's copy of article, "Can Your Children Read?" Undated manuscript, pp. 2-4. TWBSA.
6. Burgess, *Remember*, p. 208.
7. Thornton W. Burgess, "Nature as the Universal Teacher," *Natural History*, March-April 1922, pp. 137-140. TWBSA.
8. Thornton W. Burgess, "Nature Study Key to Knowledge," *Nature*, January 1924, p. 47. TWBSA.
9. Burgess, *Remember*, p. 145.
10. According to environmental historian Ralph H. Lutts, the term "environmental education" was conceived by Chuck Roth, education director of the Massachusetts Audubon Society, and William B. Stapp, professor of resource planning and conservation at the University of Michigan: "Bill told me that he and Chuck coined the phrase 'environmental education' at Chuck's kitchen table in Littleton, Massachusetts, probably in the 1960s," says Lutts.
11. Burgess, "Nature Study Key," p. 49.
12. "Lecture #8," undated, p. 2. TWBSA.
13. Information provided by Wayne W. Wright.
14. Thornton W. Burgess, *The Adventures of Bobby Coon*, (Boston: Little, Brown and Company, 1919), pp. 19-34.
15. David Brower, *For Earth's Sake* (Salt Lake City: Gibb-Smith Publisher, 1990), pp. 445-446.

Chapter Fourteen

1. Thornton W. Burgess, "Nature as the Universal Teacher," *Natural History, Vol. XXII*, No. 2, 1922, p. 139.
2. Obituary notice, *Animals Magazine*, Massachusetts Society for the Prevention of Cruelty to Animals, 1965.
3. Ralph Lutts, *The Nature Fakers* (Charlottesville: University Press of Virginia, 1990), p. 3.
4. Lutts, *Nature Fakers*, p. 103.
5. Ibid., p. 3.
6. Ibid., p. 71.
7. Ibid., p. 190.
8. Ibid., p. 176.
9. "Walt Disney Accused," *The Horn Book*, December 1965. Based on an interview with Frances Clarke Sayers conducted by Charles M. Weisenberg, public relations director of the Los Angeles Public Library.
10. Lutts, *Nature Fakers*, p. 107.
11. *Rochester Democrat-Chronicle*, July 19, 1911. TWBSA.
12. Thornton W. Burgess, *Now I Remember*, p. 302.
13. Burgess, *Remember*, pp. 326-327.
14. Correspondence between TWB and New World Productions, February 6, 1961, March 1961. TWBSA.
15. Carter Luke provided background information on George Angell and the Massachusetts Society for the Prevention of Cruelty to Animals.
16. TWB to Aida Flemming, March 18, 1958. University of New Brunswick Archives and Special Collections.
17. TWB to Aida Flemming, June 12, 1962. UNBA& SC.
18. William T. Hornaday to TWB, December 18, 1918. TWBSA.
19. Note: In 1830, the Boston Society of Natural History was formed as an organization devoted to collecting and studying natural history specimens. The Society's collections were moved in 1864 to a permanent location at Berkeley and Boylston Streets in Boston's Back Bay. The facility was named the New England Museum of Natural History. In 1951 it became the Boston Museum of Science and moved to its current site on the Charles River. Information was provided by Ken Pauley, former Education Associate at the museum.
20. Bradford Washburn to TWB. TWBSA.
21. Lou Levine, "My Most Unforgettable Character," *Reader's Digest* (reprint), 1967, p. 4.

Chapter Fifteen

1. TWB, "An Old Man's Dream," undated essay, early 1960s, p. 1. Property of author.
2. Author unknown, "Eighteenth Century Lives on in Damon Coate's Old House in Hampden," source unidentified, 1916, p. 5. *Courtesy of David Cesan.*
3. *Journal*, April 20, 1947.
4. *Journals*, July 7-11, 1945; August 11, 1939; April 28, 1949; and May 22, 1949.
5. Marion W. Gerrish, "Thornton Burgess' Hampden Place Charms Historically," source unknown, Feb. 2, 1952, p. 5. *Courtesy of David Cesan.*
6. Public notice, June 6, 1922. *Courtesy of David Cesan.*
7. Tape, oral history of Gertrude Lyons made by Josh Lane, June 15, 1983. *Courtesy of David Cesan.*
8. *Journal*, March 7, 1945.
9. Article, source unknown, July 11, 1965. *Courtesy of David Cesan.*
10. *Journal*, August 17, 1950.
11. *Journal*, August 19-20, 1950.
12. *Journal*, August 25- 29, 1950.
13. *Journal*, September 5, 1950.
14. Burgess, "An Old Man's Dream," p. 2. Copy given to author by Ernestine Johnson.
15. *Springfield Republican*, June 6, 1965. TWBSA.

16. *Journal*, March 30, 1946.
17. Richard Walton, with William E. Davis. *Massachusetts Audubon Society: The First Sixty Years* (Massachusetts Audubon Society, 2010).
18. Dalton Philpott, "Open Letter to Citizens of Western Massachusetts and Northern Connecticut," Sept. 17, 2003, pp. 1-8. *Courtesy of David Cesan.* Note: A key member of Friends of Laughing Brook, personal friend of Thornton Burgess, and Hampden town moderate, Dalton Philpott was actively involved with the acquisition, development, operation, maintenance, and fund-raising for Laughing Brook. His account and interviews provide a chronology of the development of Laughing Brook Wildlife Sanctuary.
19. Email, Mary Shanley-Koeber, director of Mass Audubon Connecticut River Valley Wildlife Sanctuaries, to author, October 26, 2010.
20. Philpott, "Open Letter."
21. Ibid.
22. Note: Thornton Burgess joined the Allen Bird Club in 1912 and was an active member for many years. The Allen Bird Club participated in the Radio Nature League, the Green Meadow Club bird sanctuary program, and signed Burgess' petition opposing flooding of Lower Klamath Lake in Oregon. On May 3, 1953, Burgess' journal noted: "Showed a special 'thrills' film to Allen Bird Club at Natural History Museum. Wonderful reception. Some sat in outer hall. Gave me rousing applause." Historian George C. Kingston provided information to this section.
23. Interview in Sandwich, Massachusetts, Frances Meigs, July 2, 1998.
24. Mary Shanley-Koeber to Hampden Select Board, September 17, 2010.
25. Mary Rogeness, "Beacon Hill Byline," Archive, Massachusetts State Representative for Second Hampden District, October 10, 1996.

Chapter Fifteen Sidebar

1. Thornton W. Burgess, *Now I Remember* (Boston: Little, Brown and Company), p. 16.
2. Note: Thornton Burgess has eleven photo credits in *Birds of the Connecticut River Valley.*

Chapter Sixteen

1. Thornton W. Burgess, *Now I Remember* (Boston: Little, Brown and Company, 1960), p. 265.
2. Information provided by the Thornton W. Burgess Society.

Chapter Seventeen

1. *Journal*, January 10, 1929.
2. Paul O'Neil, *Life*, November 14, 1960, p. 113.
3. *New York Times* obituary, June 6, 1965, p. 84.
4. Burgess, *Remember*, p. 3.
5. *Journal*, October 12, 1960.
6. *Journal*, December 23, 1944.
7. *Journal*, December 7, 1944.
8. Meigs, *Grandfather*, pp. 95-96.
9. Meigs, *Grandfather*, pp. 93-94.
10. Thornton W. Burgess will, April 25, 1966. *Courtesy of Burgess family.*
11. Letter, Kate Johnson (Wadena, Saskatchewan) to TWBS, June 2, 2009. TWBS.
12. Tony Reader, "In Search of Thornton W. Burgess," *The St. Croix Courier*, June 10, 2008. *Courtesy of Mary Howe.*
13. Meigs, *Grandfather*, p. 38.
14. Ibid., p. 24.
15. Ibid., pp. 115-116.
16. *Journal*, January 1, 1928.
17. TWB to Stuart Trueman, May 9, 1963. University of New Brunswick Archives and Special Collections (UNBASC).
18. TWB to Stuart Trueman, June 6, 1963. UNBASC.
19. Note: May 18 was the date of the birthday of Burgess' father, Thornton W. Burgess, Sr., who died when Burgess was ten months old; the birthday of his son Thornton III; and the death of his first wife Nina.
20. Louis Levine, "Unforgettable Thornton W. Burgess," *Reader's Digest* (reprint), October, 1967, p.6.
21. Ibid., pp. 5-6.
22. "Thornton Burgess: Story man felt too busy to die," *Toronto Journal*, June 5, 1993. UNBASC.

Chapter Eighteen

1. Thornton W. Burgess, *The Adventures of Reddy Fox* (Boston: Little, Brown and Company, 1915), pp. 15-17.

BIBLIOGRAPHY

Books

Boynton, Mary F. *Louis Agassiz Fuertes.* New York, New York: Oxford University Press, 1956.

Brower, David. *For Earth's Sake.* Salt Lake City, Utah: Gibbs-Smith Publisher, 1990.

Burgess, Thornton W. *50 Favorite Burgess Stories.* New York, New York: Grosset & Dunlap, 1944, 1946.

Jerry Muskrat at Home. New York, New York: Grosset & Dunlap, 1954.

The Adventures of Mr. Mocker. New York, New York: Grosset & Dunlap, 1942.

At Paddy the Beaver's Pond. Boston: Little, Brown and Company. 1950.

The Crooked Little Path. Boston, Massachusetts: Little, Brown and Company. 1947.

The Adventures of Old Man Coyote. New York, New York: Grosset & Dunlap, 1916, 1944.

The Adventures of Bob White. New York, New York: Grosset & Dunlap, 1919.

The Adventures of Blacky the Crow. New York, New York: Grosset & Dunlap, 1922/1950.

The Adventures of Sammy Jay. Boston, Massachusetts: Little, Brown, and Company, 1917.

The Burgess Book of Nature Lore. New York, New York: Bonanza Books, 1965.

The Adventures of Bob White. New York, New York: Grosset & Dunlap, 1919.

The Adventures of Peter Cottontail. Boston, Massachusetts: Little, Brown and Company, 1914; republished in 1987.

Mother West Wind "How" Stories. New York, New York: Grosset & Dunlap, 1944.

The Adventures of Lightfoot the Deer. New York, New York: Grosset & Dunlap, 1921.

Old Mother West Wind. New York, New York: Dover Publications, Inc., 1995.

The Adventures of Poor Mrs. Quack. New York, New York: Dover Publications, Inc., 1993.

The Adventures of Buster Bear's Twins. New York, New York: Grosset & Dunlap, 1951.

The Adventures of Reddy Fox. Boston, Massachusetts: Little Brown and Company, 1915.

The Adventures of Bowser the Hound. New York, New York: Grosset & Dunlap, 1948.

The Adventures of Paddy the Beaver. Boston, Massachusetts: Little, Brown and Company, 1917.

Mrs. Peter Rabbit. New York, New York: Grosset & Dunlap, 1919.

The Adventures of Danny Meadow Mouse. New York, New York: Grosset & Dunlap, 1944.

At the Smiling Pool. Boston, Massachusetts: Little, Brown and Company, 1948.

The Adventures of Bobby Coon. New York, New York: Grosset & Dunlap, 1946.

The Dear Old Briar-Patch. Boston, Massachusetts: Little, Brown and Company, 1975.

Now I Remember. Boston, Massachusetts: Little, Brown and Company, 1960.

Coles, Robert. *The Moral Intelligence of Children.* New York, New York: Random House, 1997.

Dorsey, Kurkpatrick. *The Dawn of Conservation Diplomacy.* Seattle, Washington: University of Washington Press, 1998.

Dowhan, Jr., Michael W. *Thornton W. Burgess, Harrison Cady: A Book, Magazine and Newspaper Bibliography.* New York, New York: Carlton Press, Inc., 1990.

Goldthwaite, John. *The Natural History of Make-Believe: A Guide to the Principal Works of Britain, Europe, and America.* New York, New York: Oxford University Press, 1996.

Hornaday, William T. *Our Vanishing Wild Life.* New York, New York: Charles Scribner's Sons, 1913.

Huck, Charlotte S. *Children's Literature in the Elementary School, 4th Edition.* Chicago, Illinois: Holt, Rinehart and Winston, Inc., 1987.

Kardell, Caroline and Lovell, Jr., Russell A. *Vital Records of Sandwich Massachusetts to 1885, Volume One.* Boston, Massachusetts: New England Historic Genealogical Society, 1996.

Vital Records of Sandwich Massachusetts to 1885, Volume Two. Boston, Massachusetts: New England Historic Genealogical Society, 1996.

Vital Records of Sandwich Massachusetts to 1885, Volume Three. Boston, Massachusetts: New England Historic Genealogical Society, 1996.

Kirkpatrick, Daniel L. *Twentieth-Century Children's Writers, 2nd Edition.* New York, New York: St. Martin's Press, 1983.

LaFollette, Marcel C. *Science on the Air.* Chicago, Illinois: University of Chicago Press, 2008.

Lear, Linda. *Beatrix Potter: A Life in Nature.* New York, New York: St. Martin's Griffin, 2007.

Linder, Leslie. *A History of the Writings of Beatrix Potter.* London, England: Frederick Warne & Co LTD. New York: Frederick Warne & Co Inc., 1971.

Lovell, Jr., Russell A. *Sandwich, A Cape Cod Town.* Sandwich, Massachusetts: Town of Sandwich, Massachusetts, 1984.

Lutts, Ralph H. *The Nature Fakers: Wildlife, Science and Sentiment.* Charlottesville, Virginia: University Press of Virginia, 1990.

Lutts, Ralph H., editor. *The Wild Animal Story.* Philadelphia, Pennsylvania: Temple University Press, 1998.

Mathewson, Worth. *William L. Finley: Pioneer Wildlife Photographer.* Corvallis, Oregon: Oregon State University, 1986.

Meigs, Frances B. *My Grandfather, Thornton W. Burgess.* Beverly, Massachusetts: Commonwealth Editions, 1998.

Moore, Annie C. *Roads to Childhood.* New York, New York: George H. Doran Company, 1920.

One Hundred and Fifty Years of Publishing 1837-1987. Boston, Massachusetts: Little, Brown and Company, 1987.

Peck, Robert M. *A Celebration of Birds: The Life and Art of Louis Agassiz Fuertes.* New York, New York: Walker and Company, 1982.

Pettingill Jr., Olin S. *My Way to Ornithology.* Norman, Oklahoma: University of Oklahoma Press, 1992.

Prescott, Orville. *A Father Reads to His Children.* New York, New York: E.P. Dutton & Co., Inc., 1965.

The Five-Dollar Gold Piece. New York, New York: Random House, 1956.

Rogers, Jason. *Newspaper Building.* New York, New York: Harper & Brothers, 1918.

Silverman, Al. *The Time of Their Lives* (The Golden Age of Great American Book Publishers, Their Editors and Authors). New York, New York: St. Martin's Press, 2008.

Sutherland, Zena and May Hill Arbuthnot. *Children and Books, 7th Edition.* Glenview, Illinois: Scott, Foresman and Company, 1986.

Sutton, George M. *To a Young Bird Artist: Letters from Louis Agassiz Fuertes to George M. Sutton.* Mechanicsburg, Pennsylvania: Stackpole Books, 1979.

The Cape Cod Story of Thornton W. Burgess. Sandwich, Massachusetts: Thornton W. Burgess Society, Inc., 1974.

Turner, John R. *A Bibliography of Unauthorized American Editions of The Tale of Peter Rabbit by Beatrix Potter 1904 – 1980.* London, England: Ian Hodgkins & Co. Ltd., 2012.

Wright, Wayne W. *Thornton W. Burgess: A Descriptive Book Bibliography.* Sandwich, Massachusetts: The Thornton W. Burgess Society, 2000.

Articles

Boston Herald, Rotogravure section, October 30, 1938.

Bryan III, J. "Mother Nature's Brother," *Saturday Review of Literature,* December 1940.

Burgess, Thornton W. "Making Men of Them," *Good Housekeeping,* July, 1914, pp. 3-12.

"Nature as the Universal Teacher," *Natural History* (March-April, 1922).

"Nature Study Key to Knowledge," *Nature,* January 1924, p. 47.

"Disembodied Voice Leads Multitude: Thornton W. Burgess Directs Army of Conservationists in Radio Nature League."

Dow, Harry. *Burgess Book Collectors Bulletin,* Vol. 16, November 1995.

Dunlop, Tom. "Return of the Heath Hen," Martha's Vineyard, May/June 1999, p. 49.

"Eighteenth Century Lives on in Damon Coate's Old House in Hampden," author and source unknown, 1916, p. 5.

Gerrish, Marion W. "Thornton Burgess' Hampden Place Charms Historically," source unknown, February 2, 1952.

Hornaday, William. "A Conspicuous National Service," *People's Home Journal,* p. 10.

Hough, Henry. "The Heath Hen's Journey to Extinction, 1792-1933," Dukes County Historical Society.

Landsberg, Michelle. "The Secrets of the Garden." *Washington Post,* May 5, 1996, X17.

Lutts, Ralph H. "The Trouble with Bambi: Walt Disney's Bambi and the American Vision of Nature," *Forest and Conservation History,* October 1992, pp. 160-171.

Paynter, Raymond, Jr. "In Memoriam: Alfred Otto Gross," *The Auk,* July 1971, pp. 521-527.

Pettingill, Jr., Olin. *Audubon,* September 1983, vol. 85, #5, pp. 98-101.

Register of the Ray P. Holland Papers on Enforcement of the Migratory Bird Treaty, 1872-1974, Special Collections and Archives Olin Library, Wesleyan University.

Roth, Charles E. "The Eclipse of Thornton W. Burgess," *The Outdoor Communicator,* fall/winter 1985-1986, pp. 18-23.

Rutledge, Bethany. "Caroline Burgess," *Burgess Book Collectors Bulletin,* Vol. 34, No. 3, November 2003.

"Nina: The First Mrs. Burgess," *Burgess Book Collectors' Bulletin,* Vol. 33, No 1, April 2002.

Tallmadge, Rosemary. "Introduction," *In Transit: The LaGuardia Journal on Teaching and Learning,* Vol. 5. Center for Teaching and Learning. LaGuardia Community College, New York, New York, 2011, pp. 1-15.

Trueman, Stuart. "Thornton Burgess: Story man felt too busy to die," *Toronto Journal,* June 5, 1993.

"WBZ Starts Radio Nature Association," *Christian Science Monitor,* Feb. 18, 1925, p. 9.

ACKNOWLEDGMENTS

The opportunity to examine the life and work of this important early twentieth century writer and conservationist would not have been possible without the preservation of primary source materials generously made available to me by the Thornton W. Burgess Society and the Burgess family. Special credit must be given to Thornton W. Burgess Society archivists Gwen Brown, Kristine Hastreiter, Julie Arrison, and especially Bethany Rutledge of Tucson, Arizona, who spent two years transcribing Burgess' personal journals recorded during the last third the author's life.

Access to personal correspondence and papers at the Smithsonian Institution, the National Museum of Natural History, Bowdoin College, the University of New Brunswick Archives and Special Collections, and the Provincial Archives of New Brunswick added immeasurable depth and living presence to this biography.

I am greatly indebted to historian and Smithsonian researcher Marcel C. LaFollette for so kindly facilitating access to Smithsonian Institution resources and to Dr. David and Doris Pawson for providing correspondence at the National Museum of Natural History. The articulate insight of LaFollette's chapter on Thornton Burgess in *Science on the Air* contributed significantly to my understanding of his role as a popularizer of science and radio and his important relationship with Smithsonian curator Austin Clark.

I first spoke with U.S. Fish and Wildlife historian Mark Madison in 2009 regarding Thornton Burgess' participation in the heath hen surveys on Martha's Vineyard, and I am grateful for his willingness to provide his perspective as a conservation historian in the Foreword of this book. Greg Dehler, author of *William Temple Hornaday: An American Crusader for Wildlife*, offered helpful information about a remarkable figure in Burgess' life. Ralph Lutts and his book *The Nature Fakers* lent perspective to the issue of nature faking then and now. Salem State University communications professor Peter Oehlkers used an academic sabbatical to research and develop the Thornton W. Burgess Research League weblog. It contains a wealth of reference information which I benefitted from and recommend. Dr. Tom French assistant director of the Massachusetts Division of Fisheries and Wildlife provided useful information on the history and function of the Migratory Bird Treaty Act.

The opportunity to collect interviews in the twenty-first century from people who personally knew an individual born in 1874 is a gift, not a given. Since I began researching this book in January 2009, Burgess' grandchildren Thornton W. Burgess IV and Frances B. Meigs have passed away, and Burgess' special friend Polly Philpott, a.k.a. "Old Mother West Wind," is unwell at this writing. I am privileged to include here the impressions, memories, stories, and reflections they shared with me. It was a great pleasure to meet and/or interview other Burgess' family members, including grandchildren Nancy Hughes and William Bradford and great-granddaughters Debra Hanna, Jean Parrish and Candy Walton, as well as Chuck Roth who knew Burgess well. I am grateful to them all for the stories and materials they shared.

I conducted approximately ninety interviews for this biography, and each source, named or not, was important to the overall work. I was fortunate to have interviews conducted in 1988 in Hampden with Burgess' secretary Ernestine Johnson and friends Polly Philpott and Pat Wilcox, as well as an extensive 1998 interview with Frances Meigs in Sandwich. In the mid-1980s, I conducted interviews with Nancy Titcomb, Stu Parsons and others associated with the early days of the Thornton W. Burgess Society, so had the benefit of that background material. Chuck Roth, Tom Tyning, Bob McMaster, and David Cesan, among others, provided me with a picture of Laughing Brook Wildlife Sanctuary, beginning with its days as a vital, thriving nature center. Martha's Vineyard conservationists Tom Chase and Matt Pelikan offered authoritative background information on the history of the heath hen.

In addition, I am particularly grateful for the professional assistance and interest of the following archivists, librarians, and institution staff members whose resources and counsel were generously offered and greatly valued. I apologize to anyone inadvertently omitted:

• American School in Japan: Linda Hayakawa, reference librarian

• Boston University, Thornton W. Burgess Collection of the Howard Gotlieb Archival Research Center: Alex Rankin, Assistant Director for Acquisitions

• Bowdoin College Library, George J. Mitchell Dept. of Special Collections & Archives: Richard Lindemann, director; Caroline Moseley and Kathleen A. Petersen, archivists

• Boy Scouts of America: Steven Price, archivist

• Fauquier County Public Library: Vicky Ginther, librarian

• Massachusetts Audubon Society: Mary Shanley-Koeber, director Connecticut Valley Wildlife Sanctuaries; Charles Roth, former education director.

• Massachusetts Society for the Prevention of Cruelty to Animals: Carter Luke, president

• New York State Historical Association: Wayne Wright, senior researcher

• New York Public Library: Matthew Boylan, senior reference librarian

• Operation Outreach: Judy Golden, president

• Perkins School for the Blind: Jan Seymour-Ford, reference librarian

• Provincial Archives of New Brunswick: Twila Buttimer, supervising archivist

• Saint Bridget's Church, Richmond, Virginia: Michele Healy, communications director

• Sandwich Archives and Historic Center: Barbara Gill, archivist and historian

• Sandwich Public Library: Lauren Robinson, research librarian

• Simmons College: Margaret Bush, Library and Information Science Professor Emerita

• Thornton W. Burgess Society: Mary Beers, education director; Joan DiPersio, public relations; Susie Lott, business manager; John Richmond, manager; Gene Schott, executive director; Shirley Stolte, library coordinator

• University of Massachusetts, Dartmouth: Susan Raidy Klein, collections librarian

• University of New Brunswick Archives and Special Collections: Patti Johnson, research librarian

• University of New York, Albany: David Mitchell, curator, Miriam Snow Mathes Historical Children's Literature Collection

• University of North Texas: Kim Stanton, archivist

• Williamsburg (Massachusetts) Historical Society: Ralmon Jon Black, historian; Eric Weber, historian; Geoffrey LeBaron, Audubon Society International Christmas Bird Count coordinator

To the readers who helped steer this project away from misdirection and error, I offer deep and lasting thanks: Mary Beers, Susan Fisher Curtis, Susan Klein, Rob Lowrance, Kimberly Lowrance, David Lowrance, Kaethe Maguire, Robert McMaster, Patricia Rogers, Lorie Strait, Tom Tyning, Adelaide "Fiddle" Walker, and especially, Wayne W. Wright of the New York Historical Association. My heartfelt thanks for technical help by Bill Palmer, Rob Lowrance, computer specialist extraordinaire Steve Pacino, and graphic artist Pat Morely.

I am grateful for family and friends whose words of encouragement and gestures of support over the duration of this project meant more than you can know, especially Jacqueline Loring, who always had an answer, and Judi Hensle, who always called at the right moment.

At Schiffer Publishing I remain indebted to Pete Schiffer who set the course for this book with five words: "I think it is important." Editors Doug Condon-Martin and Jennifer Marie Savage, copy-editor Tina Phelps, and marketing director Stacey McNutt offered expertise and good counsel in bringing *Nature's Ambassador* into being.

Christie Palmer Lowrance
August 1, 2012

INDEX